# How Matter Matters

*Perspectives on Process Organization Studies*
Series Editors: Ann Langley and Haridimos Tsoukas

*Perspectives on Process Organization Studies* is an annual series, linked to the International Symposium on Process Organization Studies, and is dedicated to the development of an understanding of organizations and organizing at large as processes in the making. This series brings together contributions from leading scholars, which focus on seeing dynamically evolving activities, interactions, and events as important aspects of organized action, rather than static structures and fixed templates.

**Volume 1: Process, Sensemaking, and Organizing**
Editors: Tor Hernes and Sally Maitlis

**Volume 2: Constructing Identity in and around Organizations**
Editors: Majken Schultz, Steve Maguire, Ann Langley, and Haridimos Tsoukas

**Volume 3: How Matter Matters: Objects, Artifacts, and Materiality in Organization Studies**
Editors: Paul R. Carlile, Davide Nicolini, Ann Langley, and Haridimos Tsoukas

# How Matter Matters

## Objects, Artifacts, and Materiality in Organization Studies

Edited by
Paul R. Carlile, Davide Nicolini, Ann Langley,
Haridimos Tsoukas

OXFORD
UNIVERSITY PRESS

# OXFORD

UNIVERSITY PRESS

Great Clarendon Street, Oxford, OX2 6DP,
United Kingdom

Oxford University Press is a department of the University of Oxford.
It furthers the University's objective of excellence in research, scholarship,
and education by publishing worldwide. Oxford is a registered trade mark of
Oxford University Press in the UK and in certain other countries

First Edition published in 2013
First published in paperback 2014

Impression: 1

Published in the United States of America by Oxford University Press
198 Madison Avenue, New York, NY 10016, United States of America

British Library Cataloguing in Publication Data

Data available

Library of Congress in Publication Data

Data available

ISBN 978–0–19–967153–3 (hbk.)
ISBN 978–0–19–870885–8 (pbk.)

Printed in Great Britain by
CPI Group (UK) Ltd, Croydon, CR0 4YY

# Contents

**Contents**

# Acknowledgments

We would like to express our great appreciation to the following colleagues who have generously offered their time to act as reviewers for the papers published in volume

Paul R. Carlile, Davide Nicolini, Ann Langley, Haridimos Tsoukas

## Reviewers listed alphabetically

Brian Bloomfield, University of Lancaster; Arne Carlsen, SINTEF Technology and Society; Samia Chreim, University of Ottawa; Peter Clark, Queen Mary University of London; Anne Laure Fayard, Polytechnic Institute of New York University; Jennifer Howard-Grenville, University of Oregon; Ruthanne Huising, McGill University; Matthew Jones, Cambridge Judge Business School; Dan Kärreman, Copenhagen Business School; Natalia Levina, New York University Stern School of Business; Philippe Lorino, ESSEC Business School; Alexandre Mallard, Centre de Sociologie de l'Innovation, Mines ParisTech; Jeanne Mengis, University of Lugano, Switzerland; Carsten Østerlund, iSchool, Syracuse University; Nikiforos Panourgias, Warwick Business School; Susan Scott, London School of Economics and Political Science; Viviane Sergi, HEC Montréal; Barbara Simpson, Strathclyde Business School; Inger Stensaker, NHH Norwegian School of Economics; Elden Wiebe, King's University College; Dvora Yanow, University of Amsterdam & Wageningen University; Mike Zundel, University of Liverpool.

# List of Figures

# List of Tables

# List of Contributors

**Karen Barad** Karen Barad is Professor of Feminist Studies, Philosophy, and History of Consciousness at the University of California at Santa Cruz. Her Ph.D. is in theoretical particle physics. She held a tenured appointment in a physics department before moving into more interdisciplinary spaces. She is the author of *Meeting the Universe Halfway: Quantum Physics and the Entanglement of Matter and Meaning* (Duke University Press, 2007) and numerous articles in the fields of physics, philosophy, science studies, poststructuralist theory, and feminist theory. Her research has been supported by the National Science Foundation, the Ford Foundation, the Hughes Foundation, the Irvine Foundation, the Mellon Foundation, and the National Endowment for the Humanities. She is the Co-Director of the Science & Justice Graduate Training Program at UCSC.

**Paul Carlile** An overall theme in Paul's work is how knowledge is developed and valued in contexts of cross domain innovation. The question of value reveals the problematic nature of knowledge itself; that is knowledge can be both a source of and a barrier to innovation. He has empirically examined these issues across a spectrum of products from software to new drug treatments and in a variety of settings from community based to large industrial firms. Paul brings a very unique approach to his study of innovation by focusing on the capacity of artifacts and how people use them to create, share, and value knowledge as they work with others. This provides a diagnostic stance to better understand the sources as well as the barriers to innovation. His research interests include product development, new models of innovation, and the potential for information technology to accelerate innovative outcomes in firms and communities. He has published on these topics in a variety of academic and practitioner outlets. Paul earned his Ph.D. at the University of Michigan and was an Assistant Professor of Organization Studies at MIT's Sloan School of Management. Paul studied Philosophy and Anthropology at Brigham Young University and also earned a Masters in Organizational Behavior there. Paul has also founded two information technology companies developing tools for creating and sharing knowledge.

**Paul Dourish** Paul Dourish is a Professor of Informatics in the Donald Bren School of Information and Computer Sciences at UC Irvine, with courtesy appointments in Computer Science and Anthropology. His research focuses primarily on understanding information technology as a site of social and cultural production; his work combines topics in human–computer interaction, ubiquitous computing, and science and technology studies. He was elected to the CHI Academy in 2008 in recognition of his contributions to Human-Computer Interaction. He is the author of two books: *Where the Action Is: The Foundations of Embodied Interaction* (MIT Press, 2001), which explores how phenomenological accounts of action can provide an alternative to traditional cognitive analysis for understanding the embodied experience of interactive and computational systems; and, with Genevieve Bell, *Divining a Digital Future: Mess and Mythology in Ubiquitous Computing* (MIT Press, 2011), which examines the social and cultural aspects of the ubiquitous computing research program. Before coming to UCI, he was a Senior Member of Research Staff in the Computer Science Laboratory of Xerox PARC; he has also held research positions at Apple Computer and at Rank Xerox EuroPARC. He holds a Ph. D. in Computer Science from University College, London, and a B.Sc. (Hons) in Artificial Intelligence and Computer Science from the University of Edinburgh.

**Nada Endrissat** Nada Endrissat is Assistant Professor at Bern University of Applied Sciences, Switzerland. She studied psychology at Free University of Berlin and received her Ph.D. in management from the University of Basel in Switzerland. Her current research interests include materiality, leadership, and the creative industries.

**Silvia Gherardi** Silvia Gherardi is full Professor of Sociology of Work and Organization at the Faculty of Sociology of the University of Trento, Italy, where she coordinates the Research Unit on Communication, Organizational Learning, and Aesthetics (www.unitn.it/rucola). Areas of interest include the exploration of different "soft" aspects of knowing in organizations, with a particular emphasis on aesthetic, emotional, symbolic, and discursive aspects in workplace practices. Her most recent book, co-authored with Antonio Strati, *Knowing and Learning in Practice-based Studies* (Edward Elgar, 2012), is devoted to the theme of practice-based studies

**Lucas D. Introna** Professor Lucas D. Introna lectures in Technology, Organisation and Ethics at the Centre for the Study of Technology and Organisation, Lancaster University. Previously he lectured in Information Systems at the London School of Economics and Political Science. His research interest is the social study of technology and its consequences for society. In particular he is concerned with the ethics and politics of technology and sociomateriality more generally. He is co-editor of

*Ethics and Information Technology* and acted as associate editor for *Management Information Systems Quarterly* and *Information Systems Research*. He is also a founding member of the International Society for Ethics and Information Technology (INSEIT) and an active member of IFIP WG 8.2, the Society for Philosophy in Contemporary World (SPCW), and a number of other academic and professional societies. His most recent work includes a book *Management, Information and Power* published by Macmillan, and various academic papers in journals and conference proceedings on a variety of topics such as: sociomateriality, phenomenology of technology, information and power, privacy, surveillance, information technology and postmodern ethics, and virtual organizations.

**Matthew Jones** Matthew Jones is a University Lecturer in Information Management at the Judge Business School and the Department of Engineering at the University of Cambridge. He previously held postdoctoral positions at the University of Reading and the University of Cambridge where he was involved in the development of computer-based models for public policy decision-making. His current research interests are concerned with the relationship between information systems and social and organizational change and theoretical and methodological issues in information systems research.

**Ann Langley** Ann Langley is Professor of Management at HEC Montréal and Canada research chair in strategic management in pluralistic settings. Her research focuses on strategic change, leadership, innovation, and the use of management tools in complex organizations with an emphasis on processual research approaches. She has published over 50 articles and two books.

**Paul M. Leonardi** Paul Leonardi is the Pentair-Nugent Associate Professor at Northwestern University where he teaches courses on the management of innovation and organizational change in the School of Communication, the McCormick School of Engineering, and the Kellogg School of Management. His research focuses on how companies can design organizational structures and employ advanced information technologies to more effectively create and share knowledge. He is the author of *Car Crashes Without Cars: Lessons about Simulation Technology* and *Organizational Change from Automotive Design* (MIT Press, 2012).

**Melissa Mazmanian** Melissa Mazmanian is Assistant Professor in the Department of Informatics at the Donald Bren School of Information and Computer Sciences at the University of California, Irvine. Melissa's interests revolve around the experience of communication technologies as used in-practice within personal and organizational contexts, specifically in relation to identity projection and the nature of personal and professional time in the digital age. Past research includes analyzing an organizational change effort oriented around increasing predictable time off in a consulting firm; tracing the emergence of shared expectations of availability as wireless email devices were introduced into a footwear manufacturing company; and studying the ways in which the material experience of new communication technologies resonates with the elite identities of knowledge professionals. Melissa earned a Ph.D. in Organization Studies from the MIT Sloan School of Management and a Masters in Information Economics, Management and Policy from the University of Michigan, School of Information.

**Davide Nicolini** Davide Nicolini is Professor of Organization Studies at Warwick Business School where he co-directs the IKON Research Centre and the Warwick Institute of Health. Prior to joining the University of Warwick he held positions at the Tavistock Institute in London and the University of Trento and Bergamo in Italy. His work has appeared in journals such as *Organization Science*, *Organization Studies*, *Journal of Management Studies*, *Human Relations*, *Management Learning*, and *Social Science and Medicine*. From 2009 he is associate editor of *Management Learning*. Davide is actively involved in developing a practice-based approach to the study of organizational phenomena and for several years he has explored the implications of this novel approach for the understanding of knowing, collaboration and change. His new book *Practice Theory, Work, and Organization* will be published in 2012 by Oxford University Press. Although these days most of his work is carried out in healthcare organizations where he tries to understand how hospitals learn from incidents and how top managers mobilize knowledge in their day-to-day work, he has also studied construction sites, factories, public organizations, hospices, pharmacies, and scientific labs.

**Claus Noppeney** Claus Noppeney works as a research professor at Bern University of the Arts and at the Business Department at Bern University of Applied Sciences. He studied economics and management at the University of St. Gallen and the Fuqua School of Business. The field of artistic perfumery is part of his interest in organizing practices in creative industries.

**Bjørnar Olsen** Bjørnar Olsen is Professor of Archaeology at the Department of Archaeology and Social Anthropology, University of Tromsø, Norway. He has written a number of papers and books on Northern prehistory and history, museology, material culture, and archaeological theory. His latest books are *Archaeology: The Discipline of Things* (2012) (with M. Shanks, T. Webmoor, and C. Witmore), *Hybrid Spaces: Medieval Finnmark and the Archaeology of Multi-Room Houses* (2011) (edited with P. Urbanczyk and C. Amundsen), *In Defense of Things: Archaeology and the Ontology of Objects* (2010), and *Persistent Memories: Pyramiden—a Soviet Mining Town in the High Arctic* (2010) (with E. Andreassen and H. Bjerck).

**Wanda J. Orlikowski** Wanda J. Orlikowski is the Alfred P. Sloan Professor of Information Technologies and Organization Studies in the Sloan School of Management at the Massachusetts Institute of Technology. Her research examines the dynamic relationship between organizations and information technologies, with particular emphases on organizing structures, cultural norms, communication genres, and work practices. She is currently exploring the sociomaterial entailments of social media.

**Manuela Perrotta** Manuela Perrotta received a Ph.D. in Sociology and Social Research from the Faculty of Sociology of the University of Trento, Italy. Currently she is postdoctoral research fellow at the Department of Interdisciplinary Studies of Culture, Norwegian University of Science and Technology. Her main research interests concern innovation and technological change; knowing and learning in organizations; construction of the body in medicine and life science; and the sociomateriality of scientific and biomedical practices.

**Susan V. Scott** Susan V. Scott is Senior Lecturer in the Information Systems and Innovation Group, Department of Management, at The London School of Economics and Political Science. Her research focuses on technology, work, and organization from a management studies perspective. She has published on: the implementation of information systems for risk management; electronic trading; the strategic organization of post-trade services; organizational reputation risk; enterprise resource planning and best practice. She is currently involved in research projects exploring the sociomateriality of rating and ranking mechanisms.

**John Shotter** John Shotter is Emeritus Professor of Communication in the Department of Communication, University of New Hampshire, and a tutor on the Professional Doctorate in System Practice in KCCF, London. He is the author of *Social Accountability and Selfhood* (Blackwell, 1984), *Cultural Politics of Everyday Life: Social Constructionism, Rhetoric, and Knowing of the Third Kind* (Open University, 1993), *Conversational Realities: The Construction of Life through Language* (Sage, 1993), *Conversational Realities Revisited: Life, Language, Body, and World* (Taos Publications, 2009), and *'Getting It':'Withness'-Thinking and the Dialogical...in Practice* (Hampton Press, 2010).

**Haridimos Tsoukas** Haridimos Tsoukas holds the Columbia Ship Management Chair in Strategic Management at the University of Cyprus, Cyprus and is a Professor of Organization Studies at Warwick Business School, University of Warwick, UK. He obtained his Ph.D. at the Manchester Business School (MBS), University of Manchester, and has worked at MBS, the University of Essex, the University of Strathclyde, and the ALBA Graduate Business School, Greece. He has published widely in several leading academic journals, including the *Academy of Management*

*Review, Strategic Management Journal, Organization Studies, Organization Science, Journal of Management Studies,* and *Human Relations.* He was the Editor-in-Chief of *Organization Studies* (2003–2008). His research interests include: knowledge-based perspectives on organizations; organizational becoming; the management of organizational change and social reforms; the epistemology of practice; and epistemological issues in organization theory. He is the editor (with Christian Knudsen) of *The Oxford Handbook of Organization Theory: Meta-theoretical Perspectives* (Oxford University Press, 2003). He has also edited *Organizations as Knowledge Systems* (Palgrave Macmillan, 2004 (with N. Mylonopoulos)) and *Managing the Future: Foresight in the Knowledge Economy* (Blackwell, 2004 (with J. Shepherd)). His book *Complex Knowledge: Studies in Organizational Epistemology* was published by Oxford University Press in 2005. He is also the author of the book *If Aristotle were a CEO* (in Greek, Kastaniotis, 2004). He writes regularly on political and social issues for the leading Greek newspaper *Kathimerini.* E-mail: htsoukas@ucy.ac.cy and Hari.Tsoukas@wbs.ac.uk

# Series Editorial Structure

### Editors-in-Chief

**Ann Langley**, HEC Montréal, Canada, ann.langley@hec.ca
**Haridimos Tsoukas**, University of Cyprus, Cyprus and University of Warwick, UK, process.symposium@gmail.com

### Advisory Board

Hamid Bouchikhi, ESSEC Business School, France
Michel Callon, CSI-École des Mines de Paris, France
Robert Chia, University of Strathclyde, UK
Todd Chiles, University of Missouri, USA
François Cooren, Université de Montréal, Canada
Barbara Czarniawska, University of Gothenburg, Sweden
Martha Feldman, University of California, Irvine, USA
Raghu Garud, Pennsylvania State University, USA
Silvia Gherardi, University of Trento, Italy
Cynthia Hardy, University of Melbourne, Australia
Robin Holt, University of Liverpool, UK
Paula Jarzabkowski, Aston Business School, UK
Sally Maitlis, University of British Columbia, Canada
Wanda Orlikowski, MIT, USA
Brian T. Pentland, Michigan State University, USA
Marshall Scott Poole, University of Illinois, USA
Georg Schreyögg, Freie Universität Berlin, Germany
Kathleen Sutcliffe, University of Michigan, USA
Andew Van de Ven, University of Minnesota, USA
Karl E. Weick, University of Michigan, USA

### Editorial Officer & Process Organization Studies Symposium Administrator

Sophia Tzagaraki, process.symposium@gmail.com

# Endorsements

"As we become more willing to convert reified entities into differentiated streams, the resulting images of process have become more viable and more elusive. Organization becomes organizing, being becomes becoming, construction becomes constructing. But as we see ourselves saying more words that end in 'ing', what must we be thinking? That is not always clear. But now, under the experienced guidance of editors Langley and Tsoukas, there is an annual forum that moves us toward continuity and consolidation in process studies. This book series promises to be a vigorous, thoughtful forum dedicated to improvements in the substance and craft of process articulation."

*Karl E. Weick*, Rensis Likert Distinguished University Professor of Organizational Behavior and Psychology, University of Michigan, USA

"In recent years process and practice approaches to organizational topics have increased significantly. These approaches have made significant contributions to already existing fields of study, such as strategy, routines, knowledge management, and technology adoption, and these contributions have brought increasing attention to the approaches. Yet because the contributions are embedded in a variety of different fields of study, discussions about the similarities and differences in the application of the approaches, the research challenges they present, and the potential they pose for examining taken for granted ontological assumptions are limited. This series will provide an opportunity for bringing together contributions across different areas so that comparisons can be made and can also provide a space for discussions across fields. Professors Langley and Tsoukas are leaders in the development and use of process approaches. Under their editorship, the series will attract the work and attention of a wide array of distinguished organizational scholars."

*Martha S. Feldman*, Johnson Chair for Civic Governance and Public Management, Professor of Social Ecology, Political Science, Business and Sociology, University of California, Irvine, USA

"*Perspectives on Process Organization Studies* will be the definitive annual volume of theories and research that advance our understanding of process questions dealing with how things emerge, grow, develop, and terminate over time. I applaud Professors Ann Langley and Haridimos Tsoukas for launching this important book series, and encourage colleagues to submit their process research and subscribe to *PROS*."

*Andrew H. Van de Ven*, Vernon H. Heath Professor of Organizational Innovation and Change, University of Minnesota, USA

"The new series—*Perspectives on Process Organization Studies*—is a timely and valuable addition to the organization studies literature. The ascendancy of process perspectives in recent years has signified an important departure from traditional perspectives on organizations that have tended to privilege either self-standing events or discrete entities. In contrast, by emphasizing emergent activities and recursive relations, process perspectives take seriously the ongoing production of organizational realities. Such a performative view of organizations is particularly salient today, given the increasingly complex, dispersed, dynamic, entangled, and mobile nature of current organizational phenomena. Such phenomena are not easily accounted for in traditional approaches that are premised on stability, separation, and substances. Process perspectives on organizations thus promise to offer powerful and critical analytical insights into the unprecedented and novel experiences of contemporary organizing."

*Wanda J. Orlikowski*, Alfred P. Sloan Professor of Information Technologies and Organization Studies, Massachusetts Institute of Technology, USA

"The recent decades witnessed conspicuous changes in organization theory: a slow but inexorable shift from the focus on structures to the focus on processes. The whirlwinds of the global economy made it clear that everything flows, even if change itself can become stable. While the interest in processes of organizing is not new, it is now acquiring a distinct presence, as more and more voices join in. A forum is therefore needed where such voices can speak to one another, and to the interested readers. The series *Perspectives on Process Organization Studies* will provide an excellent forum of that kind, both for those for whom a processual perspective is a matter of ontology, and those who see it as an epistemological choice."

*Barbara Czarniawska*, Professor of Management Studies, School of Business, Economics and Law at the University of Gothenburg, Sweden

"We are living in an era of unprecedented change; one that is characterized by instability, volatility, and dramatic transformations. It is a world in which the seemingly improbable, the unanticipated, and the downright catastrophic appear to occur with alarming regularity. Such a world calls for a new kind of thinking: thinking that issues from the chaotic, fluxing immediacy of lived experiences; thinking that resists or overflows our familiar categories of thought; and thinking that accepts and embraces messiness, contradictions, and change as the *sine qua non* of the human condition. Thinking in these genuinely processual terms means that the starting point of our inquiry is not so much about the *being* of entities such as 'organization', but their constant and perpetual *becoming*. I very much welcome this long overdue scholarly effort at exploring and examining the fundamental issue of *process* and its implications for organization studies. Hari Tsoukas and Ann Langley are to be congratulated on taking this very important initiative in bringing the process agenda into the systematic study of the phenomenon of organization. It promises to be a path-breaking contribution to our analysis of organization."

*Robert Chia*, Professor of Management, University of Strathclyde, UK

"This new series fits the need for a good annual text devoted to process studies. Organization theory has long required a volume specifically devoted to process research that can address process ontology, methodology, research design, and analysis. While many authors collect longitudinal data, there are still insufficient methodological tools and techniques to deal with the nature of that data. Essentially, there is still a lack of frameworks and methods to deal with good processual data or to develop process-based insights. This series will provide an important resource for all branches of organization, management, and strategy theory. The editors of the series, Professors Ann Langley and Hari Tsoukas, are excellent and very credible scholars within the process field. They will attract top authors to the series and ensure that each paper presents a high quality and insightful resource for process scholars. I expect that this series will become a staple in libraries, PhD studies, and journal editors' and process scholars' bookshelves."

*Paula Jarzabkowski*, Professor of Strategic Management, Aston Business School, UK

# 1

## How Matter Matters: Objects, Artifacts, and Materiality in Organization Studies

### Introducing the Third Volume of "Perspectives on Organization Studies"

*Paul R. Carlile, Davide Nicolini, Ann Langley, and Haridimos Tsoukas*

## 1.1 Bringing materiality back in

The idea that objects and materiality should be included in theoretical accounts of organizational phenomena is not new. More than half a century ago, for example, Tavistock researchers introduced the idea of "socio-technical systems" (STS) to indicate that organizing processes entail both people and material technologies and artifacts (Trist and Bamforth, 1951; Pasmore, 1988; Pickering, 1995). However, being separated by a hyphen, the "technical" and "social" systems were viewed as relatively self-contained and independent from one another, although it was clearly acknowledged that they impact on one another. Socio-technical systems researchers were not so much preoccupied with materiality as with a concept of narrower scope: technology. The latter were the tools organizational members work with to process inputs. The extra-human materiality of the world was largely taken for granted and, therefore, left relatively unexplored. The main thrust of research on socio-technical systems was to find ways whereby the demands of the social system and those of the technical system could be "jointly optimized" (Cherns, 1978: 63).

Yet, despite the explicit attention to technology, for several decades the attention to objects and materiality, more broadly, both in organization studies and the rest of social science has been limited. The so-called language turn in social science that took place towards the end of the twentieth century had in fact the unintended consequence of marginalizing objects and hiding materiality from view. Ironically, much as human lives towards the second half of the last century became mediated by objects and artifacts and depended on the functioning of technical systems, materiality in a broad sense became relatively marginalized as a topic of research interest. For example, Orlikowski and Scott (2008) analyzed all the articles published in leading management journals in the previous decade and found that 95 percent of them fail to take into consideration the role and influence of technology in organizational life. As Barad (2003) put it, in the brave new world of post-functional social science:

> Language matters. Discourse matters. Culture matters. There is an important sense in which the only thing that does not seem to matter anymore is matter. (Barad, 2003: 801).

Admittedly, there are strands that have emerged putting back into play "socio-technical systems" in various guises that have become a distinguishing feature of contemporary social studies of technology (Bijker and Law, 1994; Latour, 1996; Knorr Cetina, 1997; Mol, 1999). This attention for the material aspects of social and organizational life has further spilled over into management and organization studies fueled for example by an interest for boundary objects (Star, 1989; Carlile 2002; Bechky, 2003). While organizational phenomena, even when understood processually, are still largely conceived of as a confluence of minds, intentions, or as purely communicative undertakings there is thus an increasing attention to the need to bring materiality back into the study of organizational, technology, and management phenomena and ask in which ways objects, artifacts and materiality actually matter in organizational activity. A performative approach to organization and management studies (Gherardi, 2006; Czarniawska, 2008; Sandberg and Tsoukas, 2011; Nicolini, 2012) has made us realize that organizational sense-making, cognition, knowledge, learning, and perceiving, just to mention a few "mental" activities in organizations, are not merely situated in the ideational realm but deeply implicate *sociomaterial practices* through which they are enacted. For example, what an organization learns is not the mere result of information processing or interpreting but of organizational members learning to do certain things through the use of objects, the training and use of the body, and engagement in certain practices. From a performative (or practice-based) perspective, organizational learning is a practice that is carried out in socio-material contexts, in particular ways. To know and to learn involves the material world (including the human body) as much as it involves the mind.

The present volume is both a sign of this renewed sensitivity toward materiality and an attempt to elaborate further the idea that much is to be gained if we overcome the traditional humanist view of individual actors living in a world separate of things (Suchman, 2007: 261). As we shall see, the authors in this volume agree with bringing things back in, but also developing a new conceptual repertoire and vocabulary that allows us to think and talk more deeply about the social and material as being inherently entangled (Barad, 2003). One of our aims is to declare that the distinction between "subject" and "object" is a result of historically situated human activity, not an ontological condition. As Introna (this volume) puts it, in order to develop a more sophisticated understanding of how materiality participates in shaping the worlds we live in, we must free ourselves from the idea that a bifurcated ontology is "natural" and that humans and non-human are inherently distinctive before and after such encounters.

In this introduction, however, we would like to develop one particular aspect of this discussion and acknowledge an ethical dimension that arises with this new emerging sensitivity. In short, matter does matter because it generates consequences and, therefore, an ethical dimension grows out of a natural inquiry into the sources of those consequences. Such an inquiry, however, cannot be oriented toward developing normative deontological accounts (i.e., developing moral theories that tell us what we ought to do), but rather to develop a pragmatist ethics that approaches consequences as they are experienced by individuals in the confluence of a sociomaterial practice. A pragmatist ethics approach asks that we pay special attention to the future worlds disclosed and shaped by different ways of conceiving and enacting sociomaterial arrangements (Keulartz et al., 2004). Such a pragmatist ethics should not be seen as privileging the individual as subjectivity, but rather embracing such experiences as particular temporal outcomes of a sociomaterial entanglement.

We do believe that this ethical dimension has been implicit in some discussions about materiality and accountability (Scott and Orlikowski 2012), but so far it has not received any formal attention. Such attention raises particular questions about how sociomaterial entanglements are produced, how they are conceptualized and potentially separated as individuals actively draw a line between human and non-human actors as they reflect on their experiences. Our view is that such an inquiry can have a number of practical implications for current sociomaterial assemblages, some of which acknowledge deep and long-lasting consequences. In the end, matter matters not only as an intellectual effort, but also in an ontological and practical sense, i.e., it generates consequences for how we experience and act in our world.

## 1.2 What is matter and why does it matter?

We start our short exploration of how materiality matters by applying the pragmatist principle that the best way to shed light on ideas or concepts is to ask what are their concrete, practical consequences and what difference they may make in our lives (James, 1907). Building on the work of authors such as Fahlander (2008) and Leonardi (2010; this volume), we argue that materiality is an inherently polysemic concept and that different ways of conceiving materiality matter differently in practice. In modern English, materiality is conceived of in three significant different ways: as the stuff the inanimate world is made of; as that which is opposed to the formal; and as having legal implications. A quick inquiry into these different meanings of the word materiality using the pragmatist method reveals that deciding what counts as material and materiality is not neutral; attributing the category of matter to some aspects of the world we live in is thus practically consequential and ethically relevant.

The *Oxford English Dictionary* defines materiality first as "the quality of being composed of matter; material existence; solidity" (OED, 2001).[1] According to Leonardi (2010), if we foreground the fact that things are "made of matter," i.e., if we emphasize that things are made of tangible "stuff," we tend to foreground the affordances inscribed in artifacts and the environment. Gibson (1986) conceived affordances as action possibilities available to individuals. These possibilities are inscribed in the material nature of the environment or artifacts and are thus independent of the individual's ability to perceive them. While affordances only emerge when individuals act (affordances are properties of the action capabilities of actors, not simply a way to describe their experience) they are firmly rooted in the material existence of stuff. For example, doors afford open-ability and stone affords walk-ability (contrasted, for example, with water, which does not). In other words, while the idea of affordance cuts across the subjective/objective barrier and introduces the idea that the actor and the environment make an inseparable pair (McGrenere and Ho, 2000) it also highlights the importance of "stuff" in structuring our world. This in turn alerts us to the relevance of attributing materiality to something. Miller (2005), for example, notes that the idea of materiality as brute fact is historically and culturally situated. According to Miller, distinctions between materiality and immateriality have manifested themselves in idiosyncratic ways in history and societies, and organizations are often defined by their interpretation of perceptions about materiality and immateriality. The attribution of materiality can thus be seen as a powerful rhetorical device which grants significance in arguments and deliberations. If we can convincingly claim that a feature of something is inscribed in its materiality, we can also claim that such a feature is solid, certain, and immutable (Latour (2005) makes a similar point with reference to the concept of nature). While this seems inconsequential in the case of the walk-ability of water and stone—most of the time this issue does not really make a big difference in our lives—it is not inconsequential when we consider issues such as whether gender is actually dependent on the "stuffiness" of the body or whether intelligence is rooted in a particular piece of genetic code. Matter generates consequences in our life but so does the attribution of materiality.

The *Oxford English Dictionary* also defines materiality as the opposite of that which is just formal (i.e., or what remains at the level of abstract properties and essences). The principles included in the constitution of a country or organizations are formal until specific pieces of legislation or policies make them material. In this sense, something is "material" when it helps to instantiate ideas in practice, as in the pragmatist principle discussed above.

This view of what counts as material is particularly important as it helps to include in the realm of the material a number of symbolic objects such as rules, policies, and software. While a virtual environment can hardly be thought of as "made of stuff," it can nonetheless be thought of as being material in its consequences and therefore studied as also having affordances (Orlikowski, 2007; see Dourish and Mazmanian, this volume). By the same token, a piece of equipment that remains safely stored in its original package could be considered as "immaterial" although it is made of stuff since it has no way to enter the activity of a group of people. Daniel Miller (2005) observes oddly enough that matter seems to matter even more, the more immaterial it becomes. Whether in modern art *the more transcendent meaning of a piece of art "the more its material form is worth in dollars" or in religion the more abstract and resistant to representation the more defined and enforced are its material practices (2005: 28).*

Finally, there is a third and very important meaning of the word "material" which points to a further universe of consequences (see also Leonardi, 2010). The notion of materiality is also prominent in law and accounting where the word "material" emphasizes consequentiality and significance. Material is thus used to refer to those things (e.g., material witnesses or facts) that are pertinent to the task at hand (e.g., proving the defendant's innocence). A similar use can be found in accounting where the materiality of information is decided on the basis of its practical implications. For example, The US's Securities and Exchange Commission (SEC) states that "materiality concerns with the significance of an item to users of a registrants financial statements." Errors in reporting and misstatements can thus "fall into three ranges—inconsequential, consequential and material. Companies must record errors that fall within the material misstatement range for the independent auditor to give an unqualified opinion" (Vorhies, 2005). In the context of our discussion this means that what counts as material or immaterial cannot be abstracted from the activity at hand and the relationships in which something or someone are involved. An object (and even a human) can thus be material for someone and immaterial for others, or can change status in time.

In sum, the work of authors such as Miller (2005), Fahlander (2008), and Leonardi (2010) reminds us that notions such as that of "matter" and "materiality" are not neutral. Embracing one or another view is likely to have practical consequences in both inquiry and in practical deliberation (as suggested by James in the quote above). Mattering, that is the act of attaching the category of matter to something, does matter.

## 1.3 Accounting for how matter matters with the social

In the previous section we showed that when it comes to matter, semantics has significant implications. In this section we take a step further and suggest that when authors promoted the idea that the social and material are inherently entangled, their attention has been more on the agential power of materiality rather than the ethical implication of bringing matter back in. Our subtext is that the latter is an aspect that needs to receive more attention in the current debate. Earlier, we recognized that the suggestion that matter matters in human and social life is not new, rather what is new is the increasing role granted to materiality in explaining all things social and how this role has been conceptualized. Here we argue that authors who have foregrounded the inherent sociomaterial nature of human life have usually addressed the topic from two different, albeit strictly related, angles: the performativity of matter and the entanglement between social and material aspects of human life. Ethical concerns are present but they are not as prominent as we think they should be.

A wide range of authors including Haraway (1997), Law and Mol (1995), Latour (2005), Knorr Cetina (1997), Pickering (1993), Miller (2005), Ingold (2010), Clegg and Slife (2005), Barad (2003), and Suchman (2007) made a convincing case for the need to acknowledge the performative role of materials in social affairs. The effort is to overcome the traditional human-centered bias that was planted at the core of sociological disciplines by its founding father. According to Durkheim (1982 [1895]: 136):

> But it is plain that neither material nor non-material objects produce the impulsion that determines social transformations, because they both lack motivating power. Undoubtedly there is need to take them into account in the explanations which we attempt. To some extent they exert an influence upon social evolution whose rapidity and direction vary according to their nature. But they possess no elements essential to set that evolution in motion. They are the matter to which the vital forces of society are applied, but they do not themselves release any vital forces. Thus the specifically human environment remains as the active factor.

The work of the above-mentioned authors has shown the active role that objects, artifacts, and materials play in social affairs and has described how they perform some of the work entailed in establishing and maintaining social relationships. While the discussion still rages about how to conceptualize the agential capacity of materials, the main issue is not whether material elements are involved in social structuration or performative process, but rather to what degree.

At the same time, authors have also suggested the need to re-conceptualize social (and organizational) phenomena in such a way that the active role of materiality is fully taken into consideration. The aim here is to conjure a view where social and material elements are strongly entangled and mutually interpenetrate each other (see Jones, this volume, for a discussion). From this perspective, all things social are thus inherently heterogeneous and social life transpires through an inextricable assemblage of human and non-human elements. Latour (1996), for example, builds his argument on the comparison between the sociality among humans and that of other primates. He notes that a fundamental difference between the two is that for baboons "the social is always woven with the social: hence it lacks of durability" (Latour, 1996: 234). By contrast, the stability of human social orders beyond particular contexts of action can only be explained when one allows for the active role played by material objects—symbols alone do not resolve this puzzle. As Latour puts it: "by dislocating interaction so as to associate ourselves with non-humans, we can endure beyond the present, in a matter other than our body, and we can interact at a distance . . . " (Latour, 1996: 239). What makes human sociality distinctive, then, is that practices are not merely constellations of intersubjectivity, they are also constellations of "interobjectivity."

Thus, the social and the material—which includes not only artifacts but also "landscape, layout and material of buildings and settlements, trees and vegetation, animals, bodies and less evident material matters such as rain, ice and snow" (Fahlander, 2008: 136)—are posited to be ontologically inseparable and we need to acknowledge the inherent "socialness of things." This is in turn signaled by the adoption of the adjective "socio-material." The elimination of the hyphen is taken here as an attempt "to signal this ontological fusion. Any distinction of humans and technologies is analytical only, and done with the recognition that these entities necessarily entail each other in practice" (Orlikowski and Scott, 2008: 456).

The efforts of these authors have helped develop a sociomaterial sensitivity in the study of social and organizational phenomena. They have argued that materials need to be granted citizenship in the citadel of the social and that this in turn requires rethinking the social. So matter matters both agentially (i.e., the performativity of actors and artifacts) and ontologically (i.e., it is irreducibly entangled with the social). Our argument is that to these two we need to add a third, complementary angle. This is because fore-grounding the performativity of materiality and adopting an "entangled" orientation naturally raises key ethical issues of consequences, responsibility, and accountability that need to receive attention. There are at least three reasons why a sociomaterial sensitivity always has ethical implications.

First, adopting an entangled orientation means accepting that any time we either assemble sociomaterial arrangements (e.g., offices, hospitals, schools) or impose distinctions in existing ones, we distribute different and potentially unequal ontological positions for all involved in a given situation. Given that different ontological positions include different attributions of identity (what things are) and become associated with unbalanced forms of empowerment (what is included is empowered, while what is left out is relegated) assembling and cutting sociomaterial assemblages has consequences for the lives of those involved.

Second, any form of agency is made all the more poignant by the fact that its consequences will be material and can last over time. In other words, an attention to sociomateriality is not only an attention to material performativity; it also implies attention to the durable consequences of such performativity. While materiality contributes to making sociality durable (as in Latour's examples above), it does the same with its consequences. Assembling a city as a place where people and cars are inextricably entangled as, for example, politicians did in Los Angeles in the mid-twentieth century (Bottles, 1987) may have consequences that last much longer than the life of those who are responsible for it and also for those who are excluded from these arrangements, i.e., those who cannot drive or cannot afford a car (see also Star, 1991 for a similar argument in the field of technology).

Finally, upholding an ontology of separateness (Suchman, 2007: 257) between the human and the material, that is, upholding the human-centered view purported by traditional sociology, can in itself produce negative consequences when such separateness spills over to the human realm and we start treating living beings in the same way Durkheim was treating things. A passive view of materiality makes way for neutrality being placed on non-humans and humans alike; and so exploitation is not far away (see Introna, this volume).

## 1.4 A matter of consequence: Towards a sociomaterial ethical sensitivity

When we take on a sociomaterial sensitivity we must accept that this also implies embracing an ethical responsiveness to the features or conse-quences of a particular "agential cut" (Barad 2003). The principle is that while the idea of sociomaterial entanglements foregrounds work, activity, and the performativity of assemblages ("construction"), this is not just about what is in our heads as a "social construction," but also materially present and durable and so inseparable from the social. This entanglement then must be acknowledged when starting any conversation about ethics and accountability. Otherwise an ethical inquiry remains oddly inert to what is to be found in the entanglement and instead is satisfied with a deontological orientation of pre-existing rules as a guide to future actions. Further, accepting a sociomaterial ontology helps us see that relativism is not a productive orientation because it purposefully turns away from what is shared and durable thus rejecting the essence of sociomaterial as a starting point. For these reasons a sociomaterial orientation pushes ethical inquiry on to a much stronger productive footing.

Many of the chapters in this book speak directly or help us develop an ethical dimension that naturally arises from a sociomaterial sensitivity. The topic is explicitly set up by Barad (2003; this volume) in her use of the word "intra-action." Barad uses this neologism both to emphasize that the com-ponents of a phenomenon are agentially inseparable and to underscore the responsibility and accountability that comes to an individual observer making an agential cut through a given sociomaterial practice. Such a cut or actions naturally include some things and exclude others and so consequences and accountability naturally arise. Here Barad invokes her background as a physicist putting forward a quantum ontology where light is expressed as both a particle and a wave. But when it comes to empirically examining this duality, a measurement apparatus can only emphasize one or the other, a particle or a wave. Barad is not putting forward a physics-induced relativism, but what she call "agential realism" containing within it an epistemology, an ontology, and an ethics. So any observation, and the actions that follow it, is an agential cut that generates consequences toward a given "phenomenon" (Barad 2003). In her essay in this volume she plays imaginatively with the materialization of time, powerfully arguing that "matter doesn't move in time. Matter doesn't evolve in time. Matter does time." This "spacetimemattering" as she calls it then offers a significant reorientation of understanding not just of matter and time, but more thoroughly and intimately about justice and what she purposefully labels "respons-ability." This reveals that any cut is also an intra-action of other cuts whose image she reveals in the phrase "cutting together apart." Thus there is nothing simple about the ethical stance required, but also nothing impossible either. She remains complex, yet optimistic.

Shotter engages in an extensive conversation with Barad's work in his chapter. Starting with her notion of "intra-action," he builds on it by relating it to the work of Bakhtin/Voloshinov. Shotter's point of departure is a process relational ontology whereby "things," especially living entities, are not already made, independently existing entities, but always in the making, existing as dynamic stabilities forming ever-changing relations to their surroundings. Human agents "are not separate agents, but 'participant parts' within and of an indivisible, continually unfolding, stranded, flowing whole, able to set the boundaries that matter to us within it in one way at one moment and in another way the next" (Shotter, this volume). All "things" exist as agential enactments, notes Shotter, as focal things attended to *from within* a larger, ceaselessly unfolding, and fluid process. Shotter is particularly interested in bodily materiality and its role in the genesis of novelty. Attending to the particularities of our circumstances, our current ways of acting, and the bodily responses to those we have living contact with, enables us to engage dialogi-cally with the world, thus giving rise to immanent creativity. Bringing forth new events, especially through giving "'expressive shape' to the movements of feeling occurring within us as we body them forth out into the world" (Shotter, this volume), creates uniquely new events that open up previously unnoticed possibilities. Interestingly, Shotter's chapter walks the talk: he does not "intel-lectually" draw on Barad's work but his reading of it is a genuinely dialogical exercise shaped by the author's expectations engendered by other authors (notably Bakhtin/Voloshinov), giving rise to new feelings and thoughts.

Three chapters provide empirical examples that outline types of cuts that have to be made and are occurring in organizational lives. The first is Endrissat and Noppeney's chapter on perfume making. This paper not only accounts for the challenge of working across expertise boundaries and what is naturally included or excluded as that takes place, but it examines the development of a product that starts as immaterial (the emotion of a fragrance) but then has to be made material as different experts work across perfume development silos. Dourish and Mazmanian's chapter on the "consequences of digitization" looks closely at how the immaterial world of digital representations creates a new and consequential cut in existing practice when new digital technologies (digital photography and simulation modeling) are applied. This constraint not only generates consequences that impact a given industry, but fundamentally alters relationships and defines who has power and who does not. The paper by Orlikowski and Scott takes a very detailed look at how a new set of digital technologies (travel websites and "rating" algorithms) are fundamentally reconfiguring sociomaterial entanglements. The consequences of these new technologies are now becoming clear and what was once seen as greater efficiency and a democratic power shift toward the end consumer is now being seen as problematic "anonymous" user-generated content with potential negative consequences for the travel industry. This raises the question of how these new technologies naturally allow for "cuts" across a large set of "anonymous" actors that make locating accountabilities difficult if not elusive altogether.

Leonardi and Olsen's chapters speak instead to the issue of the durability of the material world and how that cannot be overlooked. Leonardi places this durability within the context of the emergence of new technologies within organizations and suggests that a sociomaterial approach must be careful not to have a focus that is too "narrow" in explaining the emergence of technology as has often been the case with STS approaches. To counteract this narrow orientation he applies a more macro-theoretical perspective to account for how a sociomaterial lens can be applied to understanding the emergence of technologies in large, more durable organizational dynamics. Olsen takes the durability argument even further and invokes an archaeological image of materiality and how it provides a necessary "stability" so that a social entity can grow in the first place and sustain itself in the second place. Olsen plays with this image as he examines the demise of Soviet "mining" cities. He invokes a powerful quote from Marx to make his point about the power and durability of human assembled materiality: "Men make their own history, but they do not make it just as they please."

In so doing, however, Olsen also raises a further issue that constitutes the central theme of the remaining chapters in this collection. Olsen suggests in fact that the capacity of materials to support the durability of social arrangements (as in Latour's example above) implies that in some ways we acknowledge the need of things to retain their "individual integrity." The "in-placeness" of things thus challenges both the dualist view implicit in the common-sense view of materiality discussed in section 1.2 above, but also its opposite, that is, the idea of a complete indistinguishability between the material and the social. The subtext here is that abandoning a naïve view of materiality should not result in the taking up of an equally naïve view of sociomateriality as some sort of uncontaminated fusion.

This issue is then examined in particular by Matthew Jones whose chapter reminds us that simply invoking a sociomaterial approach and all that is entailed by that is not without its challenges and consequences. The author takes a careful view of some the emerging sociomaterial ways of thinking and uses an empirical case to explore what are their concrete practical consequences—what they make us see and not see. Building on the results of his application of the pragmatist method, he provides the readers with a valuable cautionary note to motivate a more careful application of a socio-material lens. Conflating different ontological claims may reduce, instead of enhance, the capacity to perceive the practical and ethical consequences of the entanglement of the social and the material.

Gherardi and Perrotta's chapter introduces the idea of formativeness from Pareyson's (1960) aesthetic philosophy to argue that creative practices generate not only novel material forms but also and simultaneously consti-tute knowing about the creative process. They define formativeness as "a process realized through a doing that while it does invents 'the way of doing.'" The authors draw on narrative interviews with craftswomen to show how formativeness involves corporeality, material agency, playful-ness, hybridization, and recursive realization. The chapter provides a very vivid illustration of the sociomaterial entanglements embedded in the practices of creation, showing how these processes have consequences not only for the production of novelty in the moment, but also for the potentialities of subsequent creative activity brought into being through these practices.

Introna's chapter develops a unique position as it tries to address the consequences of sociomateriality. Building on the work of Heidegger and Harman he questions the prevailing bifurcated being ontology of humans and things and since we have historically treated "things" passively he suggests that eventually this spills over and we end up treating humans similarly. To counter this he calls for a novel ethics based on a radically new way of approaching things that he calls "an ethos of letting be." This implies an openness toward the becoming of "all things other," a "dwelling amid" orientation that like Heidegger (and Nietzsche before him) he contrasts with the typical Western attitude driven by will over things. The resulting attitude is one of "mindfully dwelling amid" which he describes as akin to the intimacy of the artisan with his or her material (recalling Gherardi and Perrotta's chapter in this volume). This new ethos of letting be introduces a therapeutic undecidability that challenges a detached and passive view of materiality and so prevents such neutrality (exploitativeness) from being placed on non-humans and humans alike. "Letting be" is thus an active orientation, not a passive one. On the other hand this could be seen as the vestigial remains of a postmodern stance that carries with it an unproductive ethics. Whatever the direction one takes from this ambiguous slogan of "letting be" one can at least see it as usefully avoiding either a preconceived normative ethical stance or a relativistic "anything goes" position that offers no sociomaterial constraint to comprehend the durability of its consequences. In any case, for matter to matter there have to be consequences and yet those consequences have to be considered and acted upon by those involved.

## Notes

1. materiality, n. Third edition, March 2001; online version March 2012. <http://www.oed.com/view/Entry/114928>, accessed April 28, 2012. An entry for this word was first included in *New English Dictionary*, 1905.

## References

Barad, K. (2003). "Posthumanist Performativity: Toward an Understanding of How Matter Comes to Matter." *Signs: Journal of Women in Culture and Society*, 28/3: 801–31.

Bechky, B. (2003). "Sharing Meaning Across Occupational Communities: The Transformation of Understanding on the Production Floor." *Organization Science*, 14: 312–30.

Bijker, W. and Law, J. (1994). *Shaping Technology/Building Society: Studies in Sociotechnical Change*. Cambridge, MA: MIT Press.

Bottles, S. L. (1987). *Los Angeles and the Automobile: The Making of the Modern City*. Berkeley, Los Angeles, and London: University of California Press.

Carlile, P. (2002). "A Pragmatic View of Knowledge and Boundaries: Boundary Objects in New Product Development." *Organization Science*, 13: 442–55.

Cherns, A. (1978). "The Principles of Sociotechnical Design," in W. Pasmore and J. Sherwood (eds.), *Sociotechnical Systems*. La Jolla, CA: University Associates, pp. 61–71.

Clegg, J. W. and Slife, B. D. (2005). "Epistemology and the Hither Side: A Levinasian Account of Relational Knowing." *European Journal of Psychotherapy, Counselling & Health*, 7/1–2: 65–76.

Czarniawska, B. (2008). *A Theory of Organizing*. Cheltenham, UK: Edward Elgar.

Durkheim, E. (1982 [1895]). *The Rules of Sociological Method*, trans W. D. Halls. New York: Free Press.

Fahlander, F. (2008). "Differences That Matter: Materialities, Material Culture and Social Practice," in H. Glørstad and L. Hedeager (eds.), *Six Essays on the Materiality of Society and Culture*. Gothenburg: Bricoleur Press, pp. 127–54.

Gherardi, S. (2006). *Organizational Knowledge*. Oxford: Blackwell.

Gibson, J. J. (1986). *The Ecological Approach to Visual Perception*. Hillsdale, NJ: Lawrence Erlbaum.

Haraway, D. J. (1997). *Modest_Witness@Second_Millennium. FemaleMan© _Meets_OncoMouse™: Feminism and Technoscience*. New York and London: Routledge.

Ingold, T. (2010). "The Textility of Making." *Cambridge Journal of Economics*, 34/1: 91–102.

James, W. (1907). "Pragmatism's Conception of Truth." *Journal of Philosophy, Psychology and Scientific Methods*, 4/6: 141–55.

Keulartz, J., Schermer, M., Korthals, M., and Swierstra, T. (2004). "Ethics in Technological Culture: A Programmatic Proposal for a Pragmatist Approach." *Science, Technology & Human Values*, 29/1: 3–29.

Knorr Cetina, K. (1997). "Sociality with Objects: Social Relations in Postsocial Knowledge Societies." *Theory, Culture and Society*, 14: 1–30.

Latour, B. (1996). "On Interobjectivity." *Mind, Culture, and Activity*, 3/4: 228–45.

—— (2005). *Reassembling the Social: An Introduction to Actor-Network-Theory*. Oxford: Oxford University Press.

Law, J. and Mol, A. (1995). "Notes on Materiality and Sociality." *Sociological Review*, 43/2: 274–84.

Leonardi, P. M. (2010). "Digital Materiality? How Artifacts Without Matter, Matter." *First Monday*, 15/6. Available at <http://www.uic.edu/htbin/cgiwrap/bin/ojs/index.php/fm/article/viewArticle/3036/2567>.

McGrenere, J. and Ho, W. (2000). "Affordances: Clarifying and Evolving a Concept." *Graphics Interface 2000* (May): 179–84.

Miller, D. (2005). "Materiality: An Introduction," in D. Miller (ed.), *Materiality*. Durham, NC: Duke University Press, pp. 1–50.

Mol, A. (1999). "Ontological Politics: A Word and Some Questions," in J. Law and J. Hassard (eds.), *Actor Network Theory and After*. Oxford and Keele: Blackwell and the Sociological Review, pp. 74–89.

Nicolini, D. (2012). *Practice Theory, Work and Organization: An Introduction*. Oxford: Oxford University Press.

Orlikowski, W. (2007). "Sociomaterial Practices: Exploring Technology at Work." *Organization Studies*, 28: 1435–48.

—— and Scott, S. V. (2008). "Sociomateriality: Challenging the Separation of Technology, Work and Organization." *Academy of Management Annals*, 2/1: 433–74.

Pareyson, L. (1960). *Estetica: teoria della formatività*. Bologna: Zanichelli.

Pasmore, W. (1988). *Designing Effective Organizations: The Sociotechnical Systems Perspective*. New York: John Wiley.

Pickering, A. (1993). "The Mangle of Practice: Agency and Emergence in the Sociology of Science." *American Journal of Sociology*, 99/3: 559–89.

—— (1995). *The Mangle of Practice: Time, Agency and Science*. Chicago: University of Chicago Press.

Sandberg, J. and Tsoukas, H. (2011). "Grasping the Logic of Practice: Theorizing through Practical Rationality." *Academy of Management Review*, 36: 338–60.

Scott, S. and Orlikowski, W. (2012). "Reconfiguring relations of accountability: Materialization of social media in the travel sector." *Accounting, Organization and Society*, 37, 1: 26–40.

Star, S. L. (1989). "The Structure of Ill-Structured Solutions: Boundary Objects and Heterogeneous Distributed Problem Solving," in M. Huhns and L. Gasser (eds.), *Readings in Distributed Artificial Intelligence*. Menlo Park, CA: Morgan Kaufman, pp. 37–54.

—— (1991). "Power, Technologies and the Phenomenology of Conventions: On Being Allergic to Onions," in J. Law (ed.), *A Sociology of Monsters: Essays on Power, Technology and Domination*. London: Routledge, pp. 26–56.

Suchman, L. (2007). *Human–Machine Reconfigurations: Plans and Situated Action*. Cambridge: Cambridge University Press.

Trist, E. and Bamforth, K. (1951). "Some Social and Psychological Consequences of Longwall Method of Coal-Getting." *Human Relations*, 4/1: 3–38.

Vorhies, J. B. (2005). "The New Importance of Materiality.", online (May). Available at <http://Nkww.aicpa.or~4/pubs/iofa/mav2005/vorhies.htm>, accessed March 17, 2012.

# 2

# Ma(r)king Time: Material Entanglements and Re-memberings: Cutting Together-Apart[1]

*Karen Barad*

**Abstract:** This keynote address engages in some imaginative play about one of matter's most intimate doings—the materialization of time. Matter doesn't move in time. Matter doesn't evolve in time. Matter does time. Matter materializes and enfolds different temporalities. This talk experiments with the disruption of temporal continuity and entanglements of different temporalities. The conference attendees were invited to participate in a performance of spacetime (re)configurings more akin to how electrons experience the world than any journey narrated though rhetorical forms that presume actors move along trajectories across a stage of spacetime (often called history). The electron was invoked as our host (an interesting body to inhabit), not in order to suggest flat-footed analogies between "macro" and "micro" worlds, concepts that already presume a given spatial scale, but rather as a way of thinking with and through dis/continuity—a dis/orienting experience of the dis/jointedness of time and space, entanglements of here and there, now and then, that is, a ghostly sense of dis/continuity, a *quantum dis/continuity*. Each scene presented diffracts various temporalities within and across the field of spacetime-mattering. Scenes never rest, but are reconfigured within, dispersed across, and threaded through one another. This dis/jointed movement is intended to produce a felt sense of différance, of *intra-activity*, of *agential separability—differentiatings that cut together/apart—that is the hauntological nature of quantum entanglements.*

Matter is not mere stuff. It is not an inanimate givenness. Matter is not in need of some supplement to put it in motion, to enliven it, to give it agency. It is not inaction incarnate—the remainder of the remainder of a body once inhabited by a spirit, or substance not even worthy of inhabitation. It is not some unresponsive indifferent stone cold dispassionate inertness that makes even death look lively, that which isn't even worthy of the grip of death, of pain, pleasure, joy, suffering. It is not an inert canvas for the inscription of culture and meanings, a static thing without memory, history, or an inheritance to call its own. It is not simply some thereness available for the taking. A mere backdrop to what really matters.

Matter is substance in its iterative intra-active becoming—not a thing, but a doing, a congealing of agency. It is morphologically active, responsive, generative, articulate, and alive. Mattering is the ongoing differentiating of the world. Matter plays an agentive role in its ongoing materialization. Physical matters, matters of fact, matters of concern, matters of care, matters of justice, are not separable.

Matter is a matter of trans/materiality—a cutting together-apart differentiating-entanglements, agential relatings and differences across, among, and "between genders, species, spaces, knowledges, sexualities, subjectivities, and temporalities. At stake are questions of being/becoming, knowing, getting along together, and living well."[2]

Today I would like to engage in some imaginative play about one of matter's most intimate doings—the materialization of time. Matter doesn't move in time. Matter doesn't evolve in time. Matter does time. Matter materializes and enfolds different temporalities.[3]

Today I would like to imagine with you possibilities for new imaginaries for time. Precisely because it is important to unsettle comfortable assumptions concerning notions of the new, the now, presence/absence, progress, tradition, evolution, extinction, stasis, restoration, remediation, return, reversal, universal, generation, production, emergence, recursion, iteration, temporary, momentary, biographic, historical, fast, slow, speeding up, intensifying, compressing, pausing, disrupting, rupturing, changing, becoming, being . . .

This is not a mere exercise in metaphysics, or physics. At stake are questions of justice and response-ability. I want to invite you to come on a journey with me, to experiment with possibilities of telling different kinds of stories, stories that put the story-teller at risk, stories that are generative of different response-abilities, all the while being attentive to the materiality of imagining.

Now I will begin my talk but not from the beginning, because the beginning has already clearly begun, or rather *the* beginning will never arrive . . .

This "beginning," like all beginnings, is always already threaded through with anticipation of where it is going but will never simply reach and of a past that has yet to come. It is not merely that the future and the past are not "there" and never sit still, but that the present is not simply here-now. Multiply heterogeneous iterations all: past, present, and future, not in a relation of linear unfolding, but threaded through one another in a non-linear enfolding of spacetimemattering, a topology that defies any suggestion of a smooth continuous manifold.

It is not only the nature of time in its disjointedness that is at stake, but also *disjointedness itself*. Indeed, the nature of "dis" and "jointedness," of discontinuity and continuity, of separation and entanglement, and their im/possible intra-relationships are at issue.

This paper is about joins and disjoins—cutting together/apart—not separate consecutive activities, but a single event that is not one. *Intra-action*, not interaction.[4]

An experiment. I've attempted to write this talk in a way that disrupts the conventions of historical narrative forms such as those that underlie stories of scientific progress: tales of the continuous accretion and refinement of scientific knowledge over the course of history, sagas of progress from an earlier time period to a later one punctuated with discoveries that lead the way out of the swamp of ignorance and uncertainty to the bedrock of solid and certain knowledge. In an effort to disrupt this kind of narrative (and not only this), I aim to provide you, the active listener, with an opportunity to engage in an imaginative journey that is akin to how electrons experience the world: that is, a dis/orienting experience of the dis/jointedness of time and space, entanglements of here and there, now and then, a ghostly sense of dis/continuity, a *quantum dis/continuity*, which is neither fully discontinuous with continuity nor even fully continuous with discontinuity, and in any case, surely not one with itself. There is no overarching sense of temporality, of continuity, in place. And no coherent sense of self is assumed as in so many time travel tales. The scenes are neither discontinuous nor continuous with one another (or themselves). There is no smooth temporal (or spatial) topology connecting beginning and end. Each scene diffracts various temporalities, iteratively differentiating-entangling, within and across, the field of spacetimemattering. Scenes never rest but are reconfigured within and are dispersed across and threaded through one another. Multiple entanglements, differences cutting through and re-splicing one another. My hope is that what comes across in this dis/jointed movement is a felt sense of différance, of *intra-activity*, of *agential separability—differentiatings that cut together/apart—that is the hauntological nature of quantum entanglements.*[5]

. . .

Particles are given to fits, to paroxysms, to spasmodic bouts of e-motion or activity.[6]

There seemed to be something queer about the quantum from the beginning. Or rather, it became evident from the start that the quantum causes trouble for the very notion of "from the beginning."

1912: Niels Bohr proposes the first quantum model of matter (i.e, the atom).

Bohr's inheritance: The planetary model of the model of the atom—electrons orbiting the nucleus like planets orbit the sun. A debt he owes to his teacher Ernest Rutherford. The planetary model has drawbacks: an orbiting electron would continuously radiate away its energy, giving off a continuous spectrum of light while it quickly spirals into the nucleus. Atoms wouldn't be stable. No small matter.

Other inheritances: In 1900, Planck proposes the quantization of energy. Energy is exchanged in discrete packets, not continuously. 1905: Einstein proposes that light itself is quantized. He wins the Nobel Prize for his "crazy idea" of the photon (light quantum), not for relativity.

Bohr's idea: The nucleus remains at the atom's center, but electrons don't *orbit* the nucleus (*pace* Rutherford). Rather, each electron *resides* in one of a finite set of discrete/quantized energy levels, and atoms only emit photons when their electrons "jump" from one level to another. In particular, when an electron "jumps" from a higher energy state to a lower one it emits a photon whose color/frequency is determined by the size of the jump, i.e., the change in energy. In this way, there is no continuous draining away of the electron's energy and no continuous spectrum of light emitted. With Bohr's model, atoms are stable and each kind of atom emits a unique discrete "line spectrum."

A tidy little mechanism? A simple causal explanation for the existence of matter that accounts for its spectral qualities. Nice. But not so fast . . . Specters abound. The very process by which a single line in the atomic spectrum is produced is spooked. Each spectral line is the result of an electron making a *quantum leap* from a higher energy level to a lower energy level. But what precisely is the nature of this "leap"?

. . .

Spacetime Coordinates: Universal time. No time. 1687 [Newton's *Principia*] diffracted through 1814 [Laplace's demon—the hero of a thought experiment, a clever chap who stops time, gathers information about the whereabouts and instantaneous movements of every particle, making for a complete data set which when plugged into Newton's equation gives Man his ultimate wish of complete knowability]. All time is calculable, laid out, the entirety of the past, of all that lays behind us, and the entirety of the future, of all that is before us, starting with but one moment, any moment, all moments made equal . . . All time in no time at all.

How much of our understanding of the nature of change has been and continues to be caught up in the notion of continuity? For Newton, physicist extraordinaire, inventor of the calculus, author of biblical prophesies, uniter of heaven and earth, continuity was everything. It gave him the calculus. And the calculus gave voice to his vision of a deterministic world: placing knowledge of the future and past, in its entirety, at Man's feet. Prediction, retrodiction. Time reversal, time universal. Man's for the asking. The price but a slim investment in what is happening in an instant, any instant. Determinism rules. Nature is a clockwork, a machine, a windup toy the Omniscient One started up at time t = 0 and then even He lost interest in and abandoned, or perhaps remembers now and again and drops in to do a little tuning up. The universe is a tidy affair.

. . .

1900: *Quantum* signifies the "smallest possible, and therefore indivisible, unit of a given quantity or quantifiable phenomenon." It is a measure of *the discreteness of nature*. Unlike any ordinary experience of jumping or leaping, when an electron makes a quantum leap it does so in a discontinuous fashion. In particular, the electron is initially at one energy level and then it is at another *without having been anywhere in between*. Talk about ghostly matters!

A photon of a given color is emitted during a leap that is outside of time. A photon of a color determined by the energy difference between where it started from and where it is going. A photon emitted neither before or as it leaves, or even after or when it arrives, or at any moment in between. A photon emitted at no determinate time at all. A photon emitted before it reaches where it will have already gone, at an indeterminate moment that troubles the very possibility of differentiating or ordering moments of leaving and arriving, in order to be just the right color. A color given by the size of a leap that will not yet have been determined, or always already had. A photon suspended in an indeterminacy cross-cut by a difference that has not yet been counted. Causality run amuck!

A quantum leap is a dis/continuous movement, and not just any discontinuous movement, but a particularly queer kind that troubles the very dichotomy between discontinuity and continuity. Indeed, *quantum dis/*

*continuity* troubles the very notion of *dicho-tomy*—the cutting into two—itself. All this "quantum weirdness" is actually "quantum *queerness*," and I don't mean simply strange. Q is for queer—the un/doing of identity. *Quantum dis/continuity* is at the crux of this im/possible, im/passible, trans/formation.

. . .

> On the dark stage, under a very dim light, the ghosts, dressed in grey, business-like attire, keep playing out the events of one night in 1941 when Heisenberg, then working for his home country of Germany, visited Niels Bohr, who was living in occupied Denmark.... Like the ghost, foretold by the opening question of *Hamlet*, [the ghostly reiterative (re)enactments of] Heisenberg's visit [mark] the spectral voice of justice.[7]

. . .

It's quite uncanny. During the early years of the twentieth century evidence came to light that light is ... well, it behaves like a particle after all—the position Newton advocated— ... *except*, when it behaves like a wave (as James Clerk Maxwell, Thomas Young, and others helped to demonstrate convincingly in the nineteenth century). And matter, it most definitely behaves like a particle ... well, except when it behaves like a wave. What nonsense is this? Has science lost its mind, gone mad?

Waves and particles are ontologically distinct kinds: waves are extended disturbances that can overlap and move through one another; particles are localized entities that singly occupy a given position in space one moment at a time. Light can't simply just *be* a wave *and* a particle, extended *and* localized, substance *and* disturbance, a thing *and* a doing.

So much for the solid confidence, the assured certainty, the bedrock consistency of science, at the brink of a new century. It was not merely that new empirical evidence concerning the nature of light seemed to contradict the established view, but during the first quarter of the twentieth century, it became increasingly difficult to understand how *any* consistent understanding of the nature of light could be possible. Desperate to make sense of all this, Bohr makes one of the strangest moves in the history of physics: he turns his attention to the question of ... *language*!

Entertaining questions that most physicists wouldn't even see as questions Bohr asks: What do we *mean* by "particle" or "wave"? What are the conditions for the possibility for the meaningful use of these concepts? What is the nature of scientific concepts? What role do they play? How do they matter?

Bohr's unique contribution is this: he proposes that we understand *concepts to be specific material arrangements* of experimental apparatuses.

There are no separately determinate individual entities that *interact* with one another; rather, the co-constitution of determinately bounded and propertied entities results from specific *intra-actions*. That is, not only concepts but also boundaries and properties of objects become determinate, not forevermore, but rather, as an inseparable part of, what Bohr calls a *phenomenon—the inseparability (differentiated indivisibility) of "object" and "agencies of observation."*

. . .

Stage Left: A ghost of Thomas Young and his famous two-slit experiment. (An experiment Thomas Young famously performed, but probably never did.) The two-slit experiment—the grand identity filter, the perfect litmus test of the character of being, the greatest ontological sorting machine of all time. Thomas Young is lecturing. Sound waves from the two speakers set up at the front of the lecture hall form a sonic diffraction pattern so that alternately spaced conic sections of the audience can hear Young's voice with clarity while the others sit with quizzical looks not hearing a word and still others have their ears plugged because the sound is so loud as to be unbearable. The words come clearly to those who are well-placed:

> This can be demonstrated using a simple instrument that I call a *two-slit apparatus*. It's very simple really. It has just three parts: a device that is the source of the entity being tested, a barrier with two holes in it, and a screen placed some distance further back. Now, if you want to know if an entity is a wave or a particle you simply fire a bunch of them at the barrier with the two open slits. One of two patterns will appear on the screen. If most of the entities hitting the screen collect directly across from the slits the entity in question is a particle. On the other hand, if a distinctive pattern with alternating bands of intensity appears on the screen, the entity in question is a wave. Note that the pattern of alternating bands, or *diffraction pattern*, is similar to the wave pattern formed by overlapping disturbances when two stones are dropped simultaneously into a pond at a small distance from one another. In summary, my device—the two-slit apparatus—gives a sure-fire method of distinguishing waves from particles. In this way, it is possible to categorize all of nature as belonging to one kind or the other.

Some audience members clap when Mr Young has finished. Others have already left in frustration and have asked for a refund of the ticket price. Someone notices that the remaining audience members form a pattern of bands radiating outwards from the stage. Interested in this phenomenon, one person raises her hand, but Mr Young has already disappeared.

. . .

An explosive end to the great friendship of two of the twentieth century's greatest scientists, Werner Heisenberg and Niels Bohr, authors of the "Copenhagen interpretation" of quantum physics. Why did Heisenberg, then head of the German atomic bomb project, go to occupied Copenhagen, in the midst of the war to see his old friend Niels Bohr, a Danish Jew? Did Heisenberg hope to find out what Bohr knew about the Allied bomb project? Did he come to warn Bohr about the German bomb project to reassure him that he was doing everything in his power to stall it? Did he want to see if he could persuade Bohr to take advantage of their status as authorities on atomic physics to convince the Axis and Allied powers to abandon their efforts to build atomic weapons? Did he hope to gain some important insight from his mentor about physics, or ethics, or the relationship between the two?

Speculation. Specularity. Spectrality.

Science and justice, matter and meaning are not separate elements that intersect now and again. They are inextricably fused together, and no event, no matter how energetic, can tear them asunder. They cannot be dissociated, not by chemical processing, or centrifuge, or nuclear blast.

"Does one as a physicist have the moral right to work on the practical exploitation of atomic energy?" Heisenberg's haunting question to Bohr hangs in the air throughout Copenhagen/*Copenhagen* (Frayn 2000), enfolded into the making of spacetime, its reverberations returning again, for the first time.

. . .

SpaceTime Coordinates: The Apocalypse 2060 AD, or thereafter [Newton's prediction for the end of time] diffracted through 2003 [discovery of Newton's seventeenth-century prediction/prophesy] diffracted through the seventeenth century [Newton—the prophet, the seer of the future, the inventor of the calculus, the great calculator, the seer of the laws of nature that determine every event for all time—kills time for a second time].

The end of time. We've heard this before, we hear it all the time. We inherit the future, not just the past.

Newton, the natural philosopher, had already done in time. His laws of physics always already make this pronouncement: in a deterministic universe there is no time—all events have already happened, time doesn't exist. The future has already happened. And yet, the Great Calculator makes a prediction to end all predictions. Newton, the theologian, the scholar of biblical prophesy, calculates the end of time. His prediction hidden away for a time not his own.

Biblical prophesy and natural philosophy, each engages in predictions.

One prediction for the end of time is uncertain ("It may end later"), the other leaving absolutely no room for uncertainty, not a hair's breadth.

Biblical prophesy was surely more than an avocation for Newton; it was an invocation of spirits dis/continuous with his natural philosophy.

Spirits took center stage in his natural philosophy, but *not* his theology. For Newton they were everything and nothing. The Ether filling all space, then banished. Appearing and disappearing. Spirits have a peculiar presence/absence throughout his work. A vanishing presence. A reappearing absence. Forever returning. Coming from the future as well as the past.

. . .

Stage Right: The lights go up on the house and reveal the ghosts of Einstein and Bohr pushing away from the craps table, where Einstein, with unchecked disdain in his voice, reports that some physicists claim they saw God playing there. Einstein has had enough. They mosey on over to another table and quickly fall into the groove of an old conversation. The table in front of them sports a two-slit apparatus at the very center of their imaginations. They are performing *gedanken* or thought experiments with the two-slit apparatus. The stakes: nothing less than the nature of reality. Bohr insists that using a two-slit apparatus he can show that with one arrangement of the two-slit apparatus, light, or even atoms, or electrons, behave as waves, and with a complementary arrangement these entities behave as particles. He explains that entities are not inherently "wave" or "particle," and that it is possible to produce wave and particle phenomena/behaviors/performances when the entity in question "intra-acts" with the appropriate apparatus, where "intra-action" contra "interaction" does not presume the existence of independent entities. Einstein is losing his patience. He picks up a large stack of chips, neatly arranges them in his hand, and confidently places them on the table. Bohr says he will bet against Einstein, but he keeps talking without laying down any determinate number of chips in any particular spot.

Bohr's exuberance is hard to contain as he explains that Einstein's which-slit experiment beautifully demonstrates his Principle of Complementarity according to which an entity *either* behaves like a wave *or* a particle *depending on how it is measured*. Einstein's reverie is broken by this last comment. Exasperated he asks, "So what you are saying is that the very nature of the entity—its ontology—changes with the experimental apparatus used to determine its nature? Or worse, that nothing is there before it is measured, as if measurements conjure things into existence?"

. . .

Newton the great natural philosopher, the first modern scientist, the greatest scientist of all time, the inventor of the calculus. Newton the theologian, the devoted student of biblical prophesy, a devout nontrinitarian Christian. Newton, the Chosen One, the reader of the Great Clockwork, the one prophet who had a God's eye view of all time. The one who evacuated time, exorcizing it of ghosts, while filling the world with spirits.

Newton the great empiricist, the great positivist, the great determinist, the great mechanist. All these honorifics left hanging as questions. All co-existing along with other ghosts of Newton that speak of the undoings of mechanism, determinism, positivism, scientism. Continuities and discontinuities.

The presumed radical disjuncture between continuity and discontinuity is the gateway to Man's stewardship, giving him full knowability and control over nature. Calculus is revealed as the escape hatch through which Man can take flight from his own finitude. Man's reward: A God's eye view of the universe, the universal viewpoint, the escape from perspective, with all the rights and privileges accorded therein. Vision that goes right to the heart of the matter, unmediated sight, knowledge without end, without responsibility. Individuals with inherent properties there for the knowing, there for the taking. Matter is discrete. Time is continuous. Place knows its place. Time too has its place. Nature and culture are split by this continuity, and objectivity is secured as externality. We know this story well, it is written into our bones, in many ways we inhabit it and it inhabits us.

And yet, Newtonian inheritance is not one, but many. No unity can hold, not from within or without, when restless spirits walk the night.

Superpositions, not oppositions. Physics has always been spooked.

. . .

SpaceTime Coordinates: untimely, no given space, no given time. The concern is "not with horizons of modified—past or future—presents, but with a 'past' that has never been present, and which never will be, whose future to come will never be a production or a reproduction in the form of presence."[8]

Physicists now claim to have empirical evidence that it is possible not only to change the past, but to change the very nature of being itself . . . in the past.[9]

Tunneling from the realm of imagination to the empirical world, from the laboratory of the mind to the laboratory of hard facts, from the 1930s to the 1990s, the two-slit apparatus at the center of the Bohr–Einstein debate is made flesh. New technological advances make it possible to actually do this great *thought* experiment *in the lab*. But much more than technological innovation is at issue. The way in which this experiment is designed is remarkable for its imaginative ingenuity as well, for this experiment is engineered to empirically test a difference in the *metaphysical* views of Bohr and Heisenberg. Experimental meta/physics! Empirical marks from the world beyond. A ghostly matter. The line between physics and meta-physics is undecidable/indeterminate.

Heisenberg understands measurements as disturbances that place a limit on knowability—that is, measurements entail epistemic uncertainties.

Whereas, for Bohr, measurement is about the conditions for possibility of semantic and ontic determination—that is, ontological indeterminacy.

So the disagreement between Bohr and Heisenberg has to do with what exists in the *absence* of a measurement—are there or are there not objects with inherent boundaries and characteristics before a measurement takes place? To be or not to be? But how can one even begin to contemplate an experiment that tests what exists *before* a measurement takes place when the very act of experimenting always already entails measurement?

It turns out that there *is* a way to determine *empirically* which, if either, of the "metaphysical" views of Bohr and Heisenberg has empirical support.

The basic idea behind this ingeniously designed experiment is the following.

The key is to use the inner workings of the atom (that is, its "internal degrees of freedom") to leave behind a telltale sign of which slit the atom passes through in a way that does not disturb its forward momentum (that is, its "external degrees of freedom"). In particular, the experiment is designed in just such a way that an atomic *electron* is excited to a higher energy level by a laser, and then once the atom is in one of the two cavities the excited electron is made to jump to a lower energy level, hence leaving a telltale photon behind in one of the two cavities/containers placed adja-cent to each of the two slits, while the atom continues on its way unaffected by this event. In this way, there is a determination of which slit the atom passes through without disturbing its forward momentum.

The result? Unambiguous confirmation of Bohr's point of view: In the absence of a which-slit detector the atom behaves like a wave. When a which-slit detector is introduced, the pattern *does* indeed change from a diffraction pattern to a scatter pattern, from wave behavior to particle behavior, and, crucially, this shift, *by design*, is *not* a result of a disturbance. This finding goes against both Heisenberg and Einstein's understandings, and strongly confirms Bohr's point of view, for it can be shown that the shift in pattern is the result of the *entanglement* of the "object" and the "agencies of observation." That is, there is empirical evidence for Bohr's performative understanding of identity: Identity is not inherent (e.g., entities are not inherently either a wave or a particle), but rather performed differently given different experimental circumstances.

Now, given the performative nature of identity, things get even more interesting, for if Bohr's hypothesis that phenomena are quantum entanglements (of "objects" and "agencies of observation") holds, then some (other) clearly impossible things become possible. First of all, keep in mind that a particle goes through one slit or another, while a wave goes through both slits at the same time. Now suppose that the which-slit detector is modified in such a way that the evidence of which slit the atom goes through—namely, the existence of the telltale photon in one container or the other—can be *erased after* the atom has already gone through one of the slits. In the absence of which-slit determination the atom should behave like a wave, indicated by a diffraction pattern. It turns out that if the which-slit information is "erased" (that is, if any sign of which-slit it passed through is eliminated and the question of which-slit is once again undecidable), then in fact a diffraction pattern characteristic of waves is once again in evidence (as in the case without a which-slit detector)! This result is remarkable, but there's more. It turns out that it doesn't matter at what point the information is "erased"—in particular, it could be "erased" *after* any given atom has already gone through the entire apparatus and made its mark on the screen, thereby contributing to the formation of the overall pattern!

This result is nothing less than spectacular! What this experiment tells us is that whether or not an entity goes through the apparatus as a wave or a particle can be determined *after* it has already gone through the apparatus, that is, *after it has already gone through as either a wave (through both slits at once) or a particle (through one slit or the other)*! In other words, it is not merely that the past behavior of some given entity has been changed, as it were, but that the entity's very nature has been changed in the past! That is, any entity's *past identity, its ontology, is never fixed, it is always open to future reworkings!*

The physicists who proposed the quantum eraser experiment interpret these results as the possibility of "changing the past"; they speak of the diffraction pattern as having been "recovered" (as if the original pattern has returned) and the which-slit information having been "erased." But this interpretation is based upon assumptions that are being called into question—*by this very experiment*—assumptions concerning the nature of being and time.

If one assumes a metaphysics of presence, that the pattern obtained results from the behavior of a group of individually determinate objects, then it seems inexplicable that the erasure of information of which slit each individual entity went through, *after* the individuals have gone through the slits, could have any effect. Otherwise, what notion of causality could account for such a strange occurrence? What could be the source of such instantaneous communication, a kind of global conspiracy of individual actors acting in concert to rig time? What kind of spooky-action-at-a-distance causality is this?! The difficulty here is the mistaken assumptions of a classical ontology based on the belief that individual determinately bounded and propertied objects are the actors on this stage, and the stage itself is the givenness of a container called space and a linear sequence of moments called time. But the evidence indicates that the world does not operate according to any such classical ontology, an ontology exorcised of ghosts. On the contrary, *this is empirical evidence for Derrida's hauntology*! As Derrida makes clear, we have to learn to live with ghosts and be accountable to them.

It's not that (in erasing the information after the fact that) the experimenter changes a past that had already been present. Rather, the point is that *the past was never simply there to begin with and the future is not simply what will unfold; the "past" and the "future" are iteratively reworked and enfolded through the iterative practices of spacetimemattering*—including conducting which-slit measurements and then subsequently erasing the which-slit information—*all are one phenomenon*. There is no conspiracy at work among individual particles separated in space or individual events separated in time. Space and time are phenomenal, that is, they are intra-actively configured and reconfigured in the ongoing materialization of phenomena. Neither space nor time exist as determinate givens, as universals, outside of matter. Matter does not reside in space and move through time. Space and time are matter's agential performances.

Furthermore, the evidence is against the claim made by some physicists that all trace of the event is "erased" when the which-slit information is destroyed and that the previous diffraction pattern is "recovered." On the contrary, the diffraction pattern produced is not the same (as the original). Unlike the "original," the new diffraction pattern is not plainly evident without explicitly tracing the (extant) entanglements. That is, the trace of all measurements remains even when information is "erased" *it takes work to make the ghostly entanglements visible*. The past is not closed (it never was), but erasure (of all traces) is not what is at issue. The past is not present. "Past" and "future" are iteratively reconfigured and enfolded through the world's ongoing intra-activity. There is no inherently determinate relationship between past and future. Phenomena are not located in space and time; rather, *phenomena are material entanglements enfolded and threaded through the spacetimemattering of the universe*. Even the return of a diffraction pattern does not signal a going back, an erasure of memory, a restoration of a present past. *Memory—the pattern of sedimented enfoldings of iterative intra-activity—is written into the fabric of the world.* The world "holds" the memory of all traces; or rather, the world *is* its memory (its enfolded materialization).

. . .

Let's pause to consider the quantum dis/continuity further. This discontinuity that queers our presumptions of continuity is neither the opposite of the continuous, nor continuous with it. Quantum "leaps" are not mere displacements in space through time, not from here-now to there-then, not when it is the rupture itself that helps constitute the here's and now's, and not once and for all. The point is not merely that something is here-now and there-then without ever having been anywhere in between, it's that here-now, there-then have become unmoored—there's no given place or time for them to be. Where and when do quantum leaps happen? Furthermore, if the nature of causality is troubled to such a degree that effect does not simply follow cause end-over-end in an unfolding of existence through time, if there is in fact no before and after by which to order cause and effect, has causality been arrested in its tracks?

This strange quantum causality entails the disruption of discontinuity/continuity, a disruption so destabilizing, so downright dizzying, that it is difficult to believe that it is that which makes for the stability of existence itself. Or rather, to put it a bit more precisely, if the indeterminate nature of existence by its nature teeters on the cusp of stability and instability, of possibility and impossibility, then the dynamic relationality between continuity and discontinuity is crucial to the open-ended becoming of the world which resists acausality as much as determinism.

I don't want to make too much of a little thing . . . but the quantum, this tiny disjuncture that exists in neither space nor time, torques the very nature of the relation between continuity and discontinuity to such a degree that the nature of change changes with each *intra-action*.

Change is a dynamism that operates at an entirely different level of existence from that of postulated brute matter situated in space and time; rather, what comes to be and is "immediately" reconfigured entails an iterative intra-active open-ended becoming of spacetimemattering.

*Quantum dis/continuity* is the un/doing. (Even un/doing itself, as well as the notion of itself.) Even its appellation is at once redundant and contradictory: a smallest unit, *a discontinuous bit . . . of discontinuity*. "Quantum," "discontinuity"—each designation marking a disruption, bringing us up short, disrupting us, disrupting itself, stopping short before getting to the next one. A rupture of the discontinuous? A disrupted disruption? A stutter? The reiteration not of what comes before, or after, but a disruption of before/after. A cut that is itself cross-cut. A passable impassability. An irresolvable internal contradiction, a logical disjunction, an im-passe (from the Latin *a-poria*), but one that can't contain that which it would hold back. Porosity is not necessary for quantum tunneling—a specifically quantum event, a means of getting through, without getting over, without burrowing through. Quantum tunneling makes mincemeat of closure, no w/holes are needed.

Cutting together-apart. Take out your quantum scissors! Identity will never be the same. It never was. Identity undone by a discontinuity at the heart of matter itself. What spooky matter is this, this *quantum discontinuity*?

## Notes

I would particularly like to thank Hari Tsoukas for his very gracious hospitality, and for inviting me to attend such a stimulating and enjoyable conference in a stunningly beautiful environment. I also want to thank Sophia Tzagaraki for helping to make everything run smoothly. I owe a debt of gratitude to my partner, Fern Feldman, who graciously accompanied me to Corfu, and who is a truly extraordinary interlocutor and invaluable intellectual companion.

1. This chapter is the text of a keynote address for the Third International Symposium on Process Organization Studies, Corfu, Greece, June 16, 2011. The talk was performed with accompaniment from an intricate, highly detailed, and (purposefully) dizzying Prezi presentation meant to stimulate a dis/orienting sense of spacetimemattering. The text of the talk draws heavily from the paper K. Barad, "Quantum Entanglements and Hauntological Relations of Inheritance: Dis/continuities, SpaceTime Enfoldings, and Justice-to-Come," *Derrida Today* (November 2010), 3/2: 240–68, edited by Nicole Anderson and Peter Steves.
2. From the poster advertising the UCSC Science Studies Cluster "Trans/materialities: Relatings Across Difference" Conference, May 22, 2009. Wording jointly authored by Martha Kenney (Graduate Student Organizer) and Karen Barad (Faculty Advisor).
3. More precisely matter materializes different spatiotemporalities.
4. *Intra-action* is a key concept of *agential realism* (Barad, 2007). In contrast to the usual "interaction," the notion of *intra-action* recognizes that distinct entities, agencies, events do not precede, but rather emerge from/through their intra-action. "Distinct" agencies are only distinct in a relational, not an absolute sense, that is, agencies are only distinct in relation to their mutual entanglement; they don't exist as individual elements. Importantly, intra-action constitutes a radical reworking of the traditional notion of causality.
5. This paper is diffracted through Barad (2007). The reader should keep in mind that there are multiple interpretations of quantum physics. This paper makes use

of my agential realist interpretation of quantum physics (Barad 2007). Schrader (2010) also engages with agential realism to offer a remarkable materialist deconstructive reading of microbiology evidence, including a consideration of specific policy implications. For other readings of quantum physics and deconstruction see works by Arkady Plotnitsky, Christopher Norris, and John Protevi, among others. For more on the method of reading insights diffractively through one another, see especially Chapter 2 of Barad (2007). Due to space limitations and the minimalist approach to footnotes used by the journal where the full paper is published, *Derrida Today*, many footnotes were deleted from the published text. I refer the reader to Barad (2007) for further details and more complete references. This paper highlights material covered especially in Chapter 7. This paper is an excerpt of a longer work in progress.

6. "'Fits', 'passions', and 'paroxysms' are all legitimate Newtonian terms for easy reflection and transmission of light" (Shapiro, 1993: xii). Newton argued that light is a particle.
7. Hennessey (2008) in a review of the play *Copenhagen* by Michael Frayn.
8. Derrida (1982: 21).
9. For more details see Barad (2007: Ch. 7).

# References

Barad, K. (2007). *Meeting the Universe Halfway: Quantum Physics and the Entanglement of Matter and Meaning*. Durham, NC: Duke University Press.

—— (2010). "Quantum Entanglements and Hauntological Relations of Inheritance: Dis/continuities, Space Time Enfoldings, and Justice-to-Come," *Derrida Today* (November 2010), 3/2: 240–68, edited by Nicole Anderson and Peter Steves.

Derrida, J. (1982). *Margins of Philosophy*, trans. Alan Bass. Chicago: University of Chicago Press.

—— (1994). *Specters of Marx: The State of the Debt, the Work of Mourning, & the New International*, trans. Peggy Kamuf. New York: Routledge.

Frayn, M. (2000). *Copenhagen*. New York: Anchor Books/Random House.

Hennessey, A. (2008). "The Mirror Up to Nature: Elsinore by Way of Copenhagen," blog review of Michael Frayn's play *Copenhagen*, January 13, 2008.

London Evening Standard (2010). "The world will end in 2060, according to Newton." Available online: http://www.thisislondon.co.uk/news/article-23401099-the-world-will-end-in-2060-according-to-newton.do (accessed August 20, 2010).

Schrader, A. (2010). "Responding to Pfiesteria Piscicida (the Fish Killer): Phantasmatic Ontologies, Indeterminacy, and Responsibility in Toxic Microbiology," in *Social Studies of Science* 40:2, 275–306.

Shapiro, A. E. (1993). *Fits, Passions and Paroxysms: Physics, Method, and Chemistry and Newton's Theories of Coloured Bodies and Fits of Easy Reflection*. Cambridge: Cambridge University Press.

**3**

# Reflections on Sociomateriality and Dialogicality in Organization Studies: From "Inter-" to "Intra-Thinking" . . . in Performing Practices

*John Shotter*

**Abstract:** What is special about all our dialogically structured exchanges is their immanent creativity: within them all, sooner or later, something uniquely new is created that is intricately related to the situation within which it is created. The *happening* of an "organizational moment" thus occurs when that *uniquely new something* opens up previously unnoticed new ways forward into the future. The creation of such uniquely new events is due, the author argues, to the way in which the spontaneous responsiveness of our bodies works, to an extent, to give "expressive shape" to the movements of feeling occurring within us as we body them forth out into the world. What changes within us in such encounters is not our learning new facts or bits of information, but our learning new *ways of relating* ourselves to the others and othernesses in the world around us. The author explores the nature of these new kinds of understanding in relation to Karen Barad's agentive realist account of sociomateriality, and how her account of intra-action, as opposed to inter-action, parallels in much close detail Bakhtin's (and Voloshinov's) account of dialogically structured activity in the realm of speech communication.

The notion of *intra-action* (in contrast to the usual "interaction," which presumes the prior existence of independent entities or relata) represents a profound conceptual shift. It is through specific agential intra-actions that the boundaries and properties of the components of phenomena become determinate and that particular concepts (that is,

particular material articulations of the world) become meaningful.
(Barad, 2007: 139)

And here we come on the difficulty of "all is in flux." Perhaps that is the
place to start.                                                   (Wittgenstein, 1980: 8)

As Karen Barad (2007: 139) notes, the notion of *intra-action* "represents a
profound conceptual shift," it means that no "things" exist for us as fixed
and permanent "things-in-themselves" in separation from their surroundings. All "things" exist as "doings," as agential enactments, as focal things
attended to *from within* a larger, ceaselessly unfolding, unbounded, fluid,
and, probably in itself, organized in a still unthinkable and also unimagin-
able reality. Thus, as beings within (and of) a world that is always in the
process of becoming other than what it was before, we must learn to think
"while in motion," so to speak, and to treat our "thinkings" as temporary
results[1] within a still continuing process of becoming.

Doing this, however, is not at all easy. It involves, not seeking yet more and
better theories but, as Wittgenstein (1980: 16) puts it, "a working on oneself
. . . on one's way of seeing things. (And what one expects of them)." For our
concern must be, not with already existing states of affairs, but with, again as
Wittgenstein (1953) puts it, "what is possible *before* all new discoveries and
inventions" (no. 126). We need, as Chia (2010: 135) suggests, "a re-directing
of the focus [in organization studies] from 'organizations' to *organizational
mentalities*," a focus on our initial *ways* of *orienting* ourselves within the
situations of our concern (see later). But to do this—to think, as he suggests,
previously unthinkable new thoughts—we need to attend to what is actually
there, now, in our current ways of acting and conducting our inquiries out
in the world, to notice particularities and details that we usually pass by and
fail to pick out for rational consideration. In beginning to do this, we need
to attend to those basic ways we have, as living beings, of bodily responding
to the activities of the others and othernesses around us with whom we are in
living contact—the pre-conceptual and pre-linguistic ways of spontaneously
responding we in fact share with infants and animals. Following Barad and
Chia, this is what I will try to do in what follows below.

## 3.1 The materiality of our experiences and of our bodily expressions of them

If we think of our "thinkings" as merely temporary results within a still
continuing and developing material process of becoming, then one of the
shifts we in fact need to make is to move away from the idea of exploratory

thought as involving an ethereal process of reflection, working in terms of *representations* of identifiable and nameable "things." So, although the first word in my title for this chapter is "reflections"—with the meaning, usually, that my aim is to meditate on the connections and relations between sociomateriality and dialogicality considered as separate, static, nameable "things-in-themselves"—I will be performing a very different kind of thinking. For reflection involves, so to speak, working with inner, mental "mirror images" supposedly representing entities or objects out in the world, whereas I will be much more concerned with what Barad (2007: 93) calls the "dynamic relationalities"—or simply "phenomena" (140)—emerging in the differences between our outgoing activities towards our surroundings and their incoming results. In particular, I will be concerned with the sensed *differences* (and *similarities*) which emerge in the course of reading Karen Barad's work when intertwined with expectations engendered by other authors—such as Bakhtin, Voloshinov, James, and Wittgenstein, who also have things to say in relation to the social and the material—in mind.

While I would say I was performing a *dialogical* reading of her work (see Shotter, 2005, 2006), she calls her approach a *diffractive reading* (Barad, 2007), and says that it involves placing "the understandings that are generated from different (inter)disciplinary practices in conversation with one another" (92–93). Do we differ? In talking of *dialogical* activities, I seem to be privileging language, whereas she says: "Language has been granted too much power. The linguistic turn, the semiotic turn, the interpretative turn, the cultural turn: it seems that at every turn lately every 'thing'—even materiality—is turned into a matter of language or some other form of cultural representation" (132). However, in resorting to a conversational metaphor, isn't she taking us back into a focus on language? How can the "anchor" (Weick, 2010: 104) image of conversational activity be of use to us in illuminating her diffractive methodology?

Precisely because when one speaks in conversation, *one addresses one's speech to others*, and as Bakhtin (1986: 94) puts it, "from the very beginning, the speaker expects a response from them, an active responsive understanding. The entire utterance is constructed, as it were, in anticipation of encountering this response"—and speakers are oriented precisely towards such an actively responsive understanding. They do not expect a passive understanding in which a listener is merely the recipient of a supposed inner, mental representation of the supposed thought represented in a speaker's words. In other words, listening is also an agential activity.

In this non-representational, dialogically structured view of language use, in which *anticipations* rather than causal influences play a crucial role in "shaping" the back-and-forth unfolding of processes, there is no gap in "between inner experience and its expression, no crossing over from one qualitative realm of reality to another" (Voloshinov, 1986: 28–29)—although, as he notes, "it often happens that in the process of outward expression a transit from one type of semiotic material (e.g., mimetic) to another (e.g., verbal) occurs, but nowhere in its entire course does the process go outside the material of signs. What, then, is the sign material of the psyche? Any organic activity or process: breathing, blood circulation, movements of the body, articulation, inner speech, mimetic motions, reaction to external stimuli (e.g., light stimuli) and so forth. In short, *anything and everything occurring within the organism can become the material of experience, since everything can acquire semiotic significance, can become expressive.*" The materiality of our experiences and of the semiotic material at work in our outward expressions of them, means that all our expressions are performative, not merely representational; we are always *doing something* in and by our expressions.

Further, what is also common to both dialogically structured processes and diffraction, is the creation or emergence of ephemeral, relational outcomes, unique outcomes, materially existing only in the moment of *intra*-action of two or more intertwining strands of flowing activity. Thus, as Bakhtin (1986)—one of the originators of the dialogical approach to human relations—remarks: "An utterance is never just a reflection or an expression of something already existing and outside it that is given and final. It always creates something that never existed before, something absolutely new and unrepeatable ... But something created is always created out of something given ... What is given is completely transformed in what is created" (119–20). And this is what is so special about all our *dialogically structured exchanges* (intra-actions) with the others and othernesses in our surroundings: within them all, sooner or later, something uniquely new *will emerge* that is intricately related to the situation within which it is created.

Barad (2007: 93), in talking of her diffractive methodology as enabling "a critical re-thinking of science and the social in their relationality"—i.e., the natural and the social sciences—points out that once they are set in conversation with each other (instead of each separately arguing for their own hegemony), then "what often appears as separate entities (and separate sets of concerns) with sharp edges does not actually entail a relation of absolute exteriority at all. Like the diffraction patterns illuminating the indefinite nature of boundaries—displaying shadows in 'light' regions and bright spots in 'dark' regions—the relation of the social and the scientific is a relation of 'exteriority within'" (93). In other words, just as Bakhtin notes above, momentary dynamic relationalities with their own distinctive character are created *within* intermingling strands of two or more flowing activities. Thus the similarities and differences which emerge in such a process of diffractive reading give rise, not to nameable sets of relations between separately existing entities "out there," but to an emergent sense of the dynamically changing possibilities which become available to us "from within" the agential processes of which, and within which, we are ourselves "aspects" or "participant parts" (if "parts" is at all a suitable word here)—in just the same way as in our dialogically structured encounters with the "others" and "othernesses" in our surroundings.

Central, then, to Karen Barad's (2007) proposal of a sociomaterial, performative understanding of scientific practices, is the view that all the matter around us, and within which we ourselves have our being, has agency, and that consequently we need to take account of the fact "that knowing does not come from standing at a distance and representing but rather from *a direct material engagement with the world*" (49).[2] And it is in this sense that *matter matters* to us: our "seeing" things, "hearing" things, "making sense," and "talking of" things, are all material practices, involving the intra-twining, or the entanglement, of certain of our material bodily processes with those of the material world. To repeat, we are not separate agents, but "participant parts" within and of an indivisible, continually unfolding, stranded, flowing whole, able to set the boundaries that matter to us within it in one way at one moment and in another way the next.

Our past belief that it is the task of science merely to represent the objective, external world "over there," of which we ourselves are not a part, has led us to ignore not only our own agency in producing a representation of it as populated by a set of quite separate "things"/"parts," but also its role in the production of the events we find happening to us.

Thus the profound conceptual shift to a process approach entails: a shift from living out our lives in *inter*-action with the others and othernesses in our surroundings to living within *intra*-actions with them; a shift from living in a world of already made things to a world of things-in-their-making; from life as being only "in" certain things (organisms) to things having their life only "within their relations" to the flowing processes occurring around them. In other words, the "things" around us, and especially what we think of as "living things," exist only as dynamic stabilities within transitory relations to their surroundings, rather than as independently existing, self-contained entities. As Barad (2007: 214) puts it: "Agency is a matter of intra-acting; it is an enactment . . . as an enactment and not something someone has, then it seems not only appropriate but important to consider agency as distributed over nonhuman as well as human forms." Indeed, as a consequence of this, we need to accept that our own human agency is an aspect—not a uniquely separate phenomenon in its own right—of the constituent entanglement of materiality and sociality.

It is this last shift that is, perhaps, the most profound and most difficult for us, experientially, to accept. Ordinarily, in our everyday experience, our surroundings do just seem to be furnished with a collection of very stable, already-existing things-in-themselves "over there," which we make sense of with our minds "in here." We fail to notice the agential processes at work in producing such a result, particularly those within our own bodies. But as Polanyi (1967: 13–14, 16) noted long ago, although we might talk of "straining our eyes" to see something, or "cocking our ears" to hear something, we do not attend to these inner efforts in themselves, "we [attend] *from* these internal processes to the qualities of things outside. These qualities are what those internal processes *mean* to us . . . Our own body is the only thing in the world which we normally never experience as an object, but experience always in terms of the world to which we are attending from our body." In Polanyi's (1967) terms, our *subsidiary* awareness of the muscular efforts required to swivel our eyes to converge and focus on a particular point in the visual space before us "over there" provides us with not only a *focal* awareness of what "is" at that point, but also of our bodily relation to it—of it as "near" or "far," a sense of how we can move in relation to it. Again, the outcomes of importance to us are understood, not as "objective" things, but as momentary *dynamic relationalities* which arise within the *intra*-play occurring between our outgoing activities, shaped by our (often linguistically influenced) anticipations, and their incoming results. The way or ways in which we *orient ourselves* in our undertakings within our otherwise bewildering, and not yet fully determinate surroundings—thus to clarify for ourselves what our task within them actually *is*—is thus of crucial importance.

## 3.2 Two kinds of difficulties we can face in life—going beyond what we already know

In the past, as a major consequence of Descartes' thought, we have assumed a sharp ontological split between subjective and objective events—between the realm of *the mind* "in here" and the realm of *the external world* "out there"—a split that seems to leave our body and its activities in the gap between with no other function than to do our mind's bidding. This split has given rise to the belief that the only form of knowledge of use to us is that which we arrive at indirectly, as a result of our deliberate investigations of our external world guided by our theories. Hertz (1956: 1) described the nature of these investigations as follows: "In endeavouring...to draw inferences as to the future from the past, we always adopt the following process. We form for ourselves images or symbols of external objects; and the form that we give them is such that the necessary consequents of the images in thought are always the images of the necessary consequents in nature of the things pictured. In order that this requirement may be satisfied, there must be a certain conformity between nature and our thought"—a procedure in which, we need to note, the initial and final state of things is represented, *but not the transitional processes* within which the change comes to pass.

Of importance here also is both the *starting point* (Chia, 2010) assumed for our inquiries, as well as what we might call the *orienting images* we use as stable "pivots" or "anchors" (Weick, 2010) in our attempts to linguistically articulate what is otherwise somewhat formless for us.[3] Again, here, we have inherited another of Descartes' (1968) anchoring images. In order not to have to continually argue with the philosophers and theologians of the day, he said: "I resolved to leave all these people to their disputes, and to speak only of what would happen in a new world, if God were to create, somewhere in imaginary space, enough matter to compose it, and if he were to agitate diversely and confusedly the different parts of this matter, so that he created a chaos as disordered as the poets could ever imagine, and afterwards did no more than to lend his usual preserving action to nature, and to let her act according to his established laws" (62). And it is the acceptance of this orienting image that allows Hertz (above) to set out what many still take to be the standard process of rational inquiry—we begin by forming images or symbols of external objects.

Chia (2010), however, very much in line with the shift from *inter-* to *intra-* thinking being explored here, suggests that: "The starting point for organizational inquiry ought not to be the stately *being* of discrete entities, be they 'institutions', 'organizations', or 'individuals', but their oftentimes unexpected and precarious coming-into-presence; their *becoming* and spontaneous emergence from an undifferentiated multitude of actions, events, and interactions" (115). And he goes on to claim: "How our worldviews, perceptions, knowledge, and modes of comprehension affect our concerns and preoccupations and shape our objects of inquiry must be correspondingly investigated if we are to grasp this wider sense of organization as a generic reality-constituting activity" (131). Our usually ignored, background, embodied feelings and assumptions need also, in our future inquiries, to be foregrounded (for an example, see Harquail and King, 2010).

Putting our task in this way raises the possibility of our facing two very different kinds of difficulties in our lives, not just one. There are those kind of difficulties that we might, following Wittgenstein (1980: 17), call "difficulties of the intellect," difficulties that we can formulate (or form) as *problems* and *solve* by constructing an appropriate theoretical system within which to "think them through." But there is another kind of difficulty which he calls a "difficulty of the will" (17), to do with, as he puts it, what most of us *"want* to see," i.e., what the culture within which we have grown up expects us to look for in searching for what a "something" *really is.*

I would like to call difficulties of this kind, orientational or relational difficulties. Overcoming them requires a very different kind of approach from our approach to solving problems—which, of course, expresses straightaway the nature of the difficulty we face: What actually is involved in our approaching a situation or circumstance which at first we find quite bewildering, confusing, or disorienting? What is involved in our moving from bewilderment, to feeling "at home" in such new situations?

Let us trace some of the steps involved: We confront a new situation; at first we are confused, bewildered, we don't know our "way about" (Wittgenstein) within it. However, as we "dwell in it" and begin to "move around" within it, a qualitatively distinct "something" begins to emerge; it emerges for us in the "time contours" or "time shapes" that become apparent to us in the dynamic relations, the differences, we can sense between our *outgoing* exploratory activities and their *incoming* results. An image comes to us, we find that we can express this "something" in terms of a similarity to something already well known to us. But not so fast, for we can find another image, and another and another—Wittgenstein (1953) uses *a city, a toolbox, the controls in the driving cab of a train,* and *many different types of games,* all as metaphors for different aspects of our experience in our usage of language. And it is only after we have made use of a number of such images to guide our further exploratory movements, that we can come to a sense of, come to feel completely acquainted with, *the actual field of possibilities* giving rise to them. And if we can come to feel confident of knowing our way around within such fields of possibility, then we can be competent in *resolving on different ways of "going on" within them* according to the different "ends in view" we might wish to pursue.

This, of course, presents us with some very different, much more practical ways of beginning our inquiries than beginning from "good ideas," or from "concepts" we already possess—for beginning in that way, as we have already seen, to the continual elaboration of what is already well-known to us. Instead, we can begin with what we might call "noticings" (which I'll present in summary form):

- *Three kinds of noticings:* (1) either being "struck by" an event or happening; or (2) the sensing of a qualitatively unique "unitary whole" as it emerges in our slow exploration of a present bewilderment or confusion; or (3) the sensing of a "something wrong"... "Things are still not 'quite right' yet, but I know not what."
- *A fourth kind of noticing—"incipient forms"*: (4) "A community or a *polis* is not something that can be made or engineered by some form of *techne* or by the administration of society. There is something of a circle here, comparable to the hermeneutical circle. The coming into being of a type of public life that can strengthen solidarity, public freedom, a willingness to talk and to listen, mutual debate, and a commitment to rational persuasion presupposes the incipient forms of such communal life" (Bernstein, 1983: 266).
- *A fifth kind—"what is not being said"* (the elephant in the room): (5) As Billig (1999) points out, in relation to Freud's case of Herr K. (an older man rejected by his wife) and Dora (the young daughter whose father was having an affair with Herr K's wife), people can make use of shared "dialogic routines" (101) to avoid raising those issues between them that would result in devastating conflicts—in contrast to Freud, who claimed that "repression took place in the head [of an individual], not outwardly in conversation" (102).
- *A sixth kind—"telling moments"*: (6) moments when "collective narratives or ideologies" begin to be revealed, e.g., when people begin to say: "This is how we do things around here."
- *A seventh kind—disquiets*: (7) a feeling that there is still a "something more" that has not yet been captured in all the articulations of "sensings" that we so far produced.

Weick (2010: 103) describes the importance of such noticings as follows: "An ineffable practice is conveyed piecemeal by drawing attention to smaller, effable, abridged episodes associated with a larger set of tacit, subsidiary sensitivities. This implies that a crucial stage in process thinking is attention-drawing."

In all of these noticings, due to their *just happening* nature, their spontaneity, there is at work, as Steiner (1989: 188) puts it, an "'otherness' which enters us [and] makes us other." And it is in this way that we can overcome the trap of simply returning again and again to what is already familiar to us. This is the power of truly dialogically structured meetings, within which all concerned are in a freely flowing, spontaneously responsive/expressive contact with each other. As Wittgenstein (1953: 211) remarks, in asking " ... is being struck looking plus thinking? No. Many of our concepts *cross* here"—as indeterminate events all these "noticings," as starting points for a new inquiry, are open to many different determinations.

But how might these determinations be arrived at? As Merleau-Ponty (1962: 178) notes: "At first sight, it might appear that speech heard can bring [a listener] nothing: it is he who gives to words and sentences their meaning ... Here, as everywhere, it seems at first sight true that consciousness can find in its experience only that which it has itself put there. Thus the experience of communication would appear to be an illusion ... Yet, the problem being how, to all appearances, consciousness learns something, the solution cannot consist in saying that it knows everything in advance. The fact is that we have the power to understand over and above what we may have spontaneously thought." But if we begin with "noticings"— noticings shared by all within the flow of communication occurring within a meeting—then we need not be reliant upon what is already known and shared amongst everyone in advance of the meeting to achieve unambiguous communication. "Moments of common reference" (Shotter, 2009)—a term that we might apply to such shared noticings—can be sufficient, if those within the meeting can agree upon their linguistic designation!

As aspects of the profound conceptual shift entailed by moving from inter- to intra-thinking, then, we have not only shifted away from Descartes' subject–object split, and his anchoring image of a world of separate particles in motion, we have also found his method of "seeking truth in the sciences," as he put it, inadequate to our needs. Our belief that knowledge arrived at by the process of inquiry as set out by Hertz above is somehow more basic, because more well-founded and more certain, must be given up. The forms of knowledge that we can arrive at in our everyday, "face-to-face" encounters with the others and othernesses around us can, at least, give us the specific starting points we need in our attempts to foreground the usually ignored, embodied, background expectations shaping people's inquiries, in the situations of our concern. We must also give up the idea that the major function of our talk, of our communication with the others around us, is to provide them with precise "pictures" of states of affairs in our external world. In the view taken above, it is its "point" that is important, what expectations it arouses in recipients as to where next to move from where they are now. Small changes in words can provide big changes in our orientations. As Weick (2010: 108) points out, "if one adds '-ing' to what one is saying (e.g., organization becomes organizing), then it is also possible that when one *sees* this form of *saying*, the process *thinking* gets triggered." An "organization" is a finished "thing," while "organizing" involved a whole multitude of dynamic relationalities.

Descartes' world, then, is/was a rather thin and impoverished world of passive, neutral bits of matter in motion, known to us only indirectly in terms of our "inner mental representations" of them, and in relation to which we face the task of trying to "make something" of them—and especially difficult for us, was to think of how such "dead" bits of stuff could possibly have a *meaning* for us. We had to think of ourselves as bringing "interpretations" to them—just as we have to bring "interpretations" to the symbolic forms used in the mathematical calculations in such activities as engineering and physics—if they are to have any useful meaning for us.

## 3.3 Process thinking, fluid thinking—the intra-activity of "the dialogical" in practice

### 3.3.1 From an impoverished world to a profusion of possibilities

But what if, instead of the thin and inert Cartesian world in which the one true reality is hidden behind appearances (as in Fig. 3.1(a)) we live in the midst of a qualitatively rich, still unfolding world of stranded, intra-mingling, flowing processes, each with their own agentive powers (as in Fig. 3.1(b))?

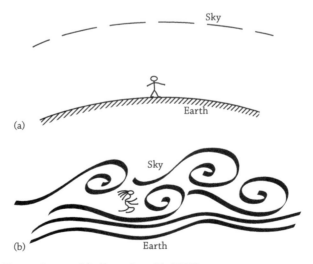

**Figure 3.1** Alternative worlds (from Ingold, 2008)

Then we will need—not yet again to start by formulating some new theories (for theory formulation is itself process in need of a performative articulation)—but to *re-orient* or to *re-relate* ourselves to our surroundings in ways very different from those into which we have been trained in recent times, a task of an unusual kind for those of us trained only in performing intellectual activities of a rational kind.

In taking some first steps towards the kind of *performative understanding* of our practices we seek, I would first like to offer a number of quotations (expressions, utterances) which, in arousing a number of preliminary expectations as to what is entailed in such a re-orientation, will help to set the scene for what is to come.

The first comes from Bergson (1911: 134–35) who, in commenting on the nature of living processes, noted that: "Like eddies of dust raised by the wind as it passes, the living turn upon themselves, [like swirls and vortices in a stream—J.S.] borne by the great blast of life. They are therefore relatively stable, and counterfeit immobility so well that we treat each of them as a *thing* rather than as a *progress,* forgetting that the very permanence of their form is only the outline of a movement." I'm quoting it for the phrase: "they . . . counterfeit immobility so well." For as Bergson makes clear to us, it is only too easy for us to think of the world as being full of nameable "things" which, once they have been named, *stay as the things we have named as*, while we are inquiring into their nature—the assumption that "words stand for things" is perniciously pervasive in all our Western forms of talk. But if we take them (or records of them) out of their context, out of the currents sustaining their formation as the dynamic stabilities *they were*, do they stay the same? If our process approach is correct, then of course they do not.

Indeed, as Harquail and King (2010: 1621) remark, in making their case for the importance of people's embodied experiences while working in organizations: "OI [Organizational Identity] research presumes that abstracted verbal representations of a member's beliefs about an organization's identity effectively express the member's perceptions and understanding of what is central, continuous, and distinctive about an organization." Clearly, in examining people's speech, it is only too easy to take the transcript of a recording (now divorced from the context of its utterance) and to find patterns in the forms so recorded, and then to take these as expressing the *meaning* of what was being communicated, i.e., to attempt to find in a collection of *already spoken words* what was accomplished by the *speaking* of those words *within face-to-face, shared surroundings*. Yet, what a speaker expresses in their speakings, and is *felt* as such by listeners, is expressed in the *bodily movements* at work in their performance of their expressions—we need to remember of our transcripts that "their form is only the outline of a movement."

Harquail and King (2010: 1628) are critical of empirical research in which this aspect of people's expressions/verbal utterances is ignored, in which the "verbal OI construals that were unmistakably informed by multiple capacities of embodied knowledge." Harquail, first an employee of the Campbell soup company and then, later, a manager at corporate headquarters, remarks about her own feelings, and how they changed as she accumulated more experiences from moving around within different spheres or arenas of activity within the organization: "Over time, her visual-spatial and bodily-kinesthetic experiences of Campbell, and the way that she understood and knew the organization, validated and substantiated her own construal, which became, at gut level, incompatible with the hegemonic narrative of Campbell's OI [what she at first had felt]. Her body felt unsettled and anxious, and she found herself thinking of Campbell as a 'fortress' or 'compound' which, in turn, structured the way she thought about and acted within the organization" (Harquail and King, 2010: 1634).

Harquail and King's (2010) emphasis on the primacy of our feelings in structuring our utterances reminds me of the stance taken by a now tragically dead family therapist friend of mine, Tom Andersen (n.d.), and his concern to work only with the feelings that arose within him in the dialogically structured activity occurring between him and his clients, and not in terms of his own impositions: "What we later come to understand (both the formed and the forming)," he said, "emerges from us being *in* language, *in* conversations, *in* movements, *in* relationships, *in* communication,[4] *in* culture, *in* nature (we do not have language, etc. 'in us'). The Being 'in' these various *ins* can best be understood by letting 'the movement of feeling that comes' (by being in these various *ins*) create its own metaphors, and let those metaphors be part of the language one searches through in order to find a meaning." Being *in* and *of* a world with, in some degree, its own agency, means that we can find events happening to us and within us—the "movement of feeling that comes" (by being in these various *ins*)—that we ourselves have not initiated. Yet these movements can be crucial in giving us guidance in how next to act in the situation within which they occur. People's intentions, the "point" of their utterances, is expressed in how they body them forth out into the world, in their facial expressions, in their eye movements, in movements of other parts of the body, and in a tone of voice expressive of agreeing, rejecting, avoiding, seeking, having, or doubting something, etc., etc.

The meaning of our words is not to be found merely in the forms or patterns of the words themselves; it is, as Wittgenstein (1953) puts it, in their *use* that they have their meaning. Thus, as he remarks: "One cannot guess how a word functions [just by looking at the word]. One has to *look at* its use and learn from that. But the difficulty is to remove the prejudice that stands in the way of doing that . . . " (no. 340). It is our *use* of words, the way we express them in our utterances, that gives them their life. Indeed, their embedding in a larger flow of activity, however, means that our "thought is surrounded by a halo," he says, "Its essence, its logic, presents an order, in fact, the a priori order of the world: that is, the order of *possibilities*, which must be common to both world and thought" (no. 97).

For my final remark in this section I would like to turn to Ingold's (2008) article (from which I took the diagram above). In it he discusses "a particular logic that has a central place in the structure of modern thought. I call it the logic of inversion . . . In a nutshell, what it does is to turn the pathways along which life is lived into boundaries within which life is contained. Life, according to this logic, is reduced to an internal property of things that occupy the world but do not properly inhabit it. A world that is occupied, I argue, is furnished with already-existing things. But one that is inhabited is woven from the strands of their continual coming-into-being" (Ingold, 2008: 1796–97). It is this logic that we must reverse if we are to restore things to the entangled flows of living activity within which they emerge, to restore them to life by returning them to the currents within which, as dynamic relationalities, they are formed and have influence in our lives.

Thus, rather than living in a Cartesian relation to our surroundings—in which we have to build up an "inner conception" of what is "out there" from the sparse data provided us by our sense organs—as we move to a performative understanding of our living, bodily relations with our surroundings, we begin to experience a profusion of possibilities. Our perceptual field spreads out in both space and time from what, at any one moment, we are focused upon: I look from my computer screen, through the window to the world outside, back into my study at the books on the shelves, and to my computer screen again—thinking of other writers and their worlds, and so on, and so on. "Nothing is more difficult," says Merleau-Ponty (1962: 58), "than to know precisely *what we see*"—what we see (and hear, and feel) is always surrounded by an indeterminate halo of a "something more." In fact, in their unfolding flow, our lived experiences are distinctive for us, not for their outcomes, but for the qualitatively unique *movements of feeling* to which they give rise as we live out our intra-actions with the others and othernesses around us.

### 3.3.2 The nature of "once-occurrent" focal events occurring within our intra-activities within the world

As has become quite clear to us, all moving matter, whether fluid or made up of particles, whether dead or alive, continually creates pattern and form as the strands of movement within it "rub up against" each other, as it were. And there is, perhaps, no greater obstacle to our conducting worthwhile investigations in organizational studies than our forgetting this. If we do forget it, as Bakhtin (1993: 1) remarks, then we are in danger of establishing "a fundamental split between the content or sense of a given act/activity and the historical actuality of its being, the actual and once-occurrent experiencing of it. And it is in consequence of this that the given act loses its valuableness and the unity of its actual becoming and self-determination. This act is truly real (it participates in once-occurrent Being-as-event) only *in its entirety*. Only this *whole* act is alive, exists fully and inescapably—comes to be, is accomplished. It is an actual living participant in the ongoing event of Being: it is in communion with the unique unity of ongoing Being." In other words, as we have already seen, the "things" of most interest to us in out study of oganiz-*ing*, are "things" which come into existence only within our relations to our surroundings, and which exist only as *dynamic stabilities* or *relationalities*, dependent for their nature upon their embedding within the larger flow of activity within which they are both formed and sustained.

Thus, what does our thinking need to be like *if it has to take place in "fluid spaces,"* in places within which there are no fixed and finished "things" in terms of which to conduct it? Can we think of such *dynamic stabilities* or *relationalities* in terms of what Law and Mol (1994: 658) call "invariant transformations" or Gibson (1979: 178) calls "formless invariants," that is, in terms not of static, pictureable and frameable forms, but in terms of sequences of continually changing forms, all of which appear as *aspects* of a stable "something" which emerges within a larger flow of activity? Like Law and Mol (1994), not only do I think it possible, but I think that, in practice—in our speech intra-twined activities—much work *is in fact done* on the basis of sensing such dynamic stabilities within such essentially fluid places.

But in starting to do this, we have, I think, not only to reject many of the well-established, taken-for-granted Cartesian notions described above, but we also have to try to install ourselves, *now*, at this moment, in a still indeterminate "flow of experience"—a flow which is both currently at work within us on us, and within which and on which we are also currently at work—a uniquely situated, pristine flow of experience within which we can begin to notice *unique features* to which we can then try to give some expression.[5] This, however, is clearly not at all easy to do. Where should we place the boundaries?

Someone who long ago wrote on the indeterminacy of the flow of experience was William James (1912: 71). About our fields of experience he wrote: "[They] have no more definite boundaries than have our fields of view. Both are fringed forever by a *more* that continuously develops, and that continuously supersedes them as life proceeds. The relations, generally speaking, are as real here as the terms are . . . "—where this "more" can be seen, to repeat, as "the order of *possibilities,* which must be common to both world and thought," described by Wittgenstein (1953, no. 97) above.

In other words, such experiences are not bounded entities with a clear beginning and a clear end, but, as he put it (James, 1890: I, 254) long ago, they are "feelings of tendency, *often so vague that we are unable to name them at all*"—even as they occur, they are on the way to somewhere else. But such feelings can, nonetheless, function, he says, as "signs of direction in thought of which we have an acutely discriminative sense, though *no definite sensorial image* plays any part in it whatsoever" (253). Further, along with such a feeling "goes the sense of its relations, near and remote, the dying echo of whence it came to us, the dawning sense of whither it is to lead . . . We all of us have this permanent consciousness of whither our thought is going. It is a feeling like any other, a feeling of what thoughts are next to arise, before they have arisen" (255–56).

There is, thus, something very special about our speech, our bodily expression of it, and the dialogically structured nature of the speech flow within which it occurs. Uniquely new understandings, appropriate to the circumstances of their occurrence, are continually created within it; yet we cannot, as individuals, be said to have caused them; they just happen, they emerge, and the entangled nature of the process of their production cannot easily be untangled. This is because the components or units into which they would need to be "analyzed" are *determined by those within the unfolding process according to the contingencies of the moment.* So, although it is the case as Bakhtin (1986: 93) points out that: "Each individual utterance is a link in the chain of speech communion. It has clear-cut boundaries that are determined by the change of speech subjects (speakers), but within these boundaries the utterance, like Leibniz's monad, reflects the speech process, others' utterances, and, above all, preceding links in the chain (sometimes close and sometimes—in areas of cultural communication—very distant)"—each individual utterance has its own unique *relational nature* in accord with its "place" within a dialogue as a whole.

In Barad's (2007) terms, the clear-cut boundaries exhibited in the speech flow determined by a change of speakers are what she calls "agential cuts," where "the agential cut enacts a resolution *within* the phenomenon of the inherent ontological indeterminacy. In other words, relata do not preexist relations; rather, relata-within-phenomena emerge through specific intra-actions. Crucially, then, intra-actions enact *agential separability*—the condition of *exteriority-within-phenomena*. The notion of agential separability is of fundamental importance, for in the absence of a classical ontological condition of exteriority between observer and observed, it provides an alternative ontological condition for the possibility of objectivity" (140), i.e., it provides a local, situated, or functional objectivity at a moment when it is needed, when it matters. Thus our utterances are not imposed, conventional units within the speech flow, but *real* units in the sense that speakers (and listeners) know/sense when an utterance, no matter how many pauses and silences there might be within its performance, has been completed. They are, however, as Barad puts it, local resolutions, and this, clearly, leaves them *open* to further scrutiny.

Thus overall, "events" as such within a bodily performed speech flow itself lack specificity; they are only partially determined; their intertwined, complex nature makes it impossible for us to characterize their nature fully: they are just as much material as mental; as much felt as thought, and thought as felt; they have neither a fully orderly nor a fully disorderly structure, neither a completely stable nor an easily changed organization, neither a fully subjective nor fully objective character. While they can exhibit progressive changes, they can also exhibit retrogressive ones too. They are also non-locatable—they are "spread out" among all those participating in them. They are neither "inside" people, but nor are they "outside" them; they are located in that space where inside and outside are one; nor is there a separate before and after (Bergson), neither an agent nor an effect, but only a meaningful, "enduring" intra-acting whole which cannot divide itself into separable inter-acting parts. It is precisely their lack of any predetermined order, and thus their openness to being specified or determined *by those involved in them, in practice*—while usually remaining quite unaware of having done so—that is one of their central defining features.

It is this that makes events occurring in this sphere of activity so interesting, for at least the following two reasons: (1) to do with the practical investigations needed into how people actually do manage to "work things out," and the part played by the ways of talking we interweave into the many different spheres of practical activity within which we are involved; and also (2) for how we might refine and elaborate these spheres of activity, and how we might extend them into novel spheres as yet unknown to us. For if what we have suggested above is true, then innovative moments, creative moments, organizational moments, dialogical moments, cannot be *planned* to occur when we want them to occur; they *just happen*; they are emergent. But this does not mean, as we will see, that we cannot *occasion* or *circumstance* them and be *sure* that, sooner or later, they will occur.

What is so important, then, about the nature of dialogically structured activities is that, as two or more strands of flowing activity intra-act, organizational moments can just happen, they can emerge. Indeed, in occurring as an intra-action (rather then an inter-action), they exemplify emergence in precisely the sense that Lewes (1875: 368–69) meant in coining the term originally: " . . . although each effect is the resultant of its components," he said, "we cannot always trace the steps of the process, so as to see in the product the mode of operation of each factor. In the latter case, I propose to call the effect an emergent. It arises out of the combined agencies, but in a form which does not display the agents in action." And this is the amazing nature of such transitional processes as these; while we can capture how things were, and what they became, we cannot—due to their emergent nature—trace out the precise lines of causality by which they came to pass.

## 3.4 How not to do it!—trying to think in terms of abstract, rational schematisms

Clearly, as Westerners, seeking well-defined, solidified end-states, we feel helpless and adrift on the waves of fortune, when trying to think "while in motion," while still "in process." And we try to settle our unease by making clear plans for how to attain our aims, to solve our problems, and we set them out in terms of clearly nameable goals and "way stations" along the way to their attainment. But in criticizing academic psychologists' attempts only to think in terms of nameable things, when trying to characterize the nature of our thought processes, William James (1890: I, 255–56, my emphasis) said: "What must be admitted is that the definite images of traditional psychology form but the very smallest part of our minds as they actually live. The traditional psychology talks like one who should say a river consists of nothing but pailsful, spoonsful, quartpotsful, barrelsful, and other moulded forms of water. Even were the pails and the pots all actually standing in the stream, still between them the free water would continue to flow. *It is just this free water of consciousness that psychologists*

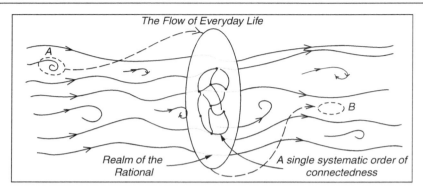

**Figure 3.2** The flow of everyday life

*resolutely overlook.* Every definite image in the mind is steeped and dyed in the free water that flows around it. With it goes the sense of its relations, near and remote, the dying echo of whence it came to us, the dawning sense of whither it is to lead."

But we often fail to observe these wise words. Instead, we do worse than thinking in terms of pailsful of water still standing in the stream. We act in relation to a dynamic stability of interest to us, *A*, say, as I depict it in Fig. 3.2—because it "counterfeits immobility" so well (Bergson)—as if we can lift it right out of the stream to take it back to our office (or laboratory) to study it more closely. And once there, we move into the Realm of the Purely Rational and convert all its intra-activities into inter-actions between a supposed set of separately named "component parts," and invent a set of rules or principles, in terms of which they can then be connected together again within a Single Systematic Order of Connectedness. We then try to take our local results from studying *A*, as a static configuration at an instant in time, i.e., as a theoretical representation, back into the flow in region *B*, where there is nothing—no "more" (James) or "field of possibilities" (Wittgenstein)—in that region to sustain it as the dynamic stability it was. In Garfinkel's (2002) terms, we *lose the phenomena*, we lose the *dynamic relationalities* that are in fact at work in producing the observed phenomena.

It is the free water flowing around the dynamic stabilities of interest to us that we cannot ignore. It is the local particularities in that free flow of water that have conditioned their emergence and which also sustain them in their existence, that we continually overlook. In other words, we continuously overlook what we might call the *determining surroundings* of the events of interest to us (Shotter, 2009)—the surroundings which, I suggested above, can *occasion* the happening of the organiz-*ing* we desire. What we lose when we try to understand what a person's words or actions mean outside of the shared sphere or arena of activity within which they are spoken,[6] is not what the words or actions can mean, but what the person actually meant in saying or doing them. In other words, to re-phrase an infamous Kantian dictum: Without the material influence of our experiences being "worded," they remain dis-organized, i.e., blind; but "wordings," i.e., utterances, without experience are empty. And this is crucial to our establishing and sustaining a practice—the knowledge informing a practice is *situated*, it is not something that can reside in the head of an individual alone.

Clearly, if we are to avoid the endless "contextualizing" needed in disambiguating abstractly stated claims, we need to move beyond an *analytical* to an *"ecological"* approach (Toulmin, 1990: 175–209) in our inquiries; an approach that is sensitive to the *particular*, the *local*, and the *timely*; that alerts us to the *incessant creation of novelty* by sentient, embodied, situated, reflexive, and responsive beings, and which emphasizes both the *open-endedness* of processes and human praxis [agency] to shape them; an approach in which our surroundings can be accounted as exerting "calls" upon us to act *responsively* in relation to them in "fitting" ways—our surroundings are also *agentive*.

Thus, in switching from an analytical to an ecological approach we switch from a mode of inquiry based on what goes on just *inside people* to inquiries focused on what people (including ourselves) go on, so to speak, *inside of*. And in this, our task cannot be that of persuasion by argument, nor to inspire others by exhortation (both of which require the use of already existing concepts), but that of creating the appropriate determining surroundings—to occasion or to circumstance—meetings within which the others around us, from their moving around within such circumstances, can come to see "connections" and "relations" they had not previously noticed. To develop the yet undeveloped potentials in existing practices, we need to seize upon, or to occasion, an opportune moment (*kairos*). I remember watching/hearing Pablo Casals in a cello master-class on TV saying to a pupil as he played: "Not like *this*, like *that*!," and feeling emotionally stunned by the subtle difference he made manifest as he made the comparison.

"In an agential realist account," says Barad (2007: 148–49), "*discursive practices are specific material (re)configurations of the world through which the determination of boundaries, properties, and meanings is differentially enacted. That is, discursive practices are ongoing agential intra-actions of the world through which specific determinacies* (along with complementary indeterminacies) are enacted within the phenomena produced." Our think-ings, speakings, and sensings, in occasioning the circumstances within which such (re)configurations can occur, are such enactments.

## 3.5 Conclusions: from impinging on experience only along the edges, to knowing from within it by direct acquaintance

What Karen Barad (2007) has provided us, then, with her agentive realism and her emphasis on intra- rather than inter-action, is not with the discov-ery of a new true theory, but with a fertile new *orientation*, with a new way (or ways) of relating ourselves to our surroundings. She has offered us a quite *new setting* for our social constructions (for our ideas, claims, concepts, etc.) than those offered us by other, still Cartesian approaches—new starting points for our inquiries and new *anchor* images in guiding what we attend to in our lookings, listenings, and so on. And what I have tried to do in these all too brief reflections (or rather, diffractions), is to explore the relations, the intra-relations, among ideas of sociomateriality and the happening of dialogically structured events, à la Bakhtin (and Voloshinov), with the aim of clarifying the nature of the profound conceptual shift she talks of above, what it means for us in our practices, in our thinking, and in our conduct of our inquiries—and especially, in what we expect of things as we go out to meet and to relate ourselves to the others and othernesses in our surroundings.

In the past, we have said that our theories are true theories if the *predic-tions* we derive from them match or "picture" the *outcomes* of the processes we study (see Hertz's formulation above). And in the past, in our social inquiries, we have talked of such entities as "society," "social relations," "culture," "organizations," "language," "communication," "persons," "the self," and so on, with the presumption that we all know perfectly well what the "it" is that is represented by the concept of the entity we are talking *about*. Clearly, we can no longer do that. Clearly also, we can no longer be satisfied with theory-driven research as providing the kind of understand-ings we need—if we are in fact to understand the sociomaterial processes within which we have our being.

So, although we can bring off some quite spectacular results in the natural sciences, we must now accept that it is just *in terms of a theory's relation to such results*, not to the whole structure of reality, that leads us to think of the theory as a *true* theory. But what is missed in all such theory-based results—which although they enable one to predict from one fixed configuration to another—is *what actually happens in the transitional flow of agentive activity* in the movement from one configuration to another. Such theory-based knowledge, as Quine (1953: 42) said long ago, "is a man-made fabric which impinges on experience only along the edges." What we now need, I think, in line with the ideas expressed above, is to pay more attention in our thinking to the "time contours" or "time shapes" that become apparent to us in the dynamic relations, the differences, emerging within us between our *outgoing* exploratory activities and their *incoming* results.

Living through this shift can, of course, be tremendously anxiety-provoking. A senior manager can be employed to produce a new leadership model, the architecture of an internal academy, an articulated strategic plan for a company's future development, etc., etc., and in taking this approach they can end up without ever producing such a product—as a seeming failure. Fernando Flores (in Spinosa et al., 1997: 45–46) describes his own experience in living through just such a circumstance thus: "Though he was trained both to develop such models [of his country's economy] and to evaluate the models others developed, he seldom found time to do this work. Instead, he was constantly talking: he explained this and that, to that and this person, put person A in touch with person B, held press conferences, and so forth ... Because he was sensitive to [this] anomaly [i.e., to the fact that his work was not producing any particular products but that he was working nonetheless], it led him to take a course on the theory of speech acts, and in that course he found the key to the anomaly ... He saw that work no longer made sense as the craftsmanship of writing this or that sentence or the skilled craftsmanship of banging this of that widget into shape but that currently work was becoming a matter of coordinating human activity—opening up conversations about one thing or another to produce a binding promise to perform an act ... Work never appears in isolation but always in a context created by conversation"—and it is *always*, in the end, in the course of conversations with the others involved that developments in an organization are achieved; they cannot simply be imposed.

The criteria for what constitutes "good work" here, as Chia (2010) makes clear—in discussing Oriental attitudes expressed in the "silent" allowing of events to take their course—are consequently very different from our Western concerns with seeking dramatic and spectacular "interventions." Bringing an organizing of people into existence is not like nut-and-bolting together a new machine. So, "although the Oriental disposition for harmony and non-intervention is sometimes construed as a debilitating passivity which accounts for its seeming indecisiveness or lack of ambition … [w]hat underpins the apparent reluctance to spectacularly intervene into the course of things is a rich historical appreciation for an immanent potentiality always already at work in the configuration of reality at each particular moment in time" (129).

Balancing between the two, between Eastern "allowing" and Western "intervening," we can see, I think, that although the "objects" of our inquiries only emerge into existence through and within intra-actions, they do so only in accord with the different agential cuts we make on the basis of the guiding expectations with which we go out to meet whatever is happening within our surroundings. And clearly, making a cut in one way, according to one way of conceptualizing or imagining events within the flow of one's experience, occludes other kinds of events.

In the world of quantum physics, clearly, complementarity is the rule—but that is also the case in our inquiries into speech communication: for we can focus like Systematizers on its orderliness, or like the Romantics on its creativity, but not on both at the same time. The situation, however, is different once we come to consider our experience of dialogically structured phenomena. While complementarity may seem to be the rule in our search for *orderly*, rationally intelligible accounts, of certain aspects of phenomena—when a focus on one aspect precludes a focus on others at the same time—in the polyphony of a truly dialogically structured meeting—in which everyone is in a spontaneously responsive connection with everyone else—then it *may be possible* for a felt unity of understanding to emerge, within which many seemingly contradictory aspects can be combined.

As Bakhtin (1984) puts it, with respect to what he feels Dostoevsky achieves in his novels: "*A plurality of independent and unmerged voices and consciousnesses, a genuine polyphony of fully valid voices is in fact the chief characteristic of Dostoevsky's novels*. What unfolds in his novels is not a multitude of characters and fates in a single objective world, illuminated by a single authorial consciousness; rather a *plurality of consciousnesses, with equal rights and each with his own world*, combine but are not merged in the unity of the event [he depicts]" (6). Thus, taking a *performative*, rather than a representational attitude towards our aims in our inquiries, leads us to the realization that their outcomes are not to be measured in terms of *their end points*, the results we arrive at. They are to be measured in terms of what we learn, what we can come to embody, along the way in making them. And just as we can distinguish someone who has comprehensive grasp of the game of chess from someone with a poor grasp—because "there are characteristic signs of it in the players' behaviour" (Wittgenstein, 1953: no. 54)—so we can also, if we take the trouble, begin to characterize (at first in a narrative account) what a comprehensive (but inevitably always unfinished) grasp of an organizational situation might be like.

So let me end where I began, by noting Wittgenstein's (1980) remark that: " . . . here we come on the difficulty of 'all is in flux'. Perhaps that is the place to start" (8), and by adding to it the fact that, as Karen Barad (2007) makes clear: "We don't obtain knowledge by standing outside of the world; we know because 'we' are *of* the world. We are part of the [matter of] world in its differential becoming" (185). In other words, we are more "at home" within this "chaos" than we have in the past acknowledged, and it is now time to begin to draw upon that fact, rather than still anxiously setting ourselves as standing over against it.[7]


## Notes

1. What Barad calls, as we shall see, "dynamic relationalities."
2. Elsewhere I have talked of our need for an understanding "from within" (Shotter, 2006).
3. "A predictable anchor in many discussions of process is the image of a stream," says Weick (2010: 104). Whereas, the notion of an "airy nothing," as in Shakespeare's *Midsummer Night's Dream*, might be a more suitable anchoring image for organizational studies, he suggests. This, however, is not to take into account the materiality of that "nothing."
4. He could have easily added "*in* organizations" also.
5. As Chia (2010: 135) puts it: "To recover this more intimate form of understanding, one must strive to abandon academic distance, immerse oneself in the initial flux and flow of reality and attempt to understand organizational emergence from within the phenomenon itself."
6. And this is Wittgenstein's (1953) point in introducing the term "language-game": as he remarks, "the term 'language-game' is meant to bring into prominence the fact that the speaking of language is part of an activity, or of a form of life" (no. 23); it is not the name of a phenomenon, but is meant to *draw our attention to* the fact that our word meanings are indeterminate outside of a shared involvement in a practical activity.
7. I would like to thank the editor (Hari Tsoukas) and two anonymous referees for their very attentive reading of a first draft of this essay and for their suggestions for its improvement. I hope I have done their efforts on my behalf justice.

## References

Andersen, T. (n.d.). *Stones and Hands*.

Bakhtin, M. M. (1984). *Problems of Dostoevsky's Poetics*, ed. and trans. C. Emerson. Minneapolis: University of Minnesota Press.

—— (1986). *Speech Genres and Other Late Essays*, trans. V. W. McGee. Austin, TX: University of Texas Press.

—— (1993). *Toward a Philosophy of the Act*, trans. and notes V. Lianpov, ed. M. Holquist. Austin, TX: University of Texas Press.

Barad, K. (2007). *Meeting the Universe Halfway: Quantum Physics and the Entanglement of Matter and Meaning*. Durham, NC & London: Duke University Press.

Bergson, H. (1911). *Creative Evolution*. London: Macmillan.

Bernstein, R. J. (1983). *Beyond Objectivism and Relativism*. Oxford: Blackwell.

Billig, M. (1999). *Freudian Repression: Conversation Creating the Unconscious*. Cambridge: Cambridge University Press.

Chia, R. (2010). "Rediscovering Becoming: Insights from an Oriental Perspective on Process Organization Studies," in T. Henes and S. Maitlis (eds.), *Process, Sensemaking, and Organization*. Oxford: Oxford University Press, pp. 112–39.

Descartes, R. (1968). *Discourse on Method and Other Writings*, trans. and introd. F. E. Sutcliffe. Harmondsworth: Penguin Books.

Garfinkel, H. (2002). *Ethnomethodology's Program: Working out Durkheim's Aphorism*, ed. and introd. A. W. Rawls. New York and Oxford: Rowman & Littlefield.

Gibson, J. (1979). *The Ecological Approach to Visual Perception*. Boston, MA: Houghton Mifflin.

Harquail, C. V. and King, A. W. (2010). "Construing Organizational Identity: The Role of Embodied Cognition," *Organization Studies*, 31/12: 1619–48.

Hertz, H. H. (1956 [1894]). *The Principles of Mechanics*. New York: Dover.

Ingold, T. (2008). "Bindings against Boundaries: Entanglements of Life in an Open World," *Environment and Planning A*, 40: 1796–1810.

James, W. (1890). *Principles of Psychology*, 2 vols. London: Macmillan.

—— (1912). "A World of Pure Experience," Chapter 2 in *Essays in Radical Empiricism*. New York: Longman Green and Co, pp. 39–91.

—— (1996 [1909]). *A Pluralistic Universe*. Lincoln, NB: University of Nebraska Press.

Law, J. and Mol, A. (1994). "Regions, Networks and Fluids: Anaemia and Social Topology," *Social Studies of Science*, 24: 641–71.

Lewes, G. H. (1875). *Problems of Life and Mind* (First Series), 2. London: Trübner.

Merleau-Ponty, M. (1962). *Phenomenology of Perception*, trans. C. Smith. London: Routledge & Kegan Paul.

Polanyi, M. (1967). *The Tacit Dimension*. London: Routledge & Kegan Paul.

Quine, W. V. (1953). "Two Dogmas of Empiricism," in *From a Logical Point of View*. Cambridge: Cambridge University Press, pp. 20–46.

Shotter, J. (2005). "Inside Processes: Transitory Understandings, Action Guiding Anticipations, and Withness Thinking," *International Journal of Action Research*, 1/1: 157–89.

——(2006). "Understanding Process from Within: An Argument for 'Withness'-Thinking," *Organization Studies*, 27/4: 585–604.

——(2009). "Moments of Common Reference in Dialogic Communication: A Basis for Unconfused Collaboration in Unique Contexts," *The International Journal of Collaborative Practices*, 1/1: 31–9, available at: http://ijcp.files.wordpress.com/2009/06/shotter-english.pdf

Spinosa, C., Flores, F., and Dreyfus, H. L. (1997). *Disclosing New Worlds: Entrepreneurship, Democratic Action, and the Cultivation of Solidarity.* Cambridge, MA: MIT Press.

Steiner, G. (1989). *Real Presences.* Chicago: University of Chicago Press.

Toulmin, S. (1990). *Cosmopolis: The Hidden Agenda of Modernity.* Chicago: University of Chicago Press.

Voloshinov, V. N. (1986 [1929]). *Marxism and the Philosophy of Language*, trans. L. Matejka and I. R. Titunik. Cambridge, MA: Harvard University Press.

Weick, K. E. (2010). "The Poetics of Process: Theorizing the Ineffable in Organization Studies," in T. Hernes and S. Maitlis (eds.), *Process, Sensemaking, and Organizing.* Oxford: Oxford University Press, pp. 102–11.

Wittgenstein, L. (1953). *Philosophical Investigations*, trans. G. E. M. Anscombe. Oxford: Blackwell.

——(1980). *Culture and Value*, trans. P. Winch, introd. G. Von Wright. Oxford: Blackwell.

**4**

# Materializing the Immaterial: Relational Movements in a Perfume's Becoming

*Nada Endrissat and Claus Noppeney*

**Abstract:** In artistic perfumery, new perfumes are not based on last year's top sellers, but on original, often unconventional ideas such as making a perfume that smells like melancholy. While this can sound promising to potential consumers, it poses a real challenge to the actors involved in the product development process: they need to organize their work in such a way that the immaterial, often deeply personal emotion can materialize into a concrete product. The chapter presents data from longitudinal, qualitative research on perfume making in artistic perfumery and outlines how the question of materializing the immaterial is approached by the creative director and two perfumers. Central to the chapter's findings is a visual concept that serves as a material representation of the emotion. Throughout the process, it takes on different roles in response to the specific situational challenges (boundaries) and relationships in which it is embedded. Together, they define the relational movements that are necessary for the product's becoming. The authors discuss insights and implications for understanding how materiality comes to matter in organization studies.

## 4.1 Introduction

Most product developments start out as ideas which need to be materialized in order to become new products. The recent turn to materiality in organization studies (Schatzki, 2006; Orlikowski, 2007; Orlikowski and Scott, 2008) has led to considerable research attention towards materiality (objects, infrastructure) and how it can support knowledge sharing, collaboration, and coordination

(Carlile, 2002, 2004; Bechky, 2003; Kellogg et al., 2006; Orlikowski, 2007; Nicolini et al., 2012) in research areas such as product development. However, less attention has been paid to the question of how people organize the means of achieving the materialization of products, that is, the question of how new products move from the "world of imagination" into the "world of concrete objects" (Aspelund, 2006). In this chapter, we adopt a sociomaterial under-standing of organizing (Orlikowski, 2007; Orlikowski and Scott, 2008) and build on research that considers the importance of materiality and boundaries in new product development (Carlile, 2002, 2004; Bechky, 2003; Ewenstein and Whyte, 2009; Nicolini et al., 2012) to help explain how immaterial, highly personal ideas can be materialized.

To make our argument, we draw from ongoing, longitudinal qualitative research on the material practices of perfume making in the emerging field of artistic perfumery. This growing niche market is characterized by con-ceptually advanced and experimental fragrances that serve highly symbolic functions. Among the European actors is Humiecki & Graef, a label that is known for its "unconventional concepts behind the highly individual perfume creations [which each] reflect a different facet of the entire spec-trum of human emotion—from fury to elation" (http://www.fragrantica.com/designers/Humiecki-%26-Graef.html).

We were able to accompany one complete perfume development process at Humiecki & Graef and their collaborators (perfumers, photographers, packaging designers) and are currently engaged in data collection for a second perfume-making process. At the beginning of each perfume's devel-opment, the creative director chooses an emotion that serves as a basic idea for the new perfume. During the development process, this emotion, which usually shows a close link to the creative director's personal experi-ence, is first materialized in the shape of a visual concept by the creative director, before it is then translated into an olfactory expression by the perfumers. The challenge is therefore to translate the highly personal, emotional experience into a visual representation and the visual into an olfactory representation. Our research questions focus on the material practices that enable the materialization of the idea and on the materiality that is produced and used during the process. Central to our findings is the visual concept that provides a representation of the emotion for the cre-ative director and the perfumers. Even though the actors show different interpretations of it, the visual concept is readable to all of them and seems to appeal to a shared sensibility that enables mutual understanding (Ewen-stein and Whyte, 2007). Our findings also show that the role and function of the visual concept change throughout the process as a consequence of situational challenges (boundaries) and the nexus of relationships in which it is embedded. Together, they define the movements that are necessary for the object to span existing boundaries and enable the materialization process. By focusing on the processes that lead to the product's becoming, we hope to contribute to existing knowledge in new product development and to a process perspective in organization studies more generally.

- First, by considering the processes of perfume making in artistic perfumery, our findings are able to shed light on how people organize as they work on products that need to cross deeply personal (emotional), visual, and olfactory boundaries. These boundaries have largely remained unexplored in organization studies and contribute to our understanding of how artistic or creative products are developed. The findings also highlight that visual materiality is able to span these boundaries and might therefore play a central role in the materialization of ideas, emotions, and personal experiences. In light of the popularity of the creative industries (Lampel et al., 2000) which "live on ideas" (Howkins, 2002), we believe that personal and sensory boundaries as well as the visual, aesthetic, or emotional functioning of materiality will play an increasingly important role in organization studies and (creative) product development processes.
- Second, by considering *when* and *how* the visual material changes its role during the process, the chapter responds to the recent call to specify the reasons for object transitions (Nicolini et al., 2012). It adds to our understanding of materiality by introducing the notion of *relational movements*. We illustrate that situational challenges (boundaries) and actor constellations require specific movements in order for the process to proceed. The visual concept is able to support these movements and gains its agency from the relationships in which it is embedded. Building on a relational process view of organizing (Langley and Tsoukas, 2010) and the notion of relational materiality (Law, 2002, 2004) we conclude that materiality matters as a consequence of its web of relationships and the relational movements that it enables.

We start with a brief overview of the role and function of objects in organization studies and then focus on the research area of new product development to highlight the ability of objects to span boundaries. After surveying current literature on the topic, we turn to our empirical case. Data are provided from three moments in time, to illustrate the process of the perfume's becoming. We show how the visual concept enables the immaterial idea to move across personal (emotional), visual, and olfactory boundaries. We conclude with a discussion of the new insights and implications for understanding how materiality matters in organization studies.

## 4.2 Objects as materiality: different roles and functions

The "turn to things" (Preda, 1999) has led to considerable research attention on how practices in organization studies are not only socially or discursively constructed, but solidly bound up with materiality (e.g., Preda, 1999; Cooren, 2004; Orlikowski, 2007). A common form of materiality in organization studies is the object. Objects are thought to play a decisive role in organizational processes, such as change or organizational learning (Wenger 2000), cross-disciplinary collaboration (Carlile, 2002, 2004; Bechky, 2003; Nicolini et al., 2012), coordination (Kellogg et al., 2006), or identity construction (Simpson and Carroll, 2008). Examples of objects that have been studied so far include timetable charts (Yakura, 2002), texts and documents (Preda, 1999; Cooren, 2004), photocopiers (Suchman, 2005), visual representations such as drawings, diagrams, and sketches (Henderson 1991, 1999; Ewenstein and Whyte, 2009), and prototypes (Bechky, 2003). Based on a comprehensive review of the literature, Rafaeli and Vilnai-Yavetz (2004) argue that objects have three functions in organizations: instrumental, symbolic, and aesthetic. In coordination research, most objects fulfill an instrumental function (Okhuysen and Bechky, 2009), which includes the enabling of communication, the motivation or activation of collaboration, and the mediation, translation, representation, or transformation of ideas, knowledge, and interests (Carlile, 2002, 2004; Boujut and Blanco, 2003; Kellogg et al., 2006; Nicolini et al., 2012).

Depending on the theoretical approach and the empirical question being studied, objects take on different roles which are reflected in the various prefixes that precede objects: activity object (Engestrom and Blackler, 2005; Nicolini et al., 2012), affiliative object (Suchman, 2005), boundary object (Star and Griesemer, 1989), boundary-negotiating artifact (Lee, 2007), epistemic object (Knorr Cetina, 1997; Rheinberger, 1997), intermediary object (Vinck and Jeantet, 1995; Boujut and Blanco, 2003), or technical object (Ewenstein and Whyte, 2009). Whether an object is going to be a boundary object or an epistemic object and whether it fulfills an instrumental or symbolic function is not pre-defined. While the object's inherent characteristics do seem to play a role, the way *in which the object is used in practice* is more important for the definition of its role and function (Bechky, 1999, 2003; Levina and Vaast, 2005; Star, 2010). For example,

Levina and Vaast (2005) were able to show that designated boundary objects that were promoted by senior management did not end up as the actual boundary objects in use. Rather, objects that were found useful in practice and were meaningful (providing a common identity) for joint work became successful boundary-spanning objects. The *situational requirement* and *actors' expectations* also define an object's role (Star and Griesemer, 1989; Henderson, 1999; Carlile, 2002, 2004; Bechky, 2003; Star, 2010; Nicolini et al., 2012). For example, in situations in which collaboration requires "coordination without consensus" or a shared understanding that is not necessarily based on identical interpretations, objects that offer "interpretive flexibility" are more likely to become boundary objects than stable/closed objects, such as operating procedures or common lexica (Star and Griesemer, 1989; Carlile, 2002). When the situational or task requirements (for example: stable, concrete, within context) are not met by the object or when the informational requirements of the actors are not fulfilled (for example, when the object is "not plastic or flexible enough" to be used by all disciplines), objects can "fail" (Bechky, 1999; Henderson, 1999). This is also emphasized by Carlile (2002), who argues that objects are no "magic bullets." Objects that work successfully in one situation do not necessarily work in another situation, because the *situational requirements* (new problem, different people) might have changed (Carlile, 2002: 452). Building on this observation, Nicolini et al. (2012) show that the same object can change its function and role over time. According to the authors, the transitions often "had to do with the material constitution of objects and their capacity to retroact on the activity" (Nicolini et al., 2012: 15), for example, to accommodate requirements of the different groups. The authors also note a "division of labor" among the objects in their study, with each object fulfilling the situational task it was best suited for (Nicolini et al., 2012). The transitional nature of objects is also stressed by Engeström and Blackler (2005) who describe a life(-cycle) for objects which follow a "career path" and become either successful products or end up in the trashcan. However, objects do not necessarily follow a one-way trajectory, but are able to change their roles and functions "back and forth," depending on the sociomaterial constellation in which they are embedded (Nicolini et al., 2012).

In sum, objects' roles and functions can vary. They are not pre-defined but appear to be a consequence of the situational challenges and web of relationships in which they are embedded. A constitutive element of a situational challenge in cross-disciplinary collaboration is a boundary, such as a knowledge, professional, or cultural boundary.

## 4.2.1 Boundaries and objects in new product development research

In the research field of new product development, the central challenge is to enable collaboration, knowledge sharing, and coordination across different practices and disciplines. This is a challenge inasmuch as each discipline carries its unique stock of knowledge, priorities, logics, and identities (Wenger, 2000), which create knowledge, cultural, disciplinary or professional boundaries (Carlile, 2002, 2004; Kellogg et al., 2006; Nicolini et al., 2012). Research has shown that these boundaries can be bridged by specific boundary-spanning mechanisms such as *boundary objects*. Originally, the notion of boundary objects was introduced by Star and Griesemer (1989) to describe a "sort of arrangement that allow different groups to work together without consensus" (Star, 2010: 602). Boundary objects are defined by their interpretive flexibility. They have "different meanings in different social worlds, but their structure is common enough to more than one world to make them recognizable, a means of translation" (Star and Griesemer, 1989: 393). What seems particularly important is that, even though they "inhabit several intersecting social worlds," they "satisfy the informational requirements of each of them" (Star and Griesemer, 1989: 393). As such, boundary objects have come to be seen as *the* way to cross social worlds (boundaries), convey technical and social information, and mobilize action (Star and Griesemer, 1989).

But other types of objects might also be suitable for crossing boundaries. In fact, Kellogg et al. (2006) argue that in dynamic organizational settings, boundary objects that are usually concrete and stable over time (Ewenstein and Whyte, 2009) and show a certain closure with respect to interpretations, values, and interests, can turn out to be counterproductive. In their stead, more flexible and concurrent forms of objects might be necessary (Kellogg et al., 2006), for example, visual representations (Henderson, 1991, 1999). Despite the fact that visual representations are often evolving and still in the making, they can be effective means for supporting collaboration processes (Ewenstein and Whyte, 2009). This is particularly the case when the collaboration is about moving forward *collectively* and *developing* or *specifying* an idea. Ewenstein and Whyte (2009) speak of visual representations as "spaces for representation" (Rheinberger, 1997). They are able to bridge the concrete and the abstract. They are themselves concrete, but also represent the abstract thing and, as such, help the crossing of boundaries, for example, between different design-disciplines in an architecture practice (Ewenstein and Whyte, 2009).

To summarize, different objects are able to cross boundaries and support collaboration. Whether an object turns out to be useful in crossing boundaries or not, largely depends on the specific requirements of the boundary and the *matching* capacities of the object. "Depending on the type of boundary faced, boundary objects with different capacities are required" (Carlile, 2004: 565).

So far, the boundaries that have been discussed in the context of new product development largely refer to two of the three capacities that Rafaeli and Vilnai-Yavetz (2004) define for objects in organizations, namely their instrumental and symbolic capacities. However, the sensory, emotional, or *aesthetic* functioning of objects and their link to aesthetic sense-making (Rafaeli and Vilnai-Yavetz, 2004), aesthetic understanding of organizations (Strati, 1992), aesthetic choices (Fine, 1992), aesthetic knowledge (Ewenstein and Whyte, 2007), or aesthetic boundaries (Mitchell, 1995) is seldom mentioned, even though aesthetics have become an important aspect of organizational life (Strati, 1992; Gagliardi, 1996; Linstead and Höpfl 2000; Guillet Monthoux, 2004). Aesthetics refers to the human senses (visual, auditory, olfactory, gustatory, and touch) and involves perception, imagination, judgments, and intuition. *Aesthetic knowledge* is "beyond words" and reflects an understanding of the "look, feel, smell, taste and sound of things in organizational life" (Ewenstein and Whyte, 2007: 689). It is embedded in practice and enables practitioners to make judgments about *when* things look, feel, sound, smell *right* (e.g., Fine, 1992; Cook and Yanow, 1993; Schulze, 2005; Ewenstein and Whyte, 2007). *Aesthetic boundaries* are characterized by different senses coming together, for example visual, hearing, and touch (Mitchell, 1995). The challenge is similar to the boundaries in product development: each sensory discipline has its own collectively shared practices which do not only involve instrumental and symbolic knowledge, but also (maybe even more so) aesthetic perceptions, intuitions, and aesthetic choices. The empirical case, to which we now turn, involves aesthetic boundaries. The materialization of a personal idea is achieved by crossing from personal experience to visual representation and then from visual representation to the olfactory product. On the one hand, these boundaries are characterized by functional differences (the creative director with a background in fashion design versus the perfume-maker); on the other hand, the boundaries are sensory and aesthetic, because they involve different senses and aesthetic knowing.

## 4.3 Research setting and approach

The Cologne-based perfumery brand Humiecki & Graef is part of the growing niche market of artistic perfumery. The collaboration with the perfumer Christophe Laudamiel goes back to 2005, when Sebastian Fischenich, the creative director of Humiecki & Graef, decided to make a perfume based on an emotion in collaboration with a globally recognized perfumer. After a first success, the collaboration was later extended to a second perfumer, Christoph Hornetz. Like Christophe Laudamiel (CL), Christoph Hornetz (CH)[1] is a perfumer at DreamAir LLC. By 2010, Humiecki & Graef had successfully launched seven perfumes on the market. Each perfume "is inspired by atypical, emotionally evocative motifs such as madness, melancholy and fury" (http://www.humieck-iandgraef.com/). Over the past three years, Humiercki & Graef launched about one perfume per year, with the official launch usually taking place in March at the artistic perfumery fair "Esxence—the scent of excellence" in Milan, Italy.

### 4.3.1 Overview of the perfume-making process

At the beginning of the perfume-making process, the creative director decides on an emotion that serves as the basic idea for the perfume. Following this decision, the creative director develops a visual concept in Zurich over a period of three to six weeks. Besides his work on the concept, he is involved in various other design projects. Once the visual concept is finished, it is used to brief the two perfumers. In mainstream perfumery, the perfume brief communicates the idea of the fragrance house to the perfumer and specifies the general scent characteristic by referencing a particular scent family (Pybus, 2006; Burr, 2008). It usually focuses on a particular target consumer segment and frequently encourages the imitation of successful competitors, rather than "new" products (Turin, 2007). The briefing at Humiecki & Graef, on the other hand, does not include information on customers or marketing, but simply consists of the visual concept which includes a sequence of three to six visual images and a few lines of text. In its visual form, the brief represents an interpretation of the particular emotion that the creative director has decided on. After the briefing, the two perfumers begin the development of the perfume formula. The perfume's development progresses over a period of three to four months at studios in Berlin and New York. The development of the perfume for Humiecki & Graef is usually not the only project the perfumers are working on. Based on our observations, we estimate that they work on about three to six projects (for different clients) simultaneously.

The visual concept is not only used as briefing information for the perfumers, but also at other stages: It is given to the packing designer, to the photographer who produces the marketing shots, and it is also used to decide on the name of the new perfume and inspires the composition of the marketing texts. Figure 4.1 provides an overview of the overall perfume-making process.

Since their first perfume development collaboration, the working relationship between the creative director and the perfumers has evolved, and their process of working together, especially the creative director's particular way of briefing the perfumers, has become a routinized practice (Feldman and Pentland, 2003).

The overall story that we are going to tell is one of a new product development process. The main challenge in our case is how the immaterial idea of the creative director can be passed on to the perfumers for them to materialize the idea into a perfume. Hence, the story is about finding an appropriate representation (materiality) of the idea which is readable to others; it is about crossing a deeply personal boundary to come to a visual materialization and about crossing a visual boundary to come to an olfactory materialization; it is about how materiality comes to matter in the process of materializing the immaterial.

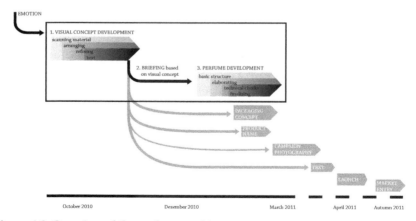

**Figure 4.1** Overview of the perfume-making process

## 4.3.2 Data collection

Our research interest was to understand how immaterial ideas are materialized. Following Schatzki (2006), our empirical approach focused on the material practices and materiality that were involved. The data presented in this chapter were mainly collected as an in-depth study of the perfume-making process over a six-month period from October 2010 to April 2011. Our data collection process was exploratory in nature and included observation, interviewing, and the review of documents (Charmaz, 2006; Corbin and Strauss, 2008). We tried to get as close as possible to the everyday activities and observed these at the design agency in Zurich and at the perfumers' studios in Berlin and New York (Emerson et al., 2007). As Charmaz (2006) suggests, we recorded what we saw as well as what we heard, including the naturally occurring talk (Silverman, 2011). We wrote extensive field notes (about 500 typed pages), took photographs (1,200 photographs), and videotaped the process (approximately 180h of video material) (Pink, 2007). We conducted and audio-recorded formal interviews (briefing and debriefing) with the creative director and the perfumers, and used the context of everyday activities for frequent informal interviews (e.g., lunch, dinner, etc.). These shorter interactions were also used to answer specific questions that arose during the observations. The people, practices, and materiality we observed included interaction partners, interruptions, timing, comments, talk, music (which the creative director and the perfumers listened to while working), emails that were written, sent, and received as well as the actors' reflections, own interpretations, and reasoning for doing things in this way or another. In addition, we collected related documents (e.g., email correspondence, sketches) and materiality (e.g., perfume versions that were disqualified and thrown out). The formal interviews that we carried out systematically after a period of observations ranged from 40 minutes to 4 hours in length. These interviews as well as some of the informal interviews (those that we considered relevant) were transcribed verbatim. The additional audio-recordings and the video-recordings were summarized by a research assistant to provide an overview of the data and their subject. The data collection process is ongoing and focuses on the making of a new (next) round of perfume development.

During the data collection process, the visual concept emerged as materiality with central importance. We therefore decided to pay particular attention to this object and to "track" it through the different stages of the overall process in order to better understand what this object does and "who it is" (Rescher, 2007). In doing so, we tried to follow "the things themselves, for their meanings are inscribed in their forms, their uses, their trajectories" (Appadurai, 1986: 3).

### 4.3.3 Data analysis

Following an inductive, qualitative analysis approach, we moved itera-tively between data collection, analysis, and the emerging theory (Char-maz, 2006; Corbin and Strauss, 2008). We transitioned between multiple readings of the interview transcripts, videotapes, field notes, coding of recurring themes, and the building of categories. Each author separately carried out open coding (Corbin and Strauss, 2008). In the course of organizing and interpreting the data, we drew upon conceptual frame-works from literature (Ewenstein and Whyte, 2009; Nicolini et al., 2012) as sensitizing concepts (Blumer, 1954) that helped us to make sense of the data and sensitized us, for example, for the different roles and functions an object can take on. The ambiguities resulting from the initial coding were taken up during the formal debriefing interviews and led to a better understanding of "what was happening" (Charmaz, 2006). For the second coding step, we focused on the visual concept and the material practices in which it was embedded. Figure 4.2 provides a summary of our empirical approach.

## 4.4 Findings

The findings are structured in chronological order and include data from three different time phases: Phase 1—the development of the visual con-cept, Phase 2—the briefing situation, and Phase 3—the development of the actual perfume (see frame in Figure 4.1). Each phase is characterized by particular challenges, boundaries, and movements.

### 4.4.1 Phase 1: From abstract to concrete, from internal to external, attachment to detachment

The development of the visual concept challenges the creative director in several ways. The initially vague emotion needs to be specified and made concrete; the emotion must be materialized so that it can serve as a com-munication device with other professionals later on in the process. For this to be possible, the personal experience (internal) has to be made

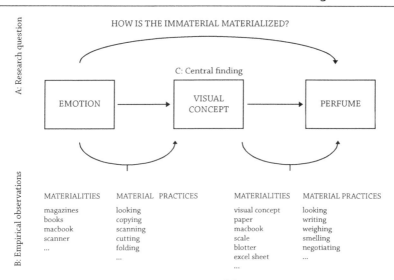

**Figure 4.2** Overview of empirical approach and focus

external and find a first materialization. The creative director has to partly detach himself from his own personal experiences and find a visual representation that can be read by others. The personal/visual boundary has to be crossed in order for others to be able to make sense of the visual concept.

On a sunny October morning in 2010, the creative director started the work on the visual concept for the new perfume that was to be launched under the label Humiecki & Graef. He started off with the vague idea that the new perfume should be about the emotion of trust. On his way to the studio, he purchased a selection of fashion and lifestyle magazines. Upon his late arrival at the studio, he started his work by going through the magazines, surfing the web for other visual associations, and consulting some reference works of cultural history. When he started talking to us, he stated that he was sure that the emotion he wanted to focus on was "trust." However, he was not yet sure "about the associations and visual representations of trust" (transcript). But this did not seem to worry him too much, he simply continued by looking through magazines, getting up from his desk to get a book, listening to music, reading emails, talking on the phone, and looking for more images that might help him develop a visual representation. Moving between digital and paper worlds, high and low culture, historical and current imagery, he continuously associated his internal world of feeling with the external world of associations. Thus, he slowly "concretized the vague feeling" (debriefing interview, transcript) he was looking for. During the making of the concept, he occasionally spoke about his idiosyncratic associations:

> *Warm, deep, warmth: inside, closed*
> *A traditional Sunday roast*
> *I have discovered that the scent needs to have something of a red wine*
> *It is something sexual, to confide in someone, to open up to someone*
> *It should be something with bast—a basketwork*

We observed how the visual concept emerged from the connections that evolved between these different aspects. Thus, the creative director seemed to come closer to what he was looking for (from transcript and field notes):

> *Creative director: There should be a woody note; the red wine is still missing; dry laurel; grey hair. [ . . . ] Grey hair mirrors the color of trust. [ . . . ] Unfortunately, this is green. [the creative director smiles]*
> *Researcher: A few minutes ago you said that it should not be green. You seem to have a concrete idea. Is it too fresh?*
> *Creative director: Yes, indeed.*

This cognitive process manifested itself in a sequence of material practices as shown in Figure 4.3: the creative director copied, scanned, and printed; he searched the internet; he cut images and folded parts of them; and he digitally assembled the visual fragments in Adobe Photoshop. Together, these different material practices propelled the overall materialization of the emotion.

All in all, the visual concept remained unfinished, open, and in the making over a period of five weeks. Throughout this period, the creative director lived an "active dialogue" (debriefing interview, transcript) with the visual images. Thus, he worked on the visual concept whenever he had an idea or was in the mood for perfecting it; for example, he worked on it at home, on a Sunday morning while still in his bed, or during his official working hours at the office. We sometimes got the impression that he was "obsessed" with it. According to him, he just continued to "polish images and words" (debriefing interview, transcript) and to make minor changes that we, as researchers, sometimes did not even notice. But to his eyes, something was still missing. There was still something he had not yet fully understood and that manifested itself in an aesthetic inconsistency. His final approval of the concept was rooted in this designerly sense of perfection:

**Figure 4.3** The making of the visual concept

> *Creative director: In every design process, there is the point where the designer knows: It is done.*
> *Researcher: What about changes?*
> *Creative director: No, no changes after it is done.*

At this point, the visual concept was "frozen" and closed. In its final state, it consists of three images and three lines of text—one under each image. As the creative director explained to us, each image serves a specific function: The first image introduces the emotion on a general, visual level. The second image visually details and concretizes the emotion further. The third image provides specific visual cues about desired olfactory notes, such as laurel or "red wine."

Overall, we observed the development of the visual concept as an associative discovery and clarification process. Like other creative processes, it was not a systematic, but rather a seemingly chaotic process with many interruptions (Michlewski, 2008). The time that the creative director needed was continuously underestimated by him and took much longer than his subjective perception of it.

The choice of the emotion of trust and the development of the visual concept involved the creative director personally. The concept worked as a reflection of his personal situation and emotional state. During a lunch break, he referred to a recent disappointment as one of the factors accounting for his motivation to have a perfume about trust. Accordingly, the search for the perfect concept corresponded with his desire to understand his own situation. The concept is not only an object he happens to be working on. It is more a true companion he literally spends his day and night with. It seems to embody what he does not yet know (Knorr-Cetina, 1997). *"Personal attachment, intimacy, and projection characterize the relationship between the concept and the creative director"* (from field notes). Reflecting on this intimate relationality in an informal interview, the creative director talks about the downsides and possible difficulties in the collaboration with the perfumers:

> *It is so hard to distance oneself from one's own biography. This is even more so when dealing with emotions . . . I have to erase the personal links. I want to see the images as mere images, because the perfumers do not share my experience. They can hardly relate to this. I must try to communicate the ideas without talking about myself.*

This quote illustrates very tellingly the necessity to partly dissociate himself from his own personal interpretation to make it communicable to the other people who are involved in the process. Because the concept materializes the creative director's personal associations, the concept makes sense to him. However, the perfumers approach the concept with a different background, a different understanding, a different personal situation. As a consequence, the concept has to effectively communicate the key idea across these boundaries. For this reason, the creative director wanted the concept to be clear and well-structured, while also allowing for enough interpretive flexibility, so that the perfumers could enjoy a certain degree of autonomy and creative freedom.

### 4.4.2 Phase 2: From personal to collective, from detached to attached

After the visual concept was considered "ready," it was sent to the perfumers by email without any additional information. As mentioned above, the actors have been working together for some time and their practices are routinized and do not need any additional explication. The main challenge during Phase 2 is to make the personal idea a collective one and to get the perfumers interested, committed, and attached to it.

The email with the attached visual concept was sent on November 9, 2010. Three weeks later, the creative director and the perfumers had a 45-minute briefing conversation on the telephone. In general, the term briefing refers to the process in which both a client and a designer or other professionals analyze and agree on the scope, aim, and budget of a project (Tumminelli, 2008). Thus, any briefing situation constitutes a boundary situation by its very nature. In our case, we observed a disciplinary (design–perfume-making), an aesthetic (visual–olfactory), a geographic (Zurich–Berlin), and a linguistic (German–English–French) boundary. In this briefing situation, the three participants discussed the special experience of trust as well as the richness, maturity, and complexity of the future scent in the light of the visual concept. The perfumers wanted to start their work from the visual concept and consequently explored the different facets of it. In an attempt to better understand it, they asked questions for clarification: "What do you mean by impartial?," "Does devotion capture the essence of page one?," "How does the feeling of being in good hands relate to trust?" (transcript). Thus, during the first part of the conversation, they jointly identified different aspects of the meaning of trust: "Longing," "passion," "nuances of melancholy," "a sense of love," "dedication," and "security." However, the different aspects remained rather unconnected in the course of the phone conference and were not merged to form a shared definition or description. The visual concept thus mediated the *internal* experience of the creative director and the perfumers as *external* recipients of it.

73

In the second part of the telephone conversation, the discussion shifted towards possible olfactory notes for the perfume. One perfumer clearly expressed his surprise at the laurel note that the visual concept suggested on the third image. In response, the creative director characterized this rather unusual note as "dry," "balsamic," and "herbaceous" (transcript). In this situation, the visual concept showed its interpretive flexibility insofar as the perfumer referred to the laurel leaves on the third image as an allusion to the "Roman Empire" (transcript), whereas the creative director wanted to capture the atmosphere of a "traditional Sunday roast" (field notes). In his reply the creative director conceded: "This is funny. I have not seen it this way [Roman Empire]. But it is true" (transcript). The visual image allowed for the coexistence of both associations. Thus, the visual concept is able to incorporate radically different meanings. At the same time, it allows for coherence across the boundaries. Even though different interpretations existed, they did not obstruct the process. Instead, its openness, its emphasis on the aesthetic dimension, and the lack of technical precision at this stage facilitated the process catalytically. In fact, the visual concept did not primarily convey factual statements that call for a logical examination in this briefing. It rather visually captured and mobilized "a surreality" as the creative director called it in the debriefing interview and introduced itself to the perfumers as a flexible source of stimulation and inspiration. As such, the visual concept allowed the perfumers to associate it with their own personal experiences and to establish a link and relationship with the concept.

> Creative director: "It is really about the connection between old and young."
> Perfumer: "Fine, this is how I understand the other pictures. I was immediately able to relate to this concept. It is more than just a mere understanding."
> Creative director: "Yes, I understand."
> Perfumer: "I can get the point of the concept, because it is really the feeling of a boy (short silence)—it has happened to me a few times."

The possibility to make sense of the visual concept by means of their own associations, intuitions, and experiences enabled the perfumers to identify and get attached to the visual concept. Thus, they were able to collectively empathize with the originally individual emotion of trust. The visual concept was then no longer the visual representation of Sebastian's experience of trust. Instead, the perfumers identified specific moments of their own biography. After this "appropriation," the phone conference quickly came to an end. The perfumers committed themselves to preparing two alternatives for an olfactory expression of the visual concept. They started to work on it one week later in their studio in Berlin.

### 4.4.3 Phase 3: From artistic openness to technical closedness, from visual to olfactory materialization

The goal of the development of a new perfume is a well-blended composition of initial top notes and long-lasting base notes—a "product of beauty" (Shiftan and Feinsilver, 1964). Technically, the process aims at a chemical formula that can be passed over to the aroma company that produces the perfume. The main challenge in this phase is thus for the perfumers to find an appropriate olfactory representation for the visual concept. Because the olfactory representation, in the end, is a chemical formula, they have to move from artistic openness or ambiguity to a technically closed representation.

The development of a new perfume begins with the work and decision on the structure of the perfume. The work proceeds with a thorough elaboration of the different notes and concludes with technical checks and minor adjustments. Technically, the perfume-making process can be described as a sequence of clearly defined steps and material practices at the perfumers' studio (Calkin and Jellinek, 1994). Initially, the perfumer determines the materials and writes down the exact formula. Based on our observations and inquiries, 4 to 6 alternative formulae capturing variations of the overall composition are usually calculated and subsequently weighed precisely in the laboratory area of the studio. Each step is documented accurately in writing. The perfume is taken to the desk area and then smelled by the perfumer. Following an analysis of the olfactory experience, the original formula is further modified: disturbing materials are left out, new materials are added, and the overall composition is changed until a convincing formula is found. In the fieldwork conducted by us, the visual concept was deeply intertwined with these material practices. The concept could be observed in numerous instances during this movement.

When we arrived at the perfumers' studio in December 2010, we found a printed version of the visual concept on Christoph's desk in a folder with a few notes from the phone conference. Christoph (CH) was the first to work on the new perfume. We saw him clearing his desk and then concentrating on the visual concept as shown in Figure 4.4. He looked in detail through the three pages and wrote down first ideas and associations. After a short while, he took two bottles from the archive section in the laboratory. While smelling the perfume structures from previous projects, he looked through the visual concept, took additional notes, and consulted his personal data (knowledge) base on the computer. What followed was an intensive phase of moving between the visual concept and the material practices of writing notes and formula, weighing in the laboratory, and smelling at the desk as documented in Figure 4.4. The visual concept provided the general direction, motivation, and meaning for his activities. For the entire day, the visual concept remained on his desk. In the debriefing interview, Christoph (CH) explained that he was looking for a symphony of the structure with the notes Sebastian had mentioned during the briefing.

After two hours of lone work on the perfume, Christophe (CL) joined his partner at the desk. He brought along his own copy of the visual concept and some ideas about a possible structure he wanted to explore. The two perfumers began by smelling what Christoph (CH) had previously worked on. Christophe (CL) liked the "ambery notes in the back" and disliked the "aniseed in the top." Verbalizing his first impressions, Christophe (CL) looked at the visual concept in front of him and pointed at the first picture with his blotter.[2] Going through the formula that expressed the olfactory impression in technical writing, the two perfumers found it difficult to identify the "aniseed" and "metallic" impression they had gotten from the scent. What followed was a discussion of different ingredients and the conclusion that the next versions should be softer.

During the entire smelling session, we observed the two perfumers sitting in front of a copy of the visual concept. The concept was part of the desk scenery and showed performative qualities, though neither of them referred to it explicitly: the visual concept functioned continuously as a subtle eye-catcher for the two perfumers and became a partner in the conversation. This "vitality and liveliness" (from the transcript of the debriefing interview with the creative director) of the visual concept became even more obvious when the two perfumers dealt with the second structure Christoph (CH) had prepared. We could witness how Christophe (CL) enjoyed the scent: "That is nice too," although after a quick look at the visual concept, he made it clear that this scent did not fit his perception of the concept:

> It is not my imagination of how I feel strongly about a professional master . . . in karate . . . because it is nice, it is comfortable—but there is not the very intense strength of a master.

Following this judgment, the dispute between the two perfumers escalated. In the end, Christophe (CL) picked up the visual concept: Swinging it with his left hand, he demonstrated the contrast between the scent and the concept as shown in Figure 4.4. According to him, the scent was "a cologne," "wishy-washy," "too nice," but a "no-brainer," whereas the concept

**Figure 4.4** The visual concept in use by the perfumers

was a "brainiac—a very intense mind connection." The current olfactory expression was not in line with his (CL) interpretation of the visual concept. His criticism was based on an aesthetic judgment that could not be traced back to specific elements of the visual concept. The concept seemed to have activated an aesthetic knowledge of the emotion of trust. While one perfumer looked for "masculine, floral notes," the other perfumer had a different association in mind. Despite these differences in interpretation, both perfumers were deeply committed to the visual concept: it had stimulated them in their professional and artistic ambition. The following excerpt from a field note summarizes our observation concerning the use and presence of the object during the beginning of Phase 3:

> The concept has been very present today. Yet, it is not so much the image or specific details, but the mere keyword "concept" that occupies the two perfumers. The briefing and the discussion of the concept must have left a strong impression on the two. Thus, the concept functions as a natural point of reference: "This fits with the concept," or: "This is not in line with the concept." The mere reference to the "concept" works without further detailing the link to the concept.

Later in the process, the debriefing interview confirmed how the visual concept triggered divergent associations: On the one hand, Christophe (CL) associated the visual concept with an "intensive, ideal type relationship between two people." On the other hand, Christoph (CH) saw an "erotic" and "sexual aspect," described it as "daring," and felt more "challenged" as perfumer when comparing the concept with the previous ones. Facing the contradiction, the visual concept is not only used as an intellectual and immaterial argument, but in its materiality: it is picked up, shown and performatively used as a material object. Another function of the concept was observable some time later: Christophe (CL) was in the midst of smelling and analyzing an advanced version of the perfume at his desk. He was not satisfied with the overall smell. We got the impression that the elaboration process had become stuck and that the perfumer was lacking orientation and focus. The perfumer interrupted his smelling and analyzing work. He briefly mentioned that he wanted to look through his "sketchbook," his knowledge base consisting of notes and archived formula, etc. Yet, before he really got into the pile of paper, he remembered the visual concept and took it out of his project folder labeled "H&G." After looking at the first picture for a few seconds, his search seemed to gain a new sense of direction. He noticed "milky," returned to the formula, and added some notes. A few minutes later, we saw him looking through the other pictures of the concept. He noted the "repetitiveness" among the pictures and sensed something "elegant." Taking this interpretation further towards the formula, he then wanted "to play with some woods." After this conclusion, the perfumer put the visual concept aside and returned to the formula on the computer for further technical modifications. Within a couple of minutes, the perfumer was able to gain new insights from the visual concept.

In these short contacts with the concept (which we frequently observed), the perfumers moved between the olfactory and the visual. The visual concept representing the emotion of trust provided the overall orientation for the more technical work on the formula. The formula defined and specified the ingredients and their composition with respect to amounts, weight, etc. It represented the technical expert knowledge of the perfumer. When immersed in the technical work on the perfume, the visual concept guided the perfumers back to the fundamental ideas of the perfume and prevented them from being lost in the technical details of perfume making (Shiftan and Feinsilver, 1964). Working with the visual concept, the perfumers could apply the olfactory ideas in terms of technical materiality, while not losing track of the ideas the perfume was intended to represent.

## 4.5 Discussion

Studying the process of perfume development allowed us to observe how an immaterial idea is materialized. Empirically, we considered the role and function of materiality, paying particular attention to the visual concept as the "main actor." The visual concept was developed by the creative director to represent and communicate the basic idea for the new perfume to the perfumers. Hence, the materialization process did not happen directly (from idea to perfume), but via a "detour" of visual materiality. However, the visual concept seems to have been worth the extra mile: It enabled the materialization of the immaterial by supporting three successive movements: from *abstract to concrete (from internal to external, from attachment to detachment)*, from *personal to collective (detachment-attachment)*, and from *artistic openness to technical closedness (ambiguous-concrete)*. These movements were necessary to overcome the situation-specific challenges and boundaries during the collaboration and product development process.

Table 4.1 provides a summary of our findings, including a characterization of the three situations, their challenges, the movements that were supported by the visual concept, the actors that were involved in the specific situation, their relationship, and the functions and roles of the visual concept over the three phases.

In the first phase (during the making of the visual concept), the visual concept can be described as an epistemic object or, better, an instantiation of the epistemic object of the emotion "trust." There is a close, personal relationship between the creative director (the originator of the idea) and the emotion. The "object of desire" (Knorr-Cetina, 2001) is evolving and in the making. To make the emotion communicable, a visual representation is necessary to cross the personal/visual boundary. The situational challenge is to move from abstract to concrete. According to Ewenstein and Whyte (2009), this is exactly what the visual concept is able to support. "Visual representations are certainly a significant, if not *the* major, way in which the abstract is linked with the concrete" (Ewenstein and Whyte, 2009: 12, emphasis added). A match between the situational requirements (crossing the boundaries from personal to visual, from abstract feeling to concrete visual representation, from internal representation to external materialization, from attachment to detachment) and the properties of the object allowed this movement.

**Table 4.1** Overview of situation-specific challenge, actors, and object's role

|  | 1. Development of visual concept | 2. Briefing | 3. Development of perfume |
|---|---|---|---|
| Situation-specific challenge | Specify emotion; turn emotion into a communication device; make sure others understand it | Opening ownership; conveying the experience of trust; making sure perfumers understand the idea<br>Make sure perfumers can identify with concept, appropriate it | Fit with concept; translating materialized emotion (visual concept) into olfactory representation |
| Movement | Vague–concrete internal–external<br><br>attach–detach from personal to visual | From personal experience—to collective<br>detach–attach | Artistic–technical Abstract/ambiguous–concrete<br>From visual to olfactory |
| Actors | Creative director–visual concept | Creative director–visual concept–Perfumers | Visual concept—perfumers |
| Characteristic of relationship | Personal, close, intense, emotional | Distanced but interested, then: identified with and appropriated it | Close, activates; object serves as "collaboration partner" |
| Object's characteristic and role | To trigger desire, create mutual dependencies; in the making, open—then suddenly "closed" | Translation device, interpretive flexibility across boundaries; stable, "closed" | Motivates the collaboration; directs activities; can lead do contradictions that are discussed and negotiated |

In the second phase (the moment of the briefing), the visual concept takes on the role of a boundary object. The main challenge is to translate the original idea to the perfumer, so that they understand the idea, identify with it, and appropriate it. The intimate relationship between the idea and the creative director needs to be replaced by the relationship between the visual representation and the perfumers. While the idea (emotion) had to be detached from the creative director by materializing it visually in the first phase, the challenge is now to get the detached perfumers *attached*. The movement is thus from *personal* to *collective* (from detachment to attachment) without losing the intended message (making a perfume about "trust—the feeling of being in good hands"). To establish a link, it is important that "the object is both plastic enough to adapt to local needs and constraints of the several parties employing them, yet robust enough to maintain a common identity across sites" (Star and Griesemer, 1989: 393). In other words, the visual concept can be read by the perfumers, even though they have a different professional background than the creative director. They can make sense of it and link it to their own (emotional) experiences. Again, we find a good "match" between the situational challenge and the properties of the object to allow the process to move forward, to overcome the challenge and the boundary that exists between the different professional backgrounds. In addition, the visual concept is also able to span the geographical boundaries between New York, Berlin, and Zurich, because it is mobile and easily circulated (electronically) and thus helps to establish a shared understanding and normative parameters (Latour, 1999; Ewenstein and Whyte, 2009). The fact that the creative director relies on a visual concept corresponds with the specific qualities of visual images that are also discussed in the literature. Being confined to two dimensions, visual images are elliptic and incomplete (Jonas, 1962). Yet, the visual expressiveness, eloquence, and complexity (Elkins, 1999) make it possible to frame different aspects in one visually consistent picture that can be perceived simultaneously. Thus, the "picture superiority effect" (Paivio, 1971) explains the efficiency and effectiveness of visual communication. In a similar vein, Ewenstein and Whyte (2007, 2009) argue that visual representations embody diverse types of knowledge, such as engineering-specific knowledge and aesthetic knowledge (Ewenstein and Whyte, 2007, 2009), which allows professionals with different perspectives to make sense of it and relate to it (Henderson, 1999; Eckert and Boujut, 2003).

In the third phase, the visual concept is constitutive to the material work practices of the perfumers. Once the perfumers started to engage with the visual concept, it became a co-creator. It prompted and motivated the succeeding activities of the perfumers. Besides its role as a translator, the concept was also a mediator that acted: It initially provided the controversial basic idea for the development of the formula as well as new ideas at critical moments during the further development of the perfume. When the refinement of the scent was about to stagnate, the perfumers regularly picked up the visual concept and quickly searched through the images and words for inspiration. Thus, it provided the overall direction and was a "driving force" (Miettinen et al., 2009: 1318) behind the perfume's development. It took on an active role and demanded definition, triggered discussion, and spurred the development on. These functions can be said to be characteristic of an activity object (Nicolini et al., 2012).

Our findings corroborate that the material constitution of an object (visual, olfactory, open-closed, abstract-concrete) needs to fit with the situational requirements (e.g., boundaries, challenges) in order for the object to become useful and relevant. While the different roles and functions of objects have already been discussed in the literature, the movements that we identified are novel; they offer insight into the possible *actions of materiality* and stress the mutual interdependence between object, situation, and actors (see Figure 4.5 for illustration).

### 4.5.1 Relational movements and materiality's agency

In the process of the materialization of immaterial ideas, different situation-specific challenges were encountered. On the one hand, they were defined by the actors who were involved at this particular moment (e.g., creative director) as well as by the object that was relevant at this moment (e.g., emotion of trust). The situational challenge (e.g., personal/visual boundary, moving from internal association to external visual materialization) was thus co-produced. At the same time, the situation-specific challenge defined the properties that were needed in the object to "fit," for example, a visual representation that would help to move from abstract idea to concrete image. The object, on the other hand, received its role not only from the situation, but also from the web of relations in which it was embedded; from the way in which it was used by the actors. For example, the intimate relationship between the creative director and his personal experience of trust influenced the making of the visual concept. At the same time, the visual concept (materiality) ensured the working-together of the social actors (creative director and perfumers) in Phase 2 and, in doing so, also responded to the situation-specific challenge (boundary). In short, situation, objects, and actors are interdependent. Their entanglement

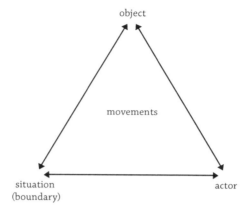

object

movements

situation
(boundary)

actor

**Figure 4.5** Interplay between situation-specific challenge (boundary), object, and actor

defines which movements are *necessary* to overcome a situation specific challenge; it also defines which movements are *possible* given the specific constellation between actors, objects, and situation. The movements, in turn, act back on the relationship constellation between object, actors, and the situation by overcoming the challenge and by moving the process of materialization to the next phase. Our findings thus corroborate the socio-material entanglement of objects, actors, and situations and help to specify the reasons for the object's transition during the process (e.g., Ewenstein and Whyte, 2009; Nicolini et al., 2012) as well as its success or failure (Bechky, 1999; Henderson 1999; Carlile, 2002, 2004). The specific chal-lenges (boundaries) do not only call for matching object characteristics (Carlile, 2004), but also for particular—boundary-specific—*movements*.

In line with a relational process view of organizing (Langley and Tsoukas, 2010) we argue that the movements are *relational*: they are enabled by the sociomaterial entanglement of actors, objects, and practices (Knorr-Cetina, 1997, 2001; Latour, 2005; Schatzki, 2006; Orlikowski, 2007; Orlikowski and Scott, 2008). According to the sociomaterial perspective, "the social and the material are considered to be inextricably related—there is no social that is not also material, and no material that is not also social" (Orlikowski, 2007: 1437). It is not the social forces alone that move material objects, but the social practices which are entangled with materiality (Latour, 1996). On the one hand, sociomateriality suggests that social relations are held in place by materiality. On the other hand, materiality receives its importance, function, role, and meaning from the social web into which it is embedded. Law (2002, 2004) speaks of *relational materiality* and explains: "Objects are an effect of stable arrays or networks of relations" (2002: 91). The object (visual concept) received its meaning and function from the way the actors were using it. The movements were possible only because of the specific relationships that existed between the actors and the object. Accordingly, materiality's agency follows from the entanglement between materiality and sociality (Barad, 2003). It is the existing web of relationships that decides which matters come to matter.

### 4.5.2 Future research

Visual images are known for being able to influence recipients emotionally. Scholars in the emerging field of visual studies emphasize the agency of images and inquire how visual images affect human emotions (Mitchell, 2005). In our case, the visual concept might have had an emotional immediacy, which could help explain why the attachment to the idea (emotion) worked so well with the perfumers. The visual concept was obviously able to trigger associations that are linked to the perfumers' own experiences which facilitated the identification with the concept's idea and the subsequent development of the perfume. In design studies, using visual material to communicate emotions is an established practice commonly referred to as "mood board." Mood boards are used in design processes "to introduce a certain mood, theme, or consumer world" (Godlewsky, 2008: 266).[3] The mood board communicates "the touch and feel" of the final product and as such refers to an aesthetic knowledge or knowing of the designers (Ewenstein and Whyte, 2007). We believe that this is also true for the visual concept that we studied: the production of the visual concept by the creative director as well as its reading and interpretation by the perfumers is largely based on an aesthetic knowing. In other words, the visual materiality is not chosen to communicate functional information, but to appeal to the senses. It is an aesthetic expression of the emotion trust which appeals to the perfumers' senses and own emotional experiences. This observation points to a new aspect in the discussion around materiality: its *aesthetic* and *emotional* side. Artistic materiality (such as artwork or other creative products) might be particularly well suited to help the materialization of immaterial ideas, emotions, or personal experiences. Future research may be able to focus on the aesthetic function (Rafaeli and Vilnai-Yavetz, 2004) and the "sensuous immediacy" of objects (Pels et al., 2002) and how these are related to emotions and aesthetic boundaries and knowing in product development and innovation processes in an economy that is increasingly driven by aesthetics (Postrel, 2003) and (sensory) experiences (Pine and Gilmore,

1999). In addition, future research could also consider in greater detail the role emotions play in the process. While the creative director presents the emotion solely as an "unconventional idea" for the new perfume, it could be argued that the emotion is always present during the development process. In principle, Sebastian organizes the work around the new perfume's development emotionally. By *organizing emotionally*, we suggest that not only the beginning is marked by an emotional experience; all subsequent processes and practices are also induced by an emotional experience. For example, the visual concept helps the perfumers relate emotionally to the concept and its idea. They engage in a form of "emotional commitment" or "emotional participation" that binds them to the development of the product. If this is the case, the emotion could be seen as vehicle for crossing boundaries. Instead of focusing on material instantiations, future research could focus more on the immaterial emotion. It would also be worthwhile to inquire whether it is this emotional relation that enables the perfumers to create a special scent that in turn induces highly emotional reactions in the consumers (as can be found on internet blogs such as www.fragrantica.com). This could be relevant for scholars working in the field of emotional design (Norman, 2003), where the focus is on the emotional side of designing, buying, and using products.

Finally, our findings suggest that objects do not only engage in relationships with human actors but also in object–object relationships. For example, the relationship between the visual concept and the fragrance or between the excel sheet (formula) and the scent; these relationships take on complementary, recursive and co-depending forms. A closer analysis of these object–object relationships could possibly take the notion of an object-centered sociality (Knorr-Cetina, 1997, 2001) a step further.

## 4.6 Conclusions

The main concern of this chapter has been to help explain the materialization of an immaterial idea. We have drawn on a study of perfume making in artistic perfumery to outline how materiality comes to matter in this process. Central to our findings has been the identification of relational movements that were enabled by the visual concept and that proved critical for the materialization to take place. The findings of our study can be linked to research in the field of new product development and the emerging stream of process organization studies. It adds to our knowledge on product development by taking into account *personal, sensory, and aesthetic boundaries* which have largely remained unexplored. We have argued that visual materiality constitutes a promising means for spanning these boundaries and called for more research to fully explore the *aesthetic* and *emotional* function of materiality in organizing processes in the creative industries and elsewhere. Second, the chapter adds to the understanding of materiality (objects) by specifying its transitions and movements. In line with a relational process view of organizing (Langley and Tsoukas, 2010) and the notion of relational materiality (Law, 2002, 2004) we argue that the objects' movements are relational and possible only when a specific constellation of situational challenges (boundaries), actors, and object characteristics match each other. In other words, materiality matters as a consequence of its web of relationships and the relational movements that it enables.

## Notes

The authors would like to thank Sebastian Fischenich (Humiecki & Graef), Christophe Laudamiel, and Christoph Hornetz (DreamAir LLC) for their openness to participate in this research project and for granting us access to the practices and processes of perfume making. We also thank the two anonymous reviewers for their intelligent and encouraging comments and Paul Carlile for his insightful feedback and guidance throughout the review process. The authors gratefully acknowledge financial support from the Swiss National Science Foundation (grant 13DPD3_132215/1).

1. Because both perfumers have the same first name, we will put their initials in parenthesis to provide the reader with a better understanding to whom we are referring.
2. Blotter refers to the paper strips used to smell and test a perfume. They are usually dipped in the perfume and then held close to the nose to smell it (Calkin and Jellinek, 1994).
3. Mood boards are seen as communication devices that mediate between different stakeholders (Eckert and Stacey, 2003), most often in client conversation. Mood boards resemble "sketchy collages" (Godlewsky, 2008) and are created from diverse material, such as images, text, textures, etc. Besides expressing a mood or evoking an emotion, the boards can provide inspiration (Eckert and Stacey, 2003) or summarize the results of a research process (Eckert, 2001).

# References

Appadurai, A. (1986). "Introduction: Commodities and the Politics of Value," in A. Appadurai (ed.), *The Social Life of Things: Commodities in Cultural Perspective*. Cambridge: Cambridge University Press, pp. 3–62.

Aspelund, K. (2006). *The Design Process*. New York: Fairchild.

Barad, K. (2003). "Posthumanist Performativity: Toward an Understanding of How Matter Comes to Matter," *Journal of Women in Culture and Society*, 28/3: 801–31.

Bechky, B. A. (1999). *Crossing Occupational Boundaries: Communication and Learning on a Production Floor*. Stanford: Stanford University Press.

—— (2003). "Sharing Meaning Across Occupational Communities: The Transformation of Understanding on a Production Floor," *Organization Science*, 14/3: 312–30.

Blumer, H. (1954). "What is Wrong with Social Theory?" *American Sociological Review*, 18: 3–10.

Boujut, J.-F. and Blanco, E. (2003). "Intermediary Objects as a Means to Foster Co-operation in Engineering Design," *Computer Supported Cooperative Work*, 12/2: 205–19.

Burr, C. (2008). *The Perfect Scent: A Year Inside the Perfume Industry in Paris and New York*. New York: Henry Holt.

Calkin, R. R. and Jellinek, J. S. (1994). *Perfumery Practice and Principles*. New York: Wiley & Sons.

Carlile, P. R. (2002). "A Pragmatic View of Knowledge and Boundaries: Boundary Objects in New Product Development," *Organization Science*, 13/4: 442–55.

—— (2004). "Transferring, Translating, and Transforming: An Integrative Framework for Managing Knowledge Across Boundaries," *Organization Science*, 15/5: 555–68.

Charmaz, K. (2006). *Constructing Grounded Theory: A Practical Guide Through Qualitative Analysis*. Los Angeles: Sage.

Cook, S. D. N. and Yanow, D. (1993). "Culture and Organizational Learning," *Journal of Management Inquiry*, 2/4: 373–90.

Cooren, F. (2004). "Textual Agency: How Texts Do Things in Organizational Settings," *Organization*, 11/3: 373–93.

Corbin, J. and Strauss A. L. (2008). *Basics of Qualitative Research: Techniques and Procedures for Developing Grounded Theory*, 3rd edn. Los Angeles: Sage.

Eckert, C. (2001). "The Communication Bottleneck in Knitwear Design: Analysis and Computing Solutions. Computer Supported Cooperative Work," *The Journal of Collaborative Computing*, 10/1: 29–74.

—— and Boujut, J. (2003). "The Role of Objects in Design Co-Operation: Communication through Physical or Virtual Objects," *Computer Supported Cooperative Work*, 12: 145–51.

—— and Stacey, M. (2003). "Sources of Inspiration in Industrial Practice: The Case of Knitwear Design," *Journal of Design Research*, 3/1: 1–30.

Elkins, J. (1999). *The Domain of Images*. Ithaca: Cornell University Press.

Emerson, R. M., Fretz, R. I., and Shaw, L. L. (2007). *Writing Ethnographic Fieldnotes* (Chicago Guides to Writing, Editing, and Publishing). Chicago: University of Chicago Press.

Engestrom, Y. and Blackler, F. (2005). "On the Life of the Object," *Organization*, 12/3: 307–30.

Ewenstein, B. and Whyte, J. (2007). "Beyond Words: Aesthetic Knowledge and Knowing in Organizations," *Organization Studies*, 28/5: 689–708.

—— (2009). "Knowledge Practices in Design: The Role of Visual Representations as 'Epistemic Objects'," *Organization Studies*, 30/1: 7–30.

Feldman, M. and Pentland, B. (2003). "Reconceptualizing Organizational Routines as a Source of Flexibility and Change," *Administrative Science Quarterly*, 48/3: 94–118.

Fine, G. A. (1992). "The Culture of Production: Aesthetic Choices and Constraints in Culinary Work," *American Journal of Sociology*, 97/5: 1268–94.

Gagliardi, P. (1996). "Exploring the Aesthetic Side of Organizational Life," in S. R. Clegg, C. Hardy, and W. R. Nord (eds.), *Handbook of Organization Studies*. London: Sage, pp. 565–80.

Godlewsky, J. (2008). "Mood Board," in M. Erlhoff and T. Marshall (eds.), *Design Dictionary: Perspectives on Design Terminology*. Basel: Birkhäuser, p. 266.

Guillet de Monthoux, P. (2004). *The Art Firm: Aesthetic Management and Metaphysical Marketing*. Stanford: Stanford University Press.

Henderson, K. (1991). "Flexible Sketches and Inflexible Data Bases: Visual Communication, Conscription Devices, and Boundary Objects in Design Engineering," *Science, Technology, & Human Values*, 16/4: 448–73.

—— (1999). *On Line and on Paper: Visual Representations, Visual Culture, and Computer Graphics in Design Engineering*. Cambridge, MA: MIT Press.

Howkins, J. (2002). *The Creative Economy: How People Make Money from Ideas*. London: Penguin.

Jonas, H. (1962). "Homo Pictor and the Differentia of Man," *Social Research*, 29/2: 201–20.

Kellogg, K. C., Orlikowski, W. J., and Yates, J. A. (2006). "Life in the Trading Zone: Structuring Coordination Across Boundaries in Postbureaucratic Organizations," *Organization Science*, 17/1: 22–44.

Knorr-Cetina, K. (1997). "Sociality with Objects: Social Relations in Postsocial Knowledge Societies," *Theory, Culture & Society*, 14/4: 1–30.

—— (2001). "Objectual Practice," in T. Schatzki, K. Knorr-Cetina, and E. von Savigny (eds.), *The Practice Turn in Contemporary Theory*. New York: Routledge, pp. 174–88.

Lampel, J., Lant, T., and Shamsie, J. (2000). "Balancing Act: Learning from Organizing Practices in Cultural Industries," *Organization Science*, 11/3: 263–9.

Langley, A. and Tsoukas, H. (2010). "Introducing 'Perspectives on Process Organization Studies'," in T. Hernes and S. Maitlis (eds.), *Processs, Sensemaking, and Organizing*. Oxford: Oxford University Press, pp. 1–26.

Latour, B. (1996). "On Interobjectivity," *Mind, Culture & Activity*, 3/4: 228–45.
—— (1999). *Pandora's Hope: Essays on the Reality of Science Studies*. Cambridge, MA: Harvard University Press.
—— (2005). *Reassembling the Social: An Introduction to Actor-Network-Theory*. Oxford: Oxford University Press.
Law, J. (2002). "Objects and Spaces," *Theory, Culture & Society*, 19/5–6: 91–105.
—— (2004). *After Method: Mess in Social Science Research*. London and New York: Routledge.
Lee, C. (2007). "Boundary Negotiating Artifacts: Unbinding the Routine of Boundary Objects and Embracing Chaos in Collaborative Work," *Computer Supported Cooperative Work*, 16/3: 307–39.
Levina, N. and Vaast, E. (2005). "The Emergence of Boundary Spanning Competence in Practice: Implications for Implementation and Use of Information Systems," *MIS Quarterly*, 29/2: 335–63.
Linstead, S. and Höpfl, H. (eds.) (2000). *The Aesthetics of Organization*. London: Sage.
McDonagh, D. and Storer, I. (2004). "Mood Boards as a Design Catalyst and Resource: Researching an Under-Researched Area," *The Design Journal*, 7/3: 16–31.
Michlewski, K. (2008). "Uncovering Design Attitude: Inside the Culture of Designers," *Organization Studies*, 29/3: 373–92.
Miettinen, R., Samra-Fredericks, D., and Yanow, D. (2009). "Re-Turn to Practice: An Introductory Essay," *Organization Studies*, 30/12: 1309–27.
Mitchell, W. J. T. (1995). "Interdisciplinarity and Visual Culture," *Art Bulletin*, 77/4: 540–44.
—— (2005). *What Do Pictures Want?* Chicago: University of Chicago Press.
Nicolini, D., Mengis, J., and Swan, J. (2012). "Understanding the Role of Objects in Cross-disciplinary Collaboration," *Organization Science*, 23/4: 000–00.
Norman, D. A. (2003). *Emotional Design: Why We Love (or Hate) Everyday Things*. New York: Basic Books.
Okhuysen, G. A. and Bechky, B. A. (2009). "Coordination in Organizations: An Integrative Perspective," *The Academy of Management Annals*, 3/1: 463–502.
Orlikowski, W. J. (2007). "Sociomaterial Practices: Exploring Technology at Work," *Organization Studies*, 28/9: 1435–48.
—— and Scott, S. V. (2008). "Sociomateriality: Challenging the Separation of Technology, Work and Organization," *The Academy of Management Annals*, 2/1: 433–74.
Paivio, A. (1971). *Imagery and Verbal Processes*. New York: Holt, Rinehart and Winston.
Pels, D., Hetherington, K., and Vandenberghe, F. (2002). "The Status of the Object: Performances, Mediations, and Techniques," *Theory, Culture & Society*, 19/5–6: 1–21.
Pine, B. J. II and Gilmore, J. H. (1999). *The Experience Economy: Work is Theatre & Every Business a Stage*. Boston, MA: Harvard Business School Press.

Pink, S. (2007). *Doing Visual Ethnography: Images, Media, and Representation in Research*, 2nd edn. London: Sage.

Postrel, V. (2003). *The Substance of Style: How the Rise of Aesthetic Value is Remaking Commerce, Culture, and Consciousness*. New York: Harper Perennial.

Preda, A. (1999). "The Turn to Things," *The Sociological Quarterly*, 40/2: 347–66.

Pybus, D. (2006). "The Perfume Brief," in C. Sell (ed.), *Chemistry of Fragrances: From Perfumer to Consumer*, 2nd edn. London: Royal Society of Chemistry, pp. 138–42.

Rafaeli, A. and Vilnai-Yavetz, I. (2004). "Emotion as a Connection of Physical Artifacts and Organizations," *Organization Science*, 15/6: 671–86.

Rescher, N. (2007). "The Promise of Process Philosophy," in C. V. Boundas (ed.), *Columbia Companion to Twentieth Century Philosophies*. New York: Columbia University Press, pp. 143–55.

Rheinberger, H.-J. (1997). *Toward a History of Epistemic Things: Synthesizing Proteins in the Test Tube*. Stanford: Stanford University Press.

Schatzki, T. R. (2006). "On Organizations as They Happen," *Organization Studies*, 27/12: 1863–73.

Schulze, H. (2005). *Heuristik: Theorie der Intentionalen Werkgenese. Sechs Theorie Erzählungen zwischen Popkultur, Privatwirtschaft und dem, was einmal Kunst genannt wurde*. Bielefeld: Transcript Verlag.

Shiftan, E. and Feinsilver, M. (1964). "Practical Research of the Art of Perfumery," *Annals of the New York Academy of Sciences*, 116/2: 692–704.

Silverman, D. (2011). *Interpreting Qualitative Data a Guide to the Principles of Qualitative Research*, 4th edn. London: Sage.

Simpson, B. and Carroll, B. (2008). "Re-viewing 'Role' in Processes of Identity Construction," *Organization*, 15/1: 29–50.

Star, S. L. (2010). "This is Not a Boundary Object: Reflections on the Origin of a Concept," *Science, Technology & Human Values*, 35/5: 601–17.

—— and Griesemer, J. R. (1989). "Institutional Ecology, 'Translations' and Boundary Objects: Amateurs and Professionals in Berkeley's Museum of Vertebrate Zoology 1907–39," *Social Studies of Science*, 19/3: 387–420.

Strati, A. (1992). "Aesthetic Understanding of Organizational Life," *Academy of Management Review*, 17/3: 568–81.

Suchman, L. (2005). "Affiliative Objects," *Organization*, 12/3: 379–99.

Tumminelli, P. (2008). "Brief," in M. Erlhoff and T. Marshall (eds.), *Design Dictionary: Perspectives on Design Terminology*. Basel: Birkhäuser, pp. 57–8.

Turin, L. (2007). *The Secret of Scent: Adventures in Perfume and the Science of Smell*. London: Faber and Faber.

Vinck, D. and Jeantet, A. (1995). "Mediating and Commissioning Objects in the Sociotechnical Process of Product Design: A Conceptual Approach," in D. MacLean, P. Saviotti, and D. Vinck (eds.), *Management and New Technology: Design, Networks and Strategy*. Brussels: COST Social Science Series.

Wenger, E. (2000). "Communities of Practice and Social Learning Systems," *Organization*, 7/2: 225–46.

Yakura, E. K. (2002). "Charting Time: Timelines as Temporal Boundary Objects," *Academy of Management Journal*, 45/5: 956–70.

# 5

# Media as Material: Information Representations as Material Foundations for Organizational Practice

*Paul Dourish and Melissa Mazmanian*

**Abstract:** Through a confluence of different disciplinary interests and trajectories, questions of the materiality of digital media and information technologies have recently come into relief. There are several different strains of work under this broad umbrella and it is valuable to distinguish between the varied concerns. This chapter has two objectives. It begins by teasing apart and describing five related ways to conceptualize the materiality of digital goods. The goal is to provide a typology for delineating current streams of research and language for analysis. Next, the authors unpack one of these conceptions, the *materiality of information representation*, by first taking a historical perspective of the material consequences of representational practices. They then analyze two empirical examples that explore the role of digitization and simulation (or the materiality of *digital* representation) in order to shed light on how social and organizational systems respond to, create practices around, and develop delineating logics about digitally rendered data.

## 5.1 An anecdote

One day, in the period when one of us (Dourish) was working as computer system manager for a university research center, a data tape arrived from the United States. It contained a corpus of research material that had been much anticipated. I mounted it in the tape drive on our DEC VAX 11/750 minicomputer, but was unable to read it successfully. The tape drive did not register any readable data on the tape at all. Since tape is occasionally an unreliable medium, I tried again using the tape drive of the other VAX in the same machine room that we shared with a neighboring research group, again without success. I subsequently tried to read it on the two other tape drives in the building, attached to computers produced by other manufacturers, with no more luck.

After consulting with some colleagues, the consensus was to take the tape to the local computing center where surely something would be able to read it. The results were frustrating (although I did get to see a whole lot of new computer systems up close). Eventually someone suggested that I take the tape to one of their long-term employees, Harry, so that he could "eyeball" it. Computer "mag tape," like old audio recording tape, comprises nothing more than a long spool of plastic material covered in brown magnetic oxide, so I was confused by the idea that it might reveal anything to the human eye—or to Harry's in particular—but, out of options, I did as suggested.

In his office, Harry unspooled a few feet of tape. He reached into his desk drawer and pulled out a small object that consisted of a metal ring about 4 cm in diameter, which held in place two thin glass sheets with a gray liquid held between them. The gray liquid turned out to be iron filings in suspension. Harry stretched out the tape on a piece of blank paper, placed his device on top, and, pencil in hand, slid it slowly up and down the tape, occasionally tapping the ring gently. The iron filings began to line up in relation to the data stored on the tape. Moving the ring up and down, Harry located a gap in the data recorded on the tape—the inter-record marker—and made a mark on the paper below; he moved the ring up the tape to find another and made a second mark. After measuring the distance between them with a ruler, and doing a quick calculation, he looked up and said, "Ah, here's your problem. It's a 400 bpi (bits-per-inch) tape. The only drive that will read this is on the ICL [mainframe]."

He was right. We got our data.

## 5.2 Introduction

Information—most particularly, digital information and the processes by which it is generated, collected, managed, distributed, and employed—has come to play such a pivotal role in all aspects of Western life that many theorists have suggested that our contemporary condition be dubbed an "information society" (or similar terms such as network society and knowledge society) (Castells, 1996; Webster, 2006). In many of these accounts, a key feature of information is its dematerialized form. Indeed, the shift to an information society is, often, a shift from material objects to digital equivalents on computer screens (as in online shopping, online movie rentals, digital libraries, electronic newspapers, and digital health records, for example). Technology pundits applaud this "substitution of bits for atoms" associated with digital technologies and suggest that the "future" will be fueled by some vague and ideal sense of digitality. As in the words of Negroponte:

> We are not waiting on any invention. It is here. It is now. It is almost genetic in its nature, in that each generation will become more digital than the preceding one. The control bits of that digital future are more than ever before in the hands of the young. Nothing could make me happier. (Negroponte, 1995: 231)

However, even in this information-rich environment, the physical world persistently makes itself felt. Networks are disrupted when undersea cables are broken and information is lost when cloud services fail. The microprocessor engineers whose work fuels the digital revolution find themselves locked in daily struggle with the limits of physical fabrication and the properties of semiconductor materials. More broadly, the information that undergirds the "information society" is encountered only ever in material form, whether that is marks on a page or magnetized regions of a spinning disk.

Increasingly, social scientists have begun to recognize these material realities and turned their attention to the intertwining of social phenomena with the material world. Coming from various disciplinary backgrounds such scholars argue that the social world manifests itself in the configuration and use of physical objects and that the properties of those physical objects and the materials from which they are made—properties like durability, density, bulk, and scarcity—condition the forms of social action that arise around them. We see organizational scientists (e.g., Orlikowski and Scott, 2008), anthropologists (e.g., Miller, 2005), sociologists (e.g., Mackenzie, 2009), STS scholars (e.g., Suchman, 2007), communication scholars (e.g., Ashcraft et al., 2009) and feminist scholars (e.g., Barad, 2003) beginning to unpack the importance of the specific material configurations of our informated world.

These writers have focused on the material aspects of social life, often taking information as itself a social phenomenon—social in both its origins and its implications. In this chapter we are similarly concerned with the material landscape of the seemingly intangible. However, rather than focus on the material aspects of social life we focus specifically on the materiality of information. More precisely we present a case for the material constructs that shape how we engage with, experience, and make sense of information. We further incorporate the technologies, objects, metaphors, and processes that shepherd, frame, and constitute information. In this chapter, we sketch a framework that begins to illuminate the various materialities of information as they arise in organizational, social, and cultural practice. We then explore the material consequences of a particular shift in the how information is represented in digital arenas for organizational processes. This perspective draws our attention to the specific representational practices associated with contemporary information science.

Focusing on information as a material object—either as it is instantiated in information systems of all sorts, or as it manifests itself in the representational systems that contribute to the shape and character of life in information society—draws specific attention to the historical particularities, cultural specificities, and political consequences of information work. Accordingly, our goal here is to provide an initial articulation necessary to begin a cross-disciplinary conversation about the various forms, effects, and implications of shifting materialities associated with information and information actions (e.g., transfer, distribution, storage, and search).

In talking of materiality here, we want to go beyond the brute fact of material manifestation. That is, what is of interest to us is not simply the fact that apparently abstract and ineffable digital "stuff" actually takes material form; rather, we want to understand the particular material properties of these forms and their consequences for how people encounter, use, and transform them. Particular material properties might include mutability, persistence, robustness, spatiality, size, durability, flexibility, and mobility. Information practice arises in conversation with these specific properties of information and its material forms. In speaking of materiality, rather than simply of material-ness, we have in mind these specific considerations.

As an illustrative example, consider the case raised by Edwards (2011) in his study of climate science, where he notes the problems faced by the U.S. National Weather Records Center in storing meteorological data on punched cards in the early 1960s. Their concern was not that they had more data than they might be able to process; rather, it was that they might have more data than their building could physically support. One gigabyte of data on punched cards weighs over 35 tons. The point is not simply that that is a lot, although it certainly is. Rather, we note that the specific material instantiations of the data have implications for where it can be stored (and therefore for the kinds of institutions that can afford to house it), for how quickly it can be moved from place to place, for how easily elements can be accessed, and so on. In turn, this shapes our ideas about the kinds of questions that can be asked of data, the sorts of information we have available to us, and what we assume is worth collecting. Transformations in storage media play out as reconsiderations not simply of the availability of information, but also of the institutional auspices under which it can be collected and managed, its lifetime, the temporalities of access, its resistance to change, and even what we think of as being practical as a data set in the first place. Yates (1993) makes similar arguments in her account of the emergence of scientific management and related phenomena around the novel technology of vertical (hanging) filing systems in the early twentieth century. The same set of documents, physically arranged in a new way, become available for drastically new forms of manipulation and use.

Further, in examining the particular material properties that characterize digital forms we take an expansive view of what is relevant for analysis. The word "material" encompasses two related meanings—that which takes physical form and that of consequence. Rather than position these meanings in opposition, our definition of materiality moves beyond the dichotomy of object vs. importance. We are interested in exploring the consequences of form and forms of consequence. By this we mean the identities, understandings, and negotiations that take place around and in relation to the physical as well as the physical manifestations of choices, lines of action, and ways of seeing that emerge from the consequence of digital infrastructures and metaphors. In other words, that which carries "material consequences" is always also physical and that which is physical occasions "material consequences."

In what follows we begin by setting out a range of perspectives of the materiality of information. The landscape is vast, and it is not our goal to attempt to explore it all here; instead, by quickly sketching a set of related research topics, we aim to provide a language for discourse that facilitates the emerging and overlapping interests arising in various fields. We then attempt to identify a smaller (although still huge) area that will command our particular attention, the materiality of digital representations. We present some initial grounding for this work, but our preliminary exploration here is conducted largely through an examination of two particular cases—the case of amateur digital photography, and the case of nuclear weapons testing. We close with broad remarks concerning potential future directions for this stream of work.

## 5.3 Aspects of the materiality of information

What do we mean by the materiality of information? Several different possibilities present themselves, and all are relevant. For practical purposes here, we begin by presenting five conceptualizations of the materiality of information in the context of digital technology. These categories emerged in our conversation as we began to survey the literature and examine how scholars—with diverse goals, perspectives, and disciplinary backgrounds—conceptualized the "materiality of information" in various ways. They are an early attempt at providing a typology for the various orientations to the materialities of information and the consequences of various material properties for how information is perceived, utilized, and brought into being. We do not suggest that these five conceptualizations are conclusive, but we feel they are a good starting point for connecting diverse conversations into a more overarching discussion of the materiality of information.

The first could broadly be described as the *material culture of digital goods*. Anthropologists have, for several decades, investigated the ways that physical objects carry symbolic value and do important cultural work; examples include studies of homes (e.g., Cieraad, 1999), cars (e.g., Miller, 2001), and the Sony Walkman (Bull, 2000). Digital goods—as icons of modernity, as fashion statements, as affiliative objects, and more—clearly play similar roles as elements of material culture. Into this category we place examinations of the cultural currency of particular digital products such as iPhones, netbooks, or the Linux operating system. Digital goods can have symbolic meaning in terms of personal histories and local significance, but more broadly—as possessions, as objects of aspiration, as demonstrations of status, as elements of interpersonal, and as projections of self-identity—digital goods in and of themselves play a broader cultural role. They make a statement and they carry symbolic weight, particularly in the transition from non-digital to digital ways of working. The materiality of digital technology, then, encompasses the study of digital technologies from the perspective of material culture as one component.

The second aspect of materiality in the realm of digital technologies might be dubbed the *transformative materiality of digital networks*. Information technologies of various sorts are increasingly woven into the fabric of everyday space, from home gateways to rural cellular telephone coverage, and these condition our experience of those spaces. Increasingly, cultural geographers and urban theorists recognize the role that information and information technologies play in the encounter with space (e.g., Graham and Marvin 2001; Kitchen and Dodge 2011). The availability of infrastructures organizes and contextualizes human action and the various meanings that space can have, both in the small (e.g., cell phone dead zones, Wi-Fi-enabled cafés, broadband-connected homes) and in the large (e.g., cities differentiated by their data infrastructure, concentrations of manufacturing industry, regions marked by different approaches to regulation of digital services or the allocation of wireless spectrum.)

In this second category we include work that concerns the physical properties of digital technologies considered as aspects of infrastructure and the built environment. So, for example, a materialist perspective on the emergence of novel forms of virtual organization in light of the spread of high-speed networks might reflect this perspective, focusing on the mutual constitution of organizational practice and technologies of communication, from open source communities to e-government to distributed teams (e.g., von Hippel and von Krogh, 2003; Olson et al., 2008). Similarly, research into the cultural geography of information technologies, from the spatial politics of digital urbanism to the reshaping of public space through Wi-Fi and WiMAX networks, reflects this second approach (e.g., Mackenzie, 2005).

The third conception concerns the *material conditions of information technology production*, or a Marxian account of the economic conditions favored by the speed, ubiquity, and manipulability of information rendered into digital forms (e.g., Harvey, 2006). Whenever we talk about digital information, we also talk, if implicitly, about a host of other elements critical to making it work: server farms located on costly real estate and with massive power costs; labor, both skilled and unskilled, to build technologies, encode information, maintain infrastructures and facilities, and deal with increasing amounts of toxic e-waste (e.g., Pellow and Park, 2002); corporate and governmental alliances and partnerships; systems of legislation, regulation, and compliance; and national and supranational regimes of governance, from telecommunications deregulation and "net neutrality" to NAFTA, GATT, and WIPO. Each of these elements involves embedded power relations that reflect resource streams, capitalist production and consumption logics, and hidden labor.

Notwithstanding the image of entrepreneurs in Silicon Valley garages and billion-dollar businesses launched from Harvard dorm rooms, building and deploying digital technologies and information systems typically requires significant capital resources. (A Harvard education, after all, costs a fair amount of money, as does Silicon Valley real estate.) Talking of the materiality of contemporary information experiences, then, most certainly includes the question of the power and resources needed to bring those systems and infrastructures into being, and the ways in which information systems themselves must reproduce the conditions of their own production (Althusser, 2001).

While emerging from different fields of scholarship (e.g., anthropology, geography, political philosophy), these first three conceptions are related and play off each other in interesting ways. Infrastructures, and the harnessing of power, resources, and ideals create the conditions—social, economic, physical—that facilitate the emergence of digitally layered spaces and the creation of information goods; issues that arise out of the third approach enable the considerations that arise in the first and second. Infrastructures of production and distribution provide the underlying structures and capacities necessary to materially transform spaces according to the logics, capacities, and actions associated with information-rich, digitally enhanced, environments. In addition, material infrastructures and technologically laden spaces contribute to how goods are produced, perceived, and layered with cultural meanings and identities. So, we can see that while our first three conceptualizations—*material culture of digital goods*, *transformative materiality of digital networks*, and *material conditions of information technology production*—are distinct in theoretical origin, level of analysis, and fundamental insights about the relationship between materiality and digital information, they also rely on and engender one another. The fourth and fifth topics focus less on digital objects and infrastructures and move instead to the realm of meaning making and lines of action associated with ways of understanding the world.

The fourth topic is the *consequential materiality of information metaphors*. Information has become one of the universal metaphors of contemporary life and this metaphor implies an informational approach to seeing and understanding the world that diminishes some forms of knowledge and authorizes others. Certainly, we see this in formalized domains, such as genomics and bioinformatics that depend on an "informational" reading of biological processes (e.g., Yockey, 1992). Such activity reshapes the domain of biology by refocusing attention and activity of those engaged in studying it and presenting this domain to others. For example, not only does an information account of the brain redirect funding dollars, reorganize the corporate competitive landscape, and reshape disciplinary structures; it shifts what are considered plausible and possible research questions and therefore the directions, goals, and insights provided by scientific enterprises. Further, an informational account of the brain re-orients us to ourselves, shaping how we understand humanity and each other.

The activities and directions engendered by information metaphors amplify the metaphorical claims of information and information science, which have been an explicit object of academic attention ever since Warren Weaver's pioneering commentary on Shannon's mathematical theory of communication set out an informational reading of human and social life (Shannon and Weaver, 1949; Day, 2008). Directing attention through informational metaphors is pervasive in everyday settings as well, where information flows, models of data processing, and computational command-and-control serve as cultural logics for understanding and narrating the world around us, whether psychological experience (how we "store" and "process" events), commercial activity ("viral" advertising draws more on the logic of computer viruses than it does on biological ones), or bedsprings ("sense-and-respond coils," in the parlance of one American television ad that occasionally graces our screens). As is often the case with such key metaphors, they begin to have material consequences as those elements of the world that do not easily fit into the metaphor (emotion, for instance) are either reframed or become invisible in public discourse (Hayles, 1999). "Information" becomes the universal solvent for both what the world is and how it can be framed.

The fifth construal of the materiality of information is a topic that we describe as the *materiality of information representation*. The central concern here is the representational consequences of the materiality of digital forms. Beyond metaphor, the particular forms that information takes—graphical and lexical expressions, columns of numbers, or records in a relational database—shape the questions that can be easily asked of it, the kinds of manipulations and analyses it supports, and how it can be used to understand the world (Goody, 1977). So, we are interested in examining the material forms in which digital data is represented and how these forms influence interpretations and lines of action—from the formal syntax of XML to the organizational schemes of relational databases and the abstractions of 1 and 0 over a substrate of continual voltage—and their consequences for particular kinds of representational practice. The ways in which information can be interpreted, negotiated, manipulated, and understood to represent then carry implications for organizational processes and social practice. Such materialities influence how data is taken up by different constituents, used to further social and political aims, and employed as an object in games of persuasion, negotiation, or identity making.

The fourth and fifth conceptualizations of the materiality of information—*consequential materiality of information metaphors*, and *materiality of information representation*—speak to the power of information in terms of digitized logics and digital objects. Metaphor and representation suggest potential lines of action, ways of engaging with the world, and techniques for understanding and approaching both the known and unknown in physical, social, and virtual environments. These information forms shape how we interpret and imagine our broader surroundings.

Each of these five accounts of information materiality—the materialities of information goods, of information infrastructures, of information production, of information metaphors, and of information representations—frames important considerations. The perspectives are united by the recognition that the ineffable "stuff" of digital abstractions is encountered only ever in material forms, and the nature of those forms has consequences for how information practice develops. Given the intense development of information models as a basic of contemporary life—in state bureaucracies, in organizations, in social life, and in cultural practice—these material considerations play potentially powerful roles in everyday experience.

What's more, it is clear that, although we can identify these strands (and possibly others) within a broad study of the materiality of information, they cannot be separated. They provide analytic distinctions, but the empirical phenomena are woven together. The robustness of representations to different forms of manipulation helps sustain the metaphors. The material conditions of information technology production incorporate and shape the networked infrastructures and spatial arrangements of digital urbanism. The prevalence of digital goods shapes the power and reach of metaphors. As a framework, then, this provides only a broad account of the different elements that might be at work in a materiality of information. And, while each construal would support detailed investigation, it is the fifth—the materiality of information representations—that we will particularly examine for the rest of this chapter.

## 5.4 Material consequences of representational practices

Our concern with the materiality and material properties of digital representations springs from similar considerations in the history of representational practice more broadly. This brief historical overview of the material consequences of representational practices provides an entry point into our discussion of digital representation in two ways. First, it provides a compelling account of how media shape perceptions of the world and possibilities for human engagement within it. And second, it suggests how the various material properties of media are directly implicated in human orientation and action.

Ong (1988), for example, examines the relationship between orality and literacy and argues that each represents not just different forms of expression but different worldviews. From the perspective of a literate culture, we might marvel at the acts of memory involved in being able to remember and recite long poems or stories accurately; however, accuracy in the sense of word-for-word reproduction is not a consideration in oral societies since there is no written record against which something can be compared. So, while the "same" words might be expressed vocally or in written format the expectations of what these words mean and the role they are expected to play in communication and coordination are quite different. We approach this phenomenon as a material consequence of representational practices.

The very idea of exact reproduction in this sense is itself an artifact or consequence of literacy. While not directly associated with digital forms of expression, spoken products are an information form with certain associated properties—high in sociality, flexibility, and relationality (one story or performance can weave into the next and integrate audiences into the narrative via the vagaries of thought and creativity) while low in mobility, persistence, and durability. With the emergence of writing and associated technologies of clay tablets, paper, ink, and the printing press, the effectiveness of a performance as a primary criterion is displaced by (or at least accompanied by) a focus on the accuracy of reproduction. Each technology modifies the possibilities for reproduction and creates the possibility for new relations and expectations to develop around the text. One could argue that the properties of text displace those of speech—persistence, durability, and mobility at the cost of intimacy, sociality, and transmutability. And with the emergence of properties such as persistence and durability come expectations of authenticity, accuracy, and legitimacy. Here the move from material to social consequences of representational practices becomes apparent.

Ingold (2007) takes this line of reason one step further, arguing that the experience of linguistic linearity is a consequence of written notations for language. The very notion of a stable and linear expression, that one thing comes before another and that processes have a beginning, middle and an end, is not inherent. Ingold suggests that our ingrained assumption that historical and natural processes are, in fact, stable and linear, emerges from the technologies of written language. When one word is placed before another in a congealed form (be it in on a clay tablet or paperback book), linearity appears fundamental. More broadly, our experience of these external representations for linguistic utterances shapes our idea of what language can be, and in particular, is critical to the sense that information is an object that can be separated from verbal performance. Mark Poster (1990) thus questions whether the move toward digitized language, with the possibility for hyper-link and cut-and-paste, fundamentally reshapes how we perceive ourselves and reality.

Goody (1977) takes a different tack in examining the power of the written word. Beyond looking simply at the properties of the written word Goody sets out the entwined history of Western knowledge practices and its *representational forms*, arguing that different representational forms provide unique structures for encountering, organizing, and knowing the world. Lists, hierarchies, and tables provide structures and techniques for presenting and manipulating information, and thus, understanding the world. As such, one can see how their development as representational strategies is harnessed to the development of the different modes of knowledge production associated with them—with classification and ordering, with generalization and grouping, and with relationality and comparison. Moving beyond the linearity of text, Goody argues that what can be set out on the page—with the representational capacities of different lexical devices—shapes what can be known. These lexical devices become information technologies with associated material properties. While lists suggest hierarchies, columns create paths for addition and subtraction; lines and arrows enable categories and groupings. Such devices provide written texts with logics of manipulability and pre-conceived relations.

Writing from a very different perspective, Green and Petre (1996) make some similar observations in the area of computer programming. Their studies of students learning to write software suggested that the types of problems that they encounter are coordinated with the lexical properties of the programming languages they are using. According to Green and Petre, programming languages, as textual objects, have "syntactic design features that help slips to occur." They show that different programming languages—not just conceptually, but lexically, as words on paper or letters on the screen—have different properties that make them subject to different kinds of problems. Green and Petre argue that it is necessary to unpack what they called the "cognitive dimensions" of programming languages as notations, including consistency, progressive evaluation (how easy it is to test a partial solution), and viscosity (a measure of how easily change can be introduced) in order to account for the material consequences of lexical properties in programming languages.

Ong and Goody, then, start to uncover the ways in which representational forms, with their associated material properties, and knowledge practices are coupled. Green and Petre provide a bridge to the domain of digital information by focusing on the notational aspects of computer systems. However, their analysis focuses largely on the aspects of notations that are immediately visible to people as an aspect of interaction with computers, not to the "internal" representations of information systems.

103

In a world of digitized information, with its associated properties of dynamic relationality, mutability, and transformation, it is necessary to take a critical look "below" various representations of information—whether it be image, table, paragraph, or line of code—and investigate the underlying logics, processes, and algorithmic actions associated

Manovich's (2002) analysis of new media provides a stronger connection to the broader world of digital representation. Manovich places new media arts in a broader historical context, arguing that the database is the major cultural form of the twenty-first century in much the same way as the novel was for the nineteenth and the film for the twentieth. In particular, he draws attention to the increasing primacy of relationality over narrative sequence. While retaining the visual and temporal aspects of film, the modality of hypertext or of computer games eschews its linear modality for the modality of the database, in which objects are linked together but their assembly into a narrative experience is in the hands of the audience. What Manovich's argument provides for us here is a connection between digital practice and the broader arguments raised by people like Goody in the context of historical knowledge production; that is, he begins to outline how the representational properties associated with digital media affect aspects of the interactional experience and, in turn, how we encounter the world through the computer. In particular, the centrality of non-linear relationality as the primary mode of database-driven interaction has broader implications for accounts of both the natural and the social world that are shaped by computer systems and ways in which information is received, organized, and interpreted via interaction with database schemes and logics. And, of course these new ways of seeing require new tools and techniques—such as analytics and network analysis—to uncover, and, dare we say, create the patterns that exist in large databases and the vast links of the web. Furthermore, as information is processed, represented, and visualized in new ways it becomes an object of political manipulation for various social and organizational factions striving to articulate certain realities and influence actions. Thus, when representational forms become mutable and manipulable in new ways the material consequences of such forms are similarly enhanced.

Curry (1998) provides many examples of this encounter with the world through the lens of the database in his account of the rise of geographical information systems. As a simple example, for instance, consider the development of geodemographic marketing. Based on the intuitive premise that "you are where you live," geodemographic marketing comprises, first, the development of a series of lifestyle profiles indexed by geographical region (in the United States, typically ZIP codes), and, second, targeted marketing based on particular localities and their specific properties. People working in the field readily acknowledge that these sorts of demographic profiles are, at best, rough and ready accounts, and that ZIP codes are scarcely the best tool for delineating regional clusters. However, when these sorts of profiles are used to target service provision, to support decisions about locating public services or commercial outlets, or to shape zoning decisions, then they become self-fulfilling prophecies. In this way, a variety of virtual boundaries that existed purely internally to the information system—both the geographical boundaries of ZIP codes and the social boundaries of market segments—are reinforced and undoubtedly take on a life of their own. It becomes apparent that the material consequences of the ZIP code are not inconsequential.

In his account of what he calls "virtualism," Miller (1998, 2005) has noted that representational models and reductive accounts of social life have a habit of migrating to centers of power where they can become tools of governance, reinforcing (and justifying) their own limits. His examples include the rules of neoclassical economics which, once they become the primary operative tools of organizations such as the World Bank and the International Monetary Fund, become prescriptive models of allowable economic process (see also Mackenzie, 2006); or the forms of audit rationality that begin as descriptive accounts but rapidly become tools to manage the provision of state services. Curry's examples, amongst others, highlight the role that information representations play within this pattern, since the models at work are ones that are often embedded in and shaped by computational tools and datasets. These models clearly do more than represent the world; the material properties of manipulation, representation, and dynamic modeling serve to "create" the world via the lines of action and ways of seeing engendered by databases, statistical analysis, and simulation. That which is assumed to be a practical and worthwhile data set is directly related to the techniques of collection, manipulation, and management of that data and the various "products" we can tease from it.

In computer science research, many people have recently become interested in what is termed "computational thinking" (Wing, 2006). As a broad manifesto, computational thinking argues that the basic elements of computational systems—structured data and algorithms—are now so central to everyday life that an understanding of their fundamentals is as important to contemporary education as an understanding of the fundamentals of mathematics, logic, and symbolic reason. The computational thinking agenda then is largely an educational one, but also one that places computer science and information science at the center of a range of scientific and policy agendas. The very argument harkens back to the work of Ong and Goody in the suggestion that new representational modes shift the nature of thought and accompanying ontological and epistemological orientations to our environment. Therefore, participation in everyday life requires formal education in these modes of thinking.

This view of computational thinking, though, is one that is largely dehistoricized and dematerialized. It is a vision that can be complicated by the idea that the computational thinking with which we are familiar is one particular computational thinking, one that has arisen in parallel with particular kinds of computer systems, particular kinds of software systems, and so particular kinds of representational and modeling practices. It is one amongst a possible range of computational thinkings. Elsewhere, we argue that it is important to recognize and to challenge the dominance of specific modes of knowledge practice embedded in computational thinking, while recognizing that there might be other ways of thinking computationally than those espoused by current computer science or information science research (Dourish, 2011). While the properties of digitized and databased information might lend themselves to certain ways of thinking, we want to resist assumptions of singularity. The metaphors and assumptions of the virtual that perspectives on the digital representations of information often inspire mask the material nature of such representations—material in terms of: the physicality of what underlies and creates the representation; the power of representations to engender new understandings of the world; and the role of representations in shaping organizational processes and human action. We hope that a focus on the material consequences of information representation can open up these lines of inquiry and suggest the multiple properties and consequences associated with the digitizing of representational forms.

In order to make these concerns more concrete, we turn now to two examples that illustrate the complexity of practical encounters with the materiality of information.

## 5.5 Examples: the materiality of digital representations

In this section, we call upon two examples from current research to demonstrate this approach to analyzing the intersection of the representations of digital information (and re-representations of data into the digital realm) and organizational practices. The first concerns the impact of digital photography on the organization of groups concerned with artistic practice;

the second focuses on the advent of digital simulation as the primary site of nuclear weapons testing.

These examples were chosen because each represents a different relationship between the process of representation (and associated practices) and the product that is represented. While a printed digital photograph might, in many cases, be indistinguishable from an image produced in a traditional darkroom, the underlying processes producing the representation are dramatically different. Nuclear simulation, however, is an inherently distinct lens on the action of exploding a bomb. Simulations might provide a deeper view into the micro-physics of an explosion, an analytical ability to simulate future reactions, or an enhanced vision on the explosion provided by three dimensional spaces; but they can never replicate driving into the desert to blow something up or, in our current geo-political climate, be validated against such explosions. As such, the digital representation, via simulation, cannot ever be confused for, or masked by, a prior representational technology.

These examples, therefore, provide insight into the material consequences of digital representation across the gamut of shifting representational technologies and suggest that the consequences of these shifts are significant across organizational forms, empirical sites, and technological upheavals.

## 5.5.1 Digital photography

Our first example focuses on the practices of voluntary organizations organized around artistic leisure pursuits, specifically camera clubs (Grinter, 2005). What becomes clear in this example is that photography denotes more than a representational form of an image on paper, and more than simply a technical process for capturing images; it denotes a system (or series of systems) of visual culture and practice. What makes a good photograph or a bad one, what distinguishes a casual snapshot from an artistic piece, the degrees of artifice and manipulation expected, and the contexts of production all reflect a series of cultural expectations about what the domain of "photography" comprises, that are grounded in, but not limited by, the material conditions of photographic production and reproduction. X-rays and satellite images are rarely thought of as examples of "photography," for example. While the emergence of cell phone cameras created the opportunities for new forms of casual and informal visual practice to emerge (only in the context of these devices did it come to make sense to regularly take and distribute photographs of food, of your new haircut, or of a pair of jeans you're trying on).

On the one hand, the physical processes and material properties of digital photography, in comparison to film photography, allow us to rethink what is "worthy" of photographic documentation—so, images are available immediately rather than after a delay for processing; images can be taken as experiments and easily deleted without wasting expensive film; images can be shared immediately, either around the camera or across networks; image libraries of tens or hundreds of thousands of photographs can be stored and accessed with relative ease. Yet, these images, and the technical and cultural practices they represent, need to be incorporated into an existing set of conventions, understandings, and procedures that surround "photography" as a practice.

The struggles that amateur photography clubs faced at the advent of consumer digital photography, as discussed by Grinter (2005), provide an interesting example of digital materiality and its entwinings with practice. At the time when Grinter's study was carried out, digital photography was becoming sufficiently popular within amateur enthusiast circles that the camera clubs needed to be able to respond to the way that the new technology questioned established community practices. These arose in particular over the way that competition categories had arisen around aspects of photographic practice, and the troublesome relationship between digital and print photography's materialities. We will focus in particular on two concerns.

The first concerns the process of photo print production. One of the categories for photographic competitions concerned maker-made prints. To be eligible for this category, photographic prints had to have been produced by the photographers themselves, rather than having been produced by commercial print processors. For the photographers, whose shared values express the strong belief that the artistry of photographic production happens at least as much in the darkroom as it does behind the viewfinder, the process of print production is critically important. However, the question of what it means to "make" a print—to have control over this process, and to possess the means to make it—is thrown into question by digital photography. Must one personally own the printer, for instance? If one makes a print on a printer at a commercial outlet, is that equivalent to personal production or to a commercial service? At which point in the process must the maker's hand be involved—pressing the print button itself? Where the production of film photography prints inherently involves an engagement with materials—development chemicals, fixer, papers, and so on—the same scope of artistic production disappears in the digital process, so that a distinction between self-made and commercially produced prints no longer makes sense. The categories by which images were judged, tied as they were to a particular material experience, had ceased to be effective as the materiality changed.

The second concern that the amateur photographers found themselves dealing with illustrates this even more starkly. Again, the artistry and creativity of darkroom practice is the practice on which things turn. This is a form of post-processing of images. Essentially, while the act of taking the photograph itself (exposing the film) constitutes a critical act in the production of an image, the actual image that results is not fixed at that moment; it is in the darkroom that specific images are produced. Manipulating the chemical process of developing an image provides many opportunities for creative engagement; cropping and photographic manipulation provides more; and some photographers might actually physically manipulate an emerging image to produce other artistic effects (e.g., through deliberate smearing or cutting.)

Digital photography is also, of course, subject to many forms of post-processing, but the material constitution of digital images allows for forms of manipulation quite different from those that film photography affords. Digital tools such as Adobe Photoshop can transform an image dramatically, introducing elements that were not present when the image was taken, or removing or reconfiguring elements that were. This presents a much more complicated set of considerations to amateur photographers. Competition categories can depend upon precise constraints. Amongst the groups that Grinter studied, for instance, "nature" shots are required to have no visual indication of human activity: no fence posts, no footpaths, and no mowed lawns, for example. However, the availability of digital manipulations of the radical sort allowed by Photoshop threatens the effectiveness of these categorical distinctions. At the same time, clearly post-processing cannot be outlawed; indeed, it is celebrated as part of the work of photography.

So the problem that the photographers found themselves grappling with was not simply that the digital material is different from the film material; it was, rather, that the nature of these different materialities potentially required a wholesale revision of the way that the practice of image-making was imagined as a community process. The stuff of images was not simply bound up with a process of image-making, although that is clearly the case; rather, the materiality was woven also into the way that the community conceived of itself, understood its own structure, celebrated and valued particular kinds of craft, interpreted images, and explored the creativity associated with the material constraints of its foundational technologies.

What is especially relevant to our argument here is that the representational forms associated with digital and film photography are not directly substitutable in terms of the sorts of practice that they enable. While a digital print may be nearly indistinguishable from a traditional film print, at least to the untrained eye, as records or outcomes of a history of practice they are quite different sorts of objects. Their material natures carry different potentialities and different constraints.

## 5.5.2 Nuclear weapons testing

Our second example also revolves around a radical change in material practice, in this case in the area of nuclear weapons testing (Gusterson, 1996, 2001, 2008). With the banning of nuclear testing emerged new forms of data about nuclear warheads and restrictions on how old data could be put into practice. As the Cold War waned and test bans became politically appealing, the government poured billions of dollars into advanced simulation technologies for the labs once built to blow things up. The purported goal of introducing such technologies was to keep the current arsenal intact (pinpointing degradation and selectively fixing warheads) while maintaining scientific innovation and excitement in a field whose vitality is considered crucial for national security.

However, within entrenched organizational logics and bureaucratic structures, Gusterson traces how this transition has been fraught with internal fissuring. The scientists themselves must figure out—as factions and as a discipline—how to make sense of the data emerging from simulation technologies purported to enable greater knowledge of nuclear warheads. The activities involved with determining and assessing understanding of the data, interpretation of what these data imply, and orientation toward future possibilities, require a faith in simulated modeling that goes against traditional logics associated with "blowing things up." Nuclear physicists were accustomed to testing assumptions in grand fashion and such practices were key to the body of shared knowledge and professional identity within the discipline. New knowledge (at both the individual and disciplinary levels) about how any model of warhead will work, and calculations about reliability and degradation, are the result of complex simulations. Yet, the implied power, danger, unpredictability, and fear of the weapon remain. The scientists themselves experience an inability to feel they can "know," in any definitive sense, what they are tasked with stewarding.

Without a direct mapping to empirical results that all can see and rally around, there is a greater ambiguity about what the simulations mean and how such meaning is calculated. In other words, simulations can be evocative, informative, and even valid without being validated against the physical reality they purport to represent. As the simulation regime continues, the disjuncture between physical weapons and their simulations grow and the simulation itself becomes the site of material engagement. This relationship has two implications.

First, simulations of nuclear warheads become simulacra in Baudrillard's (1994) sense—simulations of objects (in this case, explosions) that never themselves existed. The materiality of the simulation displaces that of the weapon. One consequence of this displacement is the fact that the development of weapons testing regimes, and hence weapons design, now becomes harnessed to a radically different technology, that of the digital simulation, both in the form of the computer systems (memory, processing capacity, etc.) and in the form of the mathematical models that these simulations implement.

In this scenario, what extends our reach as scientists is no longer breakthroughs in the design or direct testing of weapons but rather than capacity of technologies of representation. New forms of supercomputer, new technological capacities, and new system architectures do not simply make the process of simulation faster; they open up new avenues of investigation by bringing new capabilities within the realm of the thinkable and the doable, much as Fujimura (1987) has noted in her work on cancer research. The technologies of "simulation," then, become the technologies of possibility for the physical processes that they are meant to simulate, and the architectures and capacities of those technologies shape the design and research processes themselves. Edwards (2011) has noted this relationship at work in climate modeling, which rivals nuclear testing as the primary consumer of advanced supercomputer technologies; indeed, the very kinds of climate data that we collect are shaped, in part, by what our computer models can process.

Recognizing the inherent tie between representation of information and possibility for action, Gusterson outlines various "plateaus of calculation" that are accompanied by alternating narratives of the future and parties invested in bringing it to the fore as a key determinant in future lines of activity. Each of these lines of thought, relevant players, implied variables of importance, and anticipatory futures, is being established and asserted in the inescapable context of purely simulated data. Positions are taken, rallied around, and negotiated in terms of how one interprets the role and possibilities of that data. The data themselves are understood in dramatically

111

different terms as a discipline formed around nuclear testing is now forced to make sense of itself solely within the purview of the hyper-real.

In other words, this world of simulation without empiricism, that emerged from a logic of testing and visceral experiential knowledge, is stymied by competing claims as to the appropriate role of simulation-based knowledge in stewarding current warheads and building new ones. The status and meaning of information is up for grabs even among the small group of expert scientists who control and create it. This situation goes far beyond a view of science as "socially constructed" as even those invested in proving their findings cannot find grounding or shared logics to establish the meaning and validity of this new form of data. The material implications of these uncertainties manifest in an inability to agree on appropriate lines of action, future projections, or shared certainties.

Some scientists in the testing laboratories assert that simulating data is a frightening, if not disastrous, method for creating future designs (even those modified from older "pedigreed" designs). These individuals argue that without the experiential feel for how explosions happen, and the tacit knowledge of doing—that is quickly retiring out of the testing facilities— the inability to prove oneself wrong is arrogant and potentially dangerous. Others feel that movement toward simulation in nuclear design is both inevitable and beneficial, arguing that through deeper insight into how nuclear fusion works we can build more reliable and tailored warheads in a constrained political and empirical environment. Are simulated nuclear data the "grand challenge" or road to disaster? According to Gusterson, the hyperconstructed form of the data makes it difficult for these debates to settle, for dominate logics to take hold, even within the immediate scientific community of those responsible for shepherding our nuclear arsenal no less within the broader geo-political ecology of power.

What is of particular importance here is the role of digital simulation as an entity in its own right. The information *as* represented—represented as misaligned objects, implied insights, and orienting maps—becomes material in substantive and unexpected ways. The limitations of testing regimes are the limitations of technological simulation. Information technology plays more than an enabling role here, then. As simulation technologies and the platforms on which they run evolve, new forms of weapons and new ideas about weapons become possible, because the weapons and their capabilities as we know them are fundamentally entwined with the material limitations of simulation technology. The map becomes the territory.

This leads to the second implication of the relationship between the simulation and the underlying physical process it is tasked with representing. Simulation technologies were initially developed in conversation with the explosions themselves. Physical bombs were designed in tandem with the digital representation and the two were in conversation. But, the U.S. arsenal is currently facing another, equally important, physical process without this dialogue between the representation and the represented. Bombs designed for 15-year life spans are now approaching 30 years and our ability to simulate degradation is stymied by a lack of physical validation. Recent work by Bailey et al. (forthcoming) argues that the potentially dangerous ramifications of simulation without validation can be seen in the automobile industry. This lack of conversation between the physical processes and simulated representations compounds the uncertainty that plagues the institutional system of nuclear scientists.

In contrast to the example of digital photography, nuclear simulation introduces a new set of institutional, scientific, and technological materialities and practices that shatter the idea that digital representations might present the "same" product in different ways. And in this case, questions remain about whether or not the practices associated with simulation can represent the degradation of current bombs or designs of new ones. Unlike the social and cultural processes that go into producing images in a new way, we may no longer be able to produce a nuclear explosion as intended (or successfully shepherd the degradation of our current arsenal). Such disintermediation is not caused by a digital technology, but rather, shifts in the technologies of representation enabled the current material infrastructure (geo-political and technological) that now defines nuclear testing and shepherding.

## 5.6 Conclusion

Much of the rhetoric that surrounds information technologies and new media focuses on the apparently immaterial nature of digital representations (Poster, 2006). Indeed, as Hayles (1999) has noted, this separation is the foundational myth of contemporary information science. Digital information, though, is encountered only ever in material forms. Just as social scientists have increasingly recognized the significance of materiality in social and cultural practice, so too has recent attention turned to the materialities at work in information practice (e.g., Kirschenbaum, 2008; Montford and Bogost, 2009; Blanchette, 2011).

We feel that by establishing an initial typology, or language, for articulating the ways in which scholars have approached the various materialities associated with information and information goods this chapter sets the stage for cross-disciplinary dialogue. In presenting an initial framework that delineates the *material culture of information goods*, the *transformative materiality of digital networks*, the *material conditions of information technology production*, the *consequential materiality of information metaphors*, and the *materiality of information representation* we begin to outline the various materialities of information and information goods in a manner that captures both the variety of "materialities" at play as well as the ways in which "information" is tied to physical materials, digital technologies, social processes, computational logics, and organizational capabilities.

Our current work represents a contribution to this discussion with a particular focus on the materialities of information representations and their consequences. In particular, we would like to place contemporary digital practice within a historical pattern of entwined development of representational forms and knowledge practice, and so to examine the representational contexts and consequences of digital information systems. This focus calls attention the ways in which representations of information occasion possibilities for action and logics of organizing in, at least, two ways. First, information represented in different ways has material implications for how that information is used in practice, the ways in which it is "read," and the lines of action that stem from it. As such, information representations are constitutive of organizational forms and the logics that are used to motivate organizational processes (as can be seen in the case of nuclear scientists). Second, evolving technologies of representation trigger, and often necessitate, evolving organizational processes and associated ways of doing, ways of judging, and ways of understanding the various products of representations (as can be seen in the case of amateur photography clubs).

We have used the brief examples of digital photography and nuclear weapons testing to ground our discussion. These examples are evocative demonstrations of the complex interplay between organizational and social processes and the materiality of representational forms enabled by information technologies. In these vignettes, representational forms of data and response characteristics of social systems co-mingle. Together, they shape organizational practices and concomitant logics of legitimacy. We find it evocative to place digital photography alongside nuclear testing as these two narratives suggest how shifts in digital representation of information can inspire fear, aggression, and insecurity in dramatically different scenarios. Hobbyists, who enjoy photography as an outlet for artistic expression, individual identity, and social interaction were threatened, upset, and unnerved by digital photography in a manner that parallels that of scientists tasked with some of the most politically sensitive and hazardous questions of our age.

In recent years, organizational, anthropological, and digital media scholars have begun to explore, tease apart, and engage in relatively isolated discussions about the materialist foundations of digital practice (Manovich, 2002; Horst and Miller, 2006; Orlikowski, 2007; Leonardi and Barley, 2008, 2010; Orlikowski and Scott, 2008; Montford and Bogost, 2009; Blanchette, 2011). As we have noted, different forms of materiality are on display here. Our focus on material representation of digital goods highlights an underexplored facet of analysis in sociomaterial studies. Focusing on the interrelationships between digital forms, epistemology, and social process provides a nuanced and productive lens for exploring the ways in which people appropriate digital forms and digital forms shape social environments.

Materialist considerations have arisen too in new emerging fields, of which the most relevant to our exploration is "Software Studies" (Fuller, 2008). Borrowing approaches and techniques from other areas of media studies in the attempt to understand the specific conditions of new media production and use, software studies has begun to theorize the importance of digital forms in shaping thought and practice. Just as we hope to contribute to the organizational inquiry into sociomateriality by providing a more concrete elaboration of the embedding of digital materiality within a practice framework, we hope to further build on the perspective developed in software studies by emphasizing how studies of the materiality of information and information technologies need to push beyond digital as metaphor and relational logic and be strongly engaged with the specifics about the different properties, representations, and materialities of digitized information itself. That is, given that our interest in materiality is in material properties and their consequences, it is important that digital technologies are not understood merely metaphorically or analogously with media, but that their specific materialities—and the entangling of those materialities with particular forms of technological practice—must be at the center of any investigation. At the same time, in contrast to the technologically grounded approach proposed by Montford and Bogost (2009), we argue for an examination of the power and consequences of the abstractions of software systems as tools for imagining, and operating upon, the social world.

In sum, this chapter offers three contributions to the broad and burgeoning research stream on the materiality of information. First, by delineating how different strands of digital materiality can be understood and analyzed, this chapter aims to provide a foundation for developing shared understanding about how we, as an academic community, can productively engage material studies in the realm of information technologies, technological infrastructure, and information metaphors. Second, by tracing the history of the material consequences of representational practices we high-light the fundamentally human experience of information and information processing in how the limited capacity of the brain understands and orients to the world. Third, by exploring two case studies of how shifts in represen-tations of information into a digital realm affect social dynamics and discur-sive logics we hope to set the stage for future organizational research that takes data representation seriously as an object of analysis.

## Note

We owe considerable intellectual debts to many people whose provocations and inspirations shaped our thinking on these topics, including Geof Bowker, Wanda Orlikowski, Simon Penny, and Brian Cantwell Smith. We are grateful to our editor Paul Carlile and anonymous reviewers for their insightful contributions to this work. We would also like the thank Ken Cameron, Marisa Cohn, Ellie Harmon, and Silvia Lindtner for early feedback on these ideas. Finally, we would like to acknowledge the helpful conversation about this work that occurred at the Third International Sym-posium on Process Organization Studies. Our work has been supported in part by the National Science Foundation through awards 1025761 and 0968608.

## References

Althusser, L. (2001). "Ideology and Ideological State Apparatuses," in *Lenin and Philosophy and Other Essays*. New York: Monthly Review Press, pp. 121–76.

Ashcraft, K., Kuhn, T., and Cooren, F. (2009). "Constitutional Amendments: 'Material-izing' Organizational Communication," *Academy of Management Annals*, 3/1: 1–64.

Bailey, D., Leonardi, P., and Barley, S. (forthcoming). "The Lure of the Virtual," *Organization Science*.

Barad, K. (2003). "Posthumanist Performativity: Toward an Understanding of How Matter Comes to Matter," *Signs*, 28/3: 801–31.

Baudrillard, J. (1994 [1981]). *Simulacra and Simulation*. Ann Arbor: University of Michigan Press.

Blanchette, J.-F. (2011). "A Material History of Bits," *Journal of the American Society for Information Science and Technology*, 62/6: 1024–57.

Bull, M. (2000). *Sounding Out the City*. Oxford: Berg.

Castells, M. (1996). *The Rise of the Network Society*. Oxford: Blackwell.

Cieraad, I. (ed.) (1999). *At Home: An Anthropology of Domestic Space*. Syracuse, NY: Syracuse University Press.

Curry, M. (1998). *Digital Places: Living with Geographical Information Systems*. London: Routledge.

Day, R. (2008). *The Modern Invention of Information: Discourse, History, Power*. Carbondale: Southern Illinois University Press.

Dourish, P. (2011). "The View from Arnhem Land in Australia's Remote North: 'Computational Thinking' and the Postcolonial in the Teaching from Country Program," *Learning Communities: The International Journal of Learning in Social Contexts*, 2: 91–101.

Edwards, P. (2011). *A Vast Machine: Computer Models, Climate Data, and the Politics of Global Warming*. Cambridge, MA: MIT Press.

Fujimura, J. (1987). "Constructing 'Do-Able' Problems in Cancer Research: Articulating Alignment," *Social Studies of Science*, 17/2: 257–93.

Fuller, M. (2008). *Software Studies: A Lexicon*. Cambridge, MA: MIT Press.

Goody, J. (1977). *The Domestication of the Savage Mind*. Cambridge: Cambridge University Press.

Graham, S. and Marvin, S. (2001). *Splintering Urbanism: Networked Infrastructures, Technological Mobilities, and the Urban Condition*. London: Routledge.

Green, T. and Petre, M. (1996). "Usability Analysis of Visual Programming Environments: A 'Cognitive Dimensions' Framework," *Journal of Visual Languages and Computing*, 7: 131–74.

Grinter, R. (2005). "Words About Images: Coordinating Community in Amateur Photography," *Computer-Supported Cooperative Work*, 14: 161–88.

Gusterson, H. (1996). *Nuclear Rites: A Weapons Laboratory at the End of the Cold War*. Berkeley, CA: University of California Press.

—— (2001). "The Virtual Nuclear Weapons Laboratory in the New World Order," *American Ethnologist*, 28/2: 417–37.

—— (2008). "Nuclear Futures: Anticipating Knowledge, Expert Judgment and the Lack That Cannot Be Filled," *Science and Public Policy*, 35/8: 551–60.

Harvey, D. (2006). *Spaces of Global Capitalism: A Theory of Uneven Geographical Development*. London and New York: Verso.

Hayles, K. (1999). *How We Became Posthuman: Virtual Bodies in Cybernetics, Literature, and Informatics*. Chicago: University of Chicago Press.

Horst, H. and Miller, D. (2006). *The Cell Phone: An Anthropology of Communication*. Oxford: Berg.

Ingold, T. (2007). *Lines: A Brief History*. London: Routledge.

Kirschenbaum, M. (2008). *Mechanisms: New Media and the Forensic Imagination*. Cambridge, MA: MIT Press.

Kitchen, R. and Dodge, M. (2011). *Code/Space: Software and Everyday Life*. Cambridge, MA: MIT Press.

Leonardi, P. and Barley, S. (2008). "Materiality and Change: Challenges to Building Better Theory about Technology and Organizing," *Information and Organization*, 18: 159–76.

—— (2010). "What's Under Construction Here? Social Action, Materiality, and Power in Constructivist Studies of Technology and Organizing," *Academy of Management Annals*, 4/1: 1–51.

117

Mackenzie, A. (2005). "Untangling the Unwired: Wi-Fi and the Cultural Inversion of Infrastructure," *Space and Culture: International Journal of Social Spaces*, 8/3: 269–85.

—— (2006). *An Engine Not a Camera: How Financial Models Shape Markets*. Cambridge, MA: MIT Press.

—— (2009). *Material Markets: How Economic Agents Are Constructed*. Oxford: Oxford University Press.

Manovich, L. (2002). *The Language of New Media*. Cambridge, MA: MIT Press.

Miller, D. (1998). "A Theory of Virtualism," in J. Carrier and D. Miller (eds.), *Virtualism: A New Political Economy*. Oxford: Berg, pp. 187–215.

—— (ed.) (2001). *Car Cultures*. Oxford: Berg.

—— (ed.) (2005). *Materiality*. Durham, NC: Duke University Press.

Montford, N. and Bogost, I. (2009). *Racing the Beam: The Atari Video Computer System*. Cambridge, MA: MIT Press.

Negroponte, N. (1995). *Being Digital*. New York: Knopf.

Olson, G., Zimmerman, A., Bos, N., and Wulf, W. (eds.) (2008). *Scientific Collaboration on the Internet*. Cambridge, MA: MIT Press.

Ong, W. (1988). *Orality and Literacy: The Technologizing of the Word*. London: Routledge.

Orlikowski, W. (2007). "Sociomaterial Practices: Exploring Technology at Work," *Organization Studies*, 28: 1435–48.

—— and Scott, S. (2008). "Sociomateriality: Challenging the Separation of Technology, Work and Organization," *Academy of Management Annals*, 2/1: 433–74.

Pellow, D. and Park, L. (2002). *The Silicon Valley of Dreams: Environmental Injustice, Immigrant Workers, and the High-Tech Global Economy*. New York: New York University Press.

Poster, M. (1990). *The Mode of Information: Poststructuralism and Social Context*. Chicago: University of Chicago Press.

—— (2006). *Information Please: Culture and Politics in the Age of Digital Machines*. Durham, NC: Duke University Press.

Shannon, C. and Weaver, W. (1949). *The Mathematical Theory of Communication*. Urbana: University of Illinois Press.

Suchman, L. (2007). *Human–Machine Reconfigurations: Plans and Situated Actions*, 2nd edn. New York: Cambridge University Press.

von Hippel, E. and von Krogh, G. (2003). "Open Source Software and the 'Private-Collective' Innovation Model: Issues for Organizational Science," *Organization Science*, 14/2: 209–23.

Webster, F. (2006). *Theories of the Information Society*, 3rd edn. London: Routledge.

Wing, J. (2006). "Computational Thinking," *Communications of the ACM*, 49/3: 33–5.

Yates, J. (1993). *Control through Communication: The Rise of System in American Management*. Baltimore, MD: Johns Hopkins University Press.

Yockey, H. (1992). *Information Theory and Molecular Biology*. Cambridge: Cambridge University Press.

# 6

# Knowledge Eclipse: Producing Sociomaterial Reconfigurations in the Hospitality Sector

*Wanda J. Orlikowski and Susan V. Scott*

**Abstract:** Drawing on a field study of the travel site TripAdvisor, the authors explore how online reviewing, rating, and ranking mechanisms are overshadowing traditional configurations of knowledge in the hospitality sector by redistributing resources, shifting practices and habitats, and redefining what counts, who counts, and how. The authors suggest that such sociomaterial reconfigurations offer important insights into the broader issues associated with the role of social media in knowledge practices, and the ways in which expert valuation schemes are being eclipsed by ones grounded in user-generated content. They maintain that these different valuation schemes entail different kinds of work, producing different valuations of the real, and enacting different (singular and multiple) realities. As such, these reconfigurations of valuation raise not just important epistemological issues but also critical questions of ontology and accountability.

Contemporary knowledge practices are currently undergoing a significant shift as the rise of social media and online user-generated content is spreading into ever more domains of everyday life. Most of us already routinely consult Wikipedia as a valued source of knowledge. Others turn to online forums or Twitter to obtain advice on technical difficulties. And product and service recommendations are now commonly sought on websites such as Amazon, Yelp, Netflix, Angie's List, and TripAdvisor. Such sources of knowledge and advice—dependent as they are on the spontaneous contributions of large numbers of often-anonymous people distributed around the world—

raise questions about both the value of such knowledge, and its manner of valuation. We explore these questions in this chapter, focusing in particular on the hospitality sector and the recent rise in importance of user-generated knowledge about hotels through the TripAdvisor social media website. We argue that the reconfigurations of valuation exemplified by the case of TripAdvisor offer important insights into the broader issues associated with the role of social media in knowledge practices and the eclipsing of expert valuation schemes by ones grounded in user-generated content.

There has been a growing interest in the concept of value and in the processes of valuation (see Espeland and Stevens, 1998; Callon and Muniesa, 2005; Stark, 2009; Karpik, 2010; Hsu et al., 2012) and the role these play in structuring markets. This research has examined the influence of critics, standards, ratings, rankings, and judgment devices in guiding consumers' choices and actions and shaping producers' strategies, work practices, and pricing decisions. The rise of the internet and the recently burgeoning arena of social media have amplified the scale, scope, and reach of online valuation schemes. While the novelty and effect of such web-based amplification has been recognized—often referred to as "the wisdom of the crowds"—there are few detailed studies of the practices and technologies that are intricately involved in producing online valuation and their consequences for knowledge and outcomes (for a few exceptions, see David and Pinch, 2008; Jeacle and Carter, 2011).

Our research interest is in understanding the reviewing, rating, and ranking mechanisms of one such online valuation scheme—TripAdvisor—and how these are overshadowing traditional configurations of knowledge in the hospitality sector. We focus specifically here on how the practices, technologies, and outcomes of online forms of hotel valuation differ from more traditional forms of valuation, how these are reconfiguring the hospitality sector, and with what consequences.

## 6.1 Literature on valuation

Valuation is critically entangled with practices of consumption and production, and as such is central to social reproduction and transformation (Willmott, 2010). Much has been written about the role of various mechanisms of valuation—prices, standards, benchmarks, brands, reviews—that allow products and services to be identified, assessed, and exchanged (Espeland and Stevens, 1998; Callon and Muniesa, 2005; Stark, 2009; Karpik, 2010; Willmott, 2010; Hsu et al., 2012). These mechanisms are particularly significant in the case of goods and services that have uncertain market value and where multiple criteria and assessments of value are present. Karpik (2010) argues that because such goods and services cannot be easily evaluated through strictly calculative mechanisms, "judgment devices" are needed to guide people to make purchasing decisions under conditions of market uncertainty. Such devices are produced by multiple different actors such as producers, sellers, advertisers, media, and authorities and include brands, rankings (expert and popular), networks (personal and impersonal), and critics.

The role and influence of critics is central to Hsu et al.'s (2012) examination of the market for wines, a class of product for which "one cannot know the quality of a good until it has been purchased and consumed," and thus where "consumers must rely on critics' published reviews as proxies for hidden product quality" (Hsu et al., 2012: 83). Critics' ratings also influence producers, "who must adjust resource allocations, divest business units, and adopt specific missions in order to conform to the standards espoused by these mediators, precisely because of their subsequent influence over consumers." Focusing on pricing, their analysis suggests that the clearer the valuation scheme that is employed by critics, the stronger the relationship between producers' prices and the quality ratings assigned by the critics. In shaping knowledge about quality, and thus the prices that are set and realized in practice, critics configure both producers and consumers and their practices of production and consumption.

In a series of studies examining the role and influence of ranking mechanisms on practices of production and consumption, Espeland and her colleagues (Espeland and Stevens, 1998; Espeland and Sauder, 2007; Sauder and Espeland, 2009) have shown how law school rankings produced by the *U.S. News & World Report* have shaped those schools over time. Drawing on detailed fieldwork, they find that the rankings normalize and structure the law schools as particular, standardized entities making them amenable over time to certain forms of manipulations and interventions. As Sauder and Espeland write:

> By imposing a shared metric on law schools, rankings unite and objectify organizations, reinforcing their coherence as similar objects . . . . Rankings have become naturalized and internalized as a standard of comparison and success. In changing how law schools think about themselves and pressuring schools toward self-discipline, rankings are now deeply embedded within schools, directing attention, resources, and interventions. (Sauder and Espeland, 2009: 80)

Jeacle and Carter (2011) also examine ranking mechanisms, in their case the online hotel reviewing website, TripAdvisor. Drawing on Giddens'

(1991) notion of abstract systems, they argue that TripAdvisor may be understood as an "expert system" which entails "inter alia the calculation of phenomena, the labelling of entities, the process of commensuration, and the ranking and ordering of entities" (Jeacle and Carter, 2011: 4). They see TripAdvisor as a "calculative regime," exerting significant influence within the social structure of the travel industry (2011: 11). They argue that its power is located within the calculative practices constituting the Popularity Index algorithm, a ranking mechanism that orders hotels within a particular region. They note that this algorithm

> provides the independent traveller with a clear and objective form of quantification from which to make hotel discriminations, and as such is invested with the objectivity and impartiality that are oft attributed to numbers.... [A] single number instantly labels the perceived quality of an establishment and that number is invested with credibility all the more so because it was constructed from the experiences and seemingly honest opinions of fellow travellers. Moreover, the Popularity Index places hotels in hierarchical relationships to one another—highlighting which hotels are 'better' or 'worse'. As an expert system, the rankings convert the numerous individual ramblings on the site into hard and objective fact. (Jeacle and Carter, 2011: 9)

The importance of rating and ranking mechanisms, algorithms, and materiality more generally, in shaping valuation schemes and outcomes is strongly evident in Callon and Muniesa's (2005) work on the calculative character of markets. They argue that valuation is a three-step process that is "distributed among human actors and material devices" (2005: 1245). They suggest that it proceeds as follows: first, the entities to be assessed have to be "detached"—moved, arranged, and ordered in a single "calculative space"; second, the entities have to be "taken into account," associated and subjected to certain manipulations; and third, a new entity—the "result"—has be produced that corresponds to the manipulations performed in the calculative space and is able to circulate widely "without taking with it the whole calculative apparatus" (2005: 1231). For Callon and Muniesa (2005: 1232), such valuation "establishes a continuum between qualitative judgment and quantitative (or numeric) calculation," a process they refer to as "qualculation." The definition of qualculation is aimed at "collaps[ing] the distinction between the quantitative and the qualitative," and indicating its inescapable materiality. Thus, qualculation is "impossible without material arrangements: paper and pencil; the benches in a court of law; a system for tallying arrivals and departures; a supermarket" (Callon and Law, 2005: 719).

Authors such as Haraway (1988), Suchman (2002a, 2002b, 2007), and Barad (2003, 2007) remind us that integral to the materiality of valuation schemes foregrounded by Callon and Muniesa (2005) is the notion of location. This is a sense of positioning that is not confined to time and space but embraces the idea of accountability, specifically located accountabilities (Suchman, 2002a). The detachment upon which calculative apparatus depend can have the effect of de-realization, of producing valuations that are dissociated and disconnected from located practices and responsibilities. Whether they involve a laboratory, theory, technology, or metric, established valuation schemes provide distance from practicalities, but not lasting or universal absolution. In order to identify what constitutes value and for whom, we need to first acknowledge that we are analyzing a series of "partial, locatable, critical knowledges" (Haraway, 1988: 584). If knowledge is located and partial, then by implication there is no unmediated source of knowledge and no neutral process of knowledge production (Law and Urry, 2004).

Treating all knowledge as located and partial enables us to make two analytical moves. First, when framing valuation schemes from this perspective we readily identify and are receptive to the coexistence of multiple forms of knowledge. Second, we are sensitized to the particular agential cuts made by the qualculative apparatus in place (Barad, 2007); in other words, when organizing what counts as value we ask what gets included and what gets excluded from the process of knowledge production. This process of analysis draws attention to the differences that the agential cuts (inclusion/ exclusion) enacted by particular valuation schemes make in practice. The agential cuts produced by the process of qualculation are performative, as Moser and Law (2006: 67) note:

> Something is being made that was not there before. To put it differently, what counts as information is (and necessarily) being bounded in a new way. And it [is] this bounding, this simplification, this practical setting of limits, that renders qualculation possible. The decisions of qualculation determine what will perform as information and what will not. And this limit-setting is indeed practical: how the limits are done depends on the task at hand. What is included and excluded, likewise. That is what the bounding is about.

We turn now to a brief consideration of shifting historical conventions and practices in genres of valuation within the hospitality sector. We then compare two different forms of valuation currently operating within this sector—the standardized, institutionalized and expert-based valuation scheme produced by hotel grading agencies such as the Automobile Association, and the emergent, online, and user-based valuation scheme produced by social media review websites such as TripAdvisor.

## 6.2 Genres of valuation within the hospitality sector

In examining the shifting role and nature of knowledge about hotels, we need to consider these within a historical context, and so we briefly trace the development of travel writing genres across a range of forms, norms, times, and places. This review indicates that travel writing has undergone a series of shifts in practices, technologies, and conventions of valuation over time, generating significant changes in the kind of travel knowledge produced, by whom, with what purpose, and with what outcomes. These changes entail different forms of valuation that have been used, and continue to be used, to assess and legitimate knowledge about hospitality in practice.

Writing about and for travel has been traced back to the *peripli*,[1] ancient documents used by Phoenician, Greek, and Roman navigators that listed the ports, landmarks, and distances that vessels could expect to find along a coastline. Versions of these for journeys on land—such as the Roman *itineraria*—provided road maps with distances that identified the cities, villages, and landmarks that would be encountered on route. More elaborate documents were also evident, as in Pausanias' *Description of Greece*, written in the second century, which offered first-hand descriptions of the art, sculpture, and architecture of ancient Greece. In later centuries, guides were used to help pilgrims on their religious journeys. One well-known example in this genre was the series of letters written in the fourth century by a Gallic woman, Egeria. Known as the *Travels of Egeria,* it recounts her pilgrimage to the Holy Land during the years 381–384, and offers detailed descriptions not just of her route but also of the holy sites, monuments, hospitality, and liturgical customs she experienced during her journey.

The pocket travel guide, more familiar to contemporary travelers, emerged in the nineteenth century. Early examples of this genre included Samuel Latham Mitchill's 1807 guide to New York City, *The Picture of New York*,[2] Gideon Minor Davison's guidebook to Saratoga Springs, Niagara, Quebec, and Boston published in 1822 as *The Fashionable Tour*, and Mariana Starke's advice to Britons traveling to France and Italy, published in 1824 with the title *Information and Directions for Travellers on the Continent*. Starke's books, in particular, served as an early model for the modern guidebook, including practical information about passports, luggage, and the cost of food and accommodation in each city.[3] She even devised an early rating system, using exclamation marks to indicate the value of particular sights. As she notes in the introduction of her book (Starke, 1826: v), "In the following pages, the Reader will find that several of these works of Art are distinguished, according to their reputed merit, by one or more exclamation-points."

Many other travel guides followed, drawing on the journals and travelogues of adventurers such as Juliette Star Dana, Isabella Bird, and John Lloyd Stephens, and offering specific details about first-hand observations and individual experiences. The genre of travel writing was further developed by publishers such as Ward & Lock in London, John Murray III in Scotland, and Karl Baedeker in Germany, who strove to distinguish subjective accounts of individuals' travel from objective and factual guides to travel destinations. Their efforts served to produce two genres of travel writing— the personal travelogue and the impersonal travel guide. As more and more people began traveling abroad in the nineteenth and twentieth centuries, the latter guides grew in popularity, becoming widely recognized as arbiters of aesthetic and cultural judgment and indispensable to travelers venturing overseas. Gretton (1993) writing about the Murray Handbooks for Travellers quotes from an 1850 *London Times* review of the red-covered Handbooks:

> Mr. Murray has succeeded in identifying his countrymen all the world over. Into every nook which an Englishman can penetrate he carries his Red Handbook. He trusts to his Murray as he would trust to his razor, because it is thoroughly English and reliable; and for his history, hotels, exchanges, scenery, for the clue to his route and his comfort by the way, the Red Handbook is his "guide, philosopher, and friend".

In a similar vein, novelist E. M. Forster has his heroine in *A Room with a View* travel from England to Florence in 1908, taking along with her a Baedeker Guidebook to Italy so that she would know "what was beautiful, and what should be ignored" (Sattin, 2008). While Murray and Baedeker guides were primarily used to aid tourists abroad, they could also be used for more nefarious purposes, as Tisdall (2007) observes:

> On a more sinister note, in 1942 Exeter, Bath, Norwich, York and Canterbury were all blitzed in what have become known as the "Baedeker Raids"—a reference to the words of the Nazi firebrand Baron Gustav von Sturm, who reputedly declared "We shall go all out to bomb every building in Britain marked with three stars in the Baedeker guide."

Travel guides in the twentieth century expanded and grew to cover hundreds of different locations around the world. Well-known brands such as Fodor's, Frommer's, Rough Guides, Lonely Planet, and Let's Go emerged and thrived. These organizations each have a distinctive and institutionalized "house style," which directs the data gathering and writing activities of

125

the multiple individuals employed to produce and publish travel guides about particular destinations. While the format of the guides and the number of contributors have changed over time, the purpose of the guides remains markedly similar to those characterizing those of Starke and Baedeker—to provide advice and recommendations to travelers visiting unfamiliar places. As such, the knowledge in these guidebooks focuses on highlighting the specific landmarks and accommodations that are deemed worthy of endorsement and likely to produce positive experiences for the readers/travelers.

Emerging alongside these branded travel guides are guides that specialize in professional assessments and accreditations of different types of accommodation, produced by organizations such as Michelin, the RAC (Royal Automobile Club), and the AA (Automobile Association). These organizations employ full-time, trained inspectors who rate hotels according to various specifications and assign stars or letter grades to signify the quality and value of accommodation to be had in those hotels. The evaluation of hotels is based on extensive criteria that have been standardized in the hospitality industry over years and which involve routine and incognito inspections of hotels. These professionalized assessments are seen to offer the very best in objectified knowledge for prospective travelers, as noted in the descriptions of two such schemes—the AA[4] and Michelin[5] respectively:

> Hotels or guest accommodation assessed by the AA are rated under a set of common quality standards agreed by the AA and the UK tourist authorities (VisitBritain, VisitScotland and VisitWales)...The common standards make types of accommodation easy to understand and give you confidence that establishments meet the standards you require.

> A team of full-time professional restaurant and hotel inspectors anonymously evaluate establishments according to a rigorous set of criteria. Only the best restaurants and hotels are included in the guide, where every establishment is a trusted Michelin recommendation.

The most recent genre of travel writing is emerging within social media reviews—descriptions of and opinions about hotels and locales posted online by anonymous users of such websites as TripAdvisor, Yahoo!Travel, Expedia, Hotels.com, etc. Most of the content included in social media websites for the hospitality sector is provided by users of the website. Such content is growing in both size and influence. Studies suggest that social media reviews are having a substantial impact on the decision-making behavior of travelers planning and booking accommodation (Starkov and Price, 2007; Vermeulen and Seegers, 2009; Xiang and Gretzel, 2010). Almost half of all consumers making travel purchases base their decisions on online content, using it to get ideas, narrow choices, and confirm their selections (Gretzel and Yoo, 2008). Most of these consumers report that user-generated content is more relevant, reliable, and enjoyable than the information provided by traditional travel service providers such as travel agents and guidebooks (Gretzel and Yoo, 2008). As a result, the once thriving market for printed travel guides is in retreat. Sales of travel guides globally have declined 10 percent every year since 2008 (Mesquita, 2011).

In this most recent genre of social media reviews, we see a return in content if not form to the individual recounting his or her first-hand travel experiences and observations. The content is personalized, subjective, and experiential—akin to the travelogues produced by early writers, which had been eclipsed by the standardized, institutionalized genres of modern travel guides. Unlike earlier genres, however, user-generated, online reviews include content that is both positive and negative (no longer just focusing on highlights and positive recommendations), and are produced anonymously (no longer attributable to a named individual or organization whose reputation and expertise could be identified, verified, and held to account).

## 6.3 Research setting and methods

In seeking to understand the valuation scheme provided by the TripAdvisor social media website, we elected to compare it to the traditional hotel valuation scheme produced by the UK-based Automobile Association (the AA). We chose the AA scheme as it is long-standing, widely regarded, highly professionalized, and particularly influential in practice. It thus offers a useful strategic contrast to the nascent and user-based valuation scheme of TripAdvisor.

We collected data from a number of research sites: the AA, TripAdvisor, various hotels affected by both valuation schemes, and the hospitality industry more generally. We conducted 55 interviews across these sites (see Table 6.1), ranging from 45 minutes to 2 hours. Nearly all interviews were recorded and transcribed. We also examined a large amount of documentation—reports, procedures, standards, trade press articles, blog discussions, newsletters, archival materials, and hundreds of reviews of multiple hotels—from the AA, TripAdvisor, hotels, and the hospitality industry. In addition, we attended a number of academic conferences and trade events focused on the hospitality sector, and participated as users and contributors on the TripAdvisor website.

Table 6.1 Number and type of interviews

|  | Number of interviews | Positions |
|---|---|---|
| Hoteliers | 21 | 12 owners; 9 managers |
| AA employees | 11 | 2 executives; 4 editors; 5 inspectors |
| TripAdvisor employees | 14 | 3 executives; 5 directors; 6 managers |
| Industry professionals | 9 | British Hospitality Association |
|  |  | English Tourist Board |
|  |  | Institute of Hospitality |
|  |  | Association of British Travel Agents |
|  |  | VisitBritain |
|  |  | VisitEngland |
|  |  | Travel Guide Writers/Editors |
| *Total* | *55* |  |

Our data analysis was exploratory, and followed a grounded theory approach (Glaser and Strauss, 1967; Dougherty, 2002; Eisenhardt and Graebner, 2007), beginning with careful reading and content analysis of the interview transcripts, observations, evaluations, and other documentary materials. Our process was inductive and iterative, focused on identifying threads associated with the nature, influence, and implications of the two hotel evaluation schemes in practice. We anticipated that in the production of knowledge about hotels, the calculative apparatus relating to each valuation scheme would make a difference in what was valued, how, and with what consequences. Our data analysis thus focused on examining this in detail.

Our analysis generated important insights into the differences in hotel assessments performed by the TripAdvisor and AA hotel evaluation schemes. We found that TripAdvisor's user-generated ratings and rankings produce a different form of valuation of hotels than those generated by the AA's standardized and professional inspections. These differences in valuation have significant implications for hoteliers' strategies and practices. Accustomed and entrained to receiving routine, annual evaluations based on standardized criteria performed by trained inspectors, hoteliers now have to contend with the uncertainty and ambiguity of reviews and ratings performed by large numbers of anonymous, online users (who may or not have visited the hotel and experienced its facilities and services).

## 6.4 Valuation of hotels

Before comparing the traditional AA and emergent TripAdvisor hotel valuation schemes, we first offer a brief account of each of the scheme's strategies and practices.

### 6.4.1 Two valuation schemes

The UK-based Automobile Association was founded in London in 1905 by a small group of motoring enthusiasts, initially to help each other avoid speeding fines and subsequently to provide a wide range of travel services to its now 15 million members, including breakdown and road assistance, route maps, auto insurance, financial services, hotel accreditation, and travel guides. The AA is one of the UK's most widely recognized and respected brands, and in 2004 it was acquired by a group of private equity funds for $3 billion. The AA has been evaluating hotel accommodation since 1909, and for its most recent 2012 Guides, its 30 professional inspectors visited and evaluated almost 4,000 hotels throughout the UK.

The AA hotel valuation scheme is based on a well-defined set of standards, criteria, and metrics that have been developed, honed, and configured over time through detailed, on-the-ground practices, inspections, and audits, and changed in relation to shifting norms and expectations of the hospitality industry, tourist authorities, consumers and hoteliers. Updated over time, these standards are today defined in the AA's Hotel Quality Standards, a 65-page brochure that articulates the specific standards for facilities and services that must be met for a hotel to be awarded a particular star rating. The AA has an explicit system of star ratings—from one to five stars designating different classes and qualities of accommodation. This system uses black stars to denote the level of award and red stars to distinguish those hotels deemed "exceptional" at a certain level. The AA also distinguishes between types of accommodation—having different criteria and standards for hotels, B&Bs, inns, guesthouses, etc.

The process of valuation involves each hotel being visited annually by one of the AA's 30 full-time inspectors. Inspectors are hired from the hospitality industry and are then thoroughly trained over nine weeks in the inspection procedures of the AA, including the meaning and definition of the standards and criteria, the use of the "AA Dashboard"—a spreadsheet that incorporates hundreds of quantitative metrics and qualitative assessments structured in terms of facilities (e.g., bedrooms, bathrooms, lobby, etc.), services (e.g., reception, room service, food quality), and operational issues (e.g., levels of cleanliness, furnishings, maintenance, etc.). These ratings are based on the quality standards for each level of star award (from one to five). Inspectors' training, which includes a period of shadowing where more junior inspectors accompany more senior ones on their inspections, teaches the inspectors how to perform an inspection, what to look for, what to include in their notes, what to exclude.

Hotel inspections are usually conducted as an overnight stay, with the inspector booking and staying incognito. During his or her visit to the hotel, the inspector performs a detailed evaluation of the hotel that includes capturing data about its facilities and services within the AA Dashboard operating on the inspector's laptop computer. At the end of the hotel stay, the inspector uses the Dashboard to generate a report that computes a rating for each of the key categories of facilities and services and produces an overall graph summarizing the hotel's performance. This report forms the basis of the star rating that is awarded to the hotel, and the face-to-face discussion the inspector has with the manager after checking out of the hotel at the end of his/her stay.

Within three days of the inspection, the inspector sends one copy of the final report to the hotel manager and one to the editor of the AA guides, who will use this report to prepare the review published about the hotel in the annual AA travel guides. Hoteliers may seek clarification about their evaluation and even challenge their star rating. A re-evaluation may then be performed to ensure validity and consistency of rating. The AA also periodically performs "benchmarks" when multiple inspectors gather at a single hotel, individually perform their inspections, and then meet to compare their scores and ratings. In addition, and as part of a staff appraisal process, senor inspectors will periodically call hoteliers to get their feedback on the inspection process.

We turn now to the TripAdvisor hotel evaluation scheme. TripAdvisor is a social media organization founded in Boston in 2000 by four software entrepreneurs, and its mission is to "Help travelers around the world plan and have the perfect trip." After a shaky first year, TripAdvisor's growth has been rapid, and it now hosts the world's largest online travel website, including over 60 million user-generated reviews and opinions on approximately 1 million hotels, restaurants, and venues. TripAdvisor operates websites for 30 countries with content available in 18 languages, and these receive almost 50 million unique users per month. The company currently employs just over a thousand people located around the world, and in 2010 it generated revenues of nearly $500 million, derived from "click through" fees, advertising, and hotel listings.

Hotel reviews on TripAdvisor are produced by its 20 million members who have established a pseudonymous profile with the website. A review includes both qualitative assessments (in the form of free text comments) and quantitative ratings on six criteria (value, rooms, location, cleanliness, service, and sleep quality—none of which are defined). Members may also post their own photos to accompany their reviews. TripAdvisor uses the quantitative ratings to compute a Traveler Rating—an overall rating across all reviewers for each hotel—and the Popularity Index—a ranking of all hotels within a specific geographic city or region. Both the Traveler Rating and Popularity ranking are highly influential in practice, and many travelers pay considerable attention to these scores.

Hotel reviews on TripAdvisor have recently been attracting considerable attention as stories in various media outlets—NBC's *Today*, the *New York Times*, the *Guardian*, the *Telegraph*, and the *Caterer and Hotelkeeper*—draw attention to apparently false or malicious content. With over 60 million reviews and opinions on the website, verification and validation of content is clearly a difficult task. TripAdvisor uses both humans and tools to screen reviews, but problems persist. Both hoteliers and the press report concerns about the accuracy and authenticity of content that is unregulated and pseudonymous. They point to multiple reviews that contain defamatory comments or incorrect information, as well as to job posting websites that seek to hire people to post (apparently fabricated) hotel reviews for $5/review. These concerns about the quality and liability of TripAdvisor content have also triggered legal and regulatory scrutiny, including a number of lawsuits and an inquiry by the UK Advertising Standards Authority.

### 6.4.2 Comparing valuation schemes

In comparing the traditional practices of hotel evaluation performed by the AA with those performed by the TripAdvisor social media website, we found important differences in what was valued, how, and with what consequences. Our approach to understanding these schemes is to consider the arrangements through which different concepts of valuation are expressed not as merely embodied in apparatus but as enacted through practice. Each scheme is an apparatus that enacts what matters and what is excluded from mattering (Barad, 2007: 148). These differences are produced by the different agential cuts enacted by the AA and TripAdvisor valuation schemes in practice. Table 6.2 offers a sense of these differences in practice.

For example, when a hotel inspector makes observations in a hotel during an overnight mystery guest stay, he or she focuses attention on matters that fall within the criteria of the AA standards and pays no attention to those that don't. So whereas an entry in the AA Hotel Guide based upon a sample of rooms inspected may describe them as generally "well appointed," a posting on TripAdvisor may include a "room tip" that specifically categorizes room 312 as "overlooking the road with street noise at the weekend." An AA inspector takes into account 20 percent of room stock

**Table 6.2** The AA and TripAdvisor valuation schemes

|  | The AA | TripAdvisor |
|---|---|---|
| *Practices* | Dense, long-standing practices (a hundred years) honed by an institutionalized association (e.g., awarded a royal warrant), with a widely respected brand. Valuation practices entail routinized, regular, and regulated activities based on well-defined, standardized expertise embodied in a well-trained inspectorate. Inspections are done cyclically, are planned in advance, and subject to audit. | Light-weight, recent practices (ten years) of a start-up organization, that has developed an innovative and emergent social media brand on the internet. Valuation practices entail ongoing experiences of consumers reflecting multiple, diverse, and dynamic ways in which they do (or do not) experience the hotel. Reviews are posted spontaneously, at any time, and are not subject to audit. |
| *Knowledge* | Depth of knowledge of hotels—in terms of criteria, standards, facilities, and instances, articulated in the 65-page Hotel Quality Standards guide for star ratings. Each hotel receives an annual inspection conducted by a trained professional who has experienced many hundreds of hotels in his/her career. Inspection reports are formal and standardized, and discussed immediately and face-to-face with hoteliers. | Breadth of knowledge of hotels—in terms of criteria, standards, facilities, and instances, represented in 6 undefined criteria, a free-text box, and a facility to upload photos. Each hotel receives multiple, ongoing reviews by many untrained users who have each experienced a few hotels over the course of their lives. Opinions are casual and informal with reviews posted at varying times and at a remove and distance from the hoteliers. |
| *Controls* | Inspections are verified and regulated through shadowing, benchmarking, follow-up feedback, and an audit process. Hoteliers have recourse to appeal any valuation they are concerned about or do not agree with, and request a re-inspection. | Reviews are examined for inappropriate content but not verified or regulated with respect to content veracity or reviewer credibility. Hoteliers have limited recourse to appeal a review, and typically can only act by responding online to the contested review. |
| *Outputs* | Inspection reports are edited by professional writers for annual publication in the AA travel guidebooks | Reviews are posted to the website and aggregated via a proprietary algorithm into a real-time ranking for hotels within a region. |

during his/her tour of the hotel conducted with the manager and is unlikely to stay on a weekend. Whereas we discover from an anonymous reviewer on TripAdvisor that last Saturday night there was a brawl on the street below his hotel room. The boundaries defining what comes to matter are enacted differently by the AA and TripAdvisor.

The agential cuts made by each of the two hotel evaluation schemes designed to produce knowledge about travel are significant not only because of their capacity for making boundaries, but also because they enact change differently. This involves the reconfiguration of practices and actors but extends to materiality as well. We propose two metaphors with which to think about the outcomes involved here. On the one hand, we have institutionalized knowledge production through the AA. This process of knowledge production may be termed *fluvial*, a notion taken from geology to denote the formation of landscapes by the interaction of flowing water, carried through multiple regions, and across many levels and channels. In this way, the standards and criteria have flowed through the hospitality sector making differences over time. For example, to qualify for government business development grants in the 1970s and 1980s, UK hotels had to sign up with a recognized hotel accreditation scheme that would tie their practices to inspection processes and industry standards.

On the other hand, we have TripAdvisor's rating and ranking valuation scheme that has developed over a shorter timeframe and is structured by a different set of interests, priorities, practices, and technologies. TripAdvisor's founding strategy was tied to developing a travel portal for travel intermediaries, but over time it has evolved to servicing consumers directly by both providing them travel information they find useful and offering them the opportunity to share information about their own travel experiences. The operation of TripAdvisor's business model relies on a constant supply of user-generated content provided as part of consumers' ongoing practice of traveling and posting to the website. This content is aggregated by algorithms that combine users' subjective interpretations and assessments of the quality, value, and service that they have experienced at particular times in specific hotels. The knowledge thus produced by Trip Advisor is a mix of user views, algorithms, content management, weighted priorities, and filtering practices that compute specific ratings and rankings about hotels within specific regions.

This knowledge about hotels produces what Giddens (1991:26) has termed the "collage effect"—a dynamic juxtaposition of loosely linked items that is a central aspect of contemporary experience. TripAdvisor offers us review after review after review for any particular hotel, across hundreds of thousands of hotels—a process of knowledge production that may be termed *fractal*. Over time, such knowledge becomes progressively recursive and self-referential, as ratings are disconnected from any benchmarks or industry standards, reviews reference other reviews, reviewers copy themselves and each other, and the genre norms shape conformity in form and content. While the production and consumption of this knowledge is distributed and fragmented in time/space, it is always virtually present within a single time/space on the website.

In both the AA and TripAdvisor hotel valuation schemes, qualculation is being enacted as an intra-action (Barad, 2007). The specific details of this qualculation make a difference to how this intra-action is enacted in practice. For example, the AA qualculation works through industry standards, spreadsheet metrics, commensurable datasets, and a professional narrative involving identifiable relations of accountability that are threaded through its practices. The qualculation of TripAdvisor involves intersecting algorithms with non-standard and variably weighted metrics sorting through a multiplicity of personal narratives creating the perception of commensurability, all managed with a light form of (mainly) automated validation mechanisms.

Together these two hotel valuation schemes—the institutionalized star accreditations and the polysemous voices of the customer—have come to constitute the material-discursive practices characterizing value in contemporary travel. The AA configures value through its centering practices that produce fluvial knowledge honed over time, including objective criteria, professionalized standards, trained inspectors, a single dashboard, benchmarking and audit processes, and relations of accountability. A single report, a single star rating, and a single guidebook entry define an AA accredited hotel. TripAdvisor configures value through both decentering and centering practices. On the one hand, its unregulated reviews posted by many, anonymous users, using undefined criteria produce fractal knowledge that defines value in terms of the crowd—a collective, distributed, heterogeneous multiplicity. On the other hand, TripAdvisor also configures value through its calculative algorithms, mechanisms that aggregate and order, erasing difference, reducing variability, and glossing over ambiguity, inconsistency, and duplicity to produce a single ranking of hotels within a region.

## 6.5 Discussion

Reflecting on the reconfigurations of travel knowledge through the years, we see not only that multiple forms of knowledge and valuation have emerged at different times but also that they entail different "strategies of coordination"—mechanisms that work to connect and coordinate disparate elements so as to enact singularity (Law, 2002: 15). Some of these—such as the two hotel valuation schemes we studied—work in a "looplike and self-sustaining" (Law, 2002: 28) manner to hold certain things together in practice at particular times and places.

In the case of the AA hotel valuation scheme, and related accreditation mechanisms, the primary strategy of coordination is through standards. The careful development and ongoing maintenance of industry standards work to coordinate relations and practices of hoteliers and inspectors across time and place. Thus, the experiences of all guests are centered and coordinated through the inspector who draws on his/her trained experience and the AA dashboard to produce a single account of a single overnight stay. These valuation practices enact a single hotel out there, one that is assessed straightforwardly through institutional standards and the objective criteria of star ratings. The editors at the AA are conscious that this "cut" excludes the personal voice of the traveler but their efforts are focused on drawing together a guide that provides a certain standard of assurance to consumers. The report sent to the hotelier is not intended to coordinate guest feedback into a single source of truth, but rather to provide feedback to hoteliers about where and how their management strategies are aligned with industry standards and quality benchmarks, thus providing them with a mandate for action going forward.

In the case of TripAdvisor's hotel valuation scheme, users' reviews include open-ended ratings criteria and comments that are posted without verification or audit. These postings are de-centered in terms of institutionally recognized relationships such as standards, but they claim to be locatable in terms of the "truth" entailed in *in situ* accounts of how the hotel is performing at any point in time. Difference in the timing and placing of reviews produce differences in ratings, and disagreements and contradictions abound. Such valuation practices enact multiple hotels, one for each user who posts a review about his or her experiences of the hotel. Yet, alongside this user-generated multiplicity, TripAdvisor also produces singularity. Its strategy of coordination entails physical juxtaposition and algorithmic aggregation. The reviews of many anonymous users, posted at various times and places, are arranged alongside each other on the website. Its Popularity Index then performs a hierarchical ordering of these disparate ratings, achieving an algorithmically coordinated hotel that hangs together in the regional rankings displayed on the site.

Following Law (2002: 188–9), we suggest that the practices producing the AA Guidebooks enact a consistent and coherent story, one that "conforms to a tradition of continuity, of narrative," whereas the practices involving TripAdvisor are more akin to setting up a pinboard—juxtaposing traveler photos and reviews of hotels on TripAdvisor, friends' Facebook pages, entries from accreditation schemes, digital guidebook recommendations, Google Earth satellite images, and online discussion forums—claiming these are more or less equivalent, "without the necessity of a single order...[or] same narrative." Law (2002: 188) notes:

> A story and a pinboard do different jobs of work. They exist in different worlds. Crucially, they also help to *make* different kinds of worlds. And it is the making that is interesting, the performativity of storytelling on the one hand and pinboards on the other

As he argues, these differences are consequential and raise important questions (Law, 2002: 189):

> How might we think about this difference, the difference between the story and the pinboard? How might we think about the difference in the work that each does? How might we think about their performative effects?

The agential cut performed by the AA hotel valuation scheme produces a particular form of centered, locatable, relational knowledge that enacts institutionalized singularity. While this cut deliberately excludes accounts that matter to the everyday traveler, its purpose is less to efface the performances of the multiple than to provide assurance through relations and processes of accountability. The shift to social media reviews involves losing the illusion of singularity produced by institutionalized, expert-based, accreditation schemes, a singularity that enables consumers to be passive recipients of knowledge.

In contrast, social media websites such as TripAdvisor invite consumers to be active participants in knowledge construction, working through the multiple, different accounts posted on the site as well as contributing their own. Travelers making travel arrangements open multiple windows on their digital desktops, keeping TripAdvisor open as they navigate through booking engine websites and pull up hotel home pages in an effort to draw their own conclusions. While travelers lose the certainty of the AA's specialized expertise and singular valuation, they gain insights through the creative tensions afforded by TripAdvisor's juxtaposition of multiple, heterogeneous reviews. Of course, travelers need to develop the skill to engage these tensions and parse algorithmic ratings rather than be the passive recipients of them. But doing so may allow them to reclaim their status as active, critical travelers instead of having their experiences pre-digested and framed by industry experts.

Performing travel in the twenty-first century means experiencing the discomforting juxtaposition of uncertainty through the multiplicity offered by TripAdvisor. This applies to hoteliers as much as it does to travelers. Hoteliers in our study say that they live with the anxiety of "unjust" or "skewed" postings, regarding every guest as a potential bad review in process, taking reviews into staff meetings, and struggling to decide whether or not to make management changes based on user-generated content. Travelers report spending more time booking travel, making reservations at hotels they would not have otherwise chosen, drawing *in situ* comparisons with reviews, and occasionally rueing both their choices and postings.

The rise of TripAdvisor marks the tensions characterizing contemporary processes of knowing: while we continue to search for what Law (2002) describes as "neat tree-like arborescence, for singular stories," there is recognition that such singularities are illusory, one of multiple orderings in the world. In the hospitality sector, these definitive accounts and fragments coexist as each other's creatures. The enthusiasm with which TripAdvisor has been received may lie in its ability to manifest this in practice. By design, diverse accounts and multiple orderings confront each other. One could argue that TripAdvisor is realizing the generative possibilities of juxtaposition through which travelers have an explicit experience of what it means to know in tension, and to identify possibilities for action in the creative dissonance that comes from reconciling rather than concluding (Stark, 2009).

By redrawing the boundaries of travel planning practice, TripAdvisor confronts us with difficulties that may have not troubled us before and brings us to ask questions about the basis for travel knowledge that have remained dormant for many decades. To frame this in theoretical terms, it raises issues about the ordering logics of fractionally coherent objects. It also leaves us with the challenge of working out what is needed to support fractal knowing. This is important because TripAdvisor has raised many issues within the hospitality sector. To regard this decentered apparatus as entirely transparent and open is to misunderstand the specific centering cuts that are enacted. TripAdvisor has steadfastly declined to reveal the technical details of its Popularity Index algorithm on the grounds that it is proprietary and releasing it would only lead to "gaming" by hotels. Ironically then, in the midst of the multiple heterogeneity of reviews posted by the crowd, TripAdvisor's ranking algorithm reintroduces homogeneity through imposing a single ordering that determines which hotel is valued as number one in a region. Through TripAdvisor we thus learn in detail about the microphysics of power invested in the qualculative apparatus of valuation.

## 6.6 Conclusion

As part of the ongoing project of travel and knowledge about travel, we are seeing the latest knowledge eclipse (Strathern, 2000). In this case, expert valuation schemes in the hospitality sector are being supplanted by user-generated reviews posted on social media websites. Such a reconfiguration of valuation in the hospitality sector redistributes resources among businesses, shifts travel practices, redefines what counts and who counts, and changes the habitats in which these reconfigurations are realized. We suggest that such reconfigurations of valuation do not just raise epistemological issues but also raise questions of ontology. Producing stories and producing pinboards entail different kinds of work. They produce different kinds of valuations of the real, and in so doing enact different (singular and multiple) realities (Law, 2002).

The particular relations through which valuation practices are enacted raises interesting questions for scholars interested in studying the entanglement of materiality in the process of qualculation, knowledge production, and responsibility. Lucy Suchman (2002b: 142) has noted:

> As Haraway made clear, the fact that our knowing is relative to and limited by our locations does not in any sense relieve us of responsibility for it. On the contrary, it is precisely the fact that our vision of the world is a vision from somewhere—that it is based in an embodied, and therefore partial, perspective—that makes us personally responsible for it. The only possibility for the creation of effective technologies, from this perspective, is through collective awareness of the particular and multiple locations of their production and use.

Organizing a mass of data inevitably demands particular strategies of coordination. We would suggest that the current approach pursued by TripAdvisor stops short of its mission. The distinctive located accountability achieved by TripAdvisor is being offset by agential cuts that obscure its algorithms and allow anonymous, unverified postings. However, TripAdvisor has only been in operation for just over a decade, and its developments and consequences are relatively brief in the history of travel. It regularly releases new versions of its website and its policies, and its practices and technologies are thus fluid and emergent.

We believe that the reconfigurations of valuation exemplified by the case of TripAdvisor offer important insights into the broader issues associated with the role of social media in knowledge practices and the eclipsing of expert valuations by ones grounded in user-generated content. Our purpose in this chapter has been to present an account of these reconfigurations in play and to emphasize that websites hosting user-generated content are as responsible as any other form of organization for the location and partiality of the knowledge that they produce. The apparent multiplicity of valuation criteria and decentering of knowledge production to the crowd is not an excuse to lose sight of located accountabilities.

## Notes

A version of this chapter was delivered as a keynote address to the Third International Symposium on Process Organization Studies, Corfu, June 2011. We thank Hari Tsoukas for his invitation to develop these ideas here. We are grateful to Vasiliki Baka for her research assistance, and the study participants for their contributions to the fieldwork. This research was supported in part by the Centennial Visiting Professors Program at the London School of Economics.

1. http://en.wikipedia.org/wiki/Guide_book.
2. Published with the subtitle, *The Traveller's Guide through the Commercial Metropolis of the United States by a Gentleman residing in this City.*
3. http://en.wikipedia.org/wiki/Mariana_Starke.
4. http://www.theaa.com/travel/accommodation_restaurants_grading.html.
5. http://www.michelintravel.com/michelin-guides/.g

## References

Barad, K. (2003). "Posthumanist Performativity: Toward an Understanding of How Matter Comes to Matter," *Signs*, 28/3: 801–31.
—— (2007). *Meeting the University Halfway: Quantum Physics and the Entanglement of Matter and Meaning.* Durham, NC: Duke University Press.
Callon, M. and Law, J. (2005). "On Qualculation, Agency and Otherness," *Environment and Planning D: Society and Space*, 23/5: 717–33.
—— and Muniesa, F. (2005). "Economic Markets as Calculative Collective Devices," *Organization Studies*, 26/8: 1229–50.
David, S. and Pinch, T. (2008). "Six Degrees of Reputation: The Use and Abuse of Online Review and Recommendation Systems," in T. Pinch and R. Swedberg (eds.), *Living in a Material World: Economic Sociology meets Science and Technology Studies*. Cambridge, MA: MIT Press, pp. 341–74.
Dougherty, D. (2002). "Grounded Theory Building: Some Principles and Practices," in J. A. C. Baum (ed.), *Companion to Organizations*. Oxford: Blackwell Publishers, pp. 849–67.
Eisenhardt, K. M. and Graebner, M. E. (2007). "Theory Building from Cases: Opportunities and Challenges," *Academy of Management Journal*, 50/1: 25–32.

Espeland, W. N. and Sauder, M. (2007). "Ranking and Reactivity: How Public Measures Recreate Social Worlds," *American Journal of Sociology*, 113/1: 1–40.

—— and Stevens, M. (1998). "Commensuration as a Social Process," *Annual Review of Sociology*, 24: 312–43.

Giddens, A. (1991). *Modernity and Self-Identity: Self and Society in the Late Modern Age*. Stanford: Stanford University Press.

Glaser, B. G. and Strauss, A. L. (1967). *The Discovery of Grounded Theory: Strategies for Qualitative Research*. Chicago: Aldine Publishing Company.

Gretton, J. R. (1993). "Introduction," in W. B. C. Lister, *A Guide to the Microfiche Edition of Murray's Handbooks for Travellers*. Frederick, MD: University Publications of America, pp. vii–xlviii.

Gretzel, U. and Yoo, K. H. (2008). "Use and Impact of Online Travel Reviews," in P. O'Connor, W. Hopken, and U. Gretzel (eds.), *Information and Communication Technologies in Tourism*. New York: Springer, pp. 35–46.

Haraway, D. (1988). "Situated Knowledges: The Science Question in Feminism and the Privilege of Partial Perspective," *Feminist Studies*, 14: 575–99.

Hsu, G., Roberts, P. W., and Swaminathan, A.(2012). "Evaluative Schemas and the Mediating Role of Critics," *Organization Science*, 23/1: 83–97.

Jeacle, I. and Carter, C. (2011). "In TripAdvisor We Trust: Rankings, Calculative Regimes and Abstract Systems," *Accounting, Organizations and Society*, 36/4–5: 293–309.

Karpik, L. (2010). *Valuing the Unique: The Economics of Singularities*. Princeton: Princeton University Press.

Law, J. (2002). *Aircraft Stories: Decentering the Object in Technoscience*. Durham, NC: Duke University Press.

—— and Urry, J. (2004). "Enacting the Social," *Economy and Society*, 33/3: 390–410.

Mesquita, S. (2011). *Travel Publishing Yearbook*. Surrey, UK: Nielsen BookScan.

Moser, I. and Law, J. (2006). "Fluids or Flows? Information and Qualculation in Medical Practice," *Information Technology & People*, 19/1: 55–73.

Sattin, A. (2008). "Baedeker Guidebooks are Back," *Sunday Times*, January 13. http://www.timesonline.co.uk/tol/travel/holiday_type/travel_and_literature/article3159576.ece.

Sauder, M. and Espeland, W. N. (2009). "The Discipline of Rankings: Tight Coupling and Organizational Change," *American Sociological Review*, 74: 63–82.

Stark, D. (2009). *The Sense of Dissonance: Accounts of Worth in Economic Life*. Princeton: Princeton University Press.

Starke, M. (1826). *Information and Directions for Travellers On the Continent*. Paris: A. & W. Galignani Publishers.

Starkov, M. and Price, J. (2007). "Web 2.0 vs. Search Engines: Are Search Engines Becoming Obsolete in the Web 2.0 Frenzy?," *Hospitality News*, September 17, 2007. http://www.hospitalitynet.org/news/4034173.html.

Strathern, M. (2000). "The Tyranny of Transparency," *British Educational Research Journal*, 26/3: 309–21.

Suchman, L. A. (2002a). "Located Accountabilities in Technology Production," *Scandinavian Journal of Information Systems*, 14/2: 91–105.

—— (2002b). "Practice-Based Design of Information Systems: Notes from the Hyperdeveloped World," *The Information Society*, 18: 139–44.

—— (2007). *Human–Machine Reconfigurations*. Cambridge: Cambridge University Press.

Tisdall, N. (2007). "Baedeker is Back," *The Telegraph*, http://www.telegraph.co.uk/travel/artsandculture/739083/Baedeker-is-back.html.

Vermeulen, I. and Seegers, D. (2009). "Tried and Tested: The Impact of Online Hotel Reviews on Consumer Consideration," *Tourism Management*, 30: 123–7.

Willmott, H. (2010). "Creating 'Value' Beyond the Point of Production: Branding, Financialization and Market Capitalization," *Organization*, 17/5: 517–42.

Xiang, Z. and Gretzel, U. (2010). "Role of Social Media in Online Travel Information Search," *Tourism Management*, 31: 179–88.

# 7

# The Emergence of Materiality within Formal Organizations

*Paul M. Leonardi*

**Abstract:** In their demonstrations that technologies and organizations are sociomaterial, or how they become sociomaterial, scholars have not reflected in any measurable depth on the concept of materiality by itself. This chapter explores how materiality emerges from an organization's interaction with its environment. The verb "emerge" is used purposefully. To say that materiality is entirely strategically crafted would be to place an undue onus on the agency of a technology's designer or developer, an onus which the author suggests may be misplaced. Thus to say that materiality emerges is to recognize that the physical and or/digital materials that are arranged into particular forms are arranged by someone. But the selection of those materials or the ways in which people decide to arrange them may not be entirely under their control because they do so within the constraints of an organization's formal structure. By considering the insights of organizational theories that depict organizations as actively responding to environmental stimuli and other theories which propose that organizations are largely ineffective at responding to environmental pressures and are directly acted upon by their environments, the chapter demonstrates how the micro-level interpretative flexibility of artifacts, the evolution and composition of the set of relevant social groups that contribute to the artifact's construction, the processes by which an artifact reaches a point of stabilization and closure, and the structure of the technological frames shared by designers are influenced by macro-level organizational responses to and pressures from their environments.

## 7.1 Introduction

Among theorists interested in the relationship between technological and organizational change it is becoming popular to employ the concept of materiality (e.g., Dale, 2005; Orlikowski, 2007; Leonardi and Barley, 2008; Osterlund, 2008; Suchman, 2000). Students of technology and organizing appear to use this term somewhat interchangeably with the more popular word, "technology" or as something that belongs to a technology (e.g., "technology's materiality"). It seems that one reason the term is used in this way is because decades of research aimed at countering technologically deterministic claims proffered by early contingency theorists (e.g., Hickson et al., 1969; Hunt, 1970) have led organizational researchers to treat technologies like computers, software programs, and even desks and chairs as artifacts that are embedded in a web of social practice. That is to say, without people either developing or using them, the technological artifacts with which those people work daily would have no meaning nor could they bring particular affects to the organization of work.

This over-socialized view of technology has been tempered, in recent years, by a new stream of research arguing for a "sociomaterial approach" to the study of organizing. One of the goals of this approach is to bring the substance of technological artifacts back into theories of organizing. But it does so in a clever way. Rather than argue that technologies exist apart from the organizations in which they are developed and used, the sociomaterial approach argues that work occurring within organizations is not a social practice enabled or constrained by technology (Orlikowski, 2010), that technological artifacts are not simply collections of materials organized by social processes (Pinch, 2010), but rather that organizations and technologies are simultaneously social and material. That is, they are both "sociomaterial." As Leonardi (2009: 300), suggests:

> if technology is a sociomaterial process and organizing is a sociomaterial process, too, there exists no important distinction between technological and organizational change. That is, the appropriate unit of analysis for "technology" is the artifact and the people interacting with it and around it, and the appropriate unit of analysis for "organizing" is people interacting with each other and the artifacts that enable or constrain their interaction.

Given such a conceptualization, it is not surprising that many recent research papers have aimed to demonstrate, empirically, that a particular technological artifact is as much social as it is material (Svahn et al., 2009; Berente et al., 2010), that certain organizational practices are as much social as they are material (Wagner et al., 2010; Johri, 2011), or to theorize how the social and the material become, in Orlikowski's (2007: 1437) words, "constitutively entangled" (Jonsson et al., 2009; Leonardi, 2011).

In their demonstrations that technologies and organizations are sociomaterial, or to show how they become sociomaterial, scholars have not reflected in any measurable depth on the concept of materiality by itself. Materiality is defined here as the arrangement of a technological artifact's physical and/or digital materials into particular forms that endure across differences in place and time and are important to users. Of course, embedded in this definition is a paradox of sorts. The notion of arrangement implies agency and discretion on the part of a technology's designer such that the process of arranging is sociomaterial. Likewise, for physical or digital materials to become important to users also requires people making interpretations and developing perceptions—a process that is certainly sociomaterial as well. But leaving this paradox—that a technology's materiality only comes to be so through sociomaterial processes occurring during activities of development and use—aside for a moment, it seems to make good empirical sense to treat a technological artifact's materiality as something that exists at least physically (if not conceptually) apart from the people who create and use it.

Although we might agree that a technological artifact like a social media tool or an enterprise resource planning tool or a computer-simulation tool is sociomaterial in nature, it still has a certain materiality that transcends space, time, and context. For although someone arranged the digital materials out of which such tools are fashioned during development, those arrangements endure after the technology leaves the developer's desk. Similarly, when everyone leaves the office at the end of the day some part of those tools still sit on someone's hard drive on a computer on a desk. It is precisely because technological artifacts have a materiality that exists apart from people that they are useful for work. For example, because the materiality of a certain type of simulation technology is the same whether an engineer uses it at the firm's offices in Detroit or Bangalore means that offshoring of work at the task-level can occur (Leonardi and Bailey, 2008). In fact, if a technological artifact did not have a fixed materiality, extreme constructivist theorizing would not be possible. The prototypical constructivist study shows that people in two different organizations use the same new technology differently and, consequently, change (or do not change) their informal organizing in distinct ways (e.g., Zack and McKenney, 1995; Robey and Sahay, 1996; Orlikowski, 2000). The only way that scholars have been able to demonstrate these findings empirically is because the materiality of that technology was the same in both organizations under study. Given these arguments, it seems reasonable to use the term materiality to refer to those properties of the artifact that do not change from one moment to the next or across differences in location (Faulkner and Runde, 2011).

For these reasons, it would behoove organizational studies of sociomateriality to have a more theoretically informed understanding of how and why the materiality of a technological artifact emerges as it does. I use the verb "emerge" purposefully. To say that materiality is entirely strategically crafted would be to place an undue onus on the agency of technology's designer or developer, an onus which I will suggest below may be misplaced. Thus to say that materiality emerges is to recognize that the physical and or/digital materials that are arranged into particular forms are arranged by someone. But the selection of those materials or the ways in which that person decides to arrange them may not be entirely under their control because they do so within the constraints of an organization's formal structure. To discuss the emergence of materiality, then, I will focus my discussion on the development of new technologies as it is here that we see most clearly how an actor's choices—and the way that those choices are enabled or constrained—result in an artifact with a particular type of materiality.

One obvious place to begin considering choice in the design and development of new technologies is with the insights from the social construction of technology. The pioneering work on the social construction of technology (SCOT) by Pinch and Bijker (1984), which they elaborated in subsequent works (Bijker, 1992, 1995a; Pinch, 1996; Pinch and Trocco, 2002; Pinch, 2008), introduced four mechanisms to understand the social foundations of technology design and development. The first is that *relevant social groups* play a key role in the development of a technological artifact. Such groups share a particular meaning of the artifact. This meaning then can be used to explain why artifacts develop along particular paths. Pinch and Bijker describe that there were at least two relevant social groups important to the development of the bicycle: "young men of nerve," and "older men and women." Each of these groups contributed to the development of the bicycle in different ways. Second, to understand how technology is socially constructed, one must keep in mind that all newly created artifacts are interpretatively flexible. *Interpretative flexibility* is the notion that the meaning of an artifact does not reside in the technology itself, but is determined by the meanings attributed to it by its relevant social groups (Pinch, 2003). Thus, there is an interpretative flexibility over the meaning to be given to an artifact. In the case of the bicycle, the high-wheeler simultaneously had the meaning of "macho machine" for young men and "unsafe machine" for older men and women. As a result, the one artifact itself was interpretatively flexible among the various social groups and different meanings were embodied in new artifacts. The third mechanism is related to the second: All newly created artifacts reach a state of *stabilization and closure*. As Pinch and Bijker (1984: 426) describe, "closure in technology involves the stabilization of an artifact and the 'disappearance' of problems." Over time, the artifact stabilizes and interpretative flexibility is diminished as one meaning becomes dominant. Pinch and Bijker suggest that artifacts can reach a state of closure through two avenues. The first is rhetorical closure, whereby designers talk about the technology in a way that emphasizes its finality. The second is closure by redefinition of the problem. In this mechanism, designers begin to tackle a new problem of development, thus leaving the solution to the old problem satisfactorily behind, essentially closing further exploration into it. Bijker (1995a) later proposed a fourth conceptual lever to help understand the process by which technologies are socially constructed: *technological frames* structure the interactions among the actors of a relevant social group. A technological frame is comprised of the elements that influence the interactions of a group of designers and lead to the attribution of meanings to technical artifacts. Bijker (1995a) cites the development of Bakelite as a process that occurred because of the technological frames shared between the developers of the technology. Goals of the production process, for example, focused problems with the chemical composition of the material that then led to solutions that seemed "necessary" and "inevitable." As a result, artifacts come to have their meaning by the technological frames through which they are interpreted. In this frame, the technical and the social are intimately interrelated.

Although SCOT is often referenced by organizational theorists as a reminder that (though these are likely not the words they would use) the materiality of the particular technological artifact under study is the result of some prior sociomaterial process (e.g., Garud and Rappa, 1994; Rosenkopf and Tushman, 1994; Orlikowski, 2000; Pentland and Feldman, 2007), it remains today, as Klein and Kleinman (2002) argue, a decidedly "agency-centered" perspective. In other words, the agency of individual actors and, by association, their ability to profoundly and often autonomously affect the course of a technology's development figures prominently in the SCOT perspective. Perhaps this is because studies that have systematically used the SCOT framework have tended to focus on entrepreneurial ventures, embarked upon by innovators who were, at least initially, largely free from the influences of formal organizational structures. Such studies have explored the social construction of plastics (Bijker, 1987), mountain bikes

(Rosen, 1993), electrical systems (Hargadon and Douglas, 2001), and electronic synthesizers (Pinch and Trocco, 2002), as just a few examples.

At a basic level, a pronounced focus on the agency of individual actors to shape the developmental path of a new technology's materiality is to be expected from early SCOT studies. SCOT arose in response to popular and appealing deterministic notions of technological change (Bijker and Pinch, 2002). In leveling their critique against such a perspective, Pinch, Bijker, and other contributors often emphasized the interests, autonomy, and capability for action of human agents as antidotes for technologically deterministic thinking, which claimed that humans could exert little force on a technological trajectory in the face of an artifact's intrinsic logic.

Recently, however, a number of scholars have begun to cite a lack of attention to the effects of organizational and occupational structures on the development of new technologies as a major shortcoming in the SCOT approach. Klein and Kleinman (2002), for example, argue that the SCOT perspective does attempt to take into account the wider "socio-cultural and political milieu" in which artifact development takes place, yet they criticize SCOT for failing to systematically consider how such influences constrain and enable the social construction process:

> From this seminal work has flowed a body of research that is rich and diverse—but that has largely remained committed to an agency-centered approach. Despite some conceptual evolution in the direction of structural theory, most notably in Bijker's [1995a] later and more comprehensive work, *Of Bicycles, Bakelites, and Bulbs*, the SCOT approach has made only limited contributions to illuminating how social structures can influence the development of technology. (Klein and Kleinman, 2002: 28)

Kranakis (2004) has also shown that SCOT's over-emphasis on the agency of individual actors can pose problems for the analysis of technologies that are developed in large organizations. In examining the Quebec Bridge disaster of 1907, Kranakis showed how those responsible for "fixing the blame" for the bridge collapse did so without considering the ways in which the "working" of the bridge was constructed among the organizations involved in its development. Kranakis suggests that the SCOT perspective leads researchers of technology to a similar folly, ascribing the problems that emerged in the construction of the bridge to individual responsibility and error. Kranakis' careful analysis shows that the day-to-day administration of the project, how technical expertise was deployed, how complex tasks were divided and responsibility assigned, how the design process was organized and linked with other production priorities, and the choices made about who had responsibility for all these arrangements implicated organizational culture as a major contributor to the collapse of the bridge. Vaughan's (1999) study of the *Challenger* launch decision also attempts to account for structural constraints upon the social construction of technology. She shows how certain reporting structures and procedures for decision-making at NASA led the development of space shuttle technology down predictable paths and obscured the potential danger of a launch by creating administrative procedures and "go/no-go" decision criteria that were not reflective of the safety issues proposed by engineers.

The collective point that these critiques raise is that although the SCOT perspective provides four useful mechanisms for explaining the social construction process resulting in the configuration of a technological artifact's materiality, the perspective does not theorize how those mechanisms might be influenced in fundamental ways by the organizational structures in which they occur. Yet, if organizational theorists intend to continue discussing the intellectual purchase that a sociomaterial perspective can bring to studies of work in organizations, they must have in their theories a detailed understanding of how and why an artifact's materiality looks and acts the way it does.

The rest of this chapter examines how SCOT might be amended to account for the influences of formal organizational structure upon the emergence of materiality. As organizational researchers have shown, technology development processes and outcomes are quite disparate depending upon whether they were conducted by an autonomous inventor or by individuals within a formal organization (Allen, 1977; Van de Ven, 1986; Thomas, 1994; Hargadon and Douglas, 2001). This is because the process of technology development within organizations is very much linked to the formal procedures and arrangements of organizing. More than a half-century of research has convincingly shown that organizations exist in uncertain and ambiguous environments. Sometimes they seek to actively manage their environment (Pfeffer and Salancik, 1978), and sometimes the environment exerts selection pressures directly on them (Hannan and Freeman, 1977). In all cases, organizations are constantly acting and being acted upon as they interact with their environments in ways that are not always directed toward the benefit of developing new technologies. Instead, organizations make structural changes in order to respond to environmental pressures and technology development efforts are often pulled along and shaped as organizations contend with external exigencies (Davis and Taylor, 1976; Tushman and Anderson, 1986; Brown and Eisenhardt, 1995).

For SCOT to be appropriated to usefully explain the emergence of materiality within formal organizations a more empirically accurate conception of organizational influences on the social construction process is needed. In other words, researchers cannot expect to fruitfully employ the SCOT perspective, as it currently stands, to explain the emergence of materiality within formal organizations because explicit theorization of the mechanisms by which the social construction process unfolds is largely devoid of any consideration that interpretative flexibility, relevant social groups, technological frames, and stabilization/closure occur within the confines of formal organizing processes. To successfully explain the emergence of materiality within formal organizations, SCOT's agency-centered perspective must be enhanced by considering the role that formal organizations play in enabling and constraining its four mechanisms. To create a framework of this kind, one needs a detailed theory of organizations. Fortunately, the organizational studies literature has several. In the remainder of this chapter I consider how the insights provided by two dominant organizational theories—Resource Dependence and Population Ecology—might help to revise SCOT's explanations of how technology development processes unfold in ways that make it better situated to describe the emergence of materiality in formal organizations.

## 7.2 The organizational construction of materiality

Although many formal organizations are created and perpetuated with the specific goal of developing new technologies, the actual practice of technology development comprises only one part of organizational action. Organizations strive to survive and in their pursuit of survival in an ambiguous and uncertain environment they participate in many activities that are not directly aimed at new technology development (Blau et al., 1976; Chandler, 1977; DeSanctis et al., 2002). Thus, it seems reasonable to expect that the various ways in which organizational theories suggest that organizations act in and are acted upon by their environment may have the latent effect of enabling and constraining the mechanisms by which new technology development is socially constructed.

Since the mid-1970s when organizational researchers first began to take seriously an open systems perspective (Scott, 2004) which treats organizations themselves as actors in an environment of other organizations, legal regulations, and market forces, a number of theories have emerged depicting the adaptation and change of formal organizational structures in response to environmental pressures. Among these, theories such as Resource Dependence, (Aldrich and Pfeffer, 1976; Pfeffer and Salancik, 1978), New Institutionalism (DiMaggio and Powell, 1983; Tolbert and Zucker, 1999), and Transaction Cost Economics (Williamson, 1981, 1996) depict organizations as actively responding to environmental stimuli. Other theories such as Evolutionary Theory (Nelson and Winter, 1982; Dosi and Nelson, 1994) and Population Ecology (Hannan and Freeman, 1977, 1989) propose an alternative view that organizations are largely ineffective at responding to environmental pressures and are directly acted upon by their environments.

Because the goal of this chapter is to explore how formal organizational processes occurring as organizations interact with their environments may influence interpretative flexibility, relevant social groups, technological frames, and stabilization and closure—those same mechanisms through which SCOT shows that a technology's materiality emerges—I have chosen to focus in depth on one theory (Resource Dependence) that describes organizations as active entities that are capable of responding to their environment. Conversely, I have chosen another theory (Population Ecology) suggesting that organizations are often acted on (selected in favor of or against) by their environments. Using these two competing theories to consider how a technology's materiality is shaped by organization–environment relations, this analysis aims to explore how SCOT's mechanisms are implicated in the formal processes of organizing.

## 7.3 Resource Dependence

Resource Dependence theory is rooted in the assumption that organizations are open systems that actively engage in interdependent relationships with their environments. Drawing on the work of contingency theorists such as Thompson (1967) and Perrow (1970), the theory holds that no organization is self-sufficient; rather all organizations draw resources from their environment to survive. Because particular resources are critical for successful functioning, and because an organization's ability to obtain them is often uncertain, organizations find themselves in dependency relationships with other firms (Pfeffer and Salancik, 1978). To overcome dependencies, administrators seek to actively manage their environments as well as their organizations (Aldrich and Pfeffer, 1976). Depending on the level of uncertainty of a particular resource, managers regularly utilize two major mechanisms to resolve such dependencies: Buffering and Bridging strategies. The use of these strategies can have profound effects on the social construction of technology development within the organization.

## 7.3.1 Buffering

Thompson observed that when faced with environmental uncertainties that could potentially hinder its technical core—the processes that characterize its mode of production—organizations operating under norms of rationality "seek to buffer environmental influences by surrounding their technical cores with input and output components" (1967: 20). Put more plainly, organizations seek to minimize dependencies on other organizations by reducing the uncertainty of obtaining important resources. To do so, organizations buffer their technical cores through strategies such as coding: classifying inputs before inserting them into the technical core; stockpiling: collecting and holding raw materials; leveling: reducing fluctuations in its input or output environments; forecasting: anticipating changes in supply or demand conditions and attempting to adapt them; and adjusting scale: changing the scale of the technical core so as not to use so many resources (Scott, 1998: 197–8). As examples, stockpiling and adjusting scale are two processes that demonstrate how buffering strategies may affect the social construction of technology development.

When either the availability or the price of critical resources is uncertain, organizations often stockpile them; that is, they collect and hold those resources so they are assured they will be available when needed. In the process of technology development described by most SCOT research, designers begin their quest to create a new technology by addressing a particular problem and seeking a technological solution to it (Berg, 1998). In this sense, designers seek resources that will help them create a solution to a predefined problem. Once organizations stockpile certain resources such as raw materials, however, research shows that they are often compelled to find new uses for them to justify their investment (Kupperman and Smith, 1970). One popular use is to incorporate them in the design of new technologies, and there are many examples of technologies that are developed in this way (Basalla, 1988; Shane, 2000). If a designer begins with a stockpile of resources and searches for a new technology he or she can develop from them, the outcome is quite different from a process where the problem is the starting point. Sarasvathy (2001: 245) terms these "effectuation processes"—where a designer "begins with given ingredients and utensils and focuses on preparing one of many possible desirable meals with them." Thus, when organizations stockpile resources, the development of a new technology often begins by considering what existing resources are available and then what can be developed within the boundaries provided by those resources (Eppinger and Chitkara, 2006).

Designing a new technology based on an effectuation process rather than a problem–solution process dramatically affects the interpretative flexibility of the artifact. One of the key components of interpretative flexibility is that the actual functionality of the artifact is not determined by its material properties, but rather by the meanings attributed to it by relevant social groups. In Bijker's (1995a: 75) words, "the 'working' and 'nonworking' of an artifact are socially constructed assessments, rather than intrinsic properties." Thus, when a designer develops an artifact through a problem–solution process, the artifact "works" only if it is understood to "solve" the problem that spurred its development (MacKenzie, 1996). By contrast, when the designer develops the artifact through an effectuation process, starting not with a specific problem, but with a set of resources the organization has stockpiled, the "working" of the artifact is judged by much different criteria. Thus, when organizations stockpile particular resources, designers may develop new technologies aimed at utilizing those resources. In so doing, the interpretative flexibility of the artifact—the meanings they attribute to it to determine its "working"—will lead to radically different designs than if the technology was developed to combat a particular and well-defined problem (Carlson, 1992).

Organizations also adjust the scale of production in order to buffer environmental uncertainty of both materials acquisition and product sales. Economies of scale are crucial to reducing resource dependencies. Larger organizations are typically able to set prices and influence the actions of related organizations better than smaller ones (Pfeffer and Salancik, 1978). As a consequence, the degree to which an organization can use its scale to establish deals with suppliers and vendors directly affects that organization's willingness to engage in certain technological developments over others. As technology researchers have demonstrated (e.g., Christensen, 1997), more innovative designs are often only possible when developers can be assured that their investments will be returned through product sales. Pinch and Bijker (1984) argue that the stabilization and closure of an artifact is reached either rhetorically, or by redefinition of the problem. The agency-centered perspective makes the assumption that designers are free to seek additional resources if a certain technological problem has not yet been "solved." The fact that organizations use scale adjustment as a buffering mechanism, however, demonstrates that they are often limited in their ability to gain crucial resources. Thus, if an organization believes that a new technological development will be profitable, it will be more likely to increase the scale-production of the technology, enabling access to more resources (Baum et al., 2000). If such returns are not anticipated, access to crucial resources will be reduced, bringing the design of a new technology to closure before the problem is believed to be "solved." In other words, if organizations anticipate modest returns from technology development, they will adjust the scale of production so that access to new resources is reduced prematurely, resulting in the stabilization of the artifact prior to rhetorical closure or closure by redefinition of the problem.

## 7.3.2 Bridging

In addition to buffering their technical cores, organizations also seek to reduce resource dependencies by building bridges to other organizations that might affect the certainty of those resources. Researchers within the Resource Dependence perspective draw on Emerson's (1962) work on power to suggest that one of the key ways organizations can reduce their dependence on uncertain resources is to create *interdependencies* with organizations that control those resources. As a consequence, it is in each organization's best interests to help the other obtain its necessary resources. Thus, organizations conduct bridging strategies to increase interdependence through actions such as cooptation, strategic alliances, mergers, and many more. Although each of these bridging strategies may potentially influence technology development, two are considered here: cooptation and strategic alliances.

Cooptation refers to the practice of incorporating representatives of external groups into the decision-making structure of an organization. Within the Resource Dependence perspective, numerous studies of cooptation have focused on interlocking boards of directors. Board interlocks may have two important implications for technology development. First, innovations diffuse among organizations in large part through interlocks. As Davis and Greve (1997) found, "poison pills" were adopted by organizations that learned of them from their interlocking boards. Thus, the ideas or the impetus to develop a new technology may come about precisely because they have proven effective or legitimate in other organizational contexts, and board members can share first-hand information on how to develop them effectively.

In the language of SCOT, interlocks bring new relevant social groups into the development of new technologies. Relevant social groups are important to the SCOT analysis because each group shares a particular meaning for a technology, but different groups often share different meanings for it (Bijker, 1987). As information is passed among relevant social groups pertaining to the development of a specific artifact, each group's own meaning of the technology is altered slightly (Rosen, 1993). More importantly in the context of organizational technology development, the communication among relevant social groups contributes new information about how and why to design new technologies, information that may have been well out of view of technology designers themselves. Cooptation strategies may bring new relevant social groups into the social construction of technology development that may not have otherwise entered the process. Moreover, information about particular resources or methods of development and production that is shared through cooptation strategies will influence the meanings attributed to the technology by relevant social groups.

Organizations also enter into strategic alliances with other firms to reduce uncertainty and to gain legitimacy in the market. As Scott (1998: 203) defines them, "alliances involve agreements between two or more organizations to pursue joint objectives through a coordination of activities or sharing of knowledge or resources." Consequently, technology development may be shaped by the formation of organizational alliances. When firms collaborate to develop a technology, the resultant knowledge is available to all partners when they begin to develop future technologies on their own (Ahuja, 2000). Thus, alliances have the power to alter the social construction of technology development because organizations will have access to resources, tools, production methods, and patents that they did not have before.

Additionally, new entrepreneurial firms often attempt to reduce resource dependencies by developing alliances with more established market players. The results of such alliances often have the effect that the entrepreneurial firm is locked into certain modes of technology development pursuant to their agreement with another company (Santos and Eisenhardt, 2009). Thus, alliance agreements can often constrain the developmental paths along which organizations might wish to follow. This is tempered by the fact that alliances bring new resources, either in the form of material assets or information on new innovations in developmental or production procedures. From a SCOT perspective, alliances form the basis for the creation of new technological frames. A technological frame constitutes the shared structure of interpretation of an artifact among members of a relevant social group (Klein and Kleinman, 2002). Because alliances always provide a mixture of constraining and enabling forces upon organizations (Dyer and Singh, 1998), the social groups relevant to an artifact's development must create technological frames that reflect the boundaries of such agreements. These technological frames become the basis for how designers interact as they develop a new artifact. Consequently, strategic alliances between organizations may result in the creation of new technological frames that are shared by technology designers. These frames provide the boundaries for new technology development as they help to specify in what ways new designs will be constrained by agreements and in what ways they will be enabled by access to new resources.

When considering the emergence of technology's materiality through the lens of Resource Dependence theory it is clear that technology development is often influenced by the organizational arrangements made in response to environmental uncertainties. Resource Dependence theory instructs researchers adopting a SCOT perspective to consider an organization's strategic decisions in regards to inter-organizational arrangements as levers that affect the agency of technical innovators. When considering the emergence of materiality, researchers would do well to recognize that technology developers face very practical and often palpable constraints on the materials with which they work, the vendors with whom they can contract, and the information about technical innovations or consumer demands upon which they base their designs. Although a developer or a team of designers may have the autonomy to decide how they will arrange an artifact's physical or digital materials, Resource Dependence theory reminds us that they may be limited as to which materials they can use or with whom they can work to get them arranged. It is these social affordances and constraints that arise because of decisions that have little or nothing to do with the technologies under development that have profound consequences for the emergence of materiality.

## 7.4 Population Ecology

Population Ecology arose in response to models of individual organizations that were adaptive to their changing environments (i.e., Resource Dependence theory). Drawing on concepts of population ecology and natural selection in biology, ecology theory proposes that there are so many kinds of organizations because organizations are largely inert to environmental changes due in large part to the fact that initial founding conditions produce imprints on the organization's structure. Thus, when the environment changes, organizations often cannot adapt and are out-competed (Hannan and Freeman, 1977). To understand why some organizations survive and others fail, ecology researchers look to population characteristics, resources, and founder-effects to understand success and failure rates over time. Such population-level processes may very well shape the development of new technologies within individual organizations. Ecology theory draws on a number of analytic conceptualizations to explain the process of environmental selection. Of the many, three of these insights are particularly useful in explaining how organizational characteristics influence technology development: imprinting, structural inertia, and niche width.

## 7.4.1 Imprinting

In a famous essay, Stinchcombe (1965) observed that organizations are often founded with endowments that allow them to accumulate the resources they need to survive. He argued that organizations which are founded at a particular time must construct their social systems with the resources available and in line with the historically given labor market so they can recruit skills and motivate workers. Consequently, the types of organizations that emerge within a given time period are imprinted with the social structure of that founding period. Specifically, imprinting refers to a process "whereby specific environmental characteristics get mapped onto an organization's structure and affect its development and life chances" (Carroll and Hannan, 2000: 205). The concept of imprinting helps to explain why organizations develop certain forms over others. As Aldrich and Fiol (1994) suggest, imprinting is not only about constraint, but opportunity as well, because social contexts also set the conditions that create "windows of opportunity" for new organizations to carve out a piece of the market.

The circumstances in which an organization finds itself during founding play a key role in imprinting the initial form of the organization and influencing later organizational change. Thus, when organizations are set on a particular course at the time of founding, changing direction from this course may be difficult. Therefore, as research suggests (Boeker, 1988; Stuart and Sorenson, 2003), early patterns of organizing that are developed in response to the environment may limit the range of future decisions an organization will make, even if alternative options seem desirable. Research on product development processes shows that organizations often develop structures and procedures for technology development that reflect conditions at the time of their founding, including historic industry conditions (Katila and Ahuja, 2002), patent laws (Chou and Shy, 1993), inter-organizational alliances (Eisenhardt and Schoonhoven, 1996), and project team structures (Allen, 1977). All of these characteristics imprinted onto the organization at the time of founding affect the way technology development occurs not only in the short run, but over time as well.

The technological frames of varying relevant social groups are conditioned by the social contexts in which its designers are embedded (Pinch and Trocco, 2002). From an agency-centered perspective, these social contexts can change quite rapidly because there are few structural factors holding them constant (Kline and Pinch, 1996). Within formal organizations, however, the organizational structures which carry the imprint of the time of founding serve to keep the context relatively stable. Thus, technological development within large organizations may differ substantially from more autonomous situations of development precisely because the elements that comprise a technological frame are conditioned by the organization's founding imprint. Rather than changing fluidly over time, the imprinting hypothesis suggests that the technological frames that guide designers' actions may be subject to homeostasis. One would therefore expect that the environmental characteristics that are imprinted on an organization will hold the technological frames of relevant social groups constant as the organization remains locked into practices and structures developed during its time of founding, despite the fact that new procedures may be available. Whereas evolutionary theories of technology development suggest that new processes of technological development will supplant the old (Nelson and Winter, 1982), the imprinting hypothesis demonstrates that an organization's ability to adopt such innovations is often determined by environmental characteristics and less prone to designers' choices than social-shaping theories suggest (e.g., Williams and Edge, 1996).

### 7.4.2 Structural inertia

In addition to imprinting forces, Stinchcombe (1965) observed that organizations were susceptible to certain "traditionalizing forces" subsequent to founding that preserved previously adopted organizational characteristics. He argued that in attempting to overcome their "liability of newness," organizations built up a stock of resources and processes that locked them into certain patterns. Building upon this insight, ecology theory has focused on how certain organizational forms develop structural inertia—or limitations on the ability of organizations to adapt (Hannan and Freeman, 1977, 1984). Generally, three interrelated processes lead to inertia: intricacy, opacity, and asperity. Intricacy refers to the number of steps in a cascade of organizational changes (Carroll and Hannan, 2000). The more things that need to be changed, the more difficult change will be. Opacity concerns the nature of changes that one cannot see. Organizations can never fully know how the environment will change, and so they are largely unable to react to changes that have already occurred fast enough to capitalize on them. Asperity refers to the severity or rigor of the culture in which the organization is embedded. Within a given environment, certain organizational forms are legitimate and others are not. The degree to which that environment is accepting of deviations from the norm affects an organization's ability to change. Overall, if inertial forces within an organization are strong, the possibilities of adaptation in response to the changing environment are limited and attempts at reorganization might very well decrease chances of survival (Hannan and Carroll, 1995).

Ecology theory holds that organizations engage in many processes that create their own structural inertia. Some of these internal factors are sunk costs in plants, equipment, and personnel, the dynamics of political coalitions, and the tendency for precedents to become normative standards. Other factors are external to organizations, including legal regulations, exchange relations with other organizations, and loss of legitimacy during an attempted change (Hannan and Freeman, 1984: 149). Thus, organizations use their initial endowments to instantiate various mechanisms that make it difficult for them to change. This is not to say that organizations are stagnant and unproductive. In fact, inertia often confers many advantages for organizations in that firms with well-established processes and entrenched relations with other members in the environment are often able to survive in ways that fledgling organizations cannot (Hannan and Freeman, 1977; Baum, 1996). Sorenson and Stuart's (2000) investigation of the ability of semiconductor and biotechnology companies to overcome structural inertia, for example, demonstrates that the competence to produce new innovations improves with age, but that such gains in organizational competence come at the price of an organization's ability to adapt to evolving environmental demands. In other words, the more an organization works on perfecting a certain process or procedure, the more blind it becomes to impending environmental changes and is less able to absorb those changes.

One of the key assumptions from SCOT's current agency-centered perspective is that technology designers have relative autonomy to change their designs. That is to say, if an independent designer discovers a new way to patch and channel different sounds into a synthesizer, he or she will be able to adopt a new set of processes or procedures to begin to develop the technology in a new direction (Pinch and Trocco, 2002). While this may be true for independent inventors, or technologists in small, adaptive companies, ecology theory highlights the fact that once established in large formal organizations, technological development processes may be locked in forward motion because of inertial tendencies (Dobers and Strannegård 2001). In SCOT terms, closure of a problem is often reached because the structural inertia of formal organizations precludes them from adopting new procedures and process that would lead technology development down new paths. In other words, due to the structural inertia inherent in organizational forms, the design of a new technology may stabilize because of an organization's inability to adopt new practices and procedures that would otherwise influence that technology's design. While many organizational influences produce more changes in technology than a designer might anticipate, an organization's structural inertia may very well inhibit a technology from changing as much as it would if its designers were free from organizational constraints.

### 7.4.3 Niche width

The concept of "niche" is central to Population Ecology. Borrowed from biology, a niche refers to "all those combinations of [environmental] resource levels at which the population can survive and reproduce itself" (Hannan and Freeman, 1977: 947). Hannan and Freeman (1989) further defined a niche as an "n-dimensional resource space," which includes social, economic, and political dimensions, to name a few. Each population occupies a distinct niche in which individual organizations compete for scarce resources. The success of a given population can be explained by the extent to which organizations utilize the resources in a given niche. As Hannan and Freeman (1977) argued, organizations make use of the niche width differently depending on whether they are specialist or generalist organizations. Where the specialist maximizes the exploitation of the environment and accepts the risk of having the environment change, the generalist accepts lower levels of exploitation in order to enhance their security. Within the conceptualization of the niche, resource-partitioning theory (Carroll, 1985) has been useful in explaining the rise of generalist and specialist organizations. The theory predicts that generalist organizations seek to increase returns to scale by fighting over the densest resource areas of the niche, while specialists that do not have scale advantage tend to locate themselves in areas where resources are thin, and thus remain small. Resource-partitioning theory's interpretative power comes from comparing the amount of resource space available for specialists when market concentration among generalists rises (Carroll and Hannan, 2000).

A well-explored area of niche width has focused on positioning and crowding of organizations in the resource space. Dobrev et al. (2002) found that larger automobile manufacturers who occupied dense resources areas at the center of a niche were more likely to survive than the many specialists in the early history of the industry who competed in thin resource spaces by attempting to produce more customized automobiles. In a related set of studies, identity figures prominently into the positions of generalists and specialists in a niche. In their study of American breweries, Carroll and Swaminathan (2000) found that generalists who identified as mass producers had difficulty gaining acceptance as they tried to enter the micro-brewery movement because their identities were firmly based upon their generalist image. The appeal of specialist organizations came precisely from their identity as non-corporate, craft-like producers using traditional brewing methods. Mass producers could not compete with this image. Such studies demonstrate that an organization's location in a niche (resource space) matters in terms of the organization's identity and chances of survival.

Clearly, an organization's position within a given niche affects the types of resources that are available to it as well as the types of goods and services it produces. Large companies tend to produce fewer breakthrough products than smaller companies (O'Reilly and Tushman, 2008) precisely because they occupy a more general position in the environment and are less likely to take risks that jeopardize their ability to stay in the mainstream. Further, as identity becomes bound up in an organization's location within a niche, as either a specialist or a generalist, such identity may very well impede an organization from developing new technologies that conflict with that identity. As Bijker (1995b) showed with the social construction of dikes in the Netherlands' Deltaplan, and Vaughan (1996) showed with the social construction of engineering solutions to risk analysis at NASA, an organization's identity has a major effect on the process of technology development by influencing an artifact's interpretative flexibility. Developers identify a technology within a given artifact based on their perception of its functionality in relation to their specific needs. Interpretative flexibility is based on the notion that the meaning of an artifact is attributed to it by groups with particular backgrounds that influence their conceptualization of the artifact (Pinch, 1996). Given that the position of an organization in a niche dramatically affects its access to resources, and in turn its identity, we would propose that the meanings designers attribute to the artifacts they create, and thus the interpretative flexibility that artifact has, is a product of that organization's location in the niche. Thus, the interpretative flexibility of an artifact will most likely be shaped by the degree to which an organization competes in the niche's mainstream or on its periphery, and whether that organization's identity is bound up with a specialist or generalist identity.

Overall, theories of Population Ecology instruct researchers of the social construction of technology to consider the fact that organizations cannot always actively adapt to environmental changes, but are instead often selected in spite of them. Such population-level changes can place limits on the way that materiality emerges within formal organizations. Building on such recognition, one strategy that students of the sociomaterial approach might take would be to expand their analyses to include entire populations of organizations when considering how materiality emerges. Certainly, population ecologists would argue that the systemic dynamics of a particular population of organizations is the result of social processes. Although they may use evolutionary imagery to make their arguments, population ecologists no doubt envision that variation in a population and ultimately selection and retention happen as the result of decisions made by organizational leadership about how to position themselves with respect to each other. These population-level dynamics can quickly cascade down to teams of technology developers who find themselves pushed and pulled in particular directions due to strategic decisions about image, identity, and hopeful paths toward survival that are made in response to population-level dynamics, not necessarily to optimize the design of any new technology. In short, any account of how the social and the material become intertwined must recognize that organizations are jostled about on waves they cannot always directly control and that the materiality of new technologies can emerge in their wake.

## 7.5 Conclusions

This chapter began by suggesting that students adopting a sociomaterial approach to technology and organizing should not put the cart before the horse. Before showing how the social and the material become constitutively entangled, or before simply showing that they are, researchers should examine how and why a technological artifact's materiality—the arrangement of a technological artifact's physical and/or digital materials into particular forms that endure across differences in place and time and are important to users—comes to be the way it is. Focusing on the emergence of materiality is important because, if we take seriously the notion that organizational practice is sociomaterial in nature, those features of a technology that pre-exist people's interactions with it have the potential to afford or constrain work practices and the organization of work (Leonardi and Barley, 2010). In short, understanding the emergence of materiality in the first place may help to explain why certain sociomaterial practices of use arise, and why others do not.

To make explicit what has been implicit throughout most of this chapter, I argue that organizational theorists should not rush to adopt the "sociomaterial" lens and begin to view everything seen through it as inherently sociomaterial. We can talk about sociomateriality on a conceptual plane only after we recognize that the social and the material have so thoroughly saturated each other on the empirical plane. In other words, what we see when we look through a lens of sociomateriality is that the materiality of an artifact emerged as it did, in large part, because of the social dynamics of the organizations in which it was developed and this very materiality which is so thoroughly social is the same that will become enmeshed with the social dynamics of the workplace into which it is introduced so as to render it conceptually "entangled" with local practice. Consequently, it is the process of sociomaterial entanglement, not the outcome of it, which deserves our research attention if our aim is to build interesting and useful theories of organizing.

This focus both shares in and departs from the current ontology of the sociomaterial approach. It shares in the belief that organizational theorists should consider the work practices of people within organizations as sociomaterial practices and that they should also consider organizing as a sociomaterial process. But it departs from contemporary views by suggesting that people working within organizations and who make organizing happen do not confront a world that they view as sociomaterial. Instead, they confront some phenomena that they understand to be social and they deal daily with the materiality of technological artifacts with which they work—most of which appear fixed, finite, and stabilized, not inherently social and utterly malleable. It is through the work that these actors conduct as they engage in their daily tasks that they turn the social and the material into the sociomaterial.

If one subscribes to this view, theorizing materiality itself before it comes in contact with the social contexts in which it is implemented and used becomes important. It becomes important because users react to a technology's materiality—a materiality they perceived as bounded and stable—when translating it from the realm of the artifactual into the realm of the social. All theory about the sociomaterial consequences of technology use, then, begs an understanding of what materiality users confront in their work. Yet as discussed in this chapter's opening, we know from nearly three decades of constructivist research on technology development that the same materiality that users confront as objective and stable was designed and fashioned through social processes. Consequently, any theory of sociomaterial practices of technology use must theorize materiality by understanding how and why it emerged as it did because it is those sociomaterial practices of technology development that will ultimately shape, at least in part, how the technology is used.

Although the social construction of technology approach may seem like one of the most promising candidates to aid in this quest by explaining the emergence of materiality, I have argued that we know little about how the social construction of a new technology's materiality takes place in formal organizational settings. Following the work of other researchers who have begun to push SCOT to consider social structural influences, I aimed, in this chapter, to draw on influential organization theories to explore how the micro-level interpretative flexibility of artifacts, the evolution and composition of the set of relevant social groups that contribute to the artifact's construction, the processes by which the materiality of an artifact reaches a point of stabilization and closure, and the structure of the technological frames shared by designers are influenced by macro-level organizational responses to the environment.

Using the insights of Resource Dependence and Population Ecology provided a useful basis for thinking about how SCOT's mechanisms may occur differently when technologies are developed in formal organizations than when they are developed by autonomous inventors who are largely free from organizational constraints. The resulting analysis proposed that although the many organization–environment interactions that occur in the context of formal organizing may be initiated or devised without new technology development specifically in mind, they can have the latent effect of altering the mechanisms through which a technology's materiality is shaped. Organizational scholars interested in adopting a sociomaterial lens should move beyond simple descriptions of entanglement to develop a deeper understanding of the processes of entanglement because it is these processes in which organizations themselves are so implicated.

To move in this direction, theorists interested in the sociomateriality of organizational practice may start to learn much more about the organizational influences on the emergence of materiality by continuing the theoretical exercise begun above with other theories that depict organizations as actively responding to their environments, such as New Institutionalism (DiMaggio and Powell, 1983; Tolbert and Zucker, 1999) and Transaction Cost Economics (Williamson, 1981, 1996), as well as theories, such as Evolutionary Theory (Nelson and Winter, 1982; Dosi and Nelson, 1994), which suggest that organizations are directly acted upon by their environments. Ultimately, however, empirical research is needed that examines the social construction of technology within organizational contexts. Such a perspective would complement existing research on technology innovation (von Hippel, 1988; Christensen, 1997; Hargadon and Douglas, 2001), which explores how organizational arrangements lead individuals to develop breakthrough ideas, and research on product development (Clark and Fujimoto, 1991; Brown and Eisenhardt, 1995; MacCormack et al., 2001), which examines the organizational structures that lead to efficient and robust inter-and intra-organizational collaborations, with a perspective that can explain how the material features of a new technology evolve over time and come to be taken for granted as the way the technology "has to be." Understanding organizational influences on the emergence of a particular form of materiality would thus help students of technology and organization to generate a more complete understanding about how the social and material features of organizational practice become constitutively entangled, and why some sociomaterial practices change the process of organizing, and others do not.

## Note

I would like to thank Steve Barley, Woody Powell, Glenn Carroll, Pablo Boczkowski, and Paul Carlile for each offering valuable comments on sections of this manuscript.

## References

Ahuja, G. (2000). "Collaboration Networks, Structural Holes, and Innovation: A Longitudinal Study," *Administrative Science Quarterly*, 45: 425–55.

Aldrich, H. E. and Fiol, C. M. (1994). "Fools Rush In? The Institutional Context of industry Creation," *Academy of Management Review*, 19/4: 645–70.

——and Pfeffer, J. (1976). "Environments of Organizations," *Annual Review of Sociology*, 2: 79–105.

Allen, T. J. (1977). *Managing the Flow of Technology*. Cambridge, MA: MIT Press.

Basalla, G. (1988). *The Evolution of Technology*. Cambridge: Cambridge University Press.

Baum, J. A. C. (1996). "Organizational Ecology," in S. R. Clegg, C. Hardy, and W. R. Nord (eds.), *Handbook of Organizational Studies*. London: Sage, pp. 77–114.

——Calabrese, T., and Silverman, B. S. (2000). "Don't Go It Alone: Alliance Network Composition and Startups' Performance in Canadian Biotechnology," *Strategic Management Journal*, 21: 267–97.

Berente, N., Baxter, R., and Lyytinen, K. (2010). "Dynamics of Inter-Organizational Knowledge Creation and Information Technology Use Across Object Worlds: The Case of an Innovative Construction Project," *Construction Management and Economics*, 28/6: 569–88.

Berg, M. (1998). "The Politics of Technology: On Bringing Social Theory into Technological Design," *Science, Technology, and Human Values*, 23/4: 456–90.

Bijker, W. E. (1987). "The Social Construction Of Bakelite: Toward a Theory of Invention," in W. E. Bijker, T. P. Hughes, and T. Pinch (eds.), *The Social Construction of Technological Systems: New Directions in the Sociology and History of Technology.* Cambridge, MA: MIT Press, pp. 159–87.

—— (1992). "The Social Construction of Fluorescent Lighting, Or How an Artifact was Invented in its Diffusion Stage," in W. E. Bijker and J. Law (eds.), *Shaping Technology/ Building Society: Studies in Sociotechnical Change.* Cambridge, MA: MIT Press, pp. 75–104.

—— (1995a). *Of Bicycles, Bakelites, and Bulbs: Toward a Theory of Sociotechnical Change.* Cambridge, MA: MIT Press.

—— (1995b). "Sociohistorical Technology Studies," in S. Jasanoff, G. E. Markle, J. C. Peterson, and T. Pinch (eds.), *The Handbook of Science and Technology Studies.* Thousand Oaks, CA: Sage, pp. 229–56.

—— and Pinch, T. J. (2002). "SCOT Answers, Other Questions," *Technology and Culture,* 43: 361–9.

Blau, P. M., Falbe, C. M., McKinley, W., and Tracy, P. K. (1976). "Technology and Organization in Manufacturing," *Administrative Science Quarterly,* 21/1: 20–40.

Boeker, W. P. (1988). "Organizational Origins: Entrepreneurial and Environmental Imprinting at the Time of Founding," in G. R. Carroll (ed.), *Ecological Models of Organizations.* Cambridge, MA: Ballinger, pp. 33–52.

Brown, S. L. and Eisenhardt, K. M. (1995). "Product Development: Past Research, Present Findings, and Future Directions," *Academy of Management Review,* 20/2: 343–78.

Carlson, W. B. (1992). "Artifacts and Frames of Meaning: Thomas A. Edison, His Managers, and the Cultural Construction of Motion Pictures," in W. E. Bijker and J. Law (eds.), *Shaping Technology/Building Society: Studies In Sociotechnical Change.* Cambridge, MA: MIT Press, pp. 175–98.

Carroll, G. R. (1985). "Concentration and Specialization: Dynamics of Niche Width in Populations of Organizations," *American Journal of Sociology,* 90: 1262–83.

—— and Hannan, M. T. (2000). *The Demography of Corporations and Industries.* Princeton: Princeton University Press.

—— and Swaminathan, A. (2000). "Why the Microbrewery Movement? Organizational Dynamics of Resource Partitioning in the U.S. Brewing Industry," *American Journal of Sociology,* 106/3: 715–62.

Chandler, A. D. (1977). *The Visible Hand: The Managerial Revolution in American Business.* Cambridge, MA: Harvard University Press.

Chou, C.-F. and Shy, O. (1993). "The Crowding-Out Effects of Long Duration Patents," *The RAND Journal of Economics,* 24/2: 304–12.

Christensen, C. M. (1997). *The Innovators' Dilemma: When New Technologies Cause Great Firms to Fail.* Boston: Harvard Business School Press.

Clark, K. B. and Fujimoto, T. (1991). *Product Development Performance.* Boston: Harvard Business School Press.

Dale, K. (2005). "Building a Social Materiality: Spatial and Embodied Politics in Organizational Control," *Organization,* 12/5: 649–78.

Davis, G. F. and Greve, H. R. (1997). "Corporate Elite Networks and Governance Changes in the 1980s," *American Journal of Sociology,* 103/1: 1–37.

Davis, L. E. and Taylor, J. C. (1976). "Technology, Organization and Job Structure," in R. Dubin (ed.), *Handbook of Work, Organization, and Society*. Stokie, IL: Rand-McNally, pp. 379–419.

DeSanctis, G., Glass, J. T., and Ensing, I. M. (2002). "Organizational Designs for R&D," *Academy of Management Executive*, 16/3: 55–66.

DiMaggio, P. J. and Powell, W. W. (1983). "The Iron Cage Revisited: Institutional Isomorphism and Collective Rationality in Organizational Fields," *American Sociological Review*, 48: 147–60.

Dobers, P. and Strannegård, L. (2001). "Loveable Networks: A Story of Affection, Attraction and Treachery," *Journal of Organizational Change Management*, 14/1: 28–49.

Dobrev, S. D., Kim, T.-Y., and Carroll, G. R. (2002). "The Evolution of Organizational Niches: U.S. Automobile Manufacturers, 1885–1981," *Administrative Science Quarterly*, 47: 233–64.

Dosi, G. and Nelson, R. R. (1994). "An Introduction to Evolutionary Theories in Economics," *Journal of Evolutionary Economics*, 4: 153–72.

Dyer, J. H. and Singh, H. (1998). "The Relational View: Cooperative Strategy and Sources of Interorganizational Competitive Advantage," *Academy of Management Review*, 23/4: 660–79.

Eisenhardt, K. M. and Schoonhoven, C. B. (1996). "Resource-Based View of Strategic Alliance Formation: Strategic and Social Effects in Entrepreneurial Firms," *Organization Science*, 17/2: 136–50.

Emerson, R. M. (1962). "Power-Dependence Relations," *American Sociological Review*, 27: 31–40.

Eppinger, S. D. and Chitkara, A. R. (2006). "The New Practice of Global Product Development," *MIT Sloan Management Review*, 47/4: 22–30.

Faulkner, P. and Runde, J. (2011). "The Social, the Material, and the Ontology of Non-material Technological Objects," paper presented at the European Group for Organizational Studies (EGOS) Colloquium, Gothenburg.

Garud, R. and Rappa, M. A. (1994). "A Socio-Cognitive Model of Technology Evolution: The Case of Cochlear Implants," *Organization Science*, 5/3: 344–62.

Hannan, M. T. and Carroll, G. R. (1995). "An Introduction to Organizational Ecology," in G. R. Carroll and M. T. Hannan (eds.), *Organizations in Industry: Strategy, Structure, and Selection*. New York: Oxford University Press, pp. 17–31.

——and Freeman, J. (1977). "The Population Ecology of Organizations," *American Journal of Sociology*, 82/5: 929–64.

——(1984). "Structural Inertia and Organizational Change," *American Sociological Review*, 49/2: 149–64.

——(1989). *Organizational Ecology*. Cambridge, MA: Harvard University Press.

Hargadon, A. B. and Douglas, Y. (2001). "When Innovations Meet Institutions: Edison and the Design of the Electric Light," *Administrative Science Quarterly*, 46: 476–501.

Hickson, D. J., Pugh, D. S., and Pheysey, D. C. (1969). "Operations Technology and Organizational Structure: An Empirical Reappraisal," *Administrative Science Quarterly*, 14/3: 378–97.

Hunt, R. G. (1970). "Technology and Organization," *Academy of Management Journal*, 13/3: 235–52.

Johri, A. (2011). "Sociomaterial Bricolage: The Creation of Location-Spanning Work Practices by Global Software Developers," *Information and Software Technology*, 53/9: 955–68.

Jonsson, K., Holmström, J., and Lyytinen, K. (2009). "Turn to the Material: Remote Diagnostics Systems and New Forms Of Boundary-Spanning," *Information and Organization*, 19/4:, 233–52.

Katila, R. and Ahuja, G. (2002). "Something Old, Something New: A Longitudinal Study of Search Behavior and New Product Introduction," *Academy of Management Journal*, 45/6: 1183–94.

Klein, H. K. and Kleinman, D. L. (2002). "The Social Construction of Technology: Structural Considerations," *Science, Technology, & Human Values*, 27/1: 28–52.

Kline, R. and Pinch, T. J. (1996). "Users as Agents of Technological Change: The Social Construction of the Automobile in the Rural United States," *Technology and Culture*, 37/4: 763–95.

Kranakis, E. (2004). "Fixing the Blame: Organizational Culture and the Quebec Bridge Collapse," *Technology and Culture*, 45/3: 487–518.

Kupperman, R. H. and Smith, H. A. (1970). "Optimal Scale of a Commodity Stockpile," *Management Science*, 16/11: 751–8.

Leonardi, P. M. (2009). "Crossing the Implementation Line: The Mutual Constitution of Technology and Organizing across Development and Use Activities," *Communication Theory*, 19: 278–310.

——(2011). "When Flexible Routines Meet Flexible Technologies: Affordance, Constraint, and the Imbrication of Human and Material Agencies," *MIS Quarterly*, 35/1: 147–67.

——and Bailey, D. E. (2008). "Transformational Technologies and the Creation of New Work Practices: Making Implicit Knowledge Explicit in Task-Based Offshoring," *MIS Quarterly*, 32: 411–36.

——and Barley, S. R. (2008). "Materiality and Change: Challenges to Building Better Theory about Technology and Organizing," *Information and Organization*, 18: 159–76.

——(2010). "What's Under Construction Here? Social Action, Materiality, and Power in Constructivist Studies of Technology and Organizing," *Academy of Management Annals*, 4: 1–51.

MacCormack, A., Verganti, R., and Iansiti, M. (2001). "Developing Products on 'Internet Time': The Autonomy of a Flexible Development Process," *Management Science*, 47/1: 133–50.

MacKenzie, D. (1996). *Knowing Machines: Essays on Technological Change*. Cambridge, MA: MIT Press.

Nelson, R. R. and Winter, S. G. (1982). *An Evolutionary Theory of Economic Change.* Cambridge, MA: Belknap Press.

O'Reilly, C. A. and Tushman, M. L. (2008). "Ambidexterity as a Dynamic Capability: Resolving the Innovator's Dilemma," *Research in Organizational Behavior*, 28: 185–206.

Orlikowski, W. J. (2000). "Using Technology and Constituting Structures: A Practice Lens for Studying Technology in Organizations," *Organization Science*, 11/4: 404–28.

—— (2007). "Sociomaterial Practices: Exploring Technology at Work," *Organization Studies*, 28/9: 1435–48.

—— (2010). "The Sociomateriality of Organisational Life: Considering Technology in Management Research," *Cambridge Journal of Economics*, 34: 125–41.

Osterlund, C. (2008). "The Materiality of Communicative Practices," *Scandinavian Journal of Information Systems*, 20/1: 7–40.

Pentland, B. T. and Feldman, M. S. (2007). "Narrative Networks: Patterns of Technology and Organization," *Organization Science*, 18/5: 781–95.

Perrow, C. (1970). *Organizational Analysis: A Sociological View.* Belmont, CA: Wadsworth.

Pfeffer, J. and Salancik, G. (1978). *The External Control of Organizations: A Resource Dependence Perspective.* New York: Harper & Row.

Pinch, T. J. (1996). "The Social Construction of Technology: A Review," in R. Fox (ed.), *Technological Change: Methods and Themes in the History of Technology.* Amsterdam: Harwood, pp. 17–35.

—— (2003). "Giving Birth to New Users: How the Minimoog Was Sold to Rock and Roll," in N. Oudshoorn and T. Pinch (eds.), *How Users Matter: The Co-Construction of Users and Technology.* Cambridge, MA: MIT Press, pp. 247–70.

—— (2008). "Technology and Institutions: Living in a Material World," *Theory and Society*, 37: 461–83.

—— (2010). "On Making Infrastructure Visible: Putting the Non-Humans to Rights," *Cambridge Journal of Economics*, 34/1: 77–89.

—— and Bijker, W. E. (1984). "The Social Construction of Facts and Artifacts: Or How the Sociology of Science and the Sociology of Technology Might Benefit Each Other," *Social Studies of Science*, 14: 399–441.

—— and Trocco, F. (2002). *Analog Days: The Invention and Impact of the Moog Synthesizer.* Cambridge, MA: Harvard University Press.

Robey, D. and Sahay, S. (1996). "Transforming Work through Information Technology: A Comparative Case Study of Geographic Information Systems in County Government," *Information Systems Research*, 7/1: 93–110.

Rosen, P. (1993). "The Social Construction Of Mountain Bikes: Technology and Postmodernity in the Cycle Industry," *Social Studies of Science*, 23/3: 479–513.

Rosenkopf, L. and Tushman, M. L. (1994). "The Coevolution of Technology and Organization," in J. A. C. Baum and J. Singh (eds.), *Evolutionary Dynamics of Organizations.* New York: Oxford University Press, pp. 403–24.

Santos, F. M. and Eisenhardt, K. M. (2009). "Constructing Markets and Shaping Boundaries: Entrepreneurial Power in Nascent Fields," *Academy of Management Journal*, 52/4: 643–71.

Sarasvathy, S. D. (2001). "Causation and Effectuation: Toward a Theoretical Shift from Economic Inevitability to Entrepreneurial Contingency," *Academy of Management Review*, 26/2: 243–63.

Scott, W. R. (1998). *Organizations: Rational, Natural, and Open Systems*, 4th edn. Upper Saddle River, NJ: Prentice Hall.

——(2004). "Reflections on a Half-Century of Organizational Sociology," *Annual Review of Sociology*, 30: 1–21.

Shane, S. (2000). "Prior Knowledge and the Discovery of Entrepreneurial Opportunities," *Organization Science*, 11/4: 448–69.

Sorenson, J. B. and Stuart, T. E. (2000). "Aging, Obsolescence, and Organizational Innovation," *Administrative Science Quarterly*, 45: 81–112.

Stinchcombe, A. L. (1965). "Social Structure and Organizations," in J. G. March (ed.), *Handbook of Organizations*. Chicago: Rand McNally, pp. 142–93.

Stuart, T. E. and Sorenson, O. (2003). "Liquidity Events and the Geographic Distribution of Entrepreneurial Activity," *Administrative Science Quarterly*, 48: 175–201.

Suchman, L. (2000). "Embodied Practices of Engineering Work," *Mind, Culture, and Activity*, 7/1 & 2: 4–18.

Svahn, F., Henfridsson, O., and Yoo, Y. (2009). "A Threesome Dance of Agency: Mangling the Sociomateriality of Technological Regimes in Digital Innovation," *Proceedings of the International Conference on Information Systems, 2009*, available at http://aisel.aisnet.org/icis2009/2005.

Thomas, R. J. (1994). *What Machines Can't Do: Politics and Technology in the Industrial Enterprise*. Berkeley: University of California Press.

Thompson, J. D. (1967). *Organizations in Action: Social Science Bases of Administrative Theory*. New York: McGraw-Hill.

Tolbert, P. S. and Zucker, L. G. (1999). "The Institutionalization of Institutional Theory," in S. R. Clegg and C. C. Hardy (eds.), *Studying Organization: Theory and Method*. London: Sage, pp. 169–84.

Tushman, M. L. and Anderson, P. (1986). "Technological Discontinuities and Organizational Environments," *Administrative Science Quarterly*, 31: 439–65.

Van de Ven, A. H. (1986). "Central Problems in the Management of Innovation," *Management Science*, 32/5: 590–607.

Vaughan, D. (1996). *The Challenger Launch Decision: Risky Technology, Culture, and Deviance at NASA*. Chicago: University of Chicago Press.

——(1999). "The Role of the Organization in the Production of Techno-Scientific Knowledge," *Social Studies of Science*, 29/6: 913–43.

von Hippel, E. (1988). *The Sources of Innovation*. New York: Oxford University Press.

Wagner, E. L., Newell, S., and Piccolo, G. (2010). "Understanding Project Survival in an ES Environment: A Sociomaterial Practice Perspective," *Journal of the Association for Information Systems*, 11/5:, 276–97.

Williams, R. and Edge, D. (1996). "The Social Shaping of Technology," *Research Policy*, 25: 865–99.

Williamson, O. E. (1981). "The Economics of Organization: The Transaction Cost Approach," *American Journal of Sociology*, 87: 548–77.

—— (1996). *The Mechanisms of Governance*. Oxford: Oxford University Press.

Zack, M. H. and McKenney, J. L. (1995). "Social Context and Interaction in Ongoing Computer-Supported Management Groups," *Organization Science*, 6/4: 394–422.

**8**

# Reclaiming Things: An Archaeology of Matter

*Bjørnar Olsen*

**Abstract:** Late twentieth-century social and cultural research was heavily impacted by what became known as the linguistic or textual turn. Well into a new millennium we have for some time now with equal conviction and enthusiasm been told about another twist: the (re)turn to things. This chapter critically examines this repatriation campaign and discusses some of the causes for the previous neglect of things in the social sciences. The main objective, however, is to explore some key aspects of what things are in their own material constituency and how these essential thing affordances are crucial for understanding social stability and change.

Things are back! After a century of oblivion, and after decades of linguistic and textual turns, there is now much buzz in social and cultural research about a material twist: a (re)turn to things. The fascination with Saussure, Derrida, and discourse has diminished; matter has replaced symbols; discourse is substituted with flesh, also reported as the "return of the real" (Foster, 1996). In all kinds of studies, ranging from political science to English literature, things, objects, and materiality now figure prominently on the agenda. As summarized by historian Frank Trentmann, "[a]fter the turn to discourse and signs in the late twentieth century, there is a new fascination with the material stuff of life" (Trentmann, 2009: 283).

And to the extent that we should believe what we are told (though, as we shall see there may be some well-qualified doubts), it was about time. Looking at the innumerable analyses of society and culture conducted during the last century things were mostly conspicuous by their very absence. If anything they were the objects of aloofness and ridicule. As technology they were too dangerous, false, and inhuman; as everyday artifacts they were too trivial, dusty, and epiphenomenal to contribute in any meaningful way to the fields and issues which held the social scientists' concern—cultural processes, social institutions, human intentions and actions. Thus, despite their inevitable and indispensable presence, things were largely ignored or confined to the margins when the "real" spectacles of life were accounted for in cultural narratives or sociological analyses. On the main social scene they might provide a context, a setting, but were otherwise denied any purpose or agency. Ironically, as remarked by philosopher Michel Serres, while things were seen as being diagnostic of humanity ("Humanity begins with things; animals do not have things"), they played no role in the study of this humanity. Thus "in the current state of affairs the so-called human or social sciences seem best to apply only to animals" (Serres and Latour, 1995: 165–6, 199–200).

In this chapter I shall start off by discussing some possible causes of this amnesia. Why were things of such little concern to social scientists? Why did things, with a few exceptions, play hardly any role in the conceptions of society and social processes envisioned by these practitioners? It is, however, equally important to scrutinize the recent claims of things' return to the sociocultural fields. Is it really the thing in itself that has returned and which now is claimed to set a new agenda in the social sciences and elsewhere? In the second part of the chapter, I shall first explore some key aspects of what things are in their own constituency as things, before finally developing some arguments about how such essentials of matter may be helpful when addressing basic questions of stability and change. However, before I embark on this journey I find it pertinent to say something about the role of my own discipline, archaeology, whose presence in this volume may come as a slight surprise.

## 8.1 Archaeology: the discipline of things

While "archaeology" became a popular if obligation-free catchword during the textual regime, and was liberally used by philosophers, literary critics, and psychologists in need of something sufficiently metaphorically material to buttress their abstract conceptions with, the name of this brand has paradoxically almost completely vanished from view when in fact there is a material turn. Despite its persistent commitment to things, archaeology for some reason seems more or less irrelevant for those who now eagerly claim to have returned to what has always been our prime subject matter.[1] To name but one example, the 1,072 pages of Bruno Latour and Peter Weibel's

*Making Things Public* (2005) contain the work of anthropologists, art historians, artists, architects, designers, engineers, legal historians, museum curators, philosophers, psychologists, sociologists of science and technology, and even English professors, linguists, and political theorists; but no archaeologists. Not one! And this despite the fact that no other discipline has done more to make things public.

Why it is that archaeology—the discipline of things par excellence—is considered irrelevant to a discussion of things? One likely suggestion may be that archaeology deals with the distant past; its devotedness to bygone eras and moss-covered or dusty ruins renders it irrelevant, given the social sciences' concern with the modern and the "now." Against this persistent image it is probably futile, even seemingly anachronistic, to lecture how archaeology's extensive list of topics include modern beer consumption (Rathje and McCarthy, 1977; Rathje, 1984), transistor radios and electricity (Schiffer, 1991, 2008), late twentieth-century Soviet mining towns (Andreassen et al., 2010), and lunar and planetary relics of space exploration (Capelotti, 2010).

There are, however, some other issues with archaeology that may explain the unease with which it is conceived in mainstream social sciences and humanities. Doing archaeology usually brings to mind the "down and dirty" of fieldwork. On the one hand, such activities and practices are seen as slightly childish and even embarrassing (grown-up people digging in the sand), always triggering a smile or a joke. Our explorations and "discoveries" may be well suited for television formats such as *Time Team* and programs on the Discovery or National Geographic channels, and thus for popular consumption, but not for the discourses and intellectual issues with which social sciences wrestle. On the other hand, there is an element of blue-collar savagery associated with archaeological toil. Archaeologists dig ruins, sort through what our forebears regarded as trash, we handle dead bodies, and this craft (cf. Shanks and McGuire, 1996), involving direct and tough engagements with soil and rocks, working outdoors and getting dirty and weather-beaten, does not comply well with the dominant image of intellectual work. Taking into account the long-held bourgeois contempt in academia (especially in the humanities) for dirt, manual labor, and working-class life in general, it may not come as a big surprise that the craft of archaeology, and its repugnant trivia, is not considered too appropriate. This otherness, this disciplinary savagery, has also made archaeology difficult to locate within the academic landscape, a humanist discipline enmeshed with an array of instruments, methods, and practices always unfolding in close collaboration with the natural sciences (Olsen, 2010; Olsen et al., 2012).

Moreover, the archaeological objects are often bulky, fragmented, or broken; more often than not they don't stimulate aesthetic pleasure. Archaeological material comes in enormous quantities, filling up storage rooms, museum cellars, and labs. On a more general level one may speculate how these messy things, often refusing to be labeled and identified, comply with the wished-for return of objects. Things may be welcomed back, but they had better be clean, whole, and preferably discursive or photographed; and not so many and chaotic, please, and at least be easy to label (see also Hahn, 2011). As I will discuss below, these preferences may well have excluded more than dug-up objects from being permitted entry into the supposedly new, thing-friendly environment.

## 8.2 Why things were forgotten

However, before scrutinizing the now so celebrated return to things, let us look at the reasons for their previous exclusion. In our everyday routines things are mostly encountered in a mode of inconspicuous familiarity. The things we constantly engage with—the office chair, doors, the car key, the fridge, light switches, walls—all withdraw from our conscious concern. Unless broken, interrupted, or missing, such common things mostly escape our attention; they are black-boxed in their very effective ready-to-hand-ness, being at the same time "the most obvious and the best hidden" (Lefebvre, 1987: 9). This everyday shyness, however, hardly suffices to explain why they have escaped the attention of scholars. In order to understand the exclusion of things from twentieth-century social research it is necessary to dig into the foundation of modern thinking, and even into the very political economy of this thinking (Olsen, 2007, 2010; Olsen et al., 2012). Such excavations have exposed a persistent and effective historical layer of thing oblivion and displacement in Western thinking that started to form in the seventeenth century.

Included in these massive deposits left by rationalist and Enlightenment philosophers was a notion of matter as passive and inert, while the human mind was seen as active and creative. Matter and nature had no necessary immanent existence; actually, they might just prove to be an ethereal construction in our head. And if not unreal, matter was still mere surface without any powers or potential; all qualities and ideas about it had to be located in the thinking subject (cf. Matthews, 2002: 8–9, 24–6; Thomas,

2004). While sobering this skeptical attitude somewhat, Immanuel Kant's critical philosophy actually contributed more than any other to ontologize this dependency by making our experience of things an a priori product of human thought. The thing-in-itself, Kant asserted, cannot be encountered face-to-face so to speak; we can only experience it in the way it is formed by ourselves, that is, by our own thinking or reason. Kant's derivative metaphysics also made things' being solely a matter of human concern (Harman, 2002: 279, 2010).

The outcome of this philosophical legacy was that the things-in-themselves were largely out of reach. They were shut out from our immediate experience, and thus dispelled from the knowable world. It was only in their abstracted condition as objects of science that they still could be admitted (Andersson, 2001: 130). Moreover, creative engagement with the world became an asymmetrical enterprise leaving no role for the qualities and competences that could be said to already *dwell* in materials and nature, and which humans in turn helped to release or make manifest in an act of co-production. Creativity, influence, and power became the current rare commodities which only humans-in-themselves possess. Thus, the birth of man as the creative commander-in-chief brought about the simultaneous death of a lived, living, and purposeful material world (Latour, 1993; Andersson, 2001; Thomas, 2004).

A short century after Kant, things' ontological displacement was supported by perhaps an even more powerful moral and ethical denouncement. Standing trial were the swaggering representatives of things—technology and the mass-produced object. To most philosophers and social theorists from the late nineteenth century onwards consumer goods, machines, cold and inhuman technologies, became the very incarnation of our inauthentic, estranged and alienated modern being (Heidegger, 1993; Young, 2002) (Figure 8.1). Things were dangerous in their deceptive appearance; they were a threat to genuine human and social values. They were signs of an illusory world that simultaneously produced a powerful and persistent definition of freedom and emancipation as that which escapes the material (Latour, 1993: 137–8, 2002). The denouncement was surprisingly shared across otherwise very different theoretical and political positions (Olsen, 2010: 90–4). Marxism, for example, despite its conceptual alter-ego of (historical) materialism and the immense importance it assigned to things and technology as potentially revolutionary forces of production, also came to fuel the aversion for things in modern social theory (cf. Kopytoff, 1986: 84–5). Though intended as more of a critique of how things lost their social value and human involvement in the capitalist mode of production, Marxism ended up providing social theory with

**Figure 8.1** Mass-produced, cold and inhuman: Rows of finished jeeps at the Willys-Overland facility in Toledo, Ohio, June 1, 1942 (photo: Dmitri Kessel/Getty Images # 50598573)

the very vocabulary—*objectification, reification, instrumental reason*—that strongly contributed to their stigmatization. Through these metaphors, things became symbols of the destructive and humiliating physicalism of modern society, providing their social dismissal with a powerful moral justification, and paradoxically, contributing to the current self-evidently negative connotations of "materialism." Much as a consequence, as pertinently observed by Daniel Miller, most later critics of mass culture and technology have tended "to assume that the relation of persons to objects is in some way vicarious, fetishistic or wrong; that primary concern should lie with direct social relations and 'real people'" (1987: 11).

Whether intentional or not, things thus ended up being featured in the villain role as humanism's other, which at the same time gave their relegation from the disciplines studying genuine social and cultural practices a powerful moral justification (Olsen, 2003). It is therefore no wonder that during the twentieth century to study "just things" became a source of embarrassment (Olsen et al., 2012). Any attempt to address the things-in-themselves, any care for their material properties, was at best a reactionary heir of mindless antiquarianism, at worst, a pathological condition reflecting a fetishistic addiction to substances beyond the limits of experience.

## 8.3 Are things back?

According to the prevailing romantic plot this has all luckily changed. Things have been brought back from the cold and have surfaced as a new concern within a number of fields, well captured in the new slogan, "a (re)turn to things." Coming from a discipline where the study of things for the last 170 years or so has been close to a categorical imperative, this is of course great news. Indeed one gets deeply impressed, even slightly moved, by witnessing how disciplines and practitioners that not so long ago showed little more than disinterest, even distaste, for the object, now treat it with such obvious care and concern. Mindful of their previous exclusion, and tribal songs apart, we should ask: is it really the things themselves that have returned? Is it the things themselves that ground this new agenda in the social sciences? Or is it rather an appropriated and disguised version, or a counterfeit, that attracts crowds of followers? In other words, was it only when things became so deprived of their thingly content, made so socially *Heimlich*, so fluffy, fluid, quasi, and networked, that they were allowed into the academic warmth? In addressing these questions, a couple of influential stages and positions for this return will briefly be examined.

One such stage is consumption studies, as practiced especially in anthropology and sociology. In many ways, consumption studies was instrumental in making the object a matter of concern outside the traditional "thing disciplines" (archaeology, folklore, ethnology) (cf. Appadurai, 1986; Miller, 1987, 1998, 2005; Dant, 1999; Attfield, 2000; Mullins, 2004). As part of a grounding concern with how artifacts, primarily consumer goods, are actively used in social and individual self-creation, the major theoretical punchline of these studies may be labeled "objectification" or "embodiment"; the idea that social relations are externalized and made concrete and visible by being objectified or embodied in matter. Through such processes of embodiment people establish some kind of "quasi-social" relationship with objects in order to live out their abstract social relationships in a "real" material form (Dant, 1999: 2).

Despite the concept's immense popularity, it is rarely debated what the notion of embodiment—as an act, a doing—actually implies in ontological terms (cf. Olsen, 2003, 2007). Considering the confidence with which it is used, it seems to imply something a priori given or revealed about

177

human–thing relationships, rather than a way of thinking about these relationships (see Rowlands, 2005). Running counter to the conception of human–thing entanglements as a "thrown" condition (in Heidegger's existential sense), embodiment as it is widely used seems to presuppose an initial rift, by implicitly suggesting that things, bodies, and nature are not originally part of the social, but may eventually be included and endowed with history and meaning through human generosity. For example, in his introduction to what is often referred to as a major break-through in the "social" study of things, *The Social Life of Things*, Arjun Appadurai asserts that "our own approach to things is *conditioned necessarily* by the view that things have no meanings apart from those that human transactions, attributions, and motivations endow them with" (Appadurai, 1986: 5, emphasis added). Without human intervention, that is, as beings beyond or outside our cognition, things and the world are intrinsically meaningless; qualities and ideas about them are all to be located in the thinking subject. One consequence is that things' difference vanishes from view, their own voices are silenced, making their fate "always to live out the social life of men" (Pinney, 2005: 259). Appadurai's imperative is indicative of the rather paradoxical situation that the ontology responsible for the displacement of things at least to some extent also came to ground central programs of repatriation.

Interestingly, this is actually a major point of criticism raised by spokes-men of a competing candidate to the "return-to-things" commendation medal: science studies and its chief method/theory, actor-network-theory (ANT). As noted by Bruno Latour, to say that social relations are objectified in things, "such that when we are confronted with an artifact we are confronted, in effect, with social relations, is to assert a tautology, and a very implausible one at that" (Latour, 1999: 197). Both the primacy of the social and the social/material split seems to be taken for granted. However, as he insists:

> if religion, art and styles are necessary to "reflect," "reify," "materialize," "embody" society—to use some of the social theorists' favorite verbs—then are objects, not, in the end, its co-producers? Is not society built literally—not metaphorically—of gods, machines, sciences, arts and styles?...Maybe social scientists have simply forgotten that before projecting itself on to things society has to be made, built, constructed? And out of what material could it be built if not out of nonsocial, nonhuman resources? (Latour, 1993: 54)

Probably more than any other program, science studies and ANT have contributed to the rehabilitation of things in the social sciences (Latour,

1987, 1993, 1999, 2005; Callon and Law, 1997; Law and Hassard, 1999; Law and Mol, 2002). Addressing the fallacies of the oversocialized conception of society, they have had immense success in articulating how society should be conceived of rather as a complex fabric of intimate relations between people and things. In short, humans and things/non-humans are not defined by oppositions, by dualities or negativities, but by a constant exchange and mixing of energy, properties, and competences.

So far, so good. However, John Law—another prominent advocate—also tells us that ANT can be understood as "a semiotics of materiality. It takes the semiotic insight, that of the relationality of entities, the notion that they are produced in relations, and applies this ruthlessly to all materials— and not simply to those that are linguistic" (Law, 1999: 4). Despite a yearned-for correction by Latour (2005: 153), the view that "entities are produced in relations" is strong among those adhering to ANT. To be sure, things clearly do attain their relative importance through their position within systems of relations and entanglements. A petrol station is utterly marginalized without roads, cars, pipelines, oil wells, petroleum plants, oil fields, and so on. A hammer without nails, hands, and planks would be rather useless (Hodder, 2011). The question to be asked, however, is whether the identity and significance of things are appropriately grasped through such an exclusively relational stance? Or may something rather crucial about things' being actually be lost if the principles of semiotics (and relational theories at large) are "ruthlessly" applied to them? (Harman, 2002; Olsen, 2010).

While a word can be replaced by any other word as long as it retains a consistent meaning and is different from the rest, things have intrinsic qualities that seriously restrict their exchangeability. A kayak cannot be replaced by an ax, a burin with a hammer stone, or a computer with a piano, simply because they have competences or affordances that cannot be replaced as if they were just any other "empty" signifiers. In other words, despite being enrolled to serve in a network and achieving a large part of their meaning from it, "the elements of the world do retain individual integrity" (Harman, 2002: 294). They are important because each of them makes a difference, not in a negative manner for the sake of the difference itself, as in Saussurian semiotics (and poststructuralism), but because of the *positive* difference they make due to their irreplaceable uniqueness. The "weaving together of difference" that is considered constitutive of collective action (Latour, 2005: 74), depends as much on these individual and immanent qualities as on the relational web. Subjecting things to words and language has always been the preferred intellectual taming device to

179

cope with the objects' disquieting material obstinacy (cf. Barthes, 1977: 40; Simmel, 1978: 474). Making things perform like words, enslaving them in semiotic webs of relations, is another but more serious expression of this encroachment.

As this short exposition illustrates, things may be conspicuously present in current discourses and theories but in a mode heavily conditioned by the effective histories of those not-so-thing-friendly philosophies. So, the object may have returned, but it is an object that often complies surprisingly well with the expectations of previous programs, not in the least with social constructivist thought (cf. Hahn, 2011). In other words, everything solid is still melting into the air. We see this in the popularity of all kinds of "matter-in-flux" approaches where things, objects, materials, are never allowed to be hard, stable, lasting, or in place. Things are always blurred, unstable, porous, scattered and mobile, always in flow. And it also complies well with the current dominant and morally loaded intellectual hierarchy, where change, dynamics, flow, is at top and persistency, solidity, and in-placeness are always at the bottom. According to this regime, there are no intrinsic values or essences (everything is produced in relations, is hybridized or "quasi"), no secure centers, and of course stability is reactionary and out of the question.

Such norms and hierarchies may also have affected the conception of the wished-for objects of return. Just give it a thought, what kinds of things are allowed into the warmth of the social sciences? What things are spoken and written about? Are hay rackets back? Have log houses, fireplaces, and spindle back chairs become matters of concern? And what about door knobs, refrigerators, and bunk beds? They may of course be present but leafing through some of the latest volumes and journal issues carrying the concepts of matter, materiality, things, and objects on their front covers, rather suggests that what we are witnessing is a somewhat conditioned and selective return. At least these trivial artifacts, broken things and dusty museum objects are not quite in the same league as Boyle's air pump, the body, Second Life, prostheses, Henry James's novels *about* things, and intelligent design. For example, when substantiating his claim that "things are back," and that there is "new fascination for the material stuff of life," Frank Trentmann provides a seemingly extensive list of stuff which:

> range from Jane Campion's film *The Piano* (1993), biographies of objects, and exhibitions in the Fifth Berlin Biennial for Contemporary Art, "When Things Cast No Shadow" (2008), all the way to public debates about the transformation of human flesh and mind in an age of nanotechnology, cloning, and cyborgs. (Trentmann, 2009: 283).

Leaving to one side what any archaeologist could have informed him, namely that the "age of the cyborg" started some 1.5 millions years ago (and thus that we "always have been cyborgs," see Olsen et al., 2012), the selected "items" in Trentmann's list are actually quite telling: film, biographies, art exhibitions, human flesh (and mind), nanotechnology, cloning. There may be an obvious fascination with things but not just any thing. And as we have seen, the conditional restrictions of their return are not only reflected in which things are allowed back but also in which mode they are allowed to be.

## 8.4 In defense of all things solid, durable, and in place

Our everyday perception of things is intimately related to those potential actions—and reactions—created by the contacts, interfaces, and spaces between bodies and things. As noted by Henri Bergson, things act on us, they "indicate at each moment, like a compass that is being moved about, the position of a certain image, my body, in relation to the surrounding images" (Bergson 2004: 10). This enmeshment produces a material habitual competence and spatial knowledge, a "knowing-your-way-around-some-where" (Casey, 1984: 283). This competence is a knowledge for "how to go on" in a landscape, a city, or a house. Our active cohabitation with things regulates and routinizes our behavior, making it repetitive and recognizable; we repeat certain actions through habits, by bodily skills instructed and impelled by the things themselves: "Our daily life is spent among objects whose very presence invites us to play a part" (Bergson, 2004:113). Through our interchange with things, our habits and actions become standardized and predictable, producing what we like to think of as (social) structures and institutions (Durkheim, 1951: 313–14, Arendt, 1958: 137). In his characteristically vivid and uncompromising way, Michel Serres has captured the crucial roles things play in this exchange:

> The only assignable difference between animal societies and our own resides, as I have often said, in the emergence of the object. Our relationships, social bonds would have been airy as clouds were there only contracts between subjects. In fact, the object, specific to the Hominidae, stabilizes our relationships, it slows down the time of our revolutions. For an unstable band of baboons, social changes are flaring up every minute... The object, for us, makes history slow. (Serres, 1995: 87; cf. Latour, 2005: 69–70)

As Bergson also asserted, herein lies the potential for a different kind of memory, a habit memory not related to mental representations and conscious recalling but as an outcome of habitual schemes of bodily practices. In contrast to cognitive or "recollective" memory, which involves a conscious gaze at a particular past, habit memory is a bodily memory preserved by repetitious practice. The past continues by being relived in our routines and ways of dealing with things so that "it no longer represents our past to us, it *acts* it" (Bergson, 2004:93, emphasis original). Not least important is the existential security that emerges from this memory. As pertinently observed by Maurice Merleau-Ponty:

> If the past were available to us only in the form of express recollections, we should be continually tempted to recall it in order to verify its existence; and thus resemble the patient mentioned by Scheler, who was constantly turning round in order to reassure himself that things were really there—whereas in fact we feel it behind us as an incontestable acquisition. (Merleau-Ponty, 1962: 418–19)

The past endures, it accumulates in every corner and crevasse of existence becoming "now," making these presents chronological hybrids by definition and thus objecting to the common conception of time (and history) as the succession of instants. The past is made manifest as duration—as sediments constantly piling up (and gradually eroding): "Duration is the continuous progress of the past which gnaws into the future and which swells as it advances" (Bergson, 1998: 4). This layering of the past in the present is hardly conceivable without those durable qualities of things. Habit memory is thus also *material memory*; the past is made manifest, "stored up," through presences and practices. To live with this past, and to enact the habit memory it facilitates, is an inescapable part of our existence shared by all people throughout history.

Being a matrix of habitual action, the body is clearly decisive for habit memory. However, it cannot be reduced to a human corporal capacity. Habitual action would generally be very difficult or even impossible without things and their facilitating capacities and arrangements. Just try the experiment of remembering how to bike without a bicycle—or to remember your bodily skill as a pianist without a piano (cf. Merleau-Ponty, 1962: 145–7). Things are fundamentally involved, not only as a means for the action to be completed, but also in making the action and material experience familiar, repetitious, and predictable. By their very design, physiognomy, and operational affordances things assign or "instruct" bodily behavior; they require certain formalized skills to actualize *their* competences.

**Figure 8.2** Not all that is solid melts into air. Persistent past at Walltown Crags (Hadrian's Wall), Northumberland (photo: Alfredo González-Ruibal)

Crucial to things' mnemonic capacity is their persistency. The enduring past is anchored in the ever-accumulating bedrock of materials, in artifacts, streets, and monuments, and in architecture—what Benjamin called "the most binding part of the communal rhythm" (1996: 418). Thus, contrary to actions, performances, and speech, which only occur as temporary or situational presences, things *last* (cf. Olivier, 2001: 65). There are, of course, enormous differences in their duration. Nonetheless, the still present past cannot be accounted for without the lasting and gathering quality of things. Due to their persistency, the (past) material world is always directed ahead of itself into our present and future (Figure 8.2).

As long as things last they are also in place; at least enough of them to make our existence predictable and secure. When we wake up tomorrow, the bed, room, and house are still there and in place. So too are our private belongings, other houses, the streets, wires, and pipelines that connect them. Buses and cars, the shops and factories, the fences and gardens, the mountains and trees, are all there and constitute the incontestable acquisition of our shared life world. We do not expect to—nor do we—wake up to a completely new world every morning, where we have to start all over again

183

from scratch. Quite the contrary, as we expect, things are overwhelmingly *there*; they are *in place* and they manifest themselves to us as familiar, as known. In short, they are the real *Dasein*. Being in place, of course, does not imply or necessitate their immobility. To the contrary, being in place suggests that they appear where we expect them to be. The seal-hunting gear, the strike-a-light, the lasso, the yurt, the snowmobile, and the iPhone are all within reach.

This "belonging somewhere" is part of our circumspective dealings with things: we expect them to be within our "region" (Heidegger, 1962: 136–7). And again, this region is not isomorphic with the catchment area of the rural *Heimat* ridiculed by globalization theorists and cybernomads. Familiarity and situatedness are as much an a priori of the supermodern "non-places" (Augé, 1995), as of a medieval farmhouse or Sámi reindeer camp. The existential importance of this entire field of ready-to-handness, of being-in-place, becomes evident in those cases where it is disturbed or lost. It is well known how dramatic changes in the thing environment, by war or environmental catastrophe, have traumatic consequences. Losing your belongings, your home, your city or farm or hunting ground creates a loss that cannot be so easily reconciled mentally or physically. Everyone that has experienced such traumas can confirm how the existential and mnemonic importance of things lost suddenly becomes manifest (cf. Parkin, 1999: 214–15; Naum, 2008: 278–80).

Throughout human history, this reassurance of stability as the normal state of things can hardly be overstated. Even if far from being exhaustive of their qualities or equally true for all things, solidity and persistency are properties of tools, walls, rooms, houses, streets, towns, mountains, and so forth that make a vital difference to human life. Thus, despite the unquestionable variation among things, I will claim durability and "in-placeness" as their most important socioculturally constitutive qualities. This lasting quality of "being there, being operational" affords security and prediction (Gaver, 1996: 119; cf. Norman, 1988), and is probably also the primary "existential affordance" of things. This trusted durability, which also includes a "holding-in-readiness" for future (inter)actions and reenactments, also allows for another intimately related effect: the gathering or sedimentation of the past. As we shall see, this gathering itself allows for processes and outcomes that, to some extent at least, are unpredictable and subsumed to material trajectories that create their own statements of crucial significance for how the past is conceived and reenacted.

## 8.5 Sticky heritage and the material legacy of the past

As I have argued above, the materially effective past that "swells in our midst" facilitates society with the necessary firming pillar and bolts that prevent our social bonds from being "airy as clouds" (see also Olsen, 2010). However, the fact that these firming things arrest action and "slow down the time of our revolutions," to borrow another of Serres' formulations, clearly has a preservative function and this leveling of instability, of "noise," in sociopolitical terms may be also seen as reactionary and even suppressive. There is an explicit, even banal, and thus effective, aspect of this "slowing down"—although not exhaustive of its operation. The very scale, durability, and mass of a society's material reinforcement, in other words, of the things mobilized and assembled to make society work and stay together, provide at least one key to explain its historical trajectory. Moreover, I would argue that this provides a crucial key to account for the impression that the past weighs heavier on some societies than others. The stone, iron, and concrete used in the massive construction of some past and present empires left a thick and sticky heritage of materials that to some extent, at least, explains their continuous, effective history.

Consider the material legacy of the former Soviet empire. Over the last 15 years, fieldwork has frequently brought me to the Russian far north, involving encounters with metropolises, regional centers, villages, military bases, and various other contemporary sites and settlements. The impression you get from these sites, in addition to their often conspicuous decay and decline, is not so much a feeling of abandonment as that of "offlineness," postponement and waiting reserve, a feeling not least triggered by a persistent material signature of "sovietness." This signature is easily recognized by the settlements' repetitive spatial rigidity, surviving monuments, communist iconography and art, concrete architecture and iron installations. An astonishing example is provided by research conducted in the abandoned Soviet mining town of Pyramiden in the High Arctic archipelago of Svalbard (Andreassen et al., 2010).

Pyramiden was brought to an utter standstill in 1998 and little seemed changed when we arrived to do fieldwork eight years later. Buildings, gangways, monuments, piers, and various mining facilities gave a petrified face to Soviet ambitions in the High Arctic. Apartments, offices, workshops, mess halls, bars, school, hospital, etc., were all left there with most of their things in place. Things' abundant presence triggered a feeling of something postponed rather than deserted; in fact, they perpetuated the tension of a "double" postponement. Despite the seven years of post-communist existence prior to its abandonment, little of the Soviet era seemed to have ended at Pyramiden. The façade of the town was still imbued with the regime's iconic affordances bringing to mind, though not unconditionally, what Svetlana Boym has described as a "theme park of lost illusions" (2001: xiii; see also Andreassen et al., 2010: 152–5) (Figure 8.3). In the director's office of the administration building Lenin's collected works were still on the shelf.

Thus, already before its abandonment Pyramiden was postponed and out of time with conventional historical chronology, surviving as a Soviet town in a post-Soviet era (Andreassen et al., 2010: 152–5). The regime's effective and distributed extensions and constituents were, to borrow Bergson's term, "gnawing" into its future. As witnessed also in current settlements all over the vast northern Eurasian landscape this is a most effective past that not only weighs like a nightmare on the *brains* of the living (*after* Marx); but which impacts all attempts concerning "how to go on" in its currents deposits, ranging from the gauge of railways and Stalin and Khrushchev era apartment houses to power grids and city planning. These sediments may be seen as the "unintentional monuments" of the

**Figure 8.3** Stubbornly present: Lenin still alert in the abandoned High Arctic mining town of Pyramiden, Svalbard (photo: Bjørnar Olsen)

Soviet empire (Riegl, 1982), but are as much constituting its tenacious limbs and guts. This legacy is so massive, persistent, and sticky that the investment needed to get rid of it seems by far to outdo the cost of living with it.

A general comment both among foreign commentators and native intellectuals is that the serious obstacle to progress and change is an inherited Soviet mentality, a passive and obedient attitude that prevents innovative solutions and new modes of governing. "Soviet mentality is alive and well," *The Moscow Times'* commentator Georgy Bovt wrote in October 2007.[2] Without questioning the relevance of such opinions there is far less concern with the, literally speaking, *concrete* material reality which still stubbornly conditions people's lives. Take the example of the *khrushchevki* apartment house, built of precast concrete slabs and introduced in the early 1960s during the reign of its namesake Nikita Khrushchev.

The khrushchevki represented a functional and practical alternative, and contrast, to the massive and monumental Stalinist architecture. It was a quickly assembled, low-cost, and temporary solution pending the arrival of the subsequent and affluent stage of complete communism (Reid, 2009; Nagy, 2010). As this stage never arrived, the khrushchevki became a far more permanent solution. According to accounts published in *Rossiiskaia Gazeta* in March 2004 these apartment houses still comprised just shy of 0.5 billion of the entire 2.8 billion square meters of housing space in Russia (Lahusen, 2006: 738). And while currently being demolished and replaced with increasing pace in the metropolitan areas of Moscow and St. Petersburg, the less wealthy and more marginal areas offer no prospective alternatives (Figure 8.4). As remarked by Thomas Lahusen, despite their decay and breakdown, people "continue to live in these concrete ruins of socialism" (Lahusen, 2006: 738).

When did the Soviet Union end? When Gorbachev resigned or when the Supreme Soviet dissolved itself on December 26, 1991? When the Soviet Army and police forces faded out or the last KGB officer left his post? These historical events occurred; they may be dated, and they give, despite the slight discrepancy, a fairly exact and probable answer to the question. However, as we have seen, the archaeology of the former Soviet Union provides a very different answer and gives face to a far more stubborn and persistent regime. In a simplistic but effective way it also highlights some of the differences between the historical and the archaeological project (see Olivier, 2011).

**Figure 8.4** Street scene Teriberka, Kola Peninsula, Russia, July 2011: Wooden garages and Khrushchev and Stalin era apartment houses (photo: Þóra Pétursdóttir)

## 8.6 Change, habits, and the material bedrock

If materials sediment and solidify in this way, thus preserving and objectifying society, do they always come to counteract change? Is there a creative, innovative aspect of humans that is somehow combated or calmed by the slowing, sedimenting qualities of materiality? (cf. Bergson, 1998). To stay tuned, the appropriate answer is *njet*, if for no other reason than that it is hard to conceive how human creativity and agency can be realized without things. In order to adequately address the question of change we therefore need to move beyond the dominant humanist trope of creative (but unequipped) historical agents rendered in *opposition* to materiality. Moreover, we also need to refrain from always conceiving of stability and change in oppositional terms (see Olsen et al., 2012 for an argument to hold them in symmetry). To recognize change something must be preserved, something must be recognized, that is, some still-effective past that makes the novelty in the change stand out as new (Mullarkey, 2000:135). Actually, by the physiognomy they add to history things also constitute the key device in helping us to recognize historical changes.

As with things themselves and their innumerable modes of being, change operates on a vast range of levels. There are, of course, gradual shifts and small variations that are always involved in human and non-human existence. Chopping a tree, knapping a flint spear point, building a motorway, and driving a car all contribute to an impression of a "process world" that is always in transformation. Also contributing to this are the forces and rhythms of nature, which whether slowly or more abruptly are changing the physiognomy of the landscape in addition to the conditions for human life. Things themselves change, age, and wither, as the material world is also subject to the process of ruination. Thus, in addition to the solidity of the material world, there is a multitude of changes within this mass operating at different scales and at different paces. There is no contradiction between this notion of a "process world" and the notions of stability, permanence, and in-placeness; both change and stability are of course relative and egalitarian terms to be liberated from the academic hierarchical imperative used to dichotomize and rank them.

Consider Heraclitus' maxim that we never step into the same river twice, which is often used to rhetorically articulate the notion of a world in constant flux. True, the water in the river is of course running away and being replaced by new water. However, the River Thames is still there, running next to (among other places) the Embankment, Westminster, and the Millennium Dome, under London and Tower bridges. It constitutes spatial security, orientation, and an incontestable acquisition to present-day people as much as it once did to Mesolithic hunters and Neolithic farmers. The river was there. The river was wet; it contained water and fish, and deposited flotsam and jetsam on its banks. It did not suddenly appear in Scotland, as something made of wood or flying in the air.

Change, however, is often conceived of as "episodic" (Giddens, 1981), something (at least retrospectively) conceived of as bringing something new to things themselves or society at large. In Marxist social theory, these are brought together in a causal link. Things, as productive forces, are accredited a crucial role by their potential for being developed (under certain "historical conditions") to a level that causes serious contradictions and which eventually causes the transformation of society at large. The reasons why things (technology and the associated organization of production) develop are largely located outside the things themselves, such as in "social needs" or "intra-structural" contradictions within the social relations of production. These may be valid parameters, and it is not my aim here to do away with notions related either to human or "systemic" motivations. My ambition is more to ask is there is something in the material itself which contributes to its own transformation?

189

In his important book on the materiality of social change, Norwegian sociologist Tom Johansen writes about how the potential for transformation—as improvements—is somehow embedded in the materials themselves:

> Since the material manifestations are of such a solid and persistent character they become a concrete memory of the acquisitions of the past. But precisely because of this, they also lay the groundwork for improvements, developments and refinements of this memory. Moreover, they also remind us about the deficiencies of the past—as a constant challenge to the present to extend the ploughshare, improve the dwellings, refine the ornaments, etc. Because of the exteriority of the past, it enables an enduring criticism. (Johansen, 1992: 30, my translation)

Clearly this is not to say that the materialized past has been subjected to such an "enduring criticism," nor have the materials consciously been posing a constant challenge. However, the important issue here is their potential for doing; in other words, the fact that their "being-in-readiness" for such criticism and reworking is constant and enduring.

Crucial here are the two modes of tool-being explored by Heidegger. According to him, we normally deal with things in their ready-to-hand mode, encountering them in their "unobtrusive presence." They are not objects of conscious concern, subject to criticism, nor do they pose any serious challenges. They are what Latour calls black-boxed and absorbed by the "in-order-to" and silenced by their own successful operations (Latour, 1999: 183). Indeed, it is when they malfunction or are lost that these very things become "visible" as objects of concern to us. If the fridge stops working, we realize *"what* it was ready-to-hand *for"* (Heidegger, 1962: 105, emphasis in original), and thus it becomes "conspicuous" or present-at-hand to us (Heidegger, 1962; cf. Harman, 2002: chapter 4).

Discussing this process of "coming to mind," Hubert Dreyfus (1991: 70–83) has emphasized the difference between small disturbances which are normally leveled out and the more serious instances of absolute malfunctioning. When a tool is missing/lost and our work permanently interrupted "we can either stare helplessly at the remaining objects or take a new detached theoretical stance towards things and try to explain their underlying causal properties" (Dreyfus, 1991: 79). Leaving aside Dreyfus' somewhat detached philosophical approach to how to handle "total breakdown" (Olsen, 2010: 164), what should be reconsidered are those minor or partial deficiencies which are not necessarily leveled out. Precisely by such minor disturbances, things themselves may initiate a growing concern about their functioning and thus activate the potential for improvements and change. A boat that is unruly under certain wind and wave conditions will be examined, discussed, tested; changes to the sail or keel may be made, and, if successful, they will be translated and eventually black-boxed into future vessels. This process does not include a "new detached theoretical stance towards things"—it is actually grounded in the know-how of the skipper, the sailor, and the boat builder. This know-how always involves a sensibility for the "tuning" of the vessel at sea, a bodily felt awareness of how it works and how it may be improved. In this sense, ready-to-hand knowledge is crucial for the improvement of boats and also for the way they "come to mind" and for their treatment in a present-at-hand mode. Thus, there is always a latent criticism involved even in habitual living.

Social scientists may object that this might be valid for "traditional" societies, populated by craftsmen, crafting tools, and genuine raw materials; that the current instantaneity and accelerating turnover time for consumer products is a clear sign—and a reciprocal effect—of the loosening grip of the ready-to-hand. The constant offering of new products, as well as conscious marketing and advertising, makes us more conscious about things and renders an increasingly larger portion of them in a reflexive present-at-hand mode. However, this taken-for-granted assumption of a more materially reflexive (post)modernity is problematic in many ways. It is complicated by the condition that the majority of things offered to us contain and preserve their own ready-to-hand affordances, tuned in by their own effective history of being "capable of action." The spoon-like quality of the spoon and the shoe-like quality of the shoe are not replaced or seriously modified by new styles and designs. The effective history of useful design (or functional success) is evident in forms and materials that have survived throughout the millennia, adding yet another dimension to the palimpsestial accumulation of the past in the present. What comes to mind in this (post)modern prescribed imperative of replacement is more often their aesthetic and stylistic "excess" than their ready-to-hand thingness. Beyond the things we consciously notice slumbers the enormous bedrock of ready-to-hand equipment—the effective "standing reserve" of things. Although the state of "coming to mind" in terms of our dealing with things might be seen as relatively increasing historically, especially when entire industries today are devoted precisely to creating new designs and equipment, the material bedrock is still—and always will be—constituted by the ready-to-hand. Even the design industries and their conscious designers are situated firmly and dependently within this everydayness of inconspicuous materials and habit memory, which enables them to devote their time to the tiny and often extremely marginal portion of that which makes society possible.

## 8.7 Conclusion

Things, objects, materiality, matter, have become the new catchwords in the social sciences as conspicuously manifested by how these concepts increasingly find their way onto book covers, into article titles, and onto conference and session outlines. Following a century of oblivion and ignorance there *is* undoubtedly a revival and a new fascination with the material stuff of life. The question, however, is whether this fascination is caused by an interest in the things themselves and their various and sincere modes of being. Or is it due more to the fact that the object is being made so smooth and receptive, so anthropomorphized, that it now can perform in compliance with an agenda still largely set by relationalist and social constructivist thought? In this chapter I have argued in favor of what the latter question poses; a not so heroic and emancipatory option.

There are primarily two causes for my doubt. Firstly, that the categories of things allowed into the warmth seem rather restricted, leaving out not only the archaeological spoils of history, but also, and more generally, the trivial, the everyday, the numerous, dust-covered and boring; in short those things that we most commonly and inevitably encounter. Secondly, and interrelated, is the strong inclination to emphasize things as fluid, blurred, scattered, and mobile, never allowing them to be stable, hard, and lasting. As an alternative I have argued that things—from former Soviet mining towns to boats—do hold intrinsic qualities; they have integrity and do not easily melt into air. These qualities of durability and in-placeness, I have claimed, afford social life, memory, misery, and well-being. The persistency of things makes the past present and, for good or bad, impacts crucially the conditions for all human and non-human presents and futures.

"Men make their own history, but they do not make it as they please," Marx famously asserted. Archaeology can modify this statement further. However far back we go into "talkative history and silent prehistory" (Serres, 1987: 209), humans have extended their social relations to non-humans with whom they have swapped properties and formed collectives. The important lesson of this archaeology is that things, animals, natures, did not just sit in silence waiting to be used, formed, or embodied with socially constituted meanings. They possessed their own unique qualities and competences which they brought to our cohabitation with them. Sometimes these entities have served human goals and intentions; sometimes they have obeyed effectuating wishes and aspirations. Other times they have conspired against these wishes and stubbornly enacted rationales of their own device.

## Notes

I thank Chris Witmore, Davide Nicolini, and Þóra Pétursdóttir for their pertinent comments on an earlier draft of this chapter. Thanks also to Chris for his language toil and to Þóra and Alfredo González-Ruibal for letting me reproduce their photos.

1. For exceptions see the work by Tim Ingold and Ewa Domanska
2. *The Moscow Times*, October 4, 2007. http://www.themoscowtimes.com/opinion/article/the-soviet-mentality-is-alive-and-well/193895.html.

## References

Andersson, D. (2001). *Tingenes taushet, tingenes tale*. Oslo: Solum Forlag.

Andreassen, E., Bjerck, H., and Olsen, B. (2010). *Persistent Memories: Pyramiden—A Soviet Mining Town in the High Arctic*. Trondheim, Norway: Tapir.

Appadurai, A. (1986). "Introduction: Commodities and the Politics of Value," in A. Appadurai (ed.), *The Social Life of Things: Commodities in Cultural Perspective*. Cambridge: Cambridge University Press, pp. 3–63.

Arendt, H. (1958). *The Human Condition*. Chicago: University of Chicago Press.

Attfield, J. (2000). *Wild Things: The Material Culture of Everyday Life*. Oxford: Berg.

Augé, M. (1995). *Non-places: Introduction to the Anthropology of Supermodernity*. London: Verso.

Barthes, R. (1977). *Image-Music-Text*. essays selected and translated by S. Heath. London: Fontana.

Benjamin, W. (1996). *Selected Writings Volume 1: 1913–1926*. Cambridge, MA: Belknap Press.

Bergson, H. (1998). *Creative Evolution*. Mineola, NY: Dover.

—— (2004). *Matter and Memory*. Mineola, NY: Dover.

Boym, S. (2001). *The Future of Nostalgia*. New York: Basic Books.

Callon, M. and Law, J. (1997). "After the Individual in Society: Lessons on Collectivity from Science, Technology and Society," *Canadian Journal of Sociology*, 22/2: 165–82.

Capelotti, P. J. (2010). *The Human Archaeology of Space: Lunar, Planetary and Interstellar Relics of Exploration*. Jefferson, NC: McFarland Publishers.

Casey, E. (1984). "Habitual Body and Memory in Merleau-Ponty," *Man and World*, 17: 279–97.

Dant, T. (1999). *Material Culture in the Social World: Values, Activities, Lifestyles.* Maidenhead: Open University Press.

Dreyfus, H. (1991). *Being-in-the-World: A Commentary on Heidegger's "Being and Time," Division 1.* Cambridge, MA: MIT Press.

Durkheim, E. (1951). *Suicide: A Study in Sociology.* New York: Free Press.

Foster, H. (1996). *The Return of the Real: Art and Theory at the End of the Century.* Cambridge, MA: MIT Press.

Gaver, W. (1996). "Affordances for Interaction: The Social is Material for Design," *Ecological Psychology*, 8/2: 111–29.

Giddens, A. (1981). *A Contemporary Critique of Historical Materialism.* London: Macmillan.

Hahn, H. P. (2011). "Words and Things: Reflections on People's Interaction with the Material World," in J. Maran and P. W. Stockhammer (eds.), *Materiality and Social Practice: Transformative Capacities of Intercultural Encounters.* Oxford: Oxbow Books, pp. 4–12.

Harman, G. (2002). *Tool-Being: Heidegger and the Metaphysics of Objects.* Chicago: Open Court.

—— (2010). *Towards Speculative Realism: Essays and Lectures.* Ripley, UK: Zero Books.

Heidegger, M. (1962). *Being and Time.* New York: Harper & Row.

—— (1993). "The Question Concerning Technology," in D. Farell Krell (ed.), *Martin Heidegger: Basic Writings.* San Francisco: HarperCollins.

Hodder, I. (2011). "Human–Thing Entanglement: Towards an Integrated Archaeological Perspective," *Journal of the Royal Anthropological Institute*, 17: 154–77.

Johansen, T. (1992). *Kulissenes regi. En sosiomateriell analyse av forutsetningene for makt og mestring.* Oslo: Universitetsforlaget.

Kopytoff, I. (1986). "The Cultural Biography of Things: Commoditization as Process," in A. Appadurai (ed.), *The Social Life of Things: Commodities in Cultural Perspective.* Cambridge: Cambridge University Press, pp. 64–92.

Lahusen, T. (2006). "Decay or Endurance? The Ruins of Socialism," *Slavic Review*, 65/4: 736–46.

Latour, B. (1987). *Science in Action: How to Follow Scientists and Engineers through Society.* Cambridge, MA: Harvard University Press.

—— (1993). *We Have Never Been Modern.* Cambridge, MA and London: Harvard University Press.

—— (1999). *Pandora's Hope: Essays on the Reality of Science Studies.* Cambridge, MA and London: Harvard University Press.

—— (2002). "Bodies, Cyborgs and the Politics of Incarnation," in S. Sweeney and I. Hodder (eds.), *The Body.* Cambridge: Cambridge University Press, pp. 127–41.

—— (2005). *Reassembling the Social: An Introduction to Actor-Network-Theory.* Oxford: Oxford University Press.

—— and Weibel, P. (eds.) (2005). *Making Things Public: Atmospheres of Democracy.* Cambridge, MA: MIT Press.

Law, J. (1999). "After ANT: Complexity, Naming and Topology," in J. Law and J. Hassard (eds.), *Actor Network Theory and After.* Oxford: Blackwell, pp. 1–14.

—— and Hassard, J. (eds.) (1999). *Actor Network Theory and After.* Oxford: Blackwell.

—— and Mol, A. (eds.) (2002). *Complexities: Social Studies of Knowledge Practices.* Durham, NC: Duke University Press.

Lefebvre, H. (1987). "The Everyday and Everydayness," *Yale French Studies*, 73: 7–11.

Matthews, E. (2002). *The Philosophy of Merleau-Ponty.* Montreal: McGill-Queen's University Press.

Merleau-Ponty, M. (1962). *The Phenomenology of Perception.* London: Routledge & Kegan Paul.

Miller, D. (1987). *Material Culture and Mass Consumption.* Oxford: Blackwell.

—— (1998). *A Theory of Shopping.* Cambridge: Polity Press.

—— (2005). "Materiality: An Introduction," in D. Miller (ed.), *Materiality.* Durham, NC: Duke University Press, pp. 1–50.

Mullarkey, J. (2000). *Bergson and Philosophy.* Notre Dame, IN: University of Notre Dame Press.

Mullins, P. (2004). "Ideology, Power, and Capitalism: The Historical Archaeology of Consumption," in L. Meskell and R. Preucel (eds.), *A Companion to Social Archaeology.* Oxford: Blackwell, pp. 195–212.

Nagy, D. (2010). "Goodbye khrushchevki. Soviet Housing in Post-Soviet Europe," available at http://khrushchevki.wordpress.com/about/.

Naum, M. (2008). *Homelands Lost and Gained: Slavic Migration and Settlement on Bornholm in the Early Middle Ages.* Lund Studies in Historical Archaeology 9. Lund: Lund University.

Norman, D. (1988). *The Design of Everyday Things.* New York: Doubleday.

Olivier, L. (2001). "Duration, Memory and the Nature of the Archaeological Record," in H. Karlsson (ed.), *It's About Time: The Concept of Time in Archaeology.* Gothenburg: Bricoleur Press, pp. 61–70.

—— (2011). *The Dark Abyss of Time: Archaeology and Memory.* Lanham, MD: AltaMira Press.

Olsen, B. (2003). "Material Culture after Text: Re-Membering Things," *Norwegian Archaeological Review*, 36/2: 87–104.

—— (2007). "Keeping Things at Arm's Length: A Genealogy of Asymmetry," *World Archaeology*, 39/4: 579–88.

—— (2010). *In Defense of Things: Archaeology and the Ontology of Objects.* Lanham, MD: AltaMira Press.

—— Shanks, M., Webmoor, T., and Witmore, C. (2012). *Archaeology: The Discipline of Things.* Berkeley: University of California Press.

Parkin, D. (1999). "Mementoes as Transitional Objects in Human Displacement," *Journal of Material Culture*, 4/3: 303–20.

Pinney, C. (2005). "Things Happen: Or, From Which Moment Does That Object Come?" in D. Miller (ed.), *Materiality*. Durham, NC: Duke University Press, pp. 256–72.

Rathje, W. (1984). "The Garbage Decade," *American Behavioral Scientist*, 28/1: 9–29.

—— and McCarthy, M. (1977). "Regularity and Variability in Contemporary Garbage," in S. South (ed.), *Research Strategies in Historical Archaeology*. New York: Academic Press, pp. 261–86.

Reid, S. (2009). "Communist Comfort: Socialist Modernism and the Making of Cosy Homes in the Khrushchev-Era Soviet Union," *Gender and History* 21/3: 465–98.

Riegl, A. (1982). "The Modern Cult of Monuments," *Oppositions*, 25: 21–50.

Rowlands, M. (2005). "A Materialist Approach to Materiality," in D. Miller (ed.), *Materiality*. Durham, NC: Duke University Press, pp. 72–87.

Schiffer, M. (1991). *The Portable Radio in American Life*. Tucson: University of Arizona Press.

—— (2008). *Power Struggles: Scientific Authority and the Creation of Practical Electricity before Edison*. Cambridge, MA: MIT Press.

Serres, M. (1987). *Statues*. Paris: Bourin.

—— (1995). *Genesis*. Ann Arbor: University of Michigan Press.

—— with Latour, B. (1995). *Conversation on Science, Culture and Time*. Ann Arbor: University of Michigan Press.

Shanks, M. and McGuire, R. (1996). "The Craft of Archaeology," *American Antiquity*, 61/1: 75–88.

Simmel, G. (1978 [1906]). *The Philosophy of Money*. London: Routledge.

Thomas, J. (2004). *Archaeology and Modernity*. London: Routledge.

Trentmann, F. (2009). "Materiality in the Future of History: Things, Practices, and Politics," *Journal of British Studies*, 48/2: 283–307.

Young, J. (2002). *Heidegger's Later Philosophy*. Cambridge: Cambridge University Press.

# 9

# Untangling Sociomateriality

*Matthew Jones*

**Abstract:** A central metaphor in accounts of sociomateriality is that of entanglement—the social and material are not just mutually influential, but inextricably related. These accounts, however, employ several different terms, sometimes interchangeably, to characterize the nature of this entanglement, such as inseparability, interpenetration, relationality, and embodiment, and to refer to what is entangled, for example the social and the material, humans and technology, work and technology. While such variation may be justified on aesthetic or stylistic grounds, treating these terms as synonyms may be seen as conflating different ontological claims. This chapter seeks to identify these claims and to explore their consequences through an analysis of nursing in a critical care unit, a context that is, at the same time, both highly suffused by technology and intensely social. In common with the majority of sociomateriality literature much of the focus of this analysis will be on technology, but the implications for materiality more generally and for process research on organizations are also considered.

## 9.1 Introduction

Sociomateriality is doubly entangled, first in its definition and second in its ontology. The aim of this chapter will be to tease out some of these tangled strands to clarify their implications. While the discussion will refer to materiality in general and sociomaterial as an adjective (with or without a hyphen), the primary focus will be on sociomateriality specifically, and what Orlikowski and Scott (2008) refer to as the "research stream" bearing that name. Before attempting to analyze sociomateriality, therefore, it may be helpful to elaborate on this distinction.

## 9.2 Socio(-)material(ity)

The compound term socio-material or sociomaterial would seem to have been in occasional use in a range of disciplines including sociology, human geography, and economics, since at least the early 1980s, with little differentiation between the two spellings. Most references until about 2007, however, primarily employ the term, without explanation, as an adjective to describe a context, say, or a factor and it is only more recently that it has become something of a term of art, particularly in science and technology studies, organization studies, and information systems. This later work, which includes two-thirds of the more than 200 published papers using both terms, connects them with a range of theoretical approaches including: various branches of Actor Network Theory (ANT) (Latour, 1993, 2007; Law and Mol, 1993; Callon, 1996; Mol, 2002; Law, 2004; Callon and Muniesa, 2005); Mangle of Practice (Pickering, 1993); Posthumanist Performativity (Barad, 2003, 2007); Cultural and Historical Activity Theory (Engeström and Middleton, 1996; Miettinen and Virkkunen, 2005); and Practice Theory (Schatzki et al., 2001; Reckwitz, 2002). In the organization studies field, papers that use the term socio(-)material may be seen as part of a wider emerging interest in materiality and organizations (e.g. Dale, 2005; Iedema, 2007, Jensen et al., 2009), even if these other authors do not mention sociomaterial or socio-material in their work.

The main reference point for papers using the term sociomaterial (both with and without the hyphen), however, is the work of Orlikowski (2007, 2010; Orlikowski and Scott, 2008), with citations of this work outnumbering all other theoretical sources combined and often being the only reference to the term in a paper. This is perhaps not altogether surprising, as Orlikowski's account of sociomateriality draws on ideas from many of these other theoretical sources, including ANT (Callon, Latour, Law, Mol), Pickering and Barad, along with the ethnomethodological tradition of Suchman (2007) and the digital formations of Latham and Sassen (2005). Indeed, in identifying these approaches as part of a common "research stream," to which she gives the name "sociomateriality" Orlikowski provides what would appear to be the most substantive account of the concept to date. This is not to suggest that other work is not relevant to thinking about sociomateriality, but that her work would seem to be considered the key point of departure for discussion of the concept. Thus, almost without exception, the 40 journal papers (all but one published since 2007) that refer to sociomateriality specifically cite one or more of Orlikowski (2007, 2010; Orlikowski and Scott, 2008). As an "umbrella term" (Orlikowski and Scott, 2008: 434), moreover, rather than a formal integration of the various theoretical approaches, analysis of socio-materiality may also offer insight on these contributing literatures. It should be noted, however, that the focus of most of the sociomateriality literature (and to some extent also the literature using the term sociomaterial, although less so that using the term socio-material), like the papers of Orlikowski that it cites, is predominantly on technology rather than materi-ality more generally and this is reflected in the analysis below.

## 9.3 The relationship between the social and the material in the sociomateriality literature

A central metaphor in Orlikowski's account of sociomateriality is that of entanglement, a term also used in the work of Barad (2007) and Pels et al. (2002). The social and material are not just mutually influential, it is claimed, but inextricably related. Discussion of entanglement, however, would seem to conflate several different claims about the nature of this relationship.

Although Orlikowski (2007) refers to entanglement almost exclusively in association with the term constitutive (which might imply that entangle-ment has the power to establish or give organized existence to the material and social) it is also seen as having a specifically ontological connotation. This argument is developed in Orlikowski and Scott (2008: 456) who describe the term sociomaterial (no hyphen) as signaling an "ontological fusion" of the social and the material and refer to the stream of sociomaterial research as adopting a "relational ontology." What sort of ontological claim(s), there-fore, might the notion of entanglement be considered as supporting?

Even allowing for the limitations of language in expressing the nature of the relationship between the social and material, it would seem that socio-material accounts invoke several different interpretations of entanglement, not all of which are necessarily synonymous. Most of these, from an onto-logical perspective, relate to a claim that the material and social have no separate existence. In itself, however, this would not necessarily indicate that sociomateriality allows for just one ontological position. Thus, that the social and material do not exist separately from each other could imply insepar-ability, interpenetration, or relationality. Each of these terms may be found in discussions of sociomateriality, largely without any distinction being made between them, yet each may arguably have different implications.

Orlikowski and Scott (2008), for example, refer several times to socio-materiality as implying an "inherent *inseparability*" of the social and the technical (or material) and this inseparability would seem to involve two aspects: fusion and indissolubility. While evidently related, however, these terms are not necessarily equivalent. Thus fusion may be seen as referring either to the combined form, or to the process by which it was created, while indissolubility would seem more to do with the impossibility of severing the association. Nor do these aspects necessarily have the connotations that proponents of sociomateriality would appear to be seeking. Thus fusions need not be irreversible and indissoluble fusions may have been created from previously separate elements.

These semantic niceties notwithstanding, however, inseparability would seem a different and stronger claim than that of *interpenetration*, which would not seem to imply any necessary blending of elements. Rather, it would seem to refer to their mutual positioning. This would seem particularly relevant in the discussion of cyborgs (a concept linked to sociomateriality by Barad, 2003, 2007 and Suchman, 2007), which are sometimes illustrated by reference to devices such as pacemakers, insulin pumps, and prosthetic limbs (e.g., Gray et al., 1995; Laughlin, 1997) to support arguments that the boundary between humans and machines may not be clear-cut. Prosthetic devices of this sort may be expected to be of particular significance in medical settings, such as critical care, discussed below.

That the material and the social have no separate existence is also identified by Orlikowski and Scott (2008) with Slife's account of "strong" *relationality*. This argues (Slife, 2004: 159) that "all things . . . start out and forever remain in relationship. Their very qualities, properties, and identities cannot stem completely from what is inherent or 'inside' them but must depend on how they are related to each other." The existence of a relationship need not imply (irreversible) coalescence or intimate mutual positioning, however, nor does the inability of inherent properties to "completely" account for qualities, properties, and identities rule out the possibility of some influence of something that is inside. This would thus, again, seem a potentially distinct type of claim.

Another term used to refer to a relationship in which both the social and material are implicated is *embodiment*. This is particularly found in the work of Suchman (2007), who is identified by Orlikowski (2007) and Orlikowski and Scott (2008) as one of the key contributors to sociomateriality. Human action, it is argued, necessarily involves (material) bodies. Such a view of sociomaterial entanglement would seem to be of particular significance in the critical care context where, as will be discussed, the materiality of patients' bodies, their physical form, comportment, and physiological status are central to medical practice.

In identifying these particular terms as reflecting potentially distinct stances on the relationship between the material and the social, it is not intended to suggest that they constitute a complete account of the possible nuances of entanglement, or that authors writing on sociomateriality are wrong to see them as at least closely related, if not synonymous. Rather, as the discussion of critical care nursing will seek to illustrate, following through the implications of the, perhaps subtle, differences between these terms (even if these were not deliberately intended by the authors) may be helpful in clarifying the scope of sociomateriality's claims and their coherence.

This chapter therefore seeks to explore the possible ontological implications of four terms (inseparability, interpenetration, relationality, and embodiment) employed to describe the relationship between the social and the material in the work of Orlikowski and the literatures that she identifies with the sociomateriality research genre. In the next section, the connotations of these terms are considered and compared with the way they are used in these sources. In particular, the emphasis will be on highlighting potential differences between the ontological implications of the terms. A brief empirical example of critical care nursing is then presented as a basis for discussing the significance, or otherwise, of these differences in practice and their implications for process research.

## 9.4 The terminology of entanglement

As has been noted, at least four, arguably distinct, terms (inseparability, interpenetration, relationality, and embodiment) are employed in the sociomateriality literature. While it may be desirable on aesthetic or stylistic grounds to employ some variation in terminology when discussing a topic, the choice of a particular term brings with it certain associations that may have implications for how the topic is conceptualized. A brief review of the four terms would therefore seem in order to explore some possible associations evoked by describing the relationship between the social and the material in these ways and to compare these with the account in the sociomateriality literature.

### 9.4.1 Inseparability

While inseparability and the associated notions of fusion and indissolubility may not altogether avoid connotations of initially separate entities having been brought together and may imply a more contingent association than accounts of sociomateriality would seem to be seeking, they can nevertheless be considered to be advancing a relatively strong position on the relationship between the social and the material. Taken literally, they would suggest there are no circumstances in which it would be meaningful to consider the social and the material as independent of each other. Indeed, Orlikowski and Scott (2008: 456) argue that sociomateriality "does not presume independent or even interdependent entities with distinct and inherent characteristics." Rather, following Barad (2007: 33), sociomaterial phenomena are the emergent product of agential intra-action. Even if it may be possible to distinguish between the social and material analytically, in practice it is impossible to have one without the other. It is not just that we can't perceive a boundary between them or separate out their effects, "[t]here *is* no social that is not also material, and no material that is not also social" as Orlikowski (2007: 1437) puts it.

This is largely borne out by the statements in Orlikowski and Scott (2008) and Orlikowski (2010) associated with references to inseparability and fusion, as Table 9.1 illustrates.

**Table 9.1** References to inseparability in Orlikowski and Scott (2008) and Orlikowski (2010)

| | | |
|---|---|---|
| 1 | "the fusion of technology and work in organizations" | Orlikowski and Scott (2008: 434) |
| 2 | "there is an inherent inseparability between the technical and the social" | Orlikowski and Scott (2008: 434) |
| 3 | "a possible way forward is to challenge the deeply taken-for-granted assumption that technology, work, and organizations should be conceptualized separately, and to theorize their fusion" | Orlikowski and Scott (2008: 454) |
| 4 | "This is a relational ontology that presumes the social and the material are inherently inseparable . . . this is a constitutive entanglement that does not presume independent or even interdependent entities with distinct and inherent characteristics . . . Any distinction of humans and technologies is analytical only, and done with the recognition that these entities necessarily entail each other in practice" | Orlikowski and Scott (2008: 456) |
| 5 | "the social and the technical are posited to be 'ontologically inseparable from the start'" | Orlikowski (2010: 134) |
| 6 | "inseparability of 'observed object' and 'agencies of observation'" | Orlikowski (2010: 136) |

As Table 9.1 also shows, however, these statements are not always consistent on what is regarded as inseparable. Thus Orlikowski and Scott (2008: 434) refer to the fusion of "technology and work" and the inseparability between the "social and the technical," while on p. 456 they refer to the inseparability of the "social and the material" and in Orlikowski (2010) it is the "observed object" and the "agencies of observation" that are indissoluble. It may be, of course, that these terms can be considered synonyms, at least to some degree, but this is never explicitly addressed in these papers. There is sufficient inconsistency between them (not all material is necessarily technology, nor does work constitute the totality of the social, for example), however, to suggest that these distinctions may deserve greater attention.

### 9.4.2 Interpenetration

Interpenetration is mentioned just once in the three papers by Orlikowski and Orlikowski and Scott, but similar terms are employed in Orlikowski (2007) where there are references to the social and the material being "inextricably bound up" and as exhibiting "recursive intertwining" and "deep intermingling." Other authors using the term sociomaterial refer to "imbrication" (Latham and Sassen, 2005; Leonardi, 2011) or "entwinement" (Sandberg and Tsoukas, 2011). What these metaphors would seem to share is a notion of two elements being in close mutual association, but not necessarily fused. The specific statement regarding interpenetration in (Orlikowski and Scott, 2008: 455), moreover, suggests that this association is performative—"entities (whether humans or technologies) have no inherent properties, but acquire form, attributes, and capabilities through their interpenetration." It is the mutual positioning, or perhaps the process of positioning, that gives entities the properties we attribute to them.

### 9.4.3 Relationality

The theme of it being the relationship between entities that gives them their properties is extended in discussions of relationality, in which the evocation of any physical relationship is replaced by a purely topological association. Again, however, as Table 9.2 shows, there is some ambiguity about whether it is the existence of entities, the boundaries between them, or the process of mutual constitution that is being focused on. Similarly each of the statements refers to different relata—humans and artifacts, technologies and humans, people and things, material and human agency.

### 9.4.4 Embodiment

Although embodiment is not specifically used by Orlikowski to describe the entangling of the social and material, the term occurs frequently in the work of Suchman, who is identified, with Mol (2002), as one of the sources of sociomaterial thinking in Orlikowski (2007). Suchman (2007) talks of embodied competencies, action, practices, work, labors, knowing,

**Table 9.2** References to relationality in Orlikowski (2007) and Orlikowski and Scott (2008)

| | | |
|---|---|---|
| 1 | The distinction of humans and artifacts, on this view, is analytical only; these entities relationally entail or enact each other in practice. As Law puts it (2004: 42; emphasis in original): "This is a thoroughgoing *relational materiality*. Materials—and so realities—are treated as relational products. They do not exist in and of themselves." | Orlikowski (2007: 1438) |
| 2 | "a relational ontology that dissolves analytical boundaries between technologies and humans" | Orlikowski and Scott (2008: 455) |
| 3 | "people and things only exist in relation to each other" | Orlikowski and Scott (2008: 455) |
| 4 | Pickering (1993, 1995) argues for the value of a relational ontology that is premised on the "insistence that material and human agencies are mutually and emergently productive of one another" (Pickering, 1993, p. 567) | Orlikowski and Scott (2008: 459) |

and responses and in Suchman (2000: 12) she refers to embodiment in discussing the relationship between material objects and work practices.

Orlikowski and Scott (2008) also associate sociomateriality with the "practice turn" in social theory (Schatzki et al., 2001) in which cognitive capacities, activities, and understandings are all identified as embodied. The significance of embodiment to practice is further developed by Reckwitz (2002), whose theory of social practices accords bodies, in interaction with other elements such as "mental activities, 'things' and their use, a background knowledge . . . states of emotion and motivational knowledge" (Reckwitz, 2002: 249), a central role. Thus, for Reckwitz (2002: 251) "practices are routinized bodily activities; as interconnected complexes of behavioral acts they are movements of the body." From this perspective, therefore, bodies and embodied action are arguably somewhat neglected in accounts of sociomateriality.

### 9.4.5 Same but different?

Acknowledging the limitations of language in expressing indissolubility (Orlikowski and Scott, 2008) it would nevertheless appear that the terminology of entanglement, at least as employed in the three papers by Orlikowski, may allow for some differences of emphasis on the relationship between the social and the material, as shown in Table 9.3.

Although all of these terms are consistent with a necessary and close association of the social and the material, the differences in the implied nature and degree of this association may nevertheless be significant in practice. The next section therefore presents an account of critical care nursing through which these possible differences may be explored.

**Table 9.3** Possible differences in emphasis between terms used to describe entanglement in sociomateriality

| Term | Related terms | Dominant emphasis |
|---|---|---|
| Inseparability | Fusion, indissolubility | Irreversible coalescence |
| Interpenetration | Intermingling, intertwining, binding up | Intimate mutual positioning |
| Relationality | | Primacy of association |
| Embodiment | | Bodies as mediators of action |

## 9.5 Critical care

The following account of critical care nursing is derived from observations and interviews undertaken in two critical care units (CCUs) in the UK, one in a large teaching hospital and the other in a specialist cardiothoracic hospital. Observations at the first site were undertaken over a period of three months and at the second over three periods of three weeks before, during, and after the introduction of a computer-based Clinical Information System (CIS). A total of 37 interviews were also conducted with a range of the cardiothoracic CCU staff (senior and junior doctors, nurses of various grades from trainees to critical care practitioners and ward managers, dietitians, and pharmacists) during the observation periods.

### 9.5.1 The critical care context

Patients in the cardiothoracic CCU had generally undergone, or were awaiting, some form of cardiac surgery such as a coronary bypass, insertion of a metal stent in a stenosed artery, or implantation of an artificial heart valve or pacemaker. Such surgery was relatively routine at the hospital concerned and, if there were no complications, the average length of stay in CCU was three days before patients were discharged to a regular ward. Patients in the teaching hospital CCU, in contrast, were admitted for a range of conditions including acute infection, severe injuries sustained in road traffic accidents, and postoperative complications and their length of stay was generally considerably longer, in some cases up to several months. Because of the severity of the medical condition of patients in both units, however, almost all were bed-bound and many were sedated for extended periods.

In both units, the majority of patients were located in an open ward, divided into "bays" of 6–8 beds, with the remainder in side rooms (usually to control infection). By the head of each bed, against the wall, there would typically be one or more stands with bags of fluid, such as blood, saline, or parenteral nutrition with lines attached to a central venous catheter in the patient's chest or neck. Other lines attached to the catheter might be connected to syringe drivers, administering a steady dose of a drug. Sensors on, and sometimes in, the patient's body measured vital signs such as heart rate, blood pressure, blood oxygenation, and body temperature and their outputs were displayed on a monitor mounted on a unit beside the bed.

Other indicators of the patient's condition were not so easily measured or observed, however. Blood gases and chemistry, for example, required the drawing of blood samples and their analysis, either by the hospital's central biochemistry laboratory or in a blood gas analyzer situated on the unit. Similarly, microbiological samples would be sent to a central pathology laboratory. In the cardiothoracic unit digital X-rays could be taken with mobile equipment by radiographers coming on to the unit and were stored on the hospital's Picture Archiving Computer System (PACS). To see sufficient detail, however, images generally had to be displayed on a higher resolution screen than was available on a standard desktop PC, and only two such screens were installed on the unit, one in the doctors' office and the other adjacent to the central nursing station.

Depending on the patient's condition they might experience a variety of organ failures and need to be supported with breathing by a ventilator (via either a face mask or tracheal intubation), kidney function by hemofiltration, or heart/lung function by extracorporeal membrane oxygenation (ECMO). These extra machines, often quite bulky, would usually need to be positioned near the head of the bed, restricting the nurses' access to the patient's body (and potentially that of the patient in the adjacent bed too).

In the teaching hospital CCU and in the cardiothoracic CCU before the CIS was introduced, a trolley was positioned at the foot of each bed, on top of which was spread a large paper chart on which the nurses would record the patient's condition (transcribing data from the monitors, entering values that they had measured, or handwriting notes). These observations ("obs") might be done every 15 minutes throughout the day. On top of the chart (or in a rack attached to the trolley) would be additional folders (for example containing printouts from the blood gas analyzer or biochemistry or pathology reports) and charts, such as the drug chart (recording all the medication prescribed) and the "plan for the day" (recording key treatment decisions made at the morning ward round). Individual health professionals (doctors, nurses, pharmacists, dietitians, physiotherapists) would also often create additional documentation (such as "to do lists," reminders, annotated lists of patients on the unit) on loose pieces of paper that they would keep in their pocket (but sometimes on paper towels, cardboard disposable kidney dishes, or any other accessible surface that could be written on).

With the introduction of the CIS, much of the recording of patient data was automated, avoiding the risks of transcription errors and ensuring that data were recorded at the appropriate time, however busy the nurse might be with other activities. Drug charts and the "plan for the day" were also incorporated in the CIS, so the old paper charts were replaced by a computer and screen mounted on a trolley positioned at the foot of each bed and additional CIS computers were available in the doctors' office. Most, but not all, of the devices and laboratory services could interface with the CIS, enabling data to be directly entered into the record, but others still required values to be entered from print-outs. Standard CIS screens were also generally not of sufficient resolution for viewing X-rays. While the CIS integrated large amounts of the patient record, therefore, this was far from complete.

The cardiothoracic CCU had selected the particular CIS because it could be customized to their requirements and they (and the Unit Director, a consultant anesthetist, in particular) had invested considerable effort in adapting it to support evidence-based practice. Drugs that were not on the recommended protocol, for example, had been made purposefully hard (but not impossible) to prescribe, while the common prescriptions had a short cut with pre-filled boxes. Similarly, nurses' observation forms were highly structured, prompting for all the data needing to be captured or processed.

## 9.5.2 Critical care nursing

Most critical care nurses considered their work to be essentially continuous with general nursing, emphasizing the importance of bodily and emotional care of the patient, personalization of care, and empathy with the patient's feelings (insofar as it was possible for a sedated patient to indicate these). At the same time, however, with one nurse for each patient, the severe condition of the patients and the large range of medical devices used to treat them, critical care nursing is a distinct specialism, requiring high levels of vigilance and technical skill and an ability to respond effectively and knowledgeably in a medical emergency, should the patient show signs of a rapid deterioration in their condition. These characteristics of CCU work were said to attract some nurses who exhibited a preference for the technical aspects of the job rather than "care" of the patient.

Although the probability of a medical emergency may be higher in critical care than in other areas of nursing, much of the critical care nurses' work is highly routinized, for example observations need to be taken at frequent intervals, drug doses need to be prepared and administered, drips and syringe drivers need to be set up and changed regularly, monitors need to be checked and, if appropriate, reset, blood samples need to be taken and sent off for analysis, lab results need to be found. With paper-based documentation, considerable time may also be taken in entering data into the record and in calculating balances and doses, in addition to carrying out the tasks. Reducing this burden (and eliminating human error in calculations) is often cited as a reason for investing in a CIS.

Notwithstanding their commitment to the emotional and relational character of their work, nurses recognized that the technology involved in patient care and the pressures of looking after patients with often multiple life-threatening medical problems meant that they could find themselves "treating the numbers rather than the patient," paying more attention to the data displayed on the monitor, and ensuring that the equipment was working properly than to the actual condition of the patient. A few commented that they made a conscious effort to take time regularly to talk to the patient, if that was possible, and if not, at least to try to make them as comfortable as possible They also stressed the importance of touching and examining the patient's body to check that the interpretation of the patient's condition that they drew from the record was consistent with their personal observation.

Even though they indicated their awareness that "the numbers" were a necessarily mediated representation of the patient, nurses spoke and acted (in most circumstances) as if the data were direct evidence of the patient's condition. When they started a syringe driver administering a drug, for example, they would treat this as meaning that the drug was entering the patient's bloodstream, or they would consider a change in the reading of a particular parameter, on the monitor or in the CIS, as evidence of a drug's action or as a change in the patient's condition and respond accordingly. It was as if they were seeing through the technology to the patient's physiology, their actions in adjusting medical devices were actions upon the patient's body and there was nothing in between. There were sometimes incidents, of course, that could cause this to break down. It might be discovered, for example, that a sensor had become dislodged, or on one occasion it was realized at the last minute that the wrong tab had been clicked on in the CIS and the data being displayed (and about to be acted on) were from the previous day.

Since a lot of the data gathered by the technology, such as venous pressure or heart rhythm, were inaccessible to medical staff through immediate observation of the patient, however, there was not necessarily any physical correlate of the measures taken against which to assess their interpretation. Nurses and doctors talked of "gut feelings" and "experience" to explain their sense that things were "not right."

Given the critical condition of patients on the units, the mortality risk was high. While medical staff wanted to feel that "we did our best" to keep a patient alive, they recognized that they were not always successful and sought to manage the distress of failure in a number of ways. One approach, that tended to be adopted in the case of long-stay CCU patients who did not show signs of recovery or experienced frequent relapses, was to rationalize withdrawal of interventions in terms of avoiding prolongation of suffering and the, evidence-supported, low probability of recovery (although the economic considerations could not be wholly ignored either).

Medical staff also commented on the way that technology and the patient's sedation could help to reduce their sensitivity to death. It made it easier, they suggested, not to think of it solely as a person who had died, but as a set of numbers that had not worked out, or as a body that had not responded to the treatments as it could have been expected to, or for which the available treatments and technologies had been inadequate. A further consideration arose in situations where death was unexpected and where a coroner's investigation might be held, or a patient's relatives would seek explanations. Here the technology could provide evidence that correct procedures had been followed. While the transcribed data entered on paper charts were accepted as an accurate representation of the patient's condition, introduction of a CIS made this record more complete, accessible, searchable, and apparently more reliable. Functions within the CIS, such as those providing access to treatment guidelines, enforcing completion of certain procedures (or at least requiring an identifiable individual to declare that they had been completed), or presenting a recommended treatment or drug regime by default, were also seen as increasing the consistency, and defendability, of treatment.

## 9.6 Portraying the entanglement of the social and the material in critical care

With this account of critical care nursing we may now begin to consider how the terminology of entanglement, discussed above, may be used to describe the relationship between the social and the material in this setting. Each of the terms, in the various different ways in which they are employed in the sociomateriality literature, will be addressed in turn, before a general discussion, firstly of the possible significance, or otherwise, of this termino-logical diversity for our understanding of sociomateriality, secondly of some potential problems with this vocabulary, at least as a description of critical care nursing, and finally of the implications for process research in organizations.

### 9.6.1 Inseparability

As previously noted, there would appear to be three sorts of inseparability mentioned in the three papers by Orlikowski: between humans and tech-nology, between the social and the material, and between the observed object and the agencies of observation. There would seem to be clear evidence of the first of these in the context of critical care nursing. Taken literally, the survival of most patients is dependent on the technology employed in their treatment. Take away the machines and few of them would be alive. This dependence, moreover, sometimes extended beyond the immediate treatment in the critical care unit, with patients continuing to depend on implanted devices, such as stents or pacemakers, for the rest of their lives.

Similarly, while the continuing existence of these devices did not depend upon their use in the treatment of patients (they would not disappear if they were stored in a cupboard when not in use), their creation, purchase, deployment, and maintenance are the product of human actions. Take away these actions and the devices would not be on the unit to be used.

There is a sense too, in which it would seem reasonable to talk of human–machine fusion. For critical care nurses treating patients, the technology could seem to fall out of awareness. Like the cane of Merleau-Ponty's blind man (Merleau-Ponty, 1962), the devices extended the nurses' bodies such that they perceived themselves as directly observing the phenomena that the sensors were designed to measure, and as acting on the patients' bodies through the actions they took on technology. Unlike the blind man, how-ever, what the nurse observed may not be the phenomena themselves, but data that are considered (according to some understanding of the relevant physiology) to represent that phenomenon adequately (e.g., this ECG trace is evidence of a particular behavior of the patient's heart). The nurses' perception of the effects of their actions may similarly be mediated by a prior conceptualization of what is happening to the patient's body (e.g., the noradrenalin being administered will increase peripheral vascular resist-ance and raise blood pressure). In most situations these understandings are sufficiently robust that the assumptions are not called into question, but occasionally it may become apparent that the interpretation of the data or the evidence of the effects is inconsistent with assumptions and the apparent human–machine fusion may start to fragment.

It would seem debatable, however, to what extent it may be appropriate to consider the association between humans and technology as indissoluble. If there is a fusion between technology and humans in the CCU, it would appear that this association can be dissolved, at least from an ontological perspective. Thus, while the patient's body will probably have been altered, to some degree, by the technology and may bear traces from it, such as scars (so there may be some enduring legacy of the association), when patients are discharged from the unit, for the most part the technology does not go with them. Even implanted devices that may in practice be considered as an integral part of the patient's body, remain separable (for example a pacemaker can be removed), at least in principle.

Indeed it may be argued that technology fragments rather than fuses with the body. Rather than seeing the patient as a whole person, different devices generally relate to particular organ systems and the patient becomes seen as a collection of quasi-independent systems that medical staff can struggle to integrate. In contrast to Mol (2002), however, there is not a single label that different specialisms conceptualize in different ways, but a single body that the technology splits into multiple images. While it was evident that some specialisms conceptualized the body predominantly in terms of a particular component, such as cardiologists focusing on the heart, for intensivists and critical care nurses there is a need to make sense of the critical care patient as a whole. Doing this can require them to look outside the technology, to engage with the patient's body directly. This may reflect doubts about what the technology is telling them, difficulties in reconciling the different messages from different pieces of technology (that it is hoped reference to the patient's body may help to resolve), or a desire to see the patient as a whole person and not just a collection of physiological systems.

More metaphorically there is also a clear dependency of work on technology. Much of the routine activity of critical care nursing, for example, is about getting the technology to work and ensuring that it continues to work—setting up syringe drivers, changing drips, adjusting monitors, and so on. Correspondingly, technology depends on work to enable it to function, to be a "technology in use," rather than just a technological artifact (Orlikowski, 2000).

The introduction of the CIS with its checklists and guidance may be seen as a further strengthening of the association between work and technology. By making certain actions, such as prescribing a recommended drug regime, easier than others, or requiring certification that particular actions have been taken, technology influences how work is done. This does not entirely restrict human agency, however, as staff may choose, legitimately, to ignore the guidance or, unofficially, to miss steps out of a procedure, perhaps because of time pressures, but to nevertheless confirm that they have been undertaken in order to be able to get on with the job. Even with such potentially fine-grained control, therefore, technology may exert a strong influence on work, but is not determinate.

At the same time, despite all the technology involved and the work needed to get it to work, critical care nursing is more than just minding machines. It has a necessarily social dimension with respect, for example, to the conceptualization of care or the role of nurses. In both of these, technology is at least strongly implicated, if not inseparable from the social. Thus, notions of what care patients should receive and how it is delivered are strongly shaped by the technology available. The limits of how it is technologically feasible to treat patients (with given resources) become the limits of what care is delivered. As it becomes possible to keep patients alive, despite severe organ failures, for example, this becomes the measure of what treatment can be considered, even if decisions may be made not to apply such treatment on the grounds of avoiding unnecessary suffering or low probability of success. Without hemofiltration, kidney failure was often fatal. With hemofiltration, care expands to include the possibility of keeping someone alive despite acute renal failure.

The role of nurses is a subject of continuing debate within the profession in which a distinction is typically made between the "virtue script" (Gordon and Nelson, 2006), emphasizing service, altruism, emotional connection, and relationship, and technical skills, preferably credentialed, that are seen as necessary in establishing the professional identity of nurses and enhancing their status in the medical hierarchy. In this scheme, critical care nursing is generally perceived as being more aligned with the latter, as comments about the preferences of at least some CCU nurses for technology over caring indicate. Whether or not the technology means that CCU nurses do actually pay more attention to technology (and it seems that some make particular efforts to avoid any such tendency), to the extent that critical care nursing cannot be carried out without technology of some sort, being a critical care nurse necessarily involves engaging with technology and the acquisition of technical skills.

While the sociomateriality literature predominantly focuses on the inseparability of humans and technology, there is also some limited discussion of the inseparability of the social and the material more generally, primarily in the context of reference theorists such as Barad and Latour.

It can certainly be argued that the physical character of the CCU setting (such as the amount of space and its layout, the lighting, the surfaces, the installed services) is the product of social processes related to the feasibility and desirability of treating critically ill patients, and that the enactment of critical care medical practices necessarily takes place in particular material conditions, not least because patients' bodies (and those of medical staff) are themselves material. There can be no critical care, therefore, that does not simultaneously involve the social and the material.

The same can be said of any human practice, and hence, by definition, of any practice in an organizational setting. It will necessarily involve the material bodies of the participants, located in a particular material context, so there can be no social that does not involve the material. To say that the social and material are inseparable in this sense would seem little more than a truism, however, and does not imply that inseparability, per se, has any necessary consequence. That is, if there can never be a situation in which the social is separate from the material then we cannot know what the consequences of this might be.

Nor would it seem that, from an ontological perspective, the same claim can be made about the inseparability of the material from the social (i.e., pace Orlikowski (2007: 1437), there may be material without the social). The existence of material objects, such as mineral reserves (Faulkner and Runde, 2011) or stars in distant galaxies does not depend on any human practice. That our awareness of them presupposes human practices, such as astronomy or mineral exploration, and that any human engagement with these material objects will be necessarily social (if only in the sense that an individual finding the star or mineral deposit will be a social being, whether they tell anyone else about their discovery or not) would not seem to preclude their independent existence. This is not to say that such existence, per se, is socially consequential, and therefore relevant to an understanding of organizations, but it does suggest that the scope of some of the onto-logical claims made about sociomateriality may be wider than is strictly necessary for the central argument of the approach.

The final notion of inseparability, following Barad, is that of the observed object and the agencies of observation. In this sense, the CCU example may be seen as illustrating how the patient is constructed through the data provided by the technology. This would appear to operate in two ways: the first is through the phenomena that the particular sensors and tests give access to. In presenting particular data about the patient, a certain picture is created. These data may be expected to reflect elements of the biological model of disease prevalent in Western medicine, but sensors may not always provide direct access to the physiological phenomena that they seek to monitor. As technology evolves it may be possible to gain better and more complete data without necessarily achieving better access to the phenomena. The account of the patient provided by the technology defines them in terms of particular constructions of their condition.

In the second sense, as some staff recognized, the patient becomes the numbers that the technology provides. There was seen to be a danger that this could be exacerbated by the introduction of the CIS. With data automatically recorded, in greater volumes and more accessibly, the numbers provide an increasingly rich and persuasive picture. Furthermore, with doctors able to access the CIS from their office they could make treatment decisions solely on the basis of the presented data without the inconvenience and distractions of visiting the bedside. Some medical staff (and not just nurses), however, expressed concerns that this would be placing too much weight on data that were considered to be potentially unreliable or incomplete, as well as reducing the opportunities for face-to-face interaction with nurses, whose knowledge of, and experience with, the patient might be relevant to the doctor's decision.

### 9.6.2 Interpenetration

The critical care setting provides a number of examples of the interpenetration of humans and technology as mutual positioning, such as lines and sensors being inserted into the patient's body or hemofiltration or ECMO in which the patient's circulatory system is diverted via a machine to enable the blood to be treated. This association is not always symmetrical, however. It is the patient, rather than the technology, that is generally more profoundly penetrated. Devices are designed to retain their integrity even within the patient's body, but the patient may be opened up to introduce the device. In most cases the interpenetration is also only for a limited period of time, although some devices, such as artificial heart valves, may be implanted permanently.

Notions of interpenetration are evoked in discussion of cyborgs and certainly critical care patients' bodies with an artificial heart valve or a pacemaker are no longer entirely human and might not be able to survive were these implants removed. This did not seem to affect their status as humans, however, especially as the devices are generally concealed within the body and are perceived not as an augmentation, but as a restoration of normal functionality that had become impaired. It may only be other machines, such as airport body scanners, that are able to distinguish such cyborgs.

Where the machine support is more visible and active, such as with hemofiltration and ECMO, the perception of the status of the patient would seem more open to question. Decisions about the initiation and continuation of treatment invoked the idea that the patient's dependency on the device reduced their viability. That the physical boundary of the patient is breached and that vital functions are sustained only with the intervention of a machine appeared to make the machine–human boundary more ambiguous.

The claim by Orlikowski and Scott (2008) that the properties of humans and technology are *only* acquired through their interpenetration, however, would seem another overstatement unless we prejudge the conclusion by restricting the term property solely to a quality as it is defined by humans— an object has a weight only if it is measured by someone. If, however, we can consider an object to have a weight or a temperature irrespective of whether this is measured or is consequential for human practice then these properties are not dependent on mutual interpenetration of the social and the material. In the CCU context, for example, humans may be argued to have physiological properties, such as respiration, that are independent of the social—in normal circumstances they can breathe without any involvement of other people. Indeed, a major reason why patients are admitted to a CCU is the failure of these autonomous properties, and the success of their treatment is assessed by whether, or the extent to which, these properties are restored. This does not mean that their treatment is not a human practice or its outcome does not have social consequences, but that the physiological properties do not depend only on the interpenetration of humans and technology, or even of the social and the material.

The claim here is not that the interpenetration of humans and technology (or of the social and the material more generally) is not consequential or that it is unreasonable to suggest that the two acquire form, attributes, and capabilities through their interpenetration, just that they do not do so exclusively. Thus the form and attributes of a cardboard kidney dish provide the capability for it to be used as a notepad and that this capability is realized depends on the actions of medical staff with an urgent need to write something down, but with no paper to hand. That its use as both a dish and a notepad are meaningful in relation to the sociality of medical practices also does not preclude other uses, as a doorstop or a desk tidy, say. It is the properties of cardboard, as opposed to the metal from which kidney dishes were traditionally made, however, that allows it to be written on or folded to wedge open a door and thus to perform particular roles in nursing practice that a metal kidney dish could not (at least in the same way). These properties, moreover, would not seem to be *acquired only* through the uses to which the dish is put, even if they may be necessary for it to be used in these practices.

Recognizing that properties of material objects become meaningful in human practices, therefore, would not seem to require that the objects have no properties except as they are realized in these practices. A (live) patient's blood is at pressure, for example (as will be observed if a major blood vessel ruptures), whether or not anybody measures that pressure, and even if measuring it, observing the measurement, and taking action to change it, if necessary, are all human practices. Nor would it seem that the sorts of practices that the material properties can become meaningful in are wholly independent of those properties. The range of practices in which a metal kidney dish can be used may be greater than those in which it is employed in a particular setting, but are bounded by material properties that are not a product of sociomaterial interpenetration. It could not be used as fuel on a fire, for example, or for warming food in a microwave oven, as a cardboard dish could (although it could be argued that the manifestation of these properties depends on a broader social context). As with the inseparability of the social and material, therefore, the ontological implications of inter-penetration would seem neither as general nor as symmetrical as is some-times claimed.

### 9.6.3 Relationality

For Pickering (1993), it is the agency of humans and machines that is a relational product. To a considerable degree, although not entirely, critical care nurses treat patients through the technologies (including drugs and records as well as the more obvious medical devices) that they routinely employ in their work and the effects of these technologies depend on the ways in which they are used by nurses. The drug can only enter the patient's body, for example, if the right line is opened and the drip or driver is started, but if the driver does not work or the line is blocked then the nurse's actions will not have the expected effect. The dynamics of practice cannot therefore be accounted for by the actions of independent entities, but arises from their mutual engagement.

The more abstract claim of Slife (2004) that the qualities, properties, and identities of things come from their relationships may also find some support in the critical care setting. Thus, the activities and identities of CCU nurses are constituted, at least in part, through material means. A lot of CCU nursing is about doing things with machines and is generally perceived as being more technically skilled and more technology-focused than general nursing. While CCU nurses may be reluctant to abandon the virtue script, their identities would seem to be tied up with the technology that dominates their work.

The properties and identities of the technology, however, would not seem so evidently derived from the activities in which they are deployed, except insofar as devices are designed to do the things they do—a ventilator is a ventilator because it ventilates. There may be some, marginal flexibility in this identity (a kidney dish can be a notepad) but the scope of this depends on particular properties (the surface of the kidney dish being such that it can be written on, for example) that, as was argued above, are not a product of how the nurse relates to the dish, per se.

If it may be questioned whether the properties and identities of technologies depend (only) on how they are used, then the claim that materials don't exist in and of themselves, or that people and things only exist in relation to each other would seem even more extreme. At one level, as has been argued previously, it would seem reasonable to suggest that the existence of technologies is not dependent on any immediate relationship with humans (the device continues to exist in the store cupboard). At another level, however, the materiality of a CCU is necessarily a product of a relationship with people, if not of those immediately present. Medical practice in critical care is therefore always already in a relationship to technology and the material and we therefore cannot fully understand it in terms of either the social or material in isolation.

### 9.6.4 Embodiment

It would seem difficult to discuss medical practice in critical care without reference to bodies and their materiality. Patients' bodies, as physical objects, are at the centre of most work. As some medical staff commented, the technology involved in critical care may sometimes obscure this centrality, however, and conscious efforts were made to ensure that due attention was paid to the body itself, rather than just the traces it presented through the technology. Nurses' bodies may also be significant, for example in their dexterity in performing tasks, being obstructed in carrying out their work by the presence of machines around the bed, or the difficulty of more than one or two people seeing data on the CIS screen at one time due to small font sizes and the narrow viewing angle.

Although it involves considerable cognitive skills in operating devices and interpreting the patient's condition, the practice of critical care nursing is also, importantly, a movement of bodies, both of the patient and the nurse. Patients need to be turned regularly to avoid bedsores, or their position adjusted to carry out procedures, or to access or install devices. Nurses move around the bed, between devices, the record (whether on paper or computer), and the patient and sometimes away from the bed, for example to use the blood gas analyzer, to obtain drugs or equipment, or to assist colleagues. Given the need for constant vigilance over the patient's condition, however, the scope of nurses' movement is quite restricted, especially compared to doctors, and this may have consequences for the coordination of work.

Bodily knowing, as well as action, would seem essential to critical care nursing. Work is highly routinized and much of it is carried out without active reflection, indeed work can become problematic if nurses become too conscious of what they are doing. Much of this involves particular bodily movements (putting up a new bag of blood, adjusting driver rates, drawing a drug dose, making up a drip) that may be repeated many times in the course of a 12-hour shift and need to be conducted at high speed. Skillful performance of these bodily actions is a major part of critical care nursing practice.

Experienced nurses talk, too, of the body as a site of knowing, referring to "gut feelings" to explain their sense that all is not as it should be with a patient, especially where this contradicts the evidence provided by the technology. The importance of touching and examining the patient's body as a means of acquiring personal knowledge of the patient's condition to support or correct the technical understanding represents another facet of embodied knowing, as does empathic judgment of the patients' comfort through interpretation of their bodily comportment.

As an aspect of the material, therefore, bodies would seem to have a particular significance in critical care medicine. It would seem difficult, however, to argue that this is necessarily a difference in kind, rather than degree, from their significance in civil engineering (Suchman, 2007) or office work (Orlikowski and Scott, 2008). To the extent that work is done by humans then it will be organized, to some extent at least, around the physical form and capabilities of their bodies.

## 9.7 Discussion

The terminology of entanglement, in the various ways that it is discussed in the literature, would therefore seem to offer a useful vocabulary for describing the relationship between the social and the material in critical care nursing. It is also possible to identify important commonalities between the terms inseparability, interpenetration, relationality, and embodiment as they are discussed in this literature and to make comparable statements about the relationship between the social and material employing any one of them.

As the analysis of critical care nursing has sought to illustrate, however, there may be some benefit in according greater recognition to the differences between the terms and thus to their specific connotations. Where phenomena associated with the close mutual positioning of humans and machines are the particular focus of attention, for example, it may be appropriate to talk of interpenetration, or of relationality where a more abstract form of association is under consideration, or of embodiment where human bodies are significant in the association, or of inseparability where the emphasis is on the relationship being indissoluble.

It would also seem desirable to be clearer about the scope of claims, in terms of things like their level of precision or abstraction or the temporal or spatial extent of their domain of application. For example, does saying that entities have no inherent properties mean that any liquid would be as good as blood for a transfusion? Should statements about materials not existing in and of themselves be taken to apply to all materials, including Faulkner and Runde's mineral deposits, or do they refer specifically (exclusively?) to materials found in the sorts of contemporary organizational settings that are generally being discussed? Does indissolubility mean for all time and in all circumstances, or just for all practical purposes, here, now? Are we talking about how we may characterize the relationship between the social and the material in general, or how we may conceptualize a particular relationship, or making specific claims about certain specific settings, or all settings? Clarifying such claims would not be just about disarming pedants (although it might achieve that to some degree), but about trying to think through the implications of sociomaterial rhetoric in more detail.

There would also seem to be a need for greater care in treating the terms as synonyms. Is fusion a necessary requirement for inseparability, for example, or does interpenetration imply indissolubility? It may be that there are situations in which drawing connections between two different terms is appropriate to the specific claim being made or offers valuable insights, but there is a risk of metaphors becoming over-extended and losing their distinctiveness. If not all fusions are inseparable then equating the two terms may be misleading, especially in discussion of a fusion that can be separated or of an inseparable association that does not evidently involve fusion. Blurring the meanings of terms would not seem justified simply by the avoidance of stylistic clumsiness.

It is not just that different terms are used in the literature to describe the relationship, however. There is also considerable variation in the terms used to refer to the two elements seen as being related (if indeed we can talk of the elements independently of one another). Thus, taking sociomateriality as our starting point, it would seem reasonable to identify "social" and "material" as the central terms for the key relata. Elsewhere, however, we find "humans" and "work" employed as descriptions of the first element and "technology" and "artifacts" as alternatives for the second. Even if we accept that there is some overlap between these terms, they would not seem complete synonyms. While humans may be a necessary feature of phenomena described as social, for example, work is generally considered a particular subset of human activity. Compared to other literature on materiality in organizations, moreover, the sociomateriality literature would seem to pay more attention to technology than to materiality in general. This may make some arguments more clear-cut (it would seem easier to consider a patient and a dialysis machine as separate from each other, say, than to consider a patient independently of their materiality), but it also creates other problems.

As Faulkner and Runde (2010) and Leonardi (2010) discuss, for example, not all technological objects or digital artifacts are necessarily material (in the sense, as they use the term, of having a physical existence, although not all writers on sociomateriality necessarily define it in this way). This argument is primarily made in relation to computer-based information systems, such as the cardiothoracic CIS, components of which, such as applications and files, may be stored on physical media, but do not themselves have physical form. This claim can clearly be extended to other devices employed in a critical care unit which have embedded software, but there is also a sense in which critical care nursing acts upon a non-material representation of the patient constructed through data traces, whether they are recorded on paper or a computer. In accounting for the inter relationship of humans and technology, therefore, perhaps we need also to consider whether their form of existence is significant in their sociomaterial entanglement.

A further issue highlighted in the critical care setting is the significance of affect. Caring for patients is not just about keeping their bodies functioning, but is also about compassion, relationship, and emotional support. Focusing on materiality, however, can be seen as risking the neglect of the important role of emotions and motivation in nursing. While this may be attributed to the continuing influence of a "virtue script" (Gordon and

Nelson, 2006) particular to nursing, states of emotion may also be considered as essential elements of practices in general. As Reckwitz (2002: 254) argues, "every practice contains a certain practice-specific emotionality (even if that means a high control of emotions)." That focusing on technology is seen as attenuating attachment would seem supported by the comments of critical care medical staff, although, as their remarks about managing the emotional cost of patients' deaths also illustrates, this may not be regarded as wholly negative.

In drawing attention to the treatment of these two areas, the intention is not to suggest either that non-materiality and affect are the only potential problems that are overlooked in the sociomateriality literature or that the current comments have done more than point out issues that would seem to merit more substantive discussion. Both, however, may be seen to illustrate a more general point, that, in giving greater attention to the material, it would seem important that sociomaterial analysis does not overlook other dimensions of practices.

## 9.8 Socio(-)material(ity), entanglement, and process research

The literature using the term sociomaterial (with or without a hyphen) would seem to embrace a range of interpretations of entanglement. On the one hand, evident in the early literature in fields such as sociology, economics, and human geography, the term socio(-)material is merely an adjective with no specific ontological connotation. To refer to a sociomaterial factor is simply a shorthand way to highlight the social and material conditions that are seen as influencing a particular situation, rather than a claim about the inseparability of the social and material. On the other hand, Barad (2007), whose work is influential in Orlikowski's account of sociomateriality (and also in Iedema's discussion of materiality (Iedema, 2007)) rejects any a priori distinction between the social and the material. Rather they are seen as mutually constitutive of each other through situated intra-action. In between (if we can consider both Barad and the earlier literature as lying on a common spectrum) are other contributing theoretical approaches, such as the various branches of Actor Network Theory, Suchman's ethnomethodology or Practice Theory, and the sociomaterial literature drawing on them, that view materiality as integral to organizational phenomena, without necessarily dissolving any distinction between the two. Despite their shared terminology, therefore, and their grouping by

Orlikowski under the umbrella of sociomateriality, these literatures do not constitute a single, coherent perspective; indeed a number of the authors are at pains to differentiate themselves from each other.

These differences notwithstanding, however, most sociomaterial (and especially sociomateriality) literature, with the exception of those works in which the term is used simply as an adjective, would seem to adopt a "strong" process ontology (Langley, 2009). This is most evident in work drawing on Barad (2007), whose conceptualization of phenomena as the contingent outcome of sociomaterial "intra-action" can be considered inherently processual, but other sociomaterial authors who refer to inter-, rather than intra-, action would similarly emphasize the situated and emergent character of organizational practice.

The nuances of most sociomaterial thinking, therefore, would seem to be not so much about the merits, or otherwise, of a process perspective per se as about the ontological implications of this position. Is the world processual "all the way down," acquiring form only in its enactment, or can there be anything outside such instantiation? The argument presented here has sought to show both that different stands of sociomaterial thinking do not agree on the answer to this question and that an insistence that relata cannot pre-exist their relation, as Barad (2003) suggests, may not be a necessary corollary of such thinking.

In part this may be argued to be a matter of the scope of claims, where it has been suggested that some accounts of sociomateriality, while they may be reasonable in particular contexts, could be considered as over-extending the argument in relation to both the existence and properties of the material in general. While this may be countered by arguing that these general considerations are irrelevant to discussions of sociomateriality in organizational research, which is, by definition, focused on materiality within a social context, there would seem a risk of such arguments becoming tautological—the material world is always socially mediated because, as social beings, our every interaction with it is necessarily social. While this chapter cannot hope to resolve such debate, it has sought to highlight some of the assumptions that may be carried by the vocabulary employed by writers on sociomateriality to describe both the relationship between the social and the material and the relata themselves.

In terms of process research, these ontological assumptions may make a difference to, for example, the methodologies that could enable the various forms of entanglement to be studied or the types of theory that might be developed. Of greater significance for practice research, though, may be the more general argument of sociomateriality that research needs to do more than just pay greater attention to materiality, it needs to consider the social and material as mutually constitutive. We need to understand not just how "matter matters" (Barad, 2003: 803), but how the entanglement of the social and material (in its various different forms) matters. This chapter would certainly not claim to have been able to do more than indicate the potential for such understanding and there is clearly much more to be done in developing this work.

What would already seem apparent, however, is that current accounts of sociomateriality do not always seem to follow the logic of their own argument. Thus, while it may be understandable in terms of efforts to redress the perceived over-socialization of organizational research, that sociomaterial researchers promote a greater focus on materiality, this risks neglecting other aspects of organizations, such as affect, or other aspects of materiality, such as embodiment, that are perhaps under-represented in the reference literatures. The relative focus in the sociomateriality literature on technology, rather than materiality in general, is also arguably somewhat disproportionate. It is not that these lacunae are the sole preserve of sociomaterial research, but that such research might, perhaps, have been expected to show greater sensitivity to such issues.

## 9.9 Conclusion

A central claim of the sociomateriality literature, and also of many papers using the term sociomaterial (particularly without a hyphen), as well as a number that discuss materiality in organizations more generally, is that we need to consider the social and the material as "mutually enacting" (Dale, 2005: 651). As the analysis of nursing in critical care presented in this chapter has shown, this would seem a generally productive approach to understanding organizational practices, even if a number of the specific claims made in the sociomateriality literature might benefit from some qualification. It is also an approach that, for the most part, is consistent with a strong process view of organizations.

The metaphor of entanglement that is widely used in the sociomateriality literature to describe the relationship between the social and material, however, may be considered as conflating a number of potentially inconsistent ontological claims that it may be desirable to differentiate more clearly as the concept gains wider recognition and influence. The sociomateriality literature may also be seen as more focused on materiality (and technology in particular) than the arguments presented might imply, and as neglecting issues such as non-materiality and affect that may be important in understanding contemporary organizational practices.

This is not to say that the concept will in some sense fail if these points are not addressed. Indeed, a certain level of ambiguity and inconsistency may attract a wider audience, all of whom can find what they want in it, and their elimination may not be considered necessary or desirable from some points of view (Law, 2004). Nor is it to suggest that the inconsistencies and gaps identified here are definitive, or necessarily the most significant. Rather, in proposing that it may be useful to distinguish between different concepts of entanglement and what is entangled, to be more considered in the terms employed, and to pay greater attention to topics such as affect, the aim is to open debate on the future direction of research on sociomateriality. In this, there would seem a particular need for more empirical process studies to provide insight on the referents of the often abstract accounts in the literature.

## References

Barad, K. (2003). "Posthumanist Performativity: Toward an Understanding of How Matter Comes to Matter," *Signs: Journal of Women in Culture and Society*, 28/3: 801–31.
—— (2007). *Meeting the Universe Halfway*. London: Duke University Press.
Callon, M. (1986). "Some Elements of a Sociology of Translation: Domestication of the Scallops and the Fishermen of St Brieuc Bay," in J. Law (ed.), *Power, Action and Belief: A New Sociology of Knowledge*. London: Routledge & Kegan Paul, pp. 196–233.
—— and Muniesa, F. (2005). "Peripheral Vision: Economic Markets as Calculative Collective Devices," *Organization Studies*, 26/8: 1229–50.
Dale, K. (2005). "Building a Social Materiality: Spatial and Embodied Politics in Organizational Control," *Organization*, 12/5: 649–78.
Engeström, Y. and Middleton, D. (1996). *Cognition and Communication at Work*. Cambridge: Cambridge University Press.
Faulkner, P. and Runde, J. (2011). "The Social, the Material, and the Ontology of Non-Material Technological Objects," paper presented at the European Group for Organizational Studies (EGOS) Colloquium, Gothenburg, 2011.
Gordon, S. and Nelson, N. (2006). "Moving Beyond the Virtue Script in Nursing: Creating a Knowledge-Based Identity for Nurses," in S. Nelson and S. Gordon (eds.), *The Complexities of Care: Nursing Reconsidered*. Ithaca: Cornell University Press, pp. 13–29.
Gray, C. H., Mentor, S., and Figueroa-Sarriera, H. J. (1995). *The Cyborg Handbook*. London: Routledge.
Iedema, R. (2007). "On the Multi-modality, Materially and Contingency of Organization Discourse," *Organization Studies*, 28/6: 931–46.

Jensen, T., Sandström, J., and Helin, S. (2009). "Corporate Codes of Ethics and the Bending of Moral Space," *Organization*, 16/4: 529–45.

Langley, A. (2009). "Studying Processes in and around Organizations," in D. Buchanan and A. Bryman (eds.), *The SAGE Handbook of Organizational Research Methods*. London: Sage, pp. 409–429.

Latham, R. and Sassen, S. (2005). *Digital Formations: New Architectures for Global Order*. Princeton: Princeton University Press.

Latour, B. (1993). *We Have Never Been Modern*. Cambridge, MA: Harvard University Press.

—— (2007). *Reassembling the Social: An Introduction to Actor-Network-Theory*. Oxford: Oxford University Press.

Laughlin, C. D. (1997). "The Evolution of Cyborg Consciousness," *Anthropology of Consciousness*, 8/4: 144–59.

Law, J. (2004). *After Method: Mess in Social Science Research*. London: Routledge.

—— and Mol, A. (1993). "Notes on Materiality and Sociality," *Sociological Review*, 43/2: 274–94.

Leonardi, P. M. (2010). "Digital Materiality? How Artifacts Without Matter, Matter," First Monday, 15/6–7, available at http://firstmonday.org/htbin/cgiwrap/bin/ojs/index.php/fm/article/viewArticle/3036/2567.

—— (2011). "When Flexible Routines Meet Flexible Technologies: Affordance, Constraint, and the Imbrication of Human and Material Agencies," *MIS Quarterly*, 35/1: 147–67.

Merleau-Ponty, M. (1962). *The Phenomenology of Perception*. London: Routledge.

Miettinen, R. and Virkkunen, J. (2005). "Epistemic Objects, Artefacts and Organizational Change," *Organization*, 12/3: 437–56.

Mol, A. (2002). *The Body Multiple: Ontology in Medical Practice*. London: Duke University Press.

Orlikowski, W. J. (2000). "Using Technology and Constituting Structures: A Practice Lens for Studying Technology in Organizations," *Organization Science*, 11/4: 404–28.

—— (2007). "Sociomaterial Practices: Exploring Technology at Work," *Organization Studies*, 28/9: 1435–48.

—— (2010). "The Sociomateriality of Organizational Life: Considering Technology in Management Research," *Cambridge Journal of Economics*, 34/1: 125–41.

—— and Scott, S. V. (2008). "Sociomateriality: Challenging the Separation of Technology, Work and Organization," *Academy of Management Annals*, 2/1: 433–74.

Pels, D., Hetherington, K., and Vandenberghe, F. (2002). "The Status of the Object: Performances, Mediations, and Techniques," *Theory, Culture & Society*, 19/5–6: 1–21.

Pickering, A. (1993). "The Mangle of Practice: Agency and Emergence in the Sociology of Science," *American Journal of Sociology*, 99/3: 559–89.

Pickering, A. (1995). *The Mangle of Practice: Time, Agency and Science*. Chicago: University of Chicago Press.

Reckwitz, A. (2002). "Toward a Theory of Social Practices," *European Journal of Social Theory*, 5/2: 243–63.

Sandberg, J. and Tsoukas, H. (2011). "Grasping the Logic of Practice: Theorizing through Practical Rationality," *Academy of Management Review*, 36/2: 338–60.

Schatzki, T. R., Knorr-Cetina, K., and Von Savigny, E. (2001). *The Practice Turn in Contemporary Theory*. London: Routledge.

Slife, B. D. (2004). "Taking Practice Seriously: Toward a Relational Ontology," *Journal of Theoretical and Philosophical Psychology*, 24/2: 157–78.

Suchman, L. (2000). "Embodied Practices of Engineering Work," *Mind, Culture and Activity*, 7/1: 4–18.

—— (2007). *Human–Machine Reconfigurations*. Cambridge: Cambridge University Press.

# 10

# Doing by Inventing the Way of Doing: Formativeness as the Linkage of Meaning and Matter

*Silvia Gherardi and Manuela Perrotta*

**Abstract:** The chapter proposes the concept of formativeness in order to interpret how materiality comes to matter within creative practices in craftsmanship. The concept of formativeness comes from aesthetic philosophy and it denotes the process by which phenomena (for instance an object or a work of art) acquire form within working practices. Formativeness is a process realized through a doing that while it does invents "the way of doing." This concept should be added to the lexicon of practice to denote not only the process whereby the form emerges from the encounter with materials, but also a specific type of knowing process situated within practical creativity. A practice-based approach to creative practices within artisan firms informed the empirical research on which the theoretical reflection is based. A contribution to the literature on organizational creativity is thus made by complementing it with a non-linear vision of the creative process, where the following aspects of the formative process—sensible knowing, co-formation of ideas and materiality, experimenting with playfulness, translating and hybridizing materials, realization and repetition—may explain how meaning and matter are intrinsically entangled in forming.

## 10.1 Introduction

In recent years, the topic of "creativity" has given rise to a flourishing strand of analysis in organizational studies, as shown by the publication of a number of handbooks (Rickards et al., 2009; Mumford, 2012) highlighting the importance of understanding the design and aesthetics of organizations, the role of creativity in the production of innovation and the circulation of knowledge, and how organizations can encourage creativity and innovation. However, despite the large body of articles and books on the topic, the conception of what constitutes "creativity" and of the processes by which individuals and organizations produce fresh ideas for innovating products, services, and organizational processes is still tied to the instrumental view that creativity serves to give organizations an enduring competitive advantage, and to gain understanding of what can foster or impede creativity in organizations (Woodman et al., 1993; Ford, 1996; Oldham and Cummings, 1996; Boland and Collopy, 2004). Notably, a great deal of this literature concentrates on the understanding of creativity as an individual gift and therefore on the nature of creative people (Bennis and Biederman, 1997), their personality (Singh, 1986), and intelligence and cognitive abilities (Gardner, 1993). Other studies have framed creative behavior as the result of an interaction between the characteristics of the individual and those of the environment (Mumford and Gustafson, 1988; Woodman et al., 1993). Although it is recognized that organizational learning is a key component of creativity (Glynn, 1996) and an important factor for the development of new or novel knowledge that becomes accessible for problem solving (Leonard, 1995), only in a few cases has the relationship of creativity with new knowledge development and organizational learning been considered (Drazin et al., 1999; Mumford, 2000; Kazanjian and Drazin, 2012).

In contrast, in this chapter, we are interested specifically in understanding how creativity unfolds over time, how it relates to knowing as a situated activity, how affect relates to creativity, and in line with the theme of this volume how "matter matters" as an active partner in the creative process of people in workplaces. These aspects of the creative process are not totally new; nevertheless, they have not been studied within a single theoretical framework.

For example, creative activity has been recognized as an affectively charged event, and research has been conducted on how positive affect relates positively to creativity in organizations, as an antecedent to creative thought, and as a concomitant component of a creative process consisting of multiple stages (Amabile, 1988; Amabile et al., 2005). Creativity has also been studied from a process perspective. In this case, creativity has been defined (Torrence, 1988) as a process of sensing problems, making guesses, formulating hypotheses, communicating ideas to others, and contradicting conformity. These perspectives share the assumption that the nature of resources and their materiality are largely unproblematic and do not play a role in the creative process.

Nevertheless, a certain role assigned to material resources may be found in the rediscovery of Lévi-Strauss' concept of bricolage and its transformation into organizational bricolage. Scholars working in the area of organizational symbolism (Linstead and Grafton-Small, 1990) have transported the notion of bricolage from its anthropological origin and used it to oppose the rationality of linear thought, in that bricolage symbolizes a particular way of acting. Bricolage, in Lévi-Strauss' (1966: 17) terms refers to "doing things with whatever is at hand." Lévi-Strauss did not clearly define what he meant by "bricolage" and "bricoleur" and it is precisely for this reason that the term "bricolage" has been transported into organizational studies and redefined in various ways. For example, Weick (1998) has connected it with improvisation, i.e., the integration of thought and action; others have used it to describe the process of distributed agency which engages multiple actors possessing local knowledge and which results in innovation (Garud and Karnøe, 2003); others have viewed it as a strategy characteristic of information technology appropriation (Ciborra, 2002); and yet others have considered it an ideal-type of managerial practice (Duymedjian and Rüling, 2010). Prevalent in this literature is the metaphorical use of the term, in accordance with Lévi-Strauss' original view of bricolage as a particular type of relationship that human beings entertain with the world.

The aspect instead tied to intimacy with the material and whatever is at hand is more evident in the use made of it by studies on entrepreneurship, although these too attribute a passive role to materiality as an inactive presence. Consequently, small crafts businesses have been considered as forming a privileged domain in which to investigate organizational behavior in terms of entrepreneurial bricolage as "making do by applying combinations of the resources at hand to new problems and opportunities" (Baker and Nelson, 2005: 333). These authors have analytically defined entrepreneurial bricolage according to three dimensions: (i) making do, i.e., an active engagement with problems or opportunities rather than lingering over questions of whether a workable outcome can be created from what is at hand; (ii) combination of resources for new purposes, i.e., serendipitous combinations of existing programs, pasted-up solutions, or failed components put to unexpected uses; (iii) the resources at hand, i.e., physical artifacts, skills, or ideas that are accumulated on the principle that they may always come in handy. We have cited these three aspects as characteristic of practical creativity in order to distinguish the creativity of the artist—in which the work of art is an end to itself—from the creativity of the artisan who seeks to give distinctiveness to his/her product.

The symbolism of artisanal work enables Sennett to equate a master carpenter and a Linux programmer as "craftsmen." Sennett (2008: 28) defines the craftsperson as the figure representative of the specific human condition of making a personal commitment to what one does. The archetype of the artisan is therefore used—by a pragmatist—to discuss material culture and to resume classic themes of pragmatism: the relation between doing and thinking, between work and play, and between the hand and the head. In this chapter, we reprise these themes, not within the theoretical framework of pragmatism, but instead within that of a sociology of practice.

Specifically, the chapter draws on empirical research in the field of craftsmanship to explore the active role of materiality in relation to practical creativity. It proposes to perform an epistemological shift by abandoning the concept of creativity (as an individual gift or epistemic object) for that of creative practice (as a situated activity). It offers a key concept with which to interpret practical creativity as a process which gives form to material, and which in doing so relies on a dynamic which in aesthetic theory is called "formativeness": that is, doing by inventing "the way of doing." In Pareyson's aesthetic theory, formativeness is understood as the art of knowing/doing.

The chapter is structured into five main sections. Section 10.2 introduces the rationale for a practice-based approach to creative practices in crafts firms; section 10.3 presents Pareyson's concept of formativeness; section 10.4 illustrates the research design; section 10.5 sets out our interpretation of the art of knowing/doing; section 10.6 highlights the contribution of the concept of formativeness to studies of creativity in organizational settings. In the conclusions we discuss the theoretical implications of framing creativity as a practice.

## 10.2 A practice-based approach to creative practices

The main concern of a practice-based approach to creativity (i.e., focusing on creative practices) is to understand the logic of the situation and the performance of action as practical knowledge which connects working with organizing, knowing with practicing. This implies a shift toward a "practice" epistemology, moving away from an epistemology of knowledge as possession (Cook and Brown, 1999) to one of practice—that is, to a conception of knowing as a practical activity, and an activity entangling matter with meaning. The sociology of practice (Gherardi, 2011) furnishes a theory of knowledge that re-frames all material-discursive elements as practice phenomena, interpreting them in terms of collective, situated, and knowledgeable doing. It views actions as "taking place" or "happening," as being performed through a network of connections-in-action, as life-world and dwelling (Sandberg and Dall'Alba, 2009). Practice is seen by Bourdieu (1990: 52) as "the site of the dialectic of the *opus operatum* and the *modus operandi*, of the objectified products and the incorporated products of historical practice, of structure and habitus."

A central theme in the study of practices has been the knowledge hidden within practices: that is corporeal, pre-verbal and non-rational knowledge. The aesthetic analysis of organizational life (Strati, 1992) is directed to understanding the relations among aesthetics, emotions, and affectivity, and it focuses on the problematic nature of the knowledge deriving from the senses. Polanyi (1958) pointed out that, in everyday practice, we are often aware of being able to do something but unable to describe analytic-ally how we do it, to explain it scientifically, and thereby turn it into explicit rather than implicit and entirely personal knowledge. Sensible knowledge has precisely this characteristic: it evades logical-analytical description and scientific formalization and is better expressed evocatively and metaphorically.

In fact, "sensible knowledge concerns what is perceived through the senses, judged through the senses, and produced and reproduced through the senses. It resides in the visual, the auditory, the olfactory, the gustatory, the touchable and in the sensitive–aesthetic judgement. It generates dialectical relations with action and close relations with the emotions of organizational actors" (Strati, 2007: 62). Merleau-Ponty (2002) makes a crucial point in regard to sensible knowledge. He takes accounts of the subject's intimate, personal, and corporeal relation with the experience of the world and does not restrict such knowledge to the mere direct, physical, and objectively observable relation.

One of the main concerns of a practice-based approach is to understand this kind of "don't-know-what" (Strati, 2007), i.e., how people, while they are absorbed in the practice at hand, are able to discern the situated logic that connects together the inner actions, and on this basis prefigure the performance of the practice as an ongoing achievement. Knowing in prac-tice is therefore a contingent ordering, the effect of the ability of practition-ers to find their bearings using the context as a resource and articulate the matter of the world (objects, artifacts, technologies) within a form. We therefore define creative practices in terms of a knowledgeable doing that gives form to the matter at hand. In fact, objects and their material world can be construed as materialized knowledge and matter which interrogate humans and interact with them.

This aspect of practice offers organization studies a conception of organization as "a mangle of practices" (Pickering, 1995) or "a practice-order bundle" (Schatzki, 2005), or a "texture of practices" (Gherardi, 2006). These concepts, which are similar to each other, direct attention to practices as loci of the entangled forming of meaning and matter. Practices are seen as sites of knowing, working and organizing (Schatzki, 2005; Nicolini, 2010). Consequently, a key question becomes the following: how are all the elements—material and semiotic—which make up a practice assembled, held together, and interrelated?

One answer comes from practice-based studies on the practical organization of knowledge taking the form of situated methods of seeing, reasoning, and acting in an association of human and non-human elements. Very similar answers have been given to this question with concepts such as "sociotechnical ensemble" (Bijker, 1995), "sociomaterial assemblage" (Suchman, 2007), or "sociomaterial practices" (Orlikowski, 2007). The purpose of these concepts is to emphasize that "materiality is integral to organizing, positing that the social and the material are *constitutively entangled* in everyday life" (Orlikowski 2007: 1437, italics in the original). A position of constitutive entanglement privileges neither humans nor technologies, neither knowing nor doing; nor does it link them in a form of mutual interdependence.

Our aim in what follows is to add a further dimension to the above framework by focusing theoretically and empirically on the concept of formativeness and on the activity of forming within practices. While to date the specific concern has been to identify what sociomaterial elements constitute a practice, less consideration has been given to how these elements assume a form in being connected. The attention therefore moves from *what* is connected to *how* it is connected, to the process by which the form appears. This distinction has been admirably expressed by Ernst Cassirer (1944) when he writes that a great painter and a great musician are not such because of their particular sensitivity to colors or sounds, but because of their ability to draw a dynamic life of forms from static materials.

This reference to the concept of formativeness and to an aesthetic understanding of practices, which will be summarized in the next section, enables us to more clearly express our interest in how the elements of a practice are connected in a form, and in how this forming process develops in the course of the practice itself.

## 10.3 Formativeness as the art of knowing/doing

The concept of formativeness denotes the process by which phenomena (for instance an object, or a work of art) acquire form within working practices. Formativeness is a process realized through a doing that while it does invents "the way of doing." This concept should be added to the lexicon of practice to denote not only the process whereby the form emerges from the matter, but also a type of knowing process situated within creative practices.

The concept of formativeness[1] originates from the aesthetic philosophy of Pareyson[2] (1960), and it is linked not only to sensible knowledge but also to the relationship with materiality, in that it answers the question: how does practical creativity give rise to the form of its object?

Pareyson's aesthetic theory is an aesthetics of production—as opposed to an aesthetics of contemplation—and it concerns the becoming of the form, i.e., the outcome of a formation process. Pareyson is fascinated by the idea of human life as the invention of forms which acquire lives of their own: they detach themselves from their creators and become models, engendering styles. There is hence a formative character in the whole of human industriousness, and art is a specific domain of this formativeness: it is more a "doing" than an expressing or a contemplating (Pareyson, 1960: v).

Precisely because all human industriousness has an inventive and innovative side—writes Pareyson (1960: 7)—"there can be art *in* every human activity; indeed, there is an art *of* every human activity." Practical creativity can therefore be defined—borrowing from Pareyson—as that doing with art, that exercise of formativeness, which is fueled by invention and moves toward accomplishment within the routinization of creative practices.

Both in art and industriousness there is the tentative feature of intrinsic tension and union between production and invention. Simultaneously invented in doing is "the way of doing": realization is only achieved by proceeding through trial and error to the result, thus producing works that are "forms" (Pareyson, 1960: vi). Forming also requires a relationship with materiality, because forming means forming a material, and the work is nothing other than formed material. In the process of formation of matter, the work also acts as a formant even before it exists as formed.

Pareyson proposes that a work of art be regarded as pure formativeness, and the topic of his book on aesthetics is the work of art in its process of forming and being formed. But he also writes: "if all spiritual life is formative, behold the possibility of beauty possessed by every work, be it speculative, practical or utilitarian…and formative, too, is the sensible knowledge that grasps every 'thing', producing it, and 'forming thereof' the image, so that this is 'accomplished' and reveals and captures, indeed *is* the thing" (Pareyson, 1960: vii).

The knowing process is therefore a formative process in which an attempt is made to produce the image that renders the "thing"; and the outcome of knowing is seeing the "thing" formed. In the doing that invents "the way of doing" there is the sense of progressing toward the final result, attempting and correcting and re-doing; there is the inspiration and the elaboration of an intuition; there is improvisation and exercise; there is domination over the material that opposes resistance and enjoins obedience; there is technique and the language of style. Doing and knowing are not separate; neither does the one follow the other, nor does the one constitute an application of the other. In knowing-in-practice one fully grasps the co-formation and invention, between materiality and formativeness, of the knowledge produced and the process of its production.

Particularly evident in the production of objects is the performative and creative aspect that characterizes every "doing," even when it consists in thinking or acting: "one does not operate without completing, performing, producing, realizing" (Pareyson, 1960: 6). The prose of Pareyson is particularly rich with verbs and gerunds because he is interested in the process by which the outcome is achieved. His attention, like ours,[3] focuses more on the *modus operandi* than on the work accomplished (*opus operatum*). A work is "accomplished" insofar as its doing comprises the way in which it must be done. And this is both the emotion of whoever contemplates a well-accomplished work and the sense of the expression "a job done *comme il faut.*"

The empirical research now described was driven by this concept, which informed the research design.

## 10.4 The research design

The study was conducted between July 2007 and December 2009 on the "knowing-how" of craftswomen belonging to the same artisan association in all sectors of activity and in the same geographical area (Northern Italy). The research design followed the logic of grounded theory (Glaser and Strauss, 1967; Turner, 1981; Clark, 2003). Without entering into detailed discussion of how to conduct a grounded theory, we may broadly define it as an approach that makes it possible to develop theory from data and offers a way to make detailed consideration of qualitative materials in order to develop systematic interpretations about the phenomena that have been observed.

### 10.4.1 Data collection

We interviewed both craftsmen and craftswomen, trying to cover all the sectors of activities within craftsmanship (from construction to the production of artistic works). While we conducted the interviews we roughly analyzed them and wrote memos in order to coordinate and share a common view of the research process among the six persons engaged in the fieldwork.[4] All the interviews were conducted in the artisans' workplaces, which were visited and whose production processes were discussed with the respondents. For the first round of narrative interviews, we used an open protocol (Poggio, 2004; Gherardi and Poggio, 2007) which invited the interviewees to recount how they had learned their crafts, what they considered their most important skills to be, how the idea came to them to make a product, and if they remembered significant episodes in their learning processes. Their willingness and interest in taking part in a participative research process were critical for collecting interviews where "reflection" and not "information" was a common and explicit goal.[5] All the interviews, which lasted between 90 and 180 minutes, were audio-taped and professionally transcribed.

In the first round, 110 firms were involved and narrative interviews were conducted with the founder/owner, from which 60 were subsequently selected for a second round of interviews with only those craftswomen whose work involved the direct and manual production of an object. Following the typical pattern of grounded theory research, our strategy for data collection changed in order to match our theoretical understanding and therefore to focus on those craftswomen "working with their hands." Our theoretical interest in formativeness was born at that time. After the first round, we set aside craftsmen (whose narratives were rather poor) and those craftswomen whose main work was in administration (many of them had become artisans because they were involved in a family business by birth or marriage). This choice was also made because we wanted to narrow our focus on those accounts that we called "between the hand and the head" since—at that time—this was our main interpretative category.

The second round of interviews used the "episodic interview" technique (Flick, 2000), which returns to certain episodes—narrated in the previous encounter—in order to explore them further by eliciting more details.

These interviews were shorter, since an interpersonal relationship had already been established, and they lasted 30 minutes on average.

The challenge of these narratives is putting into words a knowing-how which the literature regards as ineffable or personal knowledge (Polanyi, 1958) and therefore eminently tacit, but not unsayable. We encountered the limitations of language in expressing what is taken for granted, and the main limitations were due to the difficulty of expressing sensible knowledge in words. For example, during the narrations, in order to explain a difference to the interviewer—for instance between a well-accomplished job and one only acceptable—the craftswomen resorted to objects and showed examples able "to give the idea." It was this experience in the field, where objects, material, and samples were used to sustain stories and a language rich with metaphors and sensations, that directed our attention to aesthetic philosophy. As we collected stories of situated learning and practical creativity, we realized that what was being told us was a polyphonic story of formativeness, of how material encounters ideas and how objects acquire form, and once they have been formed cancel the history of their formation, of previous failed attempts, experiments, and trial-and-error procedures.

### 10.4.2 Data analysis

For the analysis of narratives we used a double strategy. We elicited narratives and analyzed their mimetic content: that is, what the stories said about knowing in practice and in relation to materiality, leaving aside the diegetic form of stories (that is, how the story is told). This approach drew on the social constructionist assumption that language is creative in giving form to reality (Davidson, 1984) and on a reflexive assumption that narratives are co-created within narrative discourse with others (Cunliffe, 2001). The researchers were in a sense co-authors of the narratives because they shared with their interviewees (co-researchers) a single discursive space as a way to connect and create meaning at the moment of storytelling.

Nevertheless while we were collecting narratives we were also analyzing them as text, through the use of the Atlas.ti software program, which enabled us to identify the common emergent themes systematically.

### 10.4.3 Data presentation

While the use of textual analysis software provided us with a discipline for control over the contents of the texts (what was said), we subsequently returned our attention to how it was said, to how the narration was performed through the language and how certain "episodes" were selected from the flow of the account. The episode recreates the sense of a situation and uses a richness of language subjectively intended to put the listener in the situation and simultaneously to position (Davies and Harré, 1990) the ego narrating and performing a narrative identity. The episode, in fact, presents the context, which serves as the background to the logic of the practice and which contains the "inherited knowledge" with which craftswomen make sense of the task at hand. Unlike the artist, whose work is pure performativity, the craftsperson works within practices of creativity that contemporize a network of other actors, a market, and a reproducibility of works which take account of criteria of economy and not only aesthetics.

This decision to represent for the reader the episodes that gave rise to our interpretation entailed a second decision: to restrict the stories reported only to those that we regarded as representative of other similar ones which, for reasons of space we cannot report here, and which would have been repetitive.

## 10.5 Formativeness in practical creativity

Our journey through the narratives of formativeness will present five features that characterize the complex phenomenon of practical creativity, simplifying it into single elements. The isolation of discrete components of formativeness is an analytical distinction made for interpretative purposes, rather than being an ontological distinction of elements in the accomplishment of practical creativity. The elements that we shall illustrate are constitutive of formativeness and they are simultaneously present in the becoming of the form and in its knowledgeable forming.

### 10.5.1 Formativeness as corporeality

The relation with materiality and the knowledge of it are mediated by the body. This therefore concerns sensible knowledge. When narrating knowing-in-practice and the formative process of the product, the craftswomen referred to a visceral relationship with the material which could not be expressed with logical-formal language but was represented through an evocative narrative style. For instance, Emma, a fashion designer, recounted her relationship with cloth as follows:

> In my head it works in different ways ... I can be inspired by the fabric, right? I'm there, I sniff the fabrics, I touch them, I have visceral relationships with the things, so that I can be inspired by the cloth, I go and look at it, and I say "Gosh, this fabric is just right for a coat I'm working on, with the neck like this ... "

The relationship with the fabric is described through sensory perceptions: sniffing, touching, and looking are the verbs used to convey this physical and bodily relationship with an active matter. At the same time, however, sensoriality and the relationship with materiality are identified as the real sources of inspiration: not only does the fabric arouse corporeal and sensorial reactions but it is so indissolubly embedded in the formative process that it is at once an active stimulus and a passive material to be shaped. The craftswoman associates the material (the fabric) with the accomplished form ("a coat that I'm working on, with the neck like this"), discursively representing its indistinguishability. The activity/passivity dichotomy is blurred in favor of the entanglement of matter and intention.

Another example of the bodily and intimate relation with material is provided by Marta, a goldsmith who makes jewels using unusual materials like resin:

> We make a lot of things, and very different things, in the sense that we don't repeat things in series, we make things felt in the gut, we make them because we like them and realize them.

In this case, the relationship with the product is described as being "felt in the gut": the narration draws on a corporeal and pre-reflexive dimension expressly associated with pleasure. In this excerpt in particular, pleasure is narrated as the desire to realize only pieces that are liked, and which are therefore not often produced in series. But the excerpt introduces a further element of complexity: Marta expressly connects pleasure with her business idea.

The question of personal satisfaction emerges even more evidently from the story recounted by Sara, an art restorer:

> Now I've got other urgent things to attend to, I've done a small piece, but I'm not satisfied with it yet ... You see that the quality is different, because retouching is a gut thing, it's emotion, you must feel it here [points to her abdomen], if you have an off day there's nothing you can do ...

Not only does the interviewee explicitly state that satisfaction with the work done determines when a restoration is finished, but the success itself of the restoration is inextricably bound up with the emotional aspects of the work. Sara's assertion that retouching is a "gut thing," an emotion, and that it must be felt, highlights the visceral relationship between the materiality of the work and its successful outcome. Sara continues:

> It seemed like a simple job, but it's been more complicated. In a job like this you have to make contact with the work, you must understand it, but not as a graphical artistic construct but as a technical, material one. You must attune yourself to the work, because it's the work that tells you what you must do, that tells you that your approach is the right or wrong one. If you start with assumptions or preconceived ideas...without making real contact with the canvas, with the paint, with the structure of the work...you start off badly. We've sometimes begun to work on paintings from the eighteenth century, but because of haste, because of time constraints, we've found ourselves saying that this is not the right way...You can't do things because you've learned a technique; you must do things because you've understood the picture, and when you've done so, that means you've made contact and because there's you and it, you must leave the world outside. You see and feel the painting.

The viscerality of the relation with materials is in this case expressed as the craftswoman's ability to attune with, to enter into contact with, to "feel" and "understand," the painting. Yet this aesthetic understanding of the creative practice is connected with the ability to perform the restoration in "the right way." Pareyson's dictum that "the work is successful only if it is done as if it were done by itself" (1960: 74) acquires more meaningfulness in light of Sara's explanation: one must understand the work to be able to restore it; and understanding the work entails not only knowing the historical period to which it belongs (not all eighteenth-century paintings can be treated in the same way) or its graphic construction, but also understanding its materiality.

To sum up, isolating corporeality within formativeness allows us to illustrate the active presence of the material in practical creativity. As we have seen through the interview excerpts included in this subsection, the relevance of corporeality in formativeness is strictly bound up with the development of sensible knowing. On the one hand, sensible knowledge is grounded in the relation with the material; on the other, how the body "knows" and learns to know depends on how matter is enactive of sensible contexts in which the object acquires its form in an act of anticipation. Furthermore, matter arouses emotions, enacting a visceral relationship of pleasure and satisfaction.

In the next subsection we will further explore the relation of knowing and doing with materiality from a different point of view, examining the connections between form and materiality, ideation and realization.

## 10.5.2 Formativeness as material agency

There is a commonplace linear notion of the creative process according to which ideation is a phase which logically and temporally precedes the process of realization, just as abstract knowledge precedes the moment at which such knowledge is "enacted." This conception is strongly influenced by the legacy of idealism, in that it maintains that creativeness is concentrated in ideation and that realization is a temporal and causal consequence in which the idea is embodied in the passive material. For example, when it is said that the statue is already contained in the block of marble, this conveys the idea that removing "the superfluous" will reveal the form. This conception of creativeness suppresses the active role of the material in the process of practical creativeness.

The following excerpt from the interview with Elisa, a fashion stylist, shows how the process of craft creation is intrinsically and indissolubly material. The form emerges as the co-formation of idea and subject:

> I always say: stylists must know how to make models, know how to construct prototypes like model makers do. If not, it's easy to draw on paper, but it's not that model makers begin on paper and then construct. You must imagine that they first construct and then draw on the paper. Some people always make this mistake, because first they draw everything and then they have problems in constructing it . . . But stylists are different, they aren't illustrators, because stylists always have to understand how a sketch becomes three-dimensional . . .

Elisa emphasizes that the idea, the abstract form, the sketch on paper are not enough to create garments: one must "know how to make models," "construct prototypes," understand how a sketch "becomes three-dimensional." The materiality in the forming process is not something that comes after the ideation; it imposes constraints on ideas; it is simultaneous with and intrinsic to the formative process itself. Idea and materiality become entangled with each other in a single process of co-formation. Another fashion creator, Emma, described how a garment comes into being thus:

> Nobody invents anything. I always insist on saying "I may be very original in how I make things, yes, but nobody invents anything, even less in fashion . . . " So I may see a photo, the cut of a bodice, of a bra that I like, it inspires me and I decide that I'll make the bodice for the skirt in this way. How things are born is very particular, at times even from pictures, even from comic strips that I like . . . I feel like making a jacket with the shoulders like this, very like in a comic strip or a costume . . . The other day I saw this sort of super-hero with sleeves like a bat, so I tried to recreate it, after which I realized that if I put two clips on the sleeves, they were transformed, right? Ideas almost never come to

me here [in the atelier], but they come to me on the bus, they come to me when I wake up in the morning, they come to me when I'm in the shower . . .

Although Emma's story depicts the idea that induces her to create a new garment as a kind of external illumination inspired by a multiplicity of factors and everyday situations, the linearity of the process that leads from the idea to realization is only a reconstruction a posteriori, whilst the development of the creation is complex and links with the uniqueness of the formative process. Once Emma has been inspired by a certain image, she adapts her creation to the fabric, to the form of the body, to the way in which the jacket falls, inserting new elements which change the final effect (like a pair of clips holding up the sleeves) and thus aligning the formative process with the resistance of the material and the purposes of the operation (the jacket). In other words, the formative process comprises the invention of "the way of doing" in the reciprocal co-formation of idea and material. In fact, Emma continues:

> So this idea comes to me, and the only thing that I want to do is rush over here and take a piece of cloth or paper or the paper-pattern, and do it over and over again . . . I get it just right "Wow, you're a genius!" But many times it's crap, so it can't be said that an idea is always a stroke of genius. But in this job to see whether an idea works you have to realize it, the only way is to take a gamble and not be afraid of ruining a piece of fabric, not being afraid of wasting days of work, because if you have these fears it's better to do a job where you have everything guaranteed. Ideas may come from the fabric, from something that I've seen around, and then all that's needed is the stitching that I like, because then it changes into something completely different, there is not just one way, there are so many ways.

Practical creativeness develops in action, through the material realization of the craft. There is no guarantee that a certain inspiration will prove appropriate when realized. The rule is "to see whether an idea works you have to realize it," but this realization requires taking a gamble and being willing to make repeated attempts until idea and material reciprocally take form. Emma emphasizes the tentative and experimental nature of formative activity when she points out that in her work one should not be afraid of wasting time and materials, because it is tentativeness that characterizes the becoming of the form and determines the success (or otherwise) of the forming process.

However, the co-formation of idea and matter may assume different configurations. For example, the goldsmith Marta, whom we have already quoted, recounted a process the reverse of the one described by Emma:

I have moulds, or I have to make them, so I say "what shall I do now? I mix the dyes, I make the things according to whatever comes into my head, I'm clearly thinking about this summer . . . Will one thing or the other sell better, last year I did something this year I'll do something else." I try things out, I experiment, but it's a matter of the moment in the sense that things come into my head . . . so perhaps I make a resin mould and I say "I like this, it's what I had in mind." Or I make it, and it's not what I'd thought. . . . You get inspiration from one thing rather than another. Then everything comes by experimenting, because I make a resin mould and I say I don't like it and I throw it away. I chuck in the dyes to do something, and I say "I'll try and make this thing here." And I like it loads. In the end it always works like this: I think "I'll do it like this," then I make it and I say "All this messing around and I don't even like it."

Marta's narrative moves in the reverse direction to Emma's. In the above excerpt the encounter between idea and materiality arose from a stimulus external to the work setting: in this case co-formation springs from tentativeness and from the process of giving form to the material. It is during the creation of a certain product that Emma decides whether or not the formative process has produced satisfactory results. She likes some forms produced during the experimentation more than those which she had in mind; or in the material realization of a certain idea, the form actually produced does not correspond to what she had imagined. In this case, too, tentativeness is the concept that best expresses this to-and-fro movement, of a co-formation between idea and material guided by taste, but also by business experience. In the excerpt, in fact, Emma refers expressly not only to what she likes but also to what is suggested by the market. On the other hand, varying one's products from one year to the next, and imagining what will be in fashion next summer, are considerations tied more to sale of the product than to the abstract creative process, and they enable us to understand how all these elements are co-present in the practical creativeness that is at the same time a business activity.

In this subsection, we have illustrated the co-formation of ideas and materiality to show how the encounter between ideas and materiality can be an active process. We rejected the temporal and causal consequence of ideation on realization, illustrating how materiality may resist and impose constraints on ideas. The expression "in order to see if an idea works you have to realize it" gathered during the fieldwork may be taken as an icon of formativeness which expresses the entanglement of knowing/doing. Moreover, giving form to the material is a practical activity that is not detached from business activity. Tentativeness has a key role in the discovery of "the way of doing," but it is not unlimited and it must consider both taste and the market.

In the next subsection, we will illustrate how realization comes about between tentativeness and playfulness.

### 10.5.3 Formativeness as playfulness

The idea of tentativeness tied to experimentation, doing, and the practical realization of craft products has repeatedly emerged. Experimentation can assume different forms, one of the most common of which is playfulness, as the goldsmith Marta recounted:

> It all began from an experiment like a game.... From nothing, yes, from nothing. Then you know, for me these things here ... I make a series of chromatic matches, I play around with the colors, so ... I often see matches, likenesses, and I say "right, look, according to me, I could do this, I could do that, or this time I'll make a scale of colors, I'll contrast them, so I'll play around." There's no inspiration like when you say "Gotcha!" Or there may have been, or it might come to you, but most of the time you go ahead by trial and error, at least for these things here ... I like it, I like that, you take the colors and you say "beautiful, this with this, transparent with non-transparent, opaline mixed with non-opaline, mixed like this" ... it's an alchemy, you stand there, you try things out.

Marta refers to the creative experience realized through experimentation by using the evocative expression "it's an alchemy," which evokes an almost magical equilibrium not possible to explain with standardized rules, but which springs from her passion for her work and her search for innovative results through experimentation. The idea of experimentation as play is crucial. As Marta says, it is not a matter of sudden and brilliant inspiration, but rather of following a series of suggestions that arise from the formative activity itself and prompt the mixing of colors, letting oneself be led by taste in a ludic dimension.

Experimenting with materiality is an activity closely bound up with learning and the aesthetic understanding of what is done. The idea itself of playfulness, in fact, is intrinsically tied to the pleasure of the discovery of materials, techniques, and tools. The story of Katia, a ceramicist, illustrates the indissolubility of experimentation and learning:

> It takes a lot to do ceramics properly. You must know just about everything to do with techniques: enamels, glazes, slips, you have to know how to do all these things. Even the kneading of the clay, with all the procedures that follow, you have to understand the correct components to make enamels with certain

> colors ... I manipulate the clay and from that I get, and behold, a thing like this [shows a clay figurine], completely transformed. With the white, with the dyes, with the enamels. I must understand the enamels to make a complete product ... I have to manipulate, that's the most beautiful thing!

In Katia's narrative, manipulating the clay and turning it into ceramic objects is a process with two aspects: on the one hand, the narrative extols the aesthetic dimension, together with the passionate and ludic nature of experimentation ("manipulating is the most beautiful thing"); on the other, it emphasizes the non-randomness of the process and the learning by trial and error that makes it possible to foresee what the final effect of an enamel or a dye will be. Experimentation in Katia's case is the formalization of knowledge through the systematization of accumulated experience with different enamels:

> This here [showing a palette of paints] could become a blue, this violet can become a blue. You must know that it'll become a blue ... Ceramics is not an easy thing to do, also because you put something in [the oven] and it comes out completely different from what you imagined ... Not always, though, because later, with experience, you realize that you must give a color like this because later it will turn out like this ... With experience. Because the colors change. You get all the color samples, all the things, you know what you'll get from what you use. You must get all the samples. The samples are those things there [shows some palettes with small strips of color of all hues], colors like these, which you see like this, but originally are completely different.

Knowing how a color will change once the enamel has been baked in the oven makes it possible to foresee the final result and use materials and techniques expertly. Also, mistakes can be useful for the future, as in this example recounted by Sara, the restorer:

> You put things right ... also because these are not irreversible situations. The only irreversible operation is cleaning, it's the only one where you can't go back on what you've done ... If you use the wrong fixative, you can always put things right with another fixative, though obviously time and costs are involved. However, we say it's our mistake, and it helps us learn. It'll serve for the next time. When you clean a picture the color may come away. We are always cautious about this, we're always careful with cleaning. For the rest, you go by intuition, which is usually correct because it also comes from experience. The more works you restore, the more experience you have, the more you make the right decisions.

Also in this case, craft interweaves with business, because, as Sara stresses, a mistake incurs an economic loss in terms of production time and costs, but it serves for learning because it increases experience and knowing how to do things better in the future.

The extract from the interview with Sara shows what is meant by saying that intuition—historically attributed to an intrinsic, subjective, and innate capacity—is an ability learned through work, and therefore results from a learning process. Gaining experience, in this case in the restoration of paintings, allows the craftsperson "to realize" how the restoration should be done properly. In her story Sara goes into details about her skills and the materiality of paintings: we have quoted from it at length to highlight that the materiality of knowing-how and the playfulness that characterize the art of doing while discovering "the way of doing."

The interview excerpts included in this subsection, similarly to those of the previous ones, have illustrated how materiality prompts the pleasure of manipulation. However, the last excerpts make it possible to show how playfulness itself constitutes a learning process. Accordingly, experimenting is an emotional and aesthetic activity, but it is playfulness rather than calculation, even when the economic costs of experimentation are present. Finally, recognizing the playful aspect of formativeness allow us to reject the myth of intuition as innate. On the contrary, we have shown how intuition is learnt and routinized through experience. In the next subsection, we will illustrate how innovation is developed in practical creativity.

## 10.5.4 Formativeness as hybridization

We shall now consider how innovations are produced by novel uses of traditional materials or by hybridizations among different materials. The first example illustrating the "added value" of the translation of materials from one sector to another is the already-cited one of Marta the goldsmith, who used the unusual material of resin to create her jewels. Marta recounted her first experience with resin as follows:

> I had to do some work for the Academy, I wanted to take something, for decoration, I wanted to make a project and I needed something transparent but solid . . . So I tried out some things for this project and then I looked for some transparent varnishes, some transparent things, and I found the resin, I don't remember now where and how . . . And I made this block of resin . . . A series of problems, things that I didn't know, I had to create a work on movement and on traces in the air, and I needed to encase this egg in something transparent . . . something which let me see the shape of the egg, and in the end I found this resin. I put this egg in this blown pyrex, which seemed like a bubble. I began to do some tests, fine, fine . . . I like this product! And then

I looked for a different [resin], here and there, I experimented a bit, then I found these special resins used for flooring, among other things... With my husband we had to re-do this floor here, and we said "just think how beautiful it would be if it was all lacquered!" You try things, you experiment, you call, you get information...

Marta's experience with resin started when she experimented with new material to produce a particular effect of what she called "solid transparency." The excerpt reprises many of the elements that we have already discussed: the visceral bond and the pleasure of materiality; the co-formation of idea and material that leads to the production of a desired effect; experimentation; and the solution of a "series of problems" caused by the resistance of the material. However, in this case the fact that resin was a completely new material for the goldsmith introduced an innovation into the creation of jewels. As Marta says in the excerpt, in fact, the particular type of resin selected after various experiments originated from the flooring sector, where it is used as a final coating to give a "lacquered" effect. In this case, the experimentation was concerned not to find the alchemy mentioned in the previous section, nor to produce the co-formation between idea and material that satisfied the craftswoman's taste. Rather, it consisted in more profound examination of the potential of a material unknown in jewelry-making. Marta's narrative, in fact, continued as follows:

There are no courses of this kind. The firm which sells the material, one of the materials that we use, used to run courses, but for floor-layers, because the firm makes flooring products, so it showed the layers how to apply one material rather than another on a floor. But for fancy goods, for these things here, there are no courses. Above all, resin and resin products are constantly developing, there are always new ones, and there are always new surprises. So some stuff works in one way, other stuff in another; one resin is sensitive to damp, another one isn't; one resin needs a certain kind of thinner, another a different one... And so on, but nobody teaches you these things, you try them out.

The translation of resin from flooring to jewelry greatly expands the range of experimentation with that specific material and learning how to use it. Different resins have different characteristics, and for each type suitable technical solutions must be found. As Marta stresses, there are no courses on this subject, because the material is new and unknown, and the only way to obtain satisfactory results is continuous experimentation in which a process that leads to innovation by translation is also implicit.

Another type of innovation emerged from the narrative by two craftswomen, one working with glass and the other with chocolate, who were looking for an innovative way to merge their two materials into a product to present at an Exposition. Trying to create a bridge between their own materials, for a few months they asked their clients to react to the words "glass" and "chocolate." The two materials had something in common: both originate from powder, from melting and heating, both are given as gifts, both are tempered. However, the most frequent words associated with "glass" were "cold," "transparent," "movement," "blue," "neutral."

As Medea, the glassworker, told us:

> From there I worked on my material and with the chocolate.... And so the chocolate-drop necklaces were born. Chocolate melts, it would be nice to wear a chocolate drop, non-fattening chocolate, and so this was a point in common. We made a multi-sensorial track which hit the five senses, the glass to touch, the glass to feel, the glass to see, leaves of glass attached to the branches, and a glass to taste, and using the characteristics of the mental map we created a cocktail. Cold, neutral, a beautiful azure color, and this cocktail was drunk at the chocolate tasting because it could wipe away the taste of the previous chocolate. It was a beautiful experience. And I understood from these notes that cold is still perceived negatively, and from there I began to work with other colors. I began to insert form, to give a sense of warmth to the glass, because here [she works in a mountainous area] people love wood. You must make glass that gives the same sensation as wood, even if the azure glass is always present. For example, there are little bubbles where you can't tell whether they are the sky or the sea. Since then I've seen that many [other craftswomen] have switched to this style, which gives more the idea of color. Now the chocolate necklaces are being sold by retailers. It is a very simple thing, I can't sell them directly. My friend sells them, she's a sweetheart and she sells them with the slogan, "taste and wear a chocolate." It's a cute idea, a particular one.

In this case, too, the hybridization of materials firstly follows a business logic: to create a "cute" and "particular" idea, which caters to a certain segment of the market, through a circuit of authorized retailers, on the basis of a creative process which involves the clients of the two craftswomen. However, the narrative oscillates between this dimension tied to profit and a more "artisanal" one to do with the evocative-sensorial characteristics of materiality. Transforming the cold, transparent, blue, neutral, and moving glass into something warm reminiscent of wood, through the fusion of colors and alternative materials, is at once a material hybridization and a marketing strategy embedded in a non-distinguishable formative process. The chocolate necklace, which does not melt and does not fatten, is the shaped form of this common process.

247

To sum up, in this subsection we have explored the aspect of the formative process that has to do with innovation and its business value. We have shown how in practical creativity the de-contextualization of materials from one use and its re-contextualization in a new form may lead to innovation through the hybridization of materials and ideas that may lead to new products and new marketing strategies. This aspect of formativeness is the one closest to two dimensions of entrepreneurial bricolage described by Baker and Nelson (2005). One is called "resources at hand" and it refers to the set of "odds and ends" that are often collected with the idea that they may always come in handy, and firms vary significantly in their capacity to make use of inputs that are at hand and in facilitating the entrepreneurial creation of something from nothing. The other is called "combination of resources for new purposes," and the idea of recombination is not new in innovation studies, even if they say little about how these recombinations actually come about.

### 10.5.5 Formativeness as recursive realization

Our intention in this section is to evidence the repetition and recursiveness in realization. We consider another extract from the interview with Sara, the restorer:

> I am good at hiding, at disguising. Once I disguised neutral plaster with neutral, I didn't add paint, only dirty water . . . I mean . . . in slang . . . I did nothing with nothing. But the quantity of water, the technique, the stippling, the scoring, come into play. You can't explain retouching, you have to feel it. When you start explaining it, you diminish it.

When realizing a craft product, in this case a restoration, it is necessary to follow the correct way of doing things, which is often attributed to socially learned sensory skills which guide tentativeness and link it with the process of formativeness and success. The extract, however, highlights the simultaneous presence of all the above-mentioned components of realization: from feeling the re-touch to using professional techniques to do "nothing with nothing." The craftswoman's expertise resides precisely in this ability to invent her way of doing in everyday situations requiring her intervention. This example recalls what has been named "making do" in Lévi-Strauss and later in Baker and Nelson (2005) described as "creating something from nothing."

Another example of the realization of a craft product is provided by the interview with Elisabetta, a tailoress, who aptly illustrates these aspects:

Dressing impossible women, that's a real mission impossible! Dressing imperfect bodies, that's my great satisfaction! Dressing well someone who's got nothing shapely about her, that's the real challenge! Dressing a manikin is the easiest thing in the world; dressing a normal person is the easiest thing in the world; dressing defective bodies, that's an achievement, and when you're successful it's a challenge [defeated], because you have to disguise flaws, you have to emphasize the beautiful part, so the dress must be deceptive, it must hide what is wrong, enhance it at the correct point . . . The eye must fall on the beautiful part, the tailoress doesn't just make the dress, she must make . . . a miracle, well perhaps not "a miracle," but she must play . . .

The tailoress' tentativeness in making the garment and her sensory abilities, taste, and aesthetic judgment are summarized in this excerpt, which evocatively recounts success (a dress made to measure), not as a simple "manual" activity but as a miracle. Once again, the ludic dimension is at the core of the narrative: playing with materiality, experimenting with it on a body, inventing technical solutions—these are all elements that express formativeness.

But the extract illustrates another aspect crucial to our analysis: whilst Pareyson's theory of formativeness maintains that "the artist makes the work and the work makes the artist" (1960: 63), in the case of craftsmanship we may say that "the craftswoman makes the product but it is the art of knowing/doing that makes the craftswoman." In her narrative, in fact, Elisabetta shifts attention away from the "garment as product" to "knowing how to dress someone as a practical activity" distinctive of craftsmanship. Elisabetta vividly expresses the difference between the product as a material output and what we name the object of the practice. As used in activity theory, the object of a practice (be it material, like a manufactured product, or human, like a patient in a hospital) is the thing, or project, that people are working to transform, while the objectives of an activity are the intended outcomes of that process. Objects of activity are simultaneously (Blackler and Regan 2009: 164) given, socially constructed, contested, and emergent.

This aspect is now further illustrated with examples taken from the interview with Sonia, a weaver:

It's difficult to learn weaving with a course . . . The easiest thing to learn is the weaving movement, but then you need to do another course, and then another one, because it's work that you have to do over and over again to learn it properly, perfectly, to be independent. At the beginning we first learned to weave . . . but not how to set up the loom, by dint of doing it you learn, and you do it more and more precisely, more and more perfectly, so that if you prepare a perfect loom you have a perfect result. If the threads are looser on one side and tighter on the other, the result of the work is mediocre. But the more you work, the more you acquire this skill in preparation and the more you have a perfect result.... It's a matter of practice, really, of working at it. All the actions of the pedals are easily to internalize, and they stay with you; you no longer find it hard to work the pedals, you know what change of pedals you must make, you know that for one type of damask there's that type of change. When you put a type of work on the loom, you immediately weave with the method you need for that type of work. It's something that stays with you, these things are learned.

Sonia's story highlights the recursive dimension of practice as a method of learning. First you learn to weave (referring to bodily movement, to the embodiment of techniques and manual skill) and then with time you learn to prepare a perfect loom with which to produce perfect fabrics. Although Sonia states that once these two skills have been learned, they become embodied and "stay with you," she continues:

> In this work you can't do it for one day and then take four days off, you have to dedicate yourself to this kind of work. And it's also a matter of practice, you have to work every day, it take a lot of practice, it is not work that ... it doesn't pay off, it doesn't give you anything if you do it this way ... leave off for a week, then start again. Most of all, the fabric doesn't have ... you see some days later that it's been done differently, because you must also have manual skill, you must have the training, let's say, you get it day by day, skill at weaving, practically almost the same, if you weave one day ... put in more work one day and less on another ... you immediately see it in the fabric, you must have training, or it becomes uneven, you must have a certain training, and then working stimulates your curiosity and desire to change things.

This second extract instead conveys that the art of knowing-how must be constantly practiced if it is to be kept in good shape. Shifting attention from the product to formativeness and the knowing-how of craftwork highlights the crux of the matter: in craftsmanship knowing and doing are a single whole which is not exhausted in any finished product but is rather a knowing-in-practice that must be kept alive through practicing. This is not only because distance from practice and materiality means that one lacks "stimuli, curiosity and the desire to change things," as this story says, but also embodies manual skills, rhythm, sensible knowledge, and taste. In other words, there is not only the finished product but also, and above all, the art of knowing/doing.

As we have seen through the interview excerpts included in this subsection, repetition is a key element of discovering the way of doing. This knowledgeable doing is learnt from experience and within the recursiveness of practices. The main aim of this subsection, however, has been to show how the object of a practice emerges from the process of playing with materiality, experimenting, feeling the materials, connecting all the elements of a practice into a coherent whole, and within its business dimension. The expression that best represents the quality of formativeness in relation to recursiveness is "the craftswoman makes the product but it is the art of knowing/doing that makes the craftswoman."

## 10.6 Discussion: the contribution of formativeness to the theory of organizational creativity

We have not entered the debate on what constitutes "creativity," so as not to diverge from our principal interest, but from creativeness as an individual attribute, central to a large body of philosophical and psychological literature, we propose to move toward the study of the practices of creativeness and therefore toward the creative *bricolage* so well described by Lévi-Strauss (1966: 35) in terms of an engagement with tools and materials in order to discover what each of them may signify and anticipated something that has yet to materialize.

We intend to move away from what Ingold (2010: 92) called a hylomorphic model of creation, i.e., the heritage of an Aristotelian tradition that assumes that in order to create anything it is necessary to bring together form (*morphe*) and matter (*hyle*). The hylomorphic model of creation depicts form as imposed by an agent, with a particular design in mind, upon matter, thus rendered inert and passive. To this model Ingold opposes the textility of making, suggesting that the forms of things arise within fields of force and flows of material. Both Pareyson and Ingold bring forward the idea of active materials and of a vitality of materials in their own right and in relation to the art of making by aligning human movements and gestures with those of the thing in its becoming (what Heidegger called "thinging").

A practice-based understanding of creative practices contrasts the idea of the forming process as a linear one which moves through distinct stages—sensing problems, making guesses, formulating hypothesis, communicating ideas to others, and contradicting conformity—that is unsatisfactory, and it may also be misleading. More suitable for a process understanding is the image of a formative spiral in which various dynamics follow each other in a process which becomes increasingly expert and specialized but nonetheless amenable to innovation.

The study of creativity in crafts contributes to the literature on creativity by directing attention to the dimension that Sennett (2008) calls "the intelligence of the hands" and which in more general terms we have explored in terms of formativeness, that is, the knowledge process situated in practices which circumscribes the activity of doing something whilst how to do it is being discovered. This contribution has deepened the concept of entrepreneurial bricolage by enriching the three dimensions identified by Baker and Nelson (2005)—making do, combination of resources for new purposes, and using the resources at hand—with that of formativeness: that is, with the message that creativity is a situated knowing that is learned by doing and discovering how to do it in the relation with the material at hand. Entrepreneurial bricolage can be studied within a positivist theoretical frame; but we have reprised the original interpretation within organizational symbolism and continued to explore it in terms of an aesthetic understanding of creativity practices. The contribution that this approach makes to the literature on creativity consists in exploration of the non-cognitive and non-rational aspects of how people learn and enact practical creativity. Sensible knowledge, emotions, intuition, and affections are the interpretative dimensions that we have shown in relation to materiality within the formative process of the object of the practice and within the space/time of its unfolding.

More suitable for understanding creativity as an activity situated in entrepreneurial practices is the image of a texture of connections emerging from the discovery of the *modus operandi* while the *opus operatum* is anticipated. Pareyson speaks of organization as a process when he says that tentativeness is forgotten in the movement toward realization, and that the artwork acquires its definitive form as if an inner force of organization were present and all the elements were bound by necessity. In the doing that invents its way of doing there is the sense of progressing toward the final result, attempting and correcting and re-doing; there is the inspiration and the elaboration of an intuition; there is improvisation and exercise; there is domination over the material that opposes resistance and enjoys obedience; there is technique and the language of style.

We have illustrated empirically how the object of practice emerges from a texture of connections established in tentative form by experimenting, playing, and transferring from one field to another a form or a material through hybridizations and translations. It can therefore be said that formativeness is what leads the realization process to the *opus operatum* along a tortuous path and according to a logical (i.e., contingent but repeatable) practice. Bourdieu (1990: 73) points out that "the essential part of the *modus operandi* that defines practical mastery is transmitted through practice, without rising to the level of discourse, and the agents can master the *modus operandi* that enables them to perform correctly, only by making it work practically, in a real situation, in relation to practical functions."

The doing which invents "the way of doing" comprises improvisation (Weick, 1998) and reflection in action (Schön, 1983); but unlike the manner in which these responses have been analyzed by Weick and Schön, these do not arise from a breakdown or from a suspension of the action to introduce distance and therefore reflection. Instead, they are constitutive of the emergence of a course of action that tends toward realization.

## 10.7 Conclusions

The aim of this chapter has been to introduce a new term into organizational studies on creativity by analyzing the becoming of practices of creativity in craftwork. A practice lens has been used in order to show the entanglement of meaning and materiality by focusing theoretically and empirically on the concept of "formativeness" from Pareyson's aesthetic theory. We have argued that formativeness is a specific mode of knowing in practice; it constitutes that process of knowing that, in connecting all the elements of a practice, discovers its way of doing. It is a knowing that moves toward its realization through a form-taking and a forming of both the object of the practice and its mode of production.

In fact, the epistemology of practice is an epistemology of becoming (Tsoukas and Chia, 2002), in which practice or organization are not treated as separate entities or accomplished events, but as enactments, as unfolding processes that can be "understood as an 'intelligent life in between' in that it oscillates between complexification and simplification, de- and reconstruction, de- and re-territorialization" (Clegg et al., 2005: 158). Therefore, in the becoming of a practice and in the forming of its object, we looked for how the connections in action were established and made to hold. This idea of moving toward realization has been expressed by similar concepts: the concept of connection-in-action has been used by Latour (1986) to refer to the power of associating. Later Law (1994) used the term assemblage. The idea of texture of practices (Gherardi, 2006) expresses the same concern, and the French word *agencement*, used first by Deleuze and

Guattari (1980), aptly addresses in its etymology the image of the becoming of agency. Common to all these concepts is an interest in understanding how associations are established, maintained, and changed among the elements of a partially given form; the concept of formativeness offers a more nuanced interpretation in that it says that knowing how to establish connections is a form of knowledge discovered in the process of doing.

The practical knowledge used by the craftswomen as they engaged in a creative process constituted not science but art, the art of knowing/doing in situation. This art of knowing/doing proceeds from corporeal knowledge, since the body is the point of contact with the world, the source of sensible knowledge. Instead of the head as the seat of intelligibility, the crafts-women interviewed designated the gut as the "contact" with the materials that they handled. Therefore we may say that the materials and materiality in itself are active and not merely passive interlocutors. Ideas and subject are in dynamic interaction if ideas tend to shape the material; this in its turn has rules that shape the interaction.

When we described this *agencement* of bodies and materials and ideas as it happens, we used the categories of tentativeness, play, experimentation, or exercises. These are the modalities of the material agency which lead both the craftswoman and the material toward formation of the completed work. They give the idea of the practice that proceeds toward its finished form, but not through a linear process of design/execution, but instead according to a temporality and an inner rhythm to the unfolding of the formativeness that indeed proceeds toward a goal, but not in a linear and predictable manner.

In the recursiveness of practices there is always innovation, and in prac-tices of creativity this innovation is what is sought in producing something new or different. In craftwork we found that innovation is not a discontinu-ity as much as a hybridization, a copying, an improvising, a translating which in its turn is a continuation of recursiveness and repetition. The work proceeds by trial and error, by hybridizations, and by the process of change that is unique to practice—namely, repetition as the subtle and constant refinement of knowing in practice. Manual knowing-how requires "keeping your hand in," "having an eye for it," and similar expressions for embodied knowledge; but also intellectual work expresses the same.

It is therefore in the realm of practical creativity, in the relation between *modus operandi* and *opus operatum* that we have investigated how forming takes place, and how in that forming, meaning and materiality are constitutively entangled. Nevertheless, further research is needed, because formativeness—as a practical way of doing, understanding, and accounting—appeared in our empirical research as a sensitizing concept with a solid background in aesthetic philosophy. It seems promising since formativeness represents a type of knowing intrinsic to any practice and that is not limited to craft and small entrepreneurial firms. It also characterizes non-manual jobs and large professional organizations dealing with design, architecture, art, and similar creative activities. Moreover all organizational practices exhibit a tentative character in their becoming "a" practice since organizing is more an art that a science.

## Notes

We wish to thank Philippe Lorino and Antonio Strati for their helpful comments on an earlier version of this chapter. This chapter is the result of an entirely collaborative effort by the two authors. If, however, for academic reasons, individual responsibility must be assigned, Manuela Perrotta wrote the section 10.5, while Silvia Gherardi wrote all the other sections.

1. The Italian term "formatività" may be translated both as formativity and formativeness. While the former is more friendly to an English reader (as a reviewer suggested) because it recalls the idea of performativity, we prefer to keep the term formativeness as it has been already translated within aesthetic philosophy (Strati, 1999). In our opinion, the term formativeness gives more emphasis to that form of knowing which leads to a form and not only to the forming process.

2. Luigi Pareyson (1918–91) was an Italian hermeneutic and existentialist philosopher. In his book *Estetica* he "formulated the problem of dealing with inexhaustible processes of irreducible differences that concern aesthetics by stating that reality is completely independent of thought. . . . Pareyson describes interpretation as reconstruction of the process underlying the text to be interpreted" (Strati, 1999: 78). Forming means giving shape, and it involves the interpretative activity of the person and the re-proposing of difference.

3. Practice-based theorizing has developed a vocabulary made up of verbs: *learning*, *organizing*, *belonging*, *understanding*, *translating*, and *knowing*. It conjures up a world "that is always in the making, where 'doing', more than 'being', is at the centre of attention. They (the verbs) signal the constructive nature of the social and material world and convey an image of knowing as materiality, fabrication, handiwork, the craftsman's skill, conflict, and power struggle; they denote a world in which 'reality' is experienced as solid, stable, and certain matter but in which this condition is an effect, a result, a machination—in short, something that perhaps is but that could have been different" (Nicolini et al., 2003: 21).

4. We are grateful to our five co-interviewers—Attila Bruni, Francesca Gennai, Michela Giampietro, Anna Linda Musacchio, and Giulia Selmi—in the first round of interviews. Manuela Perrotta was the main interviewer for the second

round of interviews. We were helped in our research project by the local artisan association (Associazione Artigiani e Piccole Imprese della provincia di Trento) and by the presentation of our research project to each interviewed person by two of its members: Anita Da Col and Elisa Armeni, to whom we are grateful.

5. We were working with the help of Gruppo Donne Impresa dell'Associazione Artigiani e Piccole Imprese della provincia di Trento, a group of women recently formed within the association who wanted to better understand the biographies of their members and who gave us the access to 70 firms and discussed our findings while we were progressing in our research. The firms taking part in the research had the following dimensions: 61.4% have less than 5 employees, 20% have between 6 and 10 employees, and 12.9% have between 11 and 20 employees. Regarding the sector of activity, 58.6% of the firms belong to services, 22.9% is manufacturing, 15.7% is artistic, and 2.9% is both service and manufacture. The women entrepreneurs interviewed were aged between 30 and 49 years in 70% of cases.

# References

Amabile, T. M. (1988). "A Model of Creativity and Innovation in Organization," in B. M. Staw, and L. L. Cummings (eds.), *Research in Organizational Behavior.* Greenwich, CT: Jai Press, pp. 123–67.

—— Barsade, S. G., and Staw, B. M. (2005). "Affect and Creativity at Work," *Administrative Science Quarterly,* 50: 367–403.

Baker, T. and Nelson, R. (2005). "Creating Something from Nothing: Resource Construction through Entrepreneurial Bricolage," *Administrative Science Quarterly,* 50: 329–66.

Bennis, W. and Biederman, P. W. (1997). *Organizing Genius: The Secrets of Creative Collaboration.* Reading, MA: Addison-Wesley.

Bijker, W. E. (1995). *Of Bicycles, Bakelites and Bulbs: Toward a Theory of Sociotechnical Change.* Cambridge, MA: MIT Press.

Blackler, F. and Regan, S. (2009). "Intentionality, Agency, Change: Practice Theory and Management," *Management Learning,* 40/2: 161–76.

Boland, R. J. and Collopy, F. (2004). *Managing as Designing.* Stanford, CA: Stanford University Press.

Bourdieu, P. (1990). *The Logic of Practice.* Stanford: Stanford University Press.

Cassirer, E. (1944). *An Essay on Man: An Introduction to a Philosophy of Human Culture.* New Haven: Yale University Press.

Ciborra, C. (2002). *The Labyrinths of Information.* Oxford: Oxford University Press.

Clark, A. (2003). "Situational Analysis: Grounded Theory Mapping After Postmodern Turn," *Symbolic Interaction,* 26/4: 553–76.

Clegg, S. R., Kornberger, M., and Rhodes, C. (2005). "Learning/Becoming/Organizing," *Organization,* 12(2): 147–67.

Cook, S. D. and Brown, J. S. (1999). "Bridging Epistemologies: The Generative Dance Between Organizational Knowledge and Organizational Knowing," *Organization Science*, 10/4: 381–400.

Cunliffe, A. L. (2001). "Managers as Practical Authors: Reconstructing our Understanding of Management Practice," *Journal of Management Studies*, 38/3: 351–71.

Davidson, D. (1984). *Inquiries into Truth and Interpretation*. Oxford: Oxford University Press.

Davies, B. and Harré, R. (1990). "Positioning: The Discursive Production of Selves," *Journal for the Theory of Social Behaviour*, 20/1: 43–63.

Deleuze, G. and Guattari, F. (1980). *Mille Plateaux*. Paris: Editions de Minuit.

Drazin, R., Glynn, M. A., and Kazanjian, R. K. (1999). "Multilevel Theorizing about Creativity in Organizations: A Sense-Making Perspective," *Academy of Management Review*, 24: 286–308.

Duymedjian, R. and Rüling, C. (2010). "Towards a Foundation of Bricolage in Organization and Management Theory," *Organization Studies*, 31: 133–51.

Flick, U. (2000). "Episodic Interviewing," in M. W. Bauer and G. Gaskell (eds.), Qualitative Researching with Text, Image and Sound. London: Sage, pp. 75–92.

Ford, C. M. (1996). "A Theory of Individual Creativity in Multiple Social Domains," *Academy of Management Review*, 21: 1112–34.

Gardner, H. (1993). *Multiple Intelligences: The Theory in Practice*. New York: Basic Books.

Garud, R. and Karnøe, P. (2003). "Bricolage versus Breakthrough: Distributed and Embedded Agency in Technology Entrepreneurship," *Research Policy*, 32: 277–300.

Gherardi, S. (2006). *Organizational Knowledge: The Texture of Workplace Learning*. Oxford: Blackwell.

—— (2011). "Organizational Learning: The Sociology of Practice," in M. Easterby-Smith and M. Lyles (eds.), *The Blackwell Handbook of Organizational Learning and Knowledge Management*, 2nd edn. Oxford: Blackwell Publishing, pp. 43–65.

—— and Poggio, B. (2007). *Gendertelling in Organizations: Narratives from Male-Dominated Environments*. Stockholm and Malmö: Liber.

Glaser, B. G. and Strauss, A. (1967). *The Discovery of Grounded Theory: Strategies for Qualitative Research*. London: Weidenfeld & Nicolson.

Glynn, M. A. (1996). "Innovative Genius: A Framework for Relating Individual and Organizational Intelligences to Innovation," *Academy of Management Review*, 21: 1081–111.

Ingold, T. (2010). "The Textility of Making," *Cambridge Journal of Economics*, 34: 91–102.

Kazanjian, R. K. and Drazin, R. (2012). "Organizational Learning, Knowledge Management and Creativity," in M. Mumford (ed.), *Handbook of Organizational Creativity*. London: Elsevier, pp. 547–68.

Latour, B. (1986). "The Power of Association," in J. Law (ed.), *Power, Action and Belief: A New Sociology of Knowledge?* London: Routledge & Kegan Paul.

Law, J. (1994). *Organizing Modernity*. Oxford: Blackwell.

Leonard, D. (1995). *Wellsprings of Knowledge*. Boston, MA: Harvard Business School Press.

Lévi-Strauss, C. (1966) *The Savage Mind*. Chicago: University of Chicago Press.

Lindstead, S. and Grafton-Small, R. (1990). "Organizational Bricolage," in B. A. Turner (ed.), *Organizational Symbolism*. Berlin: de Gruyter, pp. 291–309.

Merleau-Ponty, M. (2002). *Causeries 1948*. Paris: Éditions du Seuil.

Mumford, M. (2000). "Managing Creative People: Strategies and Tactics for Innovation," *Human Resource Management Review*, 10: 313–51.

—— (ed.) (2012). *Handbook of Organizational Creativity*. London: Elsevier.

—— and Gustafson, S. B. (1988). "Creativity Syndrome: Integration, Application, and Innovation," *Psychological Bulletin*, 103: 27–43.

Nicolini, D. (2010). "Practice as the Site of Knowing: Insights from the Field of Telemedicine," *Organization Science*, 22: 602–20.

—— Gherardi, S., and Yanow, D. (eds.) (2003). *Knowing in Organizations: A Practice-Based Approach*. Armonk, NY: M. E. Sharpe.

Oldham, G. R. and Cummings, A. (1996). "Employee Creativity: Personal and Contextual Factors at Work," *Academy of Management Journal*, 39: 607–34.

Orlikowski, W. J. (2007). "Sociomaterial Practices: Exploring Technology at Work," *Organization Studies*, 28/9: 1435–48.

Pareyson, L. (1960). *Estetica: teoria della formatività*. Bologna: Zanichelli.

Pickering, A. (1995). *The Mangle of Practice: Time, Agency, and Science*. Chicago: University of Chicago Press.

Poggio, B. (2004). *Il metodo narrativo nelle scienze sociali*. Rome: Carocci.

Polanyi, M. (1958). *Personal Knowledge: Towards a Post-Critical Philosophy*. Chicago: University of Chicago Press.

Rickards, T., Runco, M., and Moger, S. (2009). *The Routledge Companion to Creativity*. London: Routledge.

Sandberg, J. and Dall'Alba, G. (2009). "Returning to Practice Anew: A Life-World Perspective," *Organization Studies*, 30/12: 1349–68.

Schatzki, T. R. (2005). "Peripheral Vision: The Sites of Organizations," *Organization Studies*, 26/3: 465–84.

Schön, D. (1983). *The Reflective Practitioner: How Professionals Think in Action*. New York: Basic Books.

Sennett, R. (2008). *The Craftsman*. New Haven: Yale University Press.

Singh, B. (1986). "Role Personality versus Biographical Factors in Creativity," *Psychological Studies*, 31: 90–2.

Strati, A. (1992). "Aesthetic Understanding of Organizational Life," *Academy of Management Review*, 17: 568–81.

—— (1999). *Organization and Aesthetics*. London: Sage.

—— (2007). "Sensible Knowledge and Practice-Based Learning," *Management Learning*, 38/1: 61–77.

Suchman, L. A. (2007). *Human–Machine Reconfigurations: Plans and Situated Actions*, 2nd edn. Cambridge: Cambridge University Press.

Torrence, E. P. (1988). "The Nature of Creativity as Manifest in its Testing," in R. J. Sternberg (ed.), *The Nature of Creativity: Contemporary Psychological Views.* Cambridge: Cambridge University Press, pp. 43–75.

Tsoukas, H. and Chia, R. (2002). "On Organizational Becoming: Rethinking Organizational Change," *Organization Science*, 13(5): 567–82.

Turner, B. A. (1981). "Some Practical Aspects of Qualitative Data Analysis: One Way of Organizing the Cognitive Processes Associated with the Generation of Grounded Theory," *Quality and Quantity*, 15/3: 225–47.

Weick, K. E. (1998). "Introductory Essay: Improvisation as a Mindset for Organizational Analysis," *Organization Science*, 9: 543–55.

Woodman, R. W., Sawyer, J. E., and Griffin, R. W. (1993). "Toward a Theory of Organizational Creativity," *Academy of Management Review*, 18: 293–321.

# 11

# Otherness and the Letting-be of Becoming: Or, Ethics beyond Bifurcation

*Lucas D. Introna*

**Abstract:** Why should we value things beyond their instrumental value? Such a question makes sense in a bifurcated ontology in which the human being is valued in and of itself and non-human others are mostly valued with reference to the human. This chapter attempts to move beyond such a bifurcated ontology and ethics, raising the question of the possibility of an ethical encounter with things (qua things). It argues that we are the beings that we are through our entanglements with things; we are thoroughly hybrid beings, cyborgs through and through. It suggests, with Heidegger, that a human-centered ethics of hybrids will fail to open a space for an ethical encounter with things since all beings in the sociomaterial network—humans and non-human alike—end up circulating as objects, enframed as "standing reserve," things-for-the-purposes-of the network. This suggests the need for an ethos beyond the bifurcated ethics of the Western tradition, which in turn requires a different ontology in which all beings reveal themselves as radically other. Drawing on Heidegger (and Harman's interpretation in particular) the chapter develops an account of the radical otherness of things beyond our disclosure of them as this or that particular being. This radical otherness renders possible an ethos based on the *Gelassenheit* (releasement)—a poetic dwelling, which is a letting-be of things in their becoming. This is offered as a possible starting point for a new ethos of a "community of those who have nothing in common" as suggested by Alphonso Lingis (1994).

## 11.1 Introduction

There is a long and, as some believe, venerable tradition of privileging the human when allowing for beings that ought to be taken as intrinsically worthy of ethical consideration. In the Bible this privilege is claimed as emanating from a divine decree: "God created man in his own image . . . And God blessed them, and God said unto them, be fruitful, and multiply, and replenish the earth, and subdue it: and have dominion over fish of the sea, and over fowl of the air, and over every living thing that moveth upon the earth" (Genesis 1:27–8). In the Greek tradition Aristotle, in his *Politics*, makes the same claim that "nature has made all things specifically for the sake of man." As such other beings have no intrinsic worth, in and of themselves; they are only instrumentally significant "for the sake of man." This privileging of the human has often been justified in that man is taken as a being "in the image of God." Or, as Kant argued, because they are the only beings capable of rational thought (Wood and O'Neill, 1998). In his deontological argument Kant suggests that only beings capable of reasoning out their duties and acting freely upon these—that is to say, human beings— qualify as the recipients for the duties of others. Only such beings are, according to him, the bearers of rights. For him our conduct toward the non-human is only ethically significant with reference to our rights and duties toward the human other. Singer (2002), in his book *Animal Liberation* suggests that this privileging of the human is simply a matter of "speciesism." He concludes—after a two-thousand year journey through the history of moral thought about the non-human other—that "little has changed. If animals are no longer quite outside the moral sphere, they are still in a special section near the outer rim. Their interests are allowed to count only when they do not clash with human interests. If there is a clash . . . the interests of the nonhuman are disregarded" (212). In his accusation of "speciesism" Singer is of course only calling our attention to the "sentient" non-human other. What about all other non-human others? Indeed, one might ask: how is it that this ontological (and ethical) bifurcation between us humans and them, the non-humans, has always seemed so self-evident? What is it that makes us assume that this line between them and us can be drawn in such a definitive way? That is to say, in a way that can allow us to assert, for a very long time now, that we humans are intrinsically exceptional. And, moreover, that we have these exceptional and intrinsic qualities (such as memory and reason, for example) separate from the world in which we are becoming exactly that which we assume ourselves already to be.

Every human appropriation of the world is conditioned in advance, both pragmatically and ontologically—pragmatically because we engage with the world for practical purposes and ontologically because such engagement is already constituted by a horizon of taken-for-granted assumptions about the nature of the entities so engaged. When it comes to such appropriations it seems that the most natural ontology for us humans is a *bifurcated being* ontology. That is to say, an ontology which bifurcates into the human and the non-human other, and in which these beings (the human and non-human other) *are essentially what they are before and after such an encounter*. Indeed, such a bifurcated being ontology appears to accord with the supposed reality of our encounters—bifurcations such as: social/material, culture/nature, made/given, natural/artificial, freedom/ necessity, and the like. Thus, when we engage with the entities around us we tend to find a world in which most beings already are what they are, and have their place in a "naturally" occurring order, as this or that sort of being—as human or non-human, as social or material, as spiritual or physical, and so forth. Moreover, this bifurcated ontology tends to take the human as its most original center—its measure, one might say—and the rest, the non-human, as its contrasting other.

Once we have accepted, or taken for granted, this bifurcated anthropocentric being ontology an ethics (with its implied politics) flows quite naturally from it. In this bifurcation there is an ethics for human beings that takes into account what is supposed to be essential about humans, that is to say, their human nature (living, conscious, rational beings). There is also a different ethics for the non-humans that takes into account their supposed essential non-human nature—with a complex set of distinctions about the nature of their non-human beingness (are they sentient or not, are they living or not, and so forth). This bifurcated being ontology—with its anthropocentric bias—obviously has a long history (as was pointed out above) and is also deeply embedded in the enlightenment project (Fuller, 2011)—and some might say it has served us well. This would of course depend on who the "us" is. However, I would propose that there are also very good reasons to question this ontology (and its associated ethics). There are good reasons to say that it has, in many respects, produced an agential cut (to use Barad's term) in which ethics (and politics) has become configured in such a manner as to produce the opposite of what ethics is supposed to become—that is to say, an ethics of violence and oppression of the many by the few. The purpose of this chapter is to question this ontology and its implied ethical framing. One might say the purpose of this chapter is to suggest that a different cut is possible, and perhaps desirable. The inadequacy of this ontology (and the ethics it produces) is at the heart of this discussion.

The limits of an anthropocentric ethics are evident in the work of Singer (2002), on animal rights, and Naess (1990) on the normative significance of entire ecosystems. Yet, although these authors seem to enact a cut which draws the boundaries differently, one might suggest that they only succeed in producing a different configuration of the ethically relevant "we" and the insignificant other. Indeed, any such taxonomy (located within a bifurcated being ontology) is in fact predicated on the idea that the being of things is already ontologically determined in advance. That is to say, that every entity is essentially—that is, always and already—what it is, as this or that type of being—be it social, material, human, animal, natural, artificial, or any other ontological categories that one might imagine. Or, more specifically, ontologically determined in advance as this or that particular being, be it a table, or a boy, or a chair, or a mountain, or a train, or a pen, or whatever. The work of Martin Heidegger (Heidegger, 1962, 1971,1977), Bruno Latour (Latour, 1988, 1993, 2005; Latour et al., 2011) and especially Alfred North Whitehead (1978) questions, in a profound way, such ontological predetermination.

Heidegger (1962) suggests that any being has its *be-ing* only within the constitutive horizon of a world where it is already disclosed as such a meaningful being (as a being-in-a-world). In other words that those beings become what they are when they function within a constitutive referential whole (a world). Moreover, in his later work Heidegger suggests that every revealing of being is rendered possible by a simultaneous withdrawal of its be-ing (Heidegger, 1971)—becoming is not only a bursting forth but also an essential withdrawal of such becoming. Every appropriation of any being whatsoever is always essentially partial (a caricature). Latour (1988), through his meticulous tracing of associations (or more precisely, translations), reveals that our assumed ontological boundaries simply do not add up. That we become the sort of humans that we assume ourselves to be because of our associations with a vast array of intermediaries (actors)—and likewise, they become the sort of beings they assume themselves to be because of their associations with us. That is to say, these intermediaries are not merely enacting pre-existing human qualities (agency, memory, reason), they were also performatively producing the very agent which such enactments assume. Or, as Whitehead (1978: 23) suggests: "That how an actual entity becomes constitutes what that actual entity is . . . Its 'being' is constituted by its 'becoming'. This is the principle of process." Indeed, we humans have always been becoming through the appropriation of the non-human other, from the very start, as the heterogeneous cyborgs that we now are becoming (Haraway, 1991; Leroi-Gourhan, 1993; Stiegler, 1998; Hayles, 1999).

Yet, in spite of our co-original cyborgian becoming—and locked into our assumed bifurcated being ontology—we most often do not consider the non-human others which surround us beyond their instrumental value. As we continue to appropriate them they become more and more part of who we are becoming (Whitehead, 1978). As we appropriate them the actuality of our existence emerges in these intra-relations (Barad, 2007)—as we appropriate them, or more accurately, embody them, they become *internal* to our own becoming—seemingly separate, but in actuality, insepar-able. We are, in a very profound way, each other's co-constitutive condition for our mutual ongoing becoming of what we are (Introna, 2006: 2011). If this is case, then the significance of our relationship with all other beings—especially our ethical relationship—has become (or has always been) a ques-tion that needs urgent attention. This is exactly the purpose of this chapter.

The structure and argument of the chapter unfolds in three movements. In the first movement I argue, with the science and technology studies tradition (and Latour in particular), that we are the beings that we are through our appropriation of things; we are thoroughly, and from the start, hybrid beings, cyborgs through and through. I proceed to argue, with Heidegger (1977, 1993), that a human-centered ethics of hybrids will fail to open a space for an ethical encounter with things since all beings in the sociomater-ial network—humans and non-humans alike—will end up circulating as objects, enframed as "standing reserve," things-for-the-purposes-of the net-work. I proceed to suggest that what is needed is an ethos beyond bifurcated ethics, or the overcoming of an ethics based on human willing toward an ethos of letting-be. In the second movement I prepare the ground for such an overcoming (if it is possible) by elaborating what an encounter with things beyond the traditional bifurcated ontology (or human-centered metaphys-ics) might be. Here I draw on the later work of Heidegger starting with his important essay *Letter on Humanism*. In this movement I give an account of our interaction with things, drawing on the well-known distinction between *zuhanden* (ready-to-hand) and *vorhanden* (present-at-hand), as presented in the work of Graham Harman (2002, 2005, 2011). Harman's work allows us to provide an account of the radical otherness of the thing beyond our disclos-ure of it as this or that particular being. In the final movement I elaborate an ethos, or more precisely a poetic dwelling with things, based on the *Gelas-senheit* (releasement) or the letting-be of things in their becoming. I show how such a poetic dwelling with, or ethos of *Gelassenheit*, may constitute a very otherwise way of becoming with things. I offer this as a possible starting point for a new ethos of a "community of those who have nothing in common" as suggested by Alphonso Lingis (1994).

## 11.2 Means, values, and the ethics of hybrids

### 11.2.1 We the original hybrids

Why and in what way do things—assumed to be wholly other than us—matter to us? Why should we concern ourselves with things beyond their instrumental possibilities for us? Do they have any moral significance *qua* things? One way to answer this question is to say that things matter, are morally significant, because they always already embody in some way particular values and interests (Winner, 1980; Introna and Nissenbaum, 2000; Introna, 2006). Thus, things are not merely innocent "just there" things that we appropriate, i.e., they are not merely neutral and passive objects before us—mere means toward our ends. Indeed, as actor network theorists (Callon, 1986; Latour, 1988, 2005; Law, 1991; Akrich and Latour, 1992) have argued, and shown, everyday things—doors, seat belts, keys, scallops, chairs, etc.—are indeed political "locations" where values and interests are negotiated and ultimately "inscribed" into the very materiality of the things themselves—thereby rendering these values and interests more or less permanent. In inscribing programs for action into things we make society more "durable," as Latour suggested. Through such inscriptions, which may be more or less successful, those that encounter and use these inscribed things may become, wittingly or unwittingly, enrolled into particular programs, or scripts for action. Obviously, neither the things nor those that draw upon them simply accept these inscriptions and enrolments as inevitable or unavoidable. In the flow of everyday life things often get lost, break down, and need to be maintained. Furthermore, those that draw upon them use them in unintended ways, ignoring or deliberately "misreading" the script the objects may endeavor to impose. Nevertheless, to the degree that these enrolments are successful, the consequences of such enrolments can and ought to be scrutinized.

In this view of the "ethics of things"—which we may refer to as the *ethics of hybrids*—there is clearly a moral and political debate to be had about the sort of things, and by implication the values and interests, we want to, or ought to, appropriate (Introna and Nissenbaum, 2000; Introna, 2005; Introna and Whittaker, 2006). We could argue that it is morally unacceptable to appropriate things that enroll us into programs that ultimately damage our environment or our fellow human beings—such as buying designer labels produced by child labor in a foreign country. This seems evident enough. However, such debates may ultimately prove very difficult to have in a time where things are becoming increasingly complex and interconnected. For example, it has become increasingly difficult to make ethical purchase decisions as a consumer. Do you buy Fairtrade products even if they have taken many air miles to reach your local shop? What is more important: fair compensation or the environment? Moreover, so many potentially important scripts are increasingly difficult to understand, even for the experts—as the bovine spongiform encephalopathy (BSE) crisis (commonly known as "mad cow disease") in the UK has shown. In such complex sociomaterial becomings there may be many intertwined agencies and competing incommensurable values at stake. It may prove difficult, if not impossible, to unentangle the web of agencies, values, and interests (or means and ends)—as the Kyoto Protocol clearly demonstrates (Latour, 1993).

We could nevertheless argue that it is morally desirable for the scripts of these sociomaterial becomings and their potential consequences to be made explicit (such as placing warnings on tobacco that smoking kills, or labeling food that was fairly traded)—that is, what is elsewhere referred to as disclosive ethics (Introna 2005). Thus, we could propose that we ought to "open up" the complex black boxes of our technologically advanced society and "read them out loud"—in a language accessible to those that may potentially be enrolled. This sort of ethics of hybrids is obviously very important and desperately needed. The lack of commitment to such an ethics by many in the actor network theory (ANT) field, and science and technology studies (STS) more generally, is disappointing, as confirmed by Bijker (2003). The limited awareness of the implicit and intimate link between ethics and politics, together with a commitment to a "neutral" (symmetrical) descriptive methodology, may explain this state of affairs. However, I would argue that there is no such thing as "neutral" description and that it is therefore impossible to avoid politics and by implication ethics (Radder, 1992, 1998). As such the supposed political neutrality suggested in a "descriptive" methodology—as is still relatively prevalent in STS—itself may be seen as a way to side-step the complex moral landscape of hybrids. Unfortunately such a move adds weight to the supposition that description, politics, and ethics could be separated.

Nonetheless, the ethics of hybrids, and the analysis it produces, may indeed make us acutely aware that there is no simple, easy to draw line between things and us, or, in the language of ANT, between humans and non-humans. It may show that we are the sorts of humans that we are because we appropriate, and implicitly accept the scripts of, the things that make up and mediate our contemporary way of being and becoming. Equally, the things that make up and mediate our world are the things that they are because we typically made them for our purposes—in our image as it were. Thus, in the unfolding sociomaterial networks—our contemporary technically advanced society—things and humans reflect and sustain each other as the things that they are becoming. We co-constitute each other's possibilities for becoming—as such they (we all) matter, both politically as well as ethically. Ultimately the ethical/political question of the nuclear power station is not only "is it safe?" but also "is this the sort of humans that we want to become?" The ethics of hybrids may help us to become less naive about the ethics and politics of technology but it does not address—although it does point to—the more primordial question of an ethics of the becoming of all things—that is, our intra-relation with things, *qua* things. How might we approach such a question?

The intellectual space in STS for such a consideration has become more viable as seen, for example, in the work of Latour (2002). In his paper "Morality and Technology: The End of the Means" Latour takes head-on the traditional bifurcated ontology and ethics as reflected in the *means/ends* or *fact/value* dualities or dichotomies. He argues that this dichotomy collapses when we take a closer look at the way technology folds and unfolds within human becoming. In his essay he suggests that there is an intimate (and ontological) connection between technology and morality:

> Morality is no more human than technology, in the sense that it would originate from an already constituted human who would be master of itself as well as of the universe...Morality and technology are ontological categories...and the human comes out of these modes, it is not at their origin. Or rather, it cannot become human except on condition of opening itself to these ways of being which overflow it from all sides and to which it may choose to be attached—but then at the risk of losing its soul. (Latour, 2002: 254)

What Latour is suggesting here is that technology and morality both have their being as heterogeneous networks that have as one of their performative outcomes the "human being." In other words morality (like technology) is not simply a matter of our choosing. Undeniably, his essay is a radical critique of a widely held bifurcated and anthropocentric idea of *agency and ethics*. He is suggesting that morality is a performative outcome of the heterogeneous sociomaterial nexus. In becoming moral we necessarily appropriate the non-human other. We enact our obligations of security and safety through locks, keys, safety belts, and so forth. Moreover in appropriating these devices they performatively produce exactly what they assume, that is, a responsible person (parent, driver, etc.). But this appropriation of the agency of the other always comes at a cost (Introna, 2011). The heterogeneous sociomaterial nexus does not only produce the responsible person, it produces much more besides—its performative outcomes always overflow that which was assumed in its appropriation.

Latour wants to question the categories of our bifurcated ontology, especially in their more traditional expression—such as means/ends, fact/value, is/ought, and the like. He wants to warn us that "The two modes of existence [technology and morality, or matters of fact and matters of concern] ceaselessly dislocate the dispositions of things, multiply anxieties, incite a profusion of agents, forbid the straight path, trace a labyrinth—generating possibilities for the one, and scruples and impossibilities for the other" (Latour, 2002: 257). Latour's challenge is provocative. It calls for a radically different way of thinking about the ethics of hybrid things. It points, perhaps, to an ethics beyond the idea of the hybrid, beyond, or prior to the bifurcation—perhaps even the overcoming of a bifurcated ethics as traditionally conceived. I believe the development of these ideas is very significant as it points to a convergence between the work of Latour (that is more empirically grounded) and the work of Heidegger (on the overcoming of traditional metaphysics) that I will take up below. Before I proceed to do this I would like to briefly sketch out why the bifurcated dichotomy between facts and values (is and ought), within traditional Western metaphysics and ethics leads to a nihilism that needs to be overcome in order for a different ethics (or rather ethos) of the becoming of things to be rendered possible at all.

### 11.2.2 On valuing humans, objects, and things

The ethics of hybrids (discussed above) still operates within a bifurcated ontology, that is to say, within an ontology of "them" and "us"—wherever we draw the line. In such a bifurcated ethics our ethical relationship with things is determined beforehand by us: it is anthropocentric. In this encounter with things we have already chosen, or presumed, the framework of values that will count in determining moral significance. In this ethics, things are always and already "things-for-us"—objects for our use, in our terms, for our purposes. They are always already inscribed with our intentionality—they carry it in their flesh, as it were. The defining measure of the bifurcated ethics of hybrids is the human being—the meaning of the Latin root of "man" is measure. Indeed our concern for things is what they might to do to us humans, as was suggested above. Our concern is not our instrumental use of them, the violence of our appropriation and inscription in/on them, but that such scripts may ultimately harm us. As things-for-us, or "objects" as we will refer to them, they have no moral significance as such. In the value hierarchy—of the modern, bifurcated, ethical mind— they are very far down the value line. What can be less morally significant than an inanimate object—the disposable polystyrene cup? Their moral significance is only a derivative of the way they may circulate the network as inscriptions for utility or enrolment. For example, they may become valuable if they can be sold in a market where they are valued, as is the case with works of art. The magnitude and diversity of our human projects are mirrored in the magnitude and diversity of the objects that we have appropriated, for us. As things-for-us they are at our disposal; if they fail to be useful, or when our projects drift or shift, we "dump" them. The images of endless "scrap" heaps at the edges of our cities abound. Objects are made/inscribed, used, and finally dumped. We can dispose of them because we author-ized them in the first place. Increasingly we design them in such a way that we can dispose of them as effortlessly as possible. Ideally, their demise must be as invisible as possible. Their entire moral claim on our conscience is naught, it seems.

One can legitimately ask why we should concern ourselves with things (such as inanimate objects) in a world where the ethical landscape is already overcrowded with grave and pressing matters such as untold human suffering and disappearing bio-diversity and ozone layers—to name but a few. It is my argument that our moral indifference to so many supposedly significant beings (humans, animals, nature, etc.) *starts with the idea that there are some beings that are less significant or not significant at all.*

If it is increasingly difficult (or impossible) to draw or enact the boundary between our objects and us, and if in this entangled network of human and non-humans objects lack moral significance from the start, then it is rather a small step to take for an ethics to emerge in which all things—humans and non-human alike—circulate as objects—"things-for-the-purposes-of" the network. Thus, in the sociomaterial becoming (as heterogeneous assemblages of humans and objects) our human becoming is ultimately also ordered as a "for-the-purposes-of." Thus, the irony of an anthropocentric ethics of things is that ultimately we also become "objects" in programs and scripts, at the disposal of a higher logic (capital, state, community, environment, etc). In the sociomaterial becoming others, and our objects, "objectify" us. For example, I cannot get my money out from the bank machine because I forgot my PIN number. Until I identify myself in its terms (as a five-digit number) I am of no significance to it. Equally if I cannot prove my identity by presenting inscribed objects (passport, driver's license) I cannot get a new PIN number. In Heidegger's (1977) words we have all become "standing reserve," on "stand by" for the purposes of the socio-material nexus—enframed (*Gestell*) by the calculative logic of our way of becoming. In the becoming of the sociomaterial nexus all beings become enframed, in a global network that has as its anthropocentric logic to control, manipulate, and dominate: "Enframing is the gathering together which belongs to that setting-upon which challenges man and puts him in position to reveal the actual, in the mode of ordering, as standing-reserve" (Heidegger, 1977: 305).

The value hierarchy presumed in a bifurcated anthropocentric ethics is in fact a dynamic nexus of the becoming of values and interests—there never was a hierarchy. In this nexus the becoming of our objects also becomes our fate. In the bifurcated ethics of hybrids we are also *already becoming as objects—indeed everything is already becoming as objects*. Instead of a hierarchy of values we discover a complete nihilism in which everything is leveled out, everything is potentially equally valuable/valueless; a nihilistic network in which "the highest values devaluate themselves" (Nietzsche, 1968: 9). If this is so, then I would argue that we should not "extend" our moral consideration to other things, such as inanimate objects—in a similar manner that we have done for animals and other living things, in for example environmental ethics. In other words we should not simply extend the reach of what is considered morally significant to include more things. Every possible bifurcation, every possible cut that we can make, or boundary we can draw, will be an act of violence in which some beings become valued at the expense of others—or, more fundamentally, transformed into an object of value (or valueless). Indeed, to value humans for their consciousness, their reason, or their capacity to feel pain, is already to turn them into an object—what happens if they lose these qualities? Rather we should abandon all systems of moral valuing and admit, with Heidegger, that in "the characterisation of something as 'a value' what is so valued is robbed of its worth" and admit that "what a thing is in its Being is not exhausted by its being an object, particularly when objectivity takes the form of value," furthermore, that "every valuing, even where it values positively, is a subjectivising" (Heidegger, 1993: 228). We must abandon ethics for a clearing *beyond ethics*—to let beings become in their own terms. We must admit that any attempt at moral ordering—be it egocentric, anthropocentric, biocentric (Goodpaster, 1978; Singer, 2002) or even eco-centric (Leopold, 1970; Naess, 1990) will fail. Any ethics based on "our image" is arbitrary and will eventually turn everything into an object in our image, pure will to power (Heidegger, 1977). As Lingis (1994: 9) suggests, "The man-made species we are, which produces its own nature in an environment it produces, *finds nothing within itself that is alien to itself*, opaque and impervious to its own understanding" (emphasis added). We should rather acknowledge that the existence of any being comes at the cost of denying the becoming of other beings—in ethics every being is always already implicated, and that also includes us humans. In sum: any bifurcation is arbitrary and counterproductive as it always reproduces the conditions of its own demise—the other always turns out to be already in the same. Indeed, our claim to privilege (which has endured for thousands of years) sounds hollow in the face of our instrumental destruction of the non-human other (and eventually ourselves).

Instead of creating value systems in our own humanistic terms, and categories, the absolute otherness of *every* other should be the only moral imperative—an ethics without any center whatsoever. We need an ethics of things that is radically beyond the self-identical of human beings. Such an ethics beyond metaphysics needs as its "ground," not a system for comparison, but rather a recognition of the impossibility of any comparison—every comparison is already violent in its attempt to render equal what could never be equal (Levinas, 1999). The question of what I value more, my child or the chair, when I have to make a decision is an inappropriate framing of the ethical dilemma. It allows me to dismiss the chair without going through the ethical trauma of acknowledging the otherness of them both. My child is a being other than a mere parent/child relation and the chair is, likewise, other than a mere tool for sitting. In framing the ethical dilemma as a comparison I have already violated them both—i.e., I have denied what is exactly other, and as such already "robbed them of their worth." How might we appropriate the other in its otherness? This is of course a profound aporia—one which has occupied much of the work of Levinas and the later Derrida. But for them the "other" was firstly and most definitely the human other. In his ethics Levinas (1985, 1999, 2000) has argued for the radical singularity of our fellow human beings, the *face* of the other. But what about all other others—surely the faceless non-human "third" is also calling for justice?

One might suggest that for us human beings, the wholly Other, that is indeed wholly Other, is the inanimate Other. Indeed, in many respects, the destitute face of the human Other, in the ethics of Levinas for example, is

271

already in some sense a reflection of the human face opposite it. We can indeed substitute ourselves for the human Other (become her hostage) because we can imagine—at least in some vague sense—what it must be like for the human Other to suffer violence because we also suffer violence. It is possible for us to substitute "us for them" because it could have been my friend, my child, my partner, etc.—we are a community with a common unity, our humanity. If the "forgetting of the self is what moves ethics" (as Levinas suggests), then this is hardly the forgetting of self. To grant the inanimate other (such as the disposable polystyrene cup) its otherness, in the face of the many demands of everyday life, that seems to me like a truly altruistic act. That is the nature of an ethical dilemma prior to, or beyond bifurcation. In the next section I will argue that Heidegger, especially as presented in the work of Harman, might provide us with some hints toward such an ethics beyond bifurcation, or the overcoming of ethics toward an ethos of the letting-be of all beings in their becoming—a "community of those who have nothing in common," as suggested by Alphonso Lingis (1994).

## 11.3 On the encounter with things beyond bifurcation

Graham Harman (2002, 2005, 2011) argues that Heidegger's well-known tool analysis—as, for example, presented in section three of division one of *Being and Time*—is the thread that holds together his entire philosophy. He argues against the popular pragmatic interpretation of Heidegger's tool analysis—as for example presented by Dreyfus (1991) and others—where the present-at-hand (*vorhanden*) is our detached theoretical encounter and awareness of things and where the ready-to-hand (*Zuhandenheit*) refers to our practical engagement with tools where they withdraw from view as objects and function *as* tools in order to achieve practical intentions. Instead he suggests that "both theory and practice are equally guilty of reducing things to presence-at-hand" (Harman, 2011: 42)—the nature of their present-at-handness is simply different comportments of making present. In contrast he suggests that ready-to-handness (*Zuhandenheit*) already "refers to objects insofar as they withdraw from human view into a dark subterranean reality that *never* becomes present to practical action" (Harman, 2002: 1). Thus, all entities are ontologically locked into a duality in which they reveal themselves (as *vorhanden*) but also simultaneously withdraw into the silent inaccessible underground (as tool-being/*Zuhandensein*). As such, any encounter with an entity whatsoever (as this or that particular entity) is always already present-at-hand (*vorhanden*), be it practical or theoretical. In a sense one might say that every present-at-hand entity, in its presentness, is simply a caricature—an artifice revealed in accordance with the comportment, which has as its immediate other the simultaneous withdrawal of that which is not called upon (in concept or action).

We should, however, note that, although withdrawn—except for the artifice present in each and every encounter—a thing is nonetheless a being that is thoroughly and completely deployed in reality. As Harman (2002: 21–22) suggests,

> in its fullness of being a thing is an impact irreducible to any list of properties that might be tabulated by an observer encountering it. The ongoing functioning or action of the thing, its tool-being, is *absolutely invisible*.
>
> Whatever is visible of the table in any given instant can never be its tool-being, never its ready-to-hand. However deeply we meditate on the table's act of supporting solid weights, however tenaciously we monitor its presence, any insight that is yielded will always be something quite distinct from this act [of being] itself.

This table, here before me, is more than all the perspectives, levels, or layers that we can enumerate, more than all the uses we can put it to, more than *all possible* perspectives, levels, layers, or uses. Any and all possible relations between humans and things will inevitably fail to grasp them as they are—they are irreducible to any and all of these relations.[1] Harman argues that this bursting forth of becoming (of the table, for example) is "pure event; *Erlebnis* is *Ereignis*, fully invested with significance"; however, "knowledge [or encounter] halts this event and converts it into mere *Vorgang* [occurrence] . . . to encounter an entity as the represented object of knowledge requires a kind of de-living, a de-distancing, or a de-severing" (Harman, 2002: 83).

Furthermore, Harman argues, rather controversially, that the "withdrawal of objects [*Zuhandensein*] is not some cognitive trauma that afflicts only humans and a few smart animals, but expresses the permanent inadequacy of any relation at all" (Harman, 2011: 44). All relations between entities are in a sense "broken" from the start. *Zuhandensein* is essential to the becoming of all beings themselves, their own withdrawal even as they offer their surface for such "broken" relational contact. In other words *Zuhandensein* is the incessant and ongoing eventing (or worlding) of the world in its own terms: "The world grants to things presence. Things bear world. World grants things" (Heidegger, 1971: 182). This ongoing worlding of the world is the inaccessible, always withdrawn, dense referential whole in which exists an infinite range of possibilities for things to be disclosed as this or that particular being.

One should, however, be careful to note that this withdrawn referential whole is exactly not some Platonic eternal ideal world of "forms" that exist "behind" or "above" objects, which is then made *present* in the object. In other words it is not a notion in which the world is the mere appearances (shadow) of the real world somehow behind it. For Heidegger the worlding of the world is an ongoing actuality, the sheer bursting forth of being— whether we are there to appropriate it or not. In other words the world, in its worlding, in its *Zuhandensein*, is always fully actual, fully deployed, even if it is inaccessible in any contact as such. In *An Introduction to Metaphysics* Heidegger (1964: 14) argues that *physis* denotes this self-blossoming, unfolding emergence of beings—that "manifests itself in such unfolding and preserves and endures in it: in short, the realm of things that emerges and lingers on."[2] *Physis* (sometimes translated as "physical-ity") is the unfolding event (or more accurately the ongoing eventing) in which being shows itself from itself, a revealing that is not for, or at the behest of, humans. Or, as Scott (2002: 62) puts it *"Physis* 'is' that without which nothing at all would be. It names continuous, opening eventuation of all things." The be-*ing* of beings do not need to wait (passively) for humans (or other beings) to become what they already are, they simply become. In short: the world is always and already bursting forth in its becoming. However, we should note again that this bursting forth, in its revealing, is also simultaneously an essential withdrawal. In their *Zuhan-denheit* all "things withdraw from presence into their dark subterranean reality, they distance themselves not only from human beings, but *from each other* as well.... Even inanimate things [when they appropriate each other] only unlock each other's realities to a minimal extent, reducing one another to caricatures" (Harman, 2002: 2). Whenever any being is present as a particular being (as a hammer for example) it is already a caricature.

If this argument of Heidegger (as articulated by Harman), of the irreducible nature of tool-being (or ready-to-handness), is valid then it also makes sense to talk of the radical otherness (singularity) of all other Others (in Levinas' terms)—not just of humans (as Levinas does) but also of more mundane objects such as atoms, hammers, fish, cups, trees, and pens.[3] In other words, in encountering the other (as wholly other) we ought not to bifurcate in order to reserve a special place for the becoming of human beings, over against the mute mundane world of the object. All beings are sites of becoming—a becoming that is always other than any encounter whatsoever may reveal. To defend the moral rights of humans because of their sentience, their consciousness, their rationality or whatever, is to turn the becoming of human beings into a caricature, but likewise with all other beings. The hammer appears, but also withdraws, in the disclosive eventing (*Ereignis*) of being as already *wholly other* than a mere weight to drive in nails or to smash a stone. But in what way does this bursting forth (or incessant eventing) hold sway? How can we encounter the other in ways that let it be—in a sense an action that is utterly passive? In the technological framing of *Gestell* human *Dasein* orders things—including itself—to stand forth as resources, available for human intentionality and projects. In contrast, when humans let things be, as they are, in their own terms, by dwelling in the becoming of the fourfold—as suggested by Heidegger (1971)—then a wholly otherwise relation of the letting-be of the otherness of becoming becomes an impossible possibility (to use Derrida's phrase). Heidegger (1969) calls this comportment of "letting-be" *Gelassenheit* (often translated as releasement).

## 11.4 Dwelling with things and the ethos of *Gelassenheit*

### 11.4.1 The ethos of Gelassenheit

The move beyond a bifurcated ethics (a system of values based on a meta-physics of human will to power) is for Heidegger—as it is for Latour—the move beyond the dichotomies of freedom and nature, action and passivity, *ought* and *is*.[4] In his essay *Letter on Humanism* Heidegger suggests that we should return to the more original meaning of ethics. Translating a Heraclitus fragment he proposes that *ethos* originally "means abode, dwelling place. The word names the open region in which man [all beings] dwells" (Heidegger, 1993: 233). For Heidegger *ethos* (rather than ethics) is not a relationship of humans toward other beings in which the other is valued (or not) but rather a way of dwelling where being may be encountered, an openness toward the beingness of their becoming (Zimmerman, 1983). Or as Scott suggestes:

> In the context of the question of ethics and the nurture/hostility syndrome of any ethos, the rule of being in a life dedicated to clearing release (*Gelassenheit*) gives emphasis to the allowance of differences in their disclosedness.... Preservation of disclosure is the hallmark of *Gelassenheit*'s own disclosure.... An affirmation beyond value is the guiding affection that we saw operate in [*Gelassenheit*]. (Scott, 1990: 209)

This ethos of dwelling means to cultivate and to care for the otherness in the becoming of beings (Heidegger, 1971: 147). For Heidegger this ethos of dwelling is intimately connected to his notion of freedom where freedom is taken as an act of "letting-be" which seeks to let the other be as other. Dwelling is a form of cultivating and care, but what is cultivated, and cared for, is "letting-be." *Gelassenheit* is the abandonment of that representational and calculative thinking (or comportment), that is of willing, by which human beings dispose of things *as this or that being*. This freedom is more original than willing (the setting up, or commanding forth) in that it frees itself from this incessant willing into an openness of letting be. As Heidegger (1978: 127) explains:

> Freedom now reveals itself as letting beings be . . . To let be is to engage oneself with beings. On the other hand, to be sure, this is not to be understood only as the mere management, preservation, tending, and planning of the beings in each case encountered or sought out. To let be—that is, to let beings be as the beings which they are—means to engage oneself with the open region and its openness into which every being comes to stand, bringing that openness, as it were, along with itself.

This giving up of the assumed lordship over beings—which is so central to the religious as well as the rational scientific human way of being—opens the possibility for the entry into the ethos of letting-be: "man is not the lord of beings. Man is the shepherd of Being [becoming]" (Heidegger, 1993: 221). Through the cultivation of *Gelassenheit* "we silence habitual and calculative modes of thinking and open ourselves to the promptings that come from the ontological depth of the becoming of other beings. This openness clears a space for the Being of the other to emerge as it is in itself. . . . preserving the other's irreducible otherness" (Carey, 2000: 27–8).

How do we enter the clearing of letting-be without turning the otherness of the other into a "thing-for-me" as this to that useful tool or object? First we need to note, as Harman suggests, that "*no relationality at all* can allow one object to encounter another in person [as a singularity], since it is in the nature of objects to withhold their full secrets from each other" (Harman, 2005: 169, emphasis in original). Heidegger suggests, as a hint, that there is a possible impossibility to be found in a poetic comportment—but one must also immediately say that such a comportment is a profound aporia. The poet "names all things in that which they are." This poetic comportment cannot be willed since wiling only enacts and reinforces the gravitational pull of the will to power. Rather, the poet listens, waits, and lets the disclosive event be—one could almost say, following Levinas—as a *visitation*. This waiting and listening of *Gelassenheit* lies beyond the ordinary distinction between activity and passivity, it is an undoing rather than a willing. The ethos of *Gelassenheit* is an ethos of active and ongoing passivity, accepting by letting-go. As Ziarek (2002: 182) explains:

> Lettingness is neither simply a human act nor a fate that humans accept and allow to be. Rather, letting has to be conceived in the middle voice beyond activity and passivity, the middle voice into which relations can be let. This letting, while not entirely at human disposition or will, needs to be worked on. . . . *Lassen* does not mean that humans transform being, that they enforce or make this transformation. Rather, it indicates that being transforms itself but cannot do so 'on its own', without human engagement, without human letting.

The poetic disclosure of being in the eventing of the world is immediately and wholly imminent, self-sufficient, and meaningful; no representation is necessary only letting-be. It discloses being in an event wholly "otherwise than the will to power" (Ziarek, 2002: 183).

For Harman (2007: 205) this "touching without touching" of letting-be is first and foremost an aesthetic relation which is about the singularity and supplementarity of things—things insofar as they cannot be thought, represented, utilized, or normatively regulated. Aesthetics involves feeling an object for its own sake, beyond those aspects of it that can be become content of consciousness or useful. This bursting forth of the thing in its thingness is what Harman calls *allure*: the sense of an object's existence apart from, and over and above, its own qualities (Harman, 2005: 142–4). In its allure the thing is inviting us "toward another level of reality" (179). In the event of allure, I am forced to acknowledge its integrity, entirely apart from me—that is, to let it be. The image of a young child staring with wonder into an empty glass, or a pile of toys, as if everything that is important and relevant is revealed there points to such an alluring engagement.

How might one enter into such alluring relations with all things, that is, enter into this ethos of letting-be, of *Gelassenheit*? Heidegger (1971: 215) suggests that: "Poetry first causes dwelling to be dwelling. Poetry is what really lets us dwell." If poetry causes dwelling then one might ask about the possibility of a poetry of things or a poetic dwelling with things? In this regard I will suggest two very small gestures toward such an impossible possibility; the first I will call *"things as poets"* (things naming us) and the second the *"poetry of things"* (our letting things be).

## 11.4.2 The ethos of dwelling with things

*Things as poets or the speaking of things*. In the bringing into presence of things (as present-at-hand or *vorhanden*) these things simultaneously "name" us as the beings-in-the-world that we are. Our bringing forth of them is in accordance with our willing (our needs, purposes, and desires)—caricatures in our own image, as Harman suggested above. As such they, in the manner of their presencing, disclose us as the particular beings that we are becoming. How do things disclose us? Obviously, the car refers to the driver, the pen to the writer, and the chair to the possibility of sitting down. However, the revealing of us as "users" or "manipulators" of tools and objects, is, although the most obvious disclosure, *but one possible way* in which our things disclose us. We need to listen more carefully, poetically one might say, to the "unsaid" in their coming to presence. In the eventing of the world we are not just revealed as specific beings, as "users" and "manipulators" for example, our way of becoming is also revealed in a more significant way.

Our tools—which are entangled with us in our becoming as we extend our will to power—also simultaneously point to that which withdraws in the wake of this becoming. More precisely, they also point to that which is rendered invisible in the thrusting forth of our will to power: that is to say, our finitude, our being-towards-death (Heidegger, 1962). In our *vorhanden* tools and objects we might catch a glimpse of ourselves as finite beings, thrown into the world and "lost" in our projects. The plethora of things that surround us (as they literally do) point also to our tendency to "fall away" from our possibilities to let-be by losing ourselves in the busyness of everyday life. In our calling forth of beings (as resources) we cover over the truth that our incessant willing hides what we dare not face—our own finitude. Does the silent murmur of our scrap heaps and landfills not also disclose our finitude, our mortality? Our projects run down and end, like us. The eventing of things is not just the poetry of growth, vitality, and becoming, but also the poetry of loss, decay, and finitude—like us. Moreover, do our great projects not disclose our ongoing desire for transcendence? Do we not build pyramids, cathedrals, temples, and towering office blocks as concrete expressions of our yearning for the possibility of overcoming our finitude—inscribing into the flesh of things our deepest existential desire for immortality, a "life after death"?

Furthermore, what do these things say about us when we disclose them to be disposable from the start—when our willing wills them to reveal their becoming as uniform, instantaneous, and temporary as possible? Is our need to dispose of them effortlessly (without facing them, that is) a reflection of our desire not to expose ourselves to the ethical trauma of having to deal with the fact that we are making them present merely as resources for our own egological projects? Or, maybe we do not want to face the fact that our becoming comes at the expense of other beings—beings who are now merely called forth as resources, as standing-in-reserve for our own becoming. Should we not, as an ethical act of letting-be, imagine a different kind of relation based on the letting-be of otherness (rather than ordering)—one of listening, of attuning ourselves to their otherness? This sort of listening—that is of letting-be—has a quality outside of our willing, as beautifully expressed by Alphonso Lingis (1998: 13–15) in his book *The Imperative* (when he speaks about listening, as opposed to simply hearing):

> Our hearing is not just the recording of sounds, noises and words, with silences between them. For hearing to awaken [to let-be] is to listen in to the rumble of the city or the murmur of nature, from which sounds emerge and back into which they sink . . . The elements are there by incessant oncoming. Their presence does not indicate a source from which they come. . . . Sonority floats in waves of presence which rise to shut out the distant rumble of waves to come and the echoes of its past.

On a more mundane level, is our decoration of things not also an honoring[5] of them, as an affirmation of their dignity, in the hope of reclaiming our own dignity? Or, more profoundly, do the already *silent voices*—that is, our assumption about their passivity and availability to us as resources—of our objects not disclose, to us, the excesses of our willing power over others, as we continue to enroll them in our egological projects? As we dump them in scrap heaps, landfills, and garbage cans our power over them (and others) seems to be confirmed—yet they remain unsettlingly silent, just turning the other cheek, as it were. And in their silence they also reveal to us the fact that we have already lost our otherness in the *Gestell* for which we have become mere resources. Yet, they only sometimes unsettle us as "waste," threatening us by washing up on our beaches, getting into our drinking water, and so forth. Their silent voices not only disclose their finitude and fragility but also ultimately reveal to us—if we care to listen to these poets—the tenuousness of our own existence. Their silence recalls what we have already forgotten. In the expanse and complexity of the becoming of the universe we are also already a silent voice. To the universe we humans are profoundly mute, merely resources. As Nietzsche (1968: 42) rightly concludes: "After nature had drawn a few breaths the star grew cold, and the clever animals had to die."

In the ongoing eventing of the world do we listen to these silent poets, in the withdrawal of what is *not* said? Do we attune ourselves to these poets in an active letting-be, not just now and then but as an active ongoing way of being, of dwelling? Heidegger (1971: 181) suggests that "If we let the thing be present in this thinging from out of the worlding world, then we are thinking of the thing as thing." He calls this thinking "meditative thinking." I will rather refer to it as *mindfulness*.[6] By referring to "mindfulness" I also want to invoke, following Levinas (1989), our ongoing and active *responsibility* for all Others. As Levinas suggests (1989), our primordial obligation to respond is originally tied to the fact that we have, in being, already "taken the place in the sun" of the other. *Our existence as this or that particular being is only possible by taking all others—humans and non-humans—hostage, and in so doing denying them their otherness*. Thus, this "minding" of mindfulness is not some theoretical concept, but rather an active and ongoing cultivation of a practice of the letting-be of things—all beings, human and non-human. Such a practice of mindfulness, I would suggest, would resist the "falling" or slipping into a mind-less disclosure (of making and using) of things. It would rather attune us to the infinite otherness that is already covered over by our calculative and instrumental way of becoming.

For example, rather than merely using (or dumping) a thing such a mindful practice might consider the other (even alien) possible worlds our relation with this or that thing might disclose to us; or it might consider what my use (or dumping) of this or that thing is saying about my care or minding of all others (including the thing itself) implicated in its use (or dumping). How do the disposable polystyrene cups or the techniques of cloning disclose us in our relating to the other? As we become more mindful we may ask these questions. How do our houses, our cities, our jetfighters, our motorways, and our countryside "name" or reflect us? What are the rainforests, the ozone, and the oceans saying about us and our relation to them? What are our workplaces telling us about ourselves and our relation with the other? What otherness is covered over as we make the world in our own image? In what way could our ethos be otherwise?

Moreover, as we become mindful we may also start to realize that in designing and making things we are also already designing and disclosing a way of being. As we cultivate a practice of mindful dwelling we may be able to imagine how to design *Gelassenheit* also into our world (if that is not too paradoxical). How might a world be where all things (humans and non-humans) relate to each other in a comportment of letting-be? It might be too difficult to imagine, an impossible possibility. Nevertheless, within the ethos of *Gelassenheit* designers may need to read the multiplicity of references implied (and covered over) in their designs, follow them through as much as is possible. A critic may ask: but are we not already enframed (*Gestell*) in the density of being as calculation, as Heidegger (1977) argues in the essay *The Question Concerning Technology*? This is so, but Heidegger (1969: 54) also suggests, in quite concrete terms, that we can, in the ethos of

*Gelassenheit*, "act otherwise. We can use technical devices, and yet with proper use also keep ourselves so free of them, that we may let go of them any time...I would call this comportment toward technology which expresses 'yes' and 'no' *at the same time*, by an old word, releasement [*Gelassenheit*] toward things" (emphasis added). Heidegger is here referring to our relation with thing but the same can be said with regard to their comportment toward us. Letting-be requires that we also allow them to say yes and no—for example by not strictly adhering to our scripts. Indeed designers may recall the delight (or horror) of discovering that their designs (or the way they are used) achieve many outcomes never intended. Can the aporia of letting-be, of "yes" and "no" *at the same time*, become a design practice? What and how might it be?

*The poetry of things, or, on not de-worlding things*: In revealing things as *vorhanden* tools for us, we are reducing them to our purposes, our meanings. In this sense we "de-world" them, turn them into "devices"—in Borgmann's (1987) terminology. For him devices hide much of the activity associated with them (often in pursuit of convenience). In contrast to this, he argues, things can function to gather together "focal practices." Focal practices provide a focus such that it "gathers the relations of its context and radiates into its surroundings and informs them." Focal practices—the letting-be of the thing—provide "a centre of orientation [meaning] and when we bring the surrounding technology into it, our relations to technology become clarified and well defined" (Borgmann, 1987: 16). Borgmann seems to be suggesting that as we become mindful—through letting-be—we can become attuned to things, and them to us, in a more profound way. In such a simultaneous attunement a meaningful whole comes about in which humans and things not merely reflect each other but might also allow for a multiplicity of different ways of being to emerge.

For example, one can think of the profound attunement that emerges between a skilled artisan and her tools (the artist and her material, the woodworker and his tools, the writer and her computer). It is interesting to note the *intimacy* and obvious respect that the artisan accords her tools— they reveal her and she reveals them, not as mere objects but as possibilities for being otherwise. One might say that they involve each other in a significant way, and thereby constitute each other's possibility for being otherwise (Verbeek, 2005). In this intimacy the thing becomes, in a penetrating way, a singular—it is spoken of in tenderness and maintained with care. Indeed, a singular whose loss is often experienced with anguish. This intimate dwelling of letting-be is also beautifully described by Dolores LaChapelle (1993) in her account of powder skiing. She describes how, in the unfolding event of powder skiing, there is no longer an "I" and snow and mountain, but rather a continuous flowing of interaction in which it is impossible to tell where the skier's actions begin and end and where the snow and mountain take over. One might suggest, with Harman, that in this alluring relation something new emerges, an entirely new object—a mountain-skier-snow object, that discloses the world in an entirely new and novel way. In a similar manner Rodin (1983) relates how a sculpture he is working on will fail if he tries to *make* it look like the reality he observes. However, when he works with nature (as he calls it) and allow nature to sculpt through him then his sculptures become alive—alluring one might say.

In contrast to this ethos of *Gelassenheit*, in the disclosure of *Gestell* things are revealed as mere objects (or devices) that can be dumped if broken. Through mass production we create perfect substitutes that make any thing appear as "a replacement part"—reproducing the order of the same to cover over the singular, whilst forgetting the forgetting of such covering over. As we "black-box" or de-world physical being into single-purpose sealed functional units—in the pursuit of convenience or in de-skilling—in this disclosure the possibility of poetic dwelling is excluded from the start. In the world of "standing reserve" we exclude the possibility of being otherwise by designing things as already de-worlded—that is, as a disposable thing from the start. As a disposable thing we do not decorate it (honor and dignify it)—the examples of plastic cups, spoons, or pens abound. The object becomes designed in ways that will *only* disclose its use value thereby concealing the fact that all things, including us, have already become disposable. Thus, we have no moral anxiety in throwing it away—it was supposed to be disposable from the start. As we have argued above, in a complex sociomaterial world where some things are taken as disposable all things eventually circulate as disposable (Heidegger, 1977). As we dominate things they disclose, and immediately conceal to us ourselves as already the same, as already enframed in the willing of the will—that is, as mere resources for a network that has no other purpose than appropriating all beings as becoming, always and already, resources for the network.

## 11.5 Some concluding thoughts

What now? In considering the impossible possibility of an ethos of *Gelassenheit* we have multiplied many times over our responsibility toward things. Not only are we always already responsible for the other human beings that we encounter (Levinas 1989), we may indeed also already be responsible for *every* other being—humans and non-humans. Not only must we face the face of the destitute; we must also face the silent fragility of the thing. Moreover, we are in an impossible situation—ethics is impossible. As we dwell we have to, on an everyday basis, "compare the incomparable" (Levinas, 1999). The hierarchy of values, provided by our bifurcated ontology, can no longer "simplify" ethics for us; not that it ever did, it merely helped us forget our responsibility—indeed it also helped us forget that we had forgotten. It did, however, give us a way to justify ourselves: "it was just a thing after all." The tidiness of our value hierarchy masked and continues to mask the moral complexity we do not dare face. Through our system of values we need not compare that which cannot be compared, need not face the trauma of the undecidable. As Derrida (1999: 66) argues: "there would be no decision, in the strong sense of the word, in ethics, in politics, no decision, and thus no responsibility, without the experience of some undecidability. If you don't experience some undecidability, then the decision [to discard the thing] would simply be the application of a programme [a value hierarchy] ... ethics and politics, therefore, start with undecidability." The ethos of letting-be is impossible—and so it should be. However, the insurmountable weight of our responsibility is exactly what gives our ethos its force (Levinas, 1999). It is exactly the impossibility that leads us to keep decisions open, to listen, to wait, and to reconsider again and again our choices—to let things be.

To live a life of letting-be—an ethical life—is to live in the continued shadow of doubt, *without any hope for certainty*. Clearly we must make very difficult choices on an everyday basis. However, what makes these choices real decisions—real ethical responsibility—is that no thing is excluded from the start, by default as it were. It is in the shadow of this infinite responsibility that we must work out, instance by instance, again and again, how we ought to live, with *all* others; how to dwell within a "community of those who have nothing in common," as suggested by Alphonso Lingis (1994).

## Notes

This chapter is partly based on a paper that appeared in *Theory, Culture & Society*.

1. Nathan Brown (2007) in his essay "The Inorganic Open: Nanotechnology and Physical Being" proposes the notion of "nothing-otherthan-object" to name this physical being, "this immanent otherness of that which is never nothing and yet not something" (41).

2. For a more complete discussion of *physis* refer to the discussion of Scott (2002), especially Chapter 3.
3. Extending Levinas' ethics to non-humans is not uncontroversial. We do not want to develop the argument here but it seems that the notion of tool-being of Harman (2002) and nothing-other-than-object of Brown (2007) provides some indications of how one might be able to make such an argument. Also refer to Benso (2000) and Davy (2007) for arguments to extend Levinas' ethics into the domain of the "non-human" other.
4. There is a large literature on the question of Heidegger's "ethics." We draw on some of it in this discussion. For a more comprehensive discussion refer to Caputo (1971), Zimmerman (1983), Marx (1987), Benso (1994), Hodge (1995), Schalow (2001), and McNeill (2006).
5. Latin root *decus* means to honour and dignify.
6. I would argue that mindfulness is a better term since it captures the sense of care that is fundamental in the letting-be of beings (see the essay "Building, Dwelling, Thinking" in Heidegger (1971) for a detailed discussion of meditative thinking and its relation to care).

## References

Akrich, M. and Latour, B. (1992). "A Convenient Vocabulary for the Semiotics of Human and Nonhuman Actors," in W. E. Bijker and J. Law (eds.), *Shaping Technology/Building Society: Studies in Sociotechnical Change (Inside Technology)*. Cambridge, MA: MIT Press, pp. 205–24.

Barad, K. (2007). *Meeting the Universe Halfway: Quantum Physics and the Entanglement of Matter and Meaning*. Durham, NC: Duke University Press.

Benso, S. (1994). "On the Way to an Ontological Ethics: Ethical Suggestions in Reading Heidegger," *Research in Phenomenology*, 24/1: 159–88.

—— (2000). *The Face of Things: A Different Side of Ethics*. Albany, NY: SUNY Press.

Bijker, W. E. (2003). "The Need for Public Intellectuals: A Space for STS," Pre-Presidential Address, Annual Meeting 2001, Cambridge, MA. *Science, Technology, & Human Values*, 28/4: 443–50.

Borgmann, A. (1987). *Technology and the Character of Contemporary Life: A Philosophical Inquiry*. Chicago: University of Chicago Press.

Brown, N. (2007). "The Inorganic Open: Nanotechnology and Physical Being," *Radical Philosophy*, 144 (July/August): 33–44.

Callon, M. (1986). "Some Elements of a Sociology of Translation: Domestication of the Scallops and the Fishermen of St Brieuc Bay," in J. Law (ed.), *Power, Action, and Belief: A New Sociology of Knowledge?* London: Routledge & Kegan Paul, pp. 196–233.

Caputo, D. (1971.) "Heidegger's Original Ethics," *New Scholasticism*, 45: 127–38.

Carey, S. (2000). "Cultivating Ethos through the Body," *Human Studies*, 23/1: 23–42.

Davy, B. J. (2007). "An Other Face of Ethics in Levinas," *Ethics & the Environment*, 12/1: 39–65.

Derrida, J. (1999). "Hospitality, Justice and Responsibility: A Dialogue with Jacques Derrida," in R. Kearney and M. Dooley (eds.) *Questioning Ethics: Contemporary Debates in Philosophy*. London: Routledge, pp. 65–83.

Dreyfus, H. L. (1991). *Being in the World: Commentary on Heidegger's "Being and Time,"* Division 1. Cambridge, MA: MIT Press.

Fuller, S. (2011). *Humanity 2.0: What it Means to be Human Past, Present and Future*. Basingstoke: Palgrave Macmillan.

Goodpaster, K. E. (1978). "On Being Morally Considerable," *Journal of Philosophy*, 75/6: 308–25.

Haraway, D. J. (1991). *Simians, Cyborgs, and Women: The Reinvention of Nature*, 1st edn. London and New York: Routledge.

Harman, G. (2002). *Tool-Being: Heidegger and the Metaphysics of Objects*. Chicago: Open Court.

—— (2005). *Guerrilla Metaphysics: Phenomenology and the Carpentry of Things*. Chicago: Open Court.

—— (2007). "On Vicarious Causation," *Collapse*, 2: 171–205.

—— (2011). *The Quadruple Object*. Winchester, UK: Zero Books.

Hayles, N. K. (1999). *How We Became Posthuman: Virtual Bodies in Cybernetics, Literature, and Informatics*. Chicago: University of Chicago Press.

Heidegger, M. (1962). *Being and Time*. Oxford: Wiley-Blackwell.

—— (1964). *An Introduction to Metaphysics*. New Haven: Yale University Press.

—— (1969). *Discourse on Thinking*. New York: Harper Perennial.

—— (1971). *Poetry, Language, Thought*. New York: Harper & Row.

—— (1977). *The Question Concerning Technology, and Other Essays*. New York: Harper & Row.

—— (1978). *Basic Writings from Being and Time (1927) to The Task of Thinking (1964)*, ed. D. F. Krell. London: Taylor & Francis.

—— (1993). *Basic Writings*. London and New York: Routledge.

Hodge, J. (1995). *Heidegger and Ethics*. London: Routledge.

Introna, L. D. (2005). "Disclosive Ethics and Information Technology: Disclosing Facial Recognition Systems," *Ethics and Information Technology*, 7/2: 75–86.

—— (2006). "Maintaining the Reversibility of Foldings: Making the Ethics (Politics) of Information Technology Visible," *Ethics and Information Technology*, 9/1: 11–25.

—— (2011). "The Enframing of Code: Agency, Originality and the Plagiarist," *Theory, Culture & Society*, 28/6: 113–41.

—— and Nissenbaum, H. (2000). "Shaping the Web: Why the Politics of Search Engines Matters," *The Information Society*, 16/3: 169–85.

—— and Whittaker, L. (2006). "Power, Cash, and Convenience: Translations in the Political Site of the ATM," *The Information Society*, 22/5: 325–40.

Lachapelle, D. (1993). *Deep Powder Snow: Forty-Years of Ecstatic Skiing, Avalanches, and Earth Wisdom*. Durango, CO: Kivaki Pr.

Latour, B. (1988). *The Pasteurization of France*. Cambridge, MA: Harvard University Press.

—— (1993). *We Have Never Been Modern*. Cambridge, MA: Harvard University Press.

—— (2002). "Morality and Technology: The End of the Means," *Theory, Culture & Society*, 19/5–6: 247–60.

—— (2005). *Reassembling the Social: An Introduction to Actor-Network-Theory*. Oxford: Oxford University Press.

—— Harman, G., and Erdelyi, P. (2011). *The Prince and the Wolf: Latour and Harman at the LSE*. Alresford, UK: Zero Books.

Law, J. (1991). *A Sociology of Monsters: Essays on Power, Technology, and Domination*. London: Routledge.

Leopold, A. (1970). *A Sand County Almanac: With Essays on Conservation from Round River*. New York: Ballantine Books.

Leroi-Gourhan, A. (1993). *Gesture and Speech*. Cambridge, MA: MIT Press.

Levinas, E. (1985). *Ethics and Infinity*. Pittsburgh: Duquesne University Press.

—— (1989). "Ethics as First Philosophy," in S. Hand (ed.), *The Levinas Reader*. London: Wiley-Blackwell, pp. 75–87.

—— (1999). *Otherwise Than Being, or, Beyond Essence*. Pittsburgh: Duquesne University Press.

—— (2000). *Alterity and Transcendence*. New York: Columbia University Press.

Lingis, A. (1994). *The Community of Those Who Have Nothing in Common*. Bloomington: Indiana University Press.

—— (1998). *The Imperative*. Bloomington: Indiana University Press.

McNeill, W. (2006). *The Time of Life: Heidegger and Ethos*. Albany, NY: SUNY Press.

Marx, W. (1987). *Is There a Measure on Earth? Foundations for a Nonmetaphysical Ethics*. Chicago: University of Chicago Press.

Naess, A. (1990). *Ecology, Community, and Lifestyle: Outline of an Ecosophy*. Cambridge: Cambridge University Press.

Nietzsche, F.W. (1968). *The Will to Power*, ed. W. A. Kaufmann and R. J. Hollingdale. New York: Vintage Books.

Radder, H. (1992). "Normative Reflexions on Constructivist Approaches to Science and Technology," *Social Studies of Science*, 22/1: 141–73.

—— (1998). "The Politics of STS," *Social Studies of Science*, 28/2: 325–31.

Rodin, A. and Gsell, P. (1983). *Rodin on Art and Artists: Conversations with Paul Gsell*. New York: Courier Dover Publications.

Schalow, F. (2001). "At the Crossroads of Freedom: Ethics Without Values," in R. F. H. Polt and G. Fried (eds.), *A Companion to Heidegger's Introduction to Metaphysics*. New Haven: Yale University Press, pp. 250–62.

Scott, C. E. (1990). *The Question of Ethics: Nietzsche, Foucault, Heidegger*. Indianapolis: Indiana University Press.

—— (2002). *The Lives of Things*. Indianapolis: Indiana University Press.

Singer, P. (2002). *Animal Liberation*. New York: Ecco Press.

Stiegler, B. (1998). *Technics and Time: The Fault of Epimetheus*. Stanford: Stanford University Press.

Verbeek, P.-P. (2005). *What Things Do: Philosophical Reflections on Technology, Agency, and Design*. Pennsylvania: Pennsylvania State University Press.

Whitehead, A. N. (1978). *Process and Reality: An Essay in Cosmology*. New York: Free Press.

Winner, L. (1980). "Do Artifacts Have Politics?" *Daedalus*, 109/1: 121–36.

Wood, A. and O'Neill, O. (1998). "Kant on Duties Regarding Nonrational Nature," *Proceedings of the Aristotelian Society*, 72: 189–228.

Ziarek, K. (2002). "Art, Power, and Politics: Heidegger on Machenschaft and Poiêsis," *Contretemps*, 3: 175–85.

Zimmerman, M. (1983). "Toward a Heideggerean Ethos for Radical Environmentalism," *Environmental Ethics*, 5/2: 99–131.

# Index